New Music Theatre in Europe

Between 1955 and 1975 music theatre became a central preoccupation for European composers digesting the consequences of the revolutionary experiments in musical language that followed the end of the Second World War. The 'new music theatre' wrought multiple, significant transformations, serving as a crucible for the experimental rethinking of theatrical traditions, artistic genres, the conventions of performance, and the composer's relation to society. This volume brings together leading specialists from across Europe to offer a new appraisal of the genre. It is structured according to six themes that investigate: the relation of new music theatre to earlier and contemporaneous theories of drama; the use of new technologies; the relation of new music theatre to progressive politics; the role of new venues and environments; the advancement of new conceptions of the performer; and the challenges that new music theatre lays down for music analysis. Contributing authors address canonical works by composers such as Berio, Birtwistle, Henze, Kagel, Ligeti, Nono, and Zimmermann, but also expand the field to figures and artistic developments not regularly represented in existing music histories. Particular attention is given to new music theatre as a site of intense exchange – between practitioners of different art forms, across national borders, and with diverse mediating institutions.

Robert Adlington holds the Queen's Anniversary Prize Chair in Contemporary Music at the University of Huddersfield. He is author of books on Harrison Birtwistle, Louis Andriessen, and avant-garde music in 1960s Amsterdam, and editor of volumes on avant-garde music in the 1960s, and music and communism outside the communist bloc. He has written articles and chapters on Nono, Berio, musical modernism, new music theatre, and musical temporality.

Musical Cultures of the Twentieth Century

Series Director:
Gianmario Borio, University of Pavia and Giorgio Cini Foundation, Italy

Editorial Board:
Robert Adlington, University of Huddersfield, UK
Esteban Buch, EHESS, Paris, France
Mark Delaere, University of Leuven, Belgium
Giovanni Giuriati, Università Roma La Sapienza, Italy
Wolfgang Rathert, Ludwig Maximilians-Universität, Munich, Germany
Iwona Lindstedt, University of Warsaw, Poland

The series *Musical Cultures of the Twentieth Century* adopts a collaborative model for the study of key issues in twentieth-century music. The basis for each volume is a conference drawing together leading scholars from across Europe and beyond; conference themes are determined by the series' distinguished international advisory board, with a view to developing new knowledge and understanding that reflects dialogue between scholars of different nationalities and theoretical backgrounds. Particular emphasis is placed upon recognition of the multiplicity of conceptions, artefacts, events and communities which characterised musical life in the last century. Accordingly, individual volumes seek to interrogate themes that encompass diverse musical genres and disciplinary perspectives.

The series was conceived as a project of the Institute of Music of the Giorgio Cini Foundation, Venice, where many of the conferences are convened.

Musical Listening in the Age of Technological Reproduction
Edited by Gianmario Borio

Composing for the State
Music in Twentieth-Century Dictatorships
Edited by Esteban Buch, Igor Contreras Zubillaga and Manuel Deniz Silva

Music-Dance
Sound and Motion in Contemporary Discourse
Edited by Patrizia Veroli and Gianfranco Vinay

New Music Theatre in Europe
Transformations between 1955–1975
Edited by Robert Adlington

For more information about this series, please visit: www.routledge.com/music/series/MUSCULT

New Music Theatre in Europe
Transformations between 1955–1975

Edited by Robert Adlington

LONDON AND NEW YORK

First published 2019
by Routledge
2 Park Square, Milton Park, Abingdon, Oxon OX14 4RN

and by Routledge
605 Third Avenue, New York, NY 10017

First issued in paperback 2020

Routledge is an imprint of the Taylor & Francis Group, an informa business

© 2019 selection and editorial matter, Robert Adlington; individual chapters, the contributors

The right of Robert Adlington to be identified as the author of the editorial material, and of the authors for their individual chapters, has been asserted in accordance with sections 77 and 78 of the Copyright, Designs and Patents Act 1988.

All rights reserved. No part of this book may be reprinted or reproduced or utilised in any form or by any electronic, mechanical, or other means, now known or hereafter invented, including photocopying and recording, or in any information storage or retrieval system, without permission in writing from the publishers.

Trademark notice: Product or corporate names may be trademarks or registered trademarks, and are used only for identification and explanation without intent to infringe.

British Library Cataloguing-in-Publication Data
A catalogue record for this book is available from the British Library

Library of Congress Cataloging-in-Publication Data
Names: Adlington, Robert.
Title: New music theatre in Europe : transformations between 1955–1975 /
   edited by Robert Adlington.
Description: Abingdon, Oxon; New York, NY: Routledge, 2019. | Series:
   Musical cultures of the twentieth century | Includes bibliographical
   references and index.
Identifiers: LCCN 2018052279 (print) | LCCN 2018052692 (ebook) | ISBN
   9780429451669 (ebook) | ISBN 9781138323018 (hardback : alk. paper)
Subjects: LCSH: Music theater—Europe—20th century—History and
   criticism.
Classification: LCC ML1720.5 (ebook) | LCC ML1720.5 .N38 2019 (print)
   | DDC 782.1094/09045—dc23
LC record available at https://lccn.loc.gov/2018052279

ISBN 13: 978-0-367-73094-9 (pbk)
ISBN 13: 978-1-138-32301-8 (hbk)

Typeset in Times New Roman
by Swales & Willis Ltd, Exeter, Devon, UK

Contents

List of figures, tables, and music examples	vii
Notes on contributors	xii
Acknowledgements	xvi

Introduction: why 'new music theatre' now?	1
ROBERT ADLINGTON	

PART I
Between the avant-gardes: new music theatre and new conceptions of drama

13

1	The definition of a new performance code: from the avant-garde to 'new theatre'	15
	STEFANIA BRUNO	
2	Total theatre and music theatre: tracing influences from pre- to post-war avant-gardes	33
	JULIA H. SCHRÖDER	
3	Theatre as problem: modern drama and its influence in Ligeti, Pousseur and Berio	52
	VINCENZINA C. OTTOMANO	

PART II
Expansions of technology

77

4	Audio-visual collisions: moving image technology and the Laterna Magika aesthetic in new music theatre	79
	HOLLY ROGERS	
5	Composing new media: magnetic tape technology in new music theatre, *c.* 1950–1970	101
	ANDREAS MÜNZMAY	

vi *Contents*

PART III

The critique of established power

127

6 Guerrilla in the polder: music-theatrical protests in the
Low Countries, 1968–1969
HARM LANGENKAMP

129

7 René Leibowitz's *Todos caerán*: grand opéra as
(critique of) new music theatre
ESTEBAN BUCH

153

PART IV

New venues and environments

175

8 A survey of new music theatre in Rome, 1961–1973:
'Anni favolosi'?
ALESSANDRO MASTROPIETRO

177

9 Avant-garde music theatre at the Festival d'Avignon
between 1967 and 1969
JEAN-FRANÇOIS TRUBERT

203

PART V

Reconceiving the performer

225

10 Reconceptualising the performer in new music theatre:
collaborations with actors, mimes and musicians
DAVID BEARD

227

11 Embodied commitments: solo performance and the
making of new music theatre
FRANCESCA PLACANICA

255

PART VI

Analysing new music theatre

271

12 New music theatre and theories of embodied cognition
BJÖRN HEILE

273

13 Analysing new music theatre: theme and variations (from a
multimedia perspective)
ANGELA IDA DE BENEDICTIS

294

Index

319

Figures, tables, and music examples

Figures

2.1 Erwin Piscator's staging of *Rasputin* (1927): on stage the actors play an event from the historical past; over the stage a film shows the historical future; and on the side of the stage, a text-projection gives chronological data to contextualize the two represented events. The collage, consisting of a stage photograph and a film still, was published in Erwin Piscator's book *Das politische Theater* (1929)   39

3.1 Last part of *La Cantatrice chauve* by Eugène Ionesco (*Théâtre*, volume I, 1954, p. 53). © Gallimard.   58

5.1 Marshall McLuhan, *Understanding Media*, dust jacket (designed by Abner Graboff) of the out-of-print first edition, 1964, with contemporary sound recording and reproduction technology occurring twice (record player; microphone).   104

5.2 Mauricio Kagel, *Sur scène*, 'Elektro-akustische Ausrüstung', n.p. (detail). © Copyright 1962 by Henry Litolff's Verlag Ltd & Co. KG, Leipzig. Reproduced by kind permission of Peters Edition Limited, London.   107

6.1 Soldiers taking orders from their captain. Action scene from *Hyperion en het Geweld*, 17 May 1968. Photo: Oscar Vanden Brugge, the Royal Theatre of the Mint, Brussels.   138

6.2 Cast in front of the Guevara statue. Action scene from *Reconstructie*, 28 June 1969. Photo: Joost Evers, National Archives of the Netherlands/Anefo, CC0.   143

7.1 Francisco de Goya, *Todos caerán* (*Los caprichos* no. 19).   162

8.1 Domenico Guaccero, *Scene del potere* (first version), preparatory sketch. Reproduced by courtesy of the Institute of Music of the Fondazione Giorgio Cini and Guaccero's heirs.   181

8.2 Domenico Guaccero, *Scene del potere* (final version), preparatory sketch. Reproduced by courtesy of the Institute of Music of the Fondazione Giorgio Cini and Guaccero's heirs.   182

viii *Figures, tables, and music examples*

8.3 Domenico Guaccero, *Scene del potere* (first version), preparatory sketch. Reproduced by courtesy of the Institute of Music of the Fondazione Giorgio Cini and Guaccero's heirs. 183

8.4 Musica Elettronica Viva, *Zuppa*, 25–26 October 1968, L'Attico, Piazza di Spagna; courtesy Fabio Sargentini, L'Attico Archive; photo Marco Cresci. 191

9.1 Preparatory notes for the 1968 festival programming. Maison Jean Vilar archives, 4-JV-180-1, 1967. 211

9.2 Preparatory notes for the 1969 festival programming, October 1968. Maison Jean Vilar archives, 4-JV-182-1. 217

9.3 Preparatory notes for the 1969 festival programming, October 1968. Maison Jean Vilar archives 4-JV-182-1. 218

9.4 Note by Jean Vilar during the 1968 Festival. Maison Jean Vilar archives, Avignon, 4-JV-182. 220

9.5 *Musiques Éclatées*, collective works of the ACGRM. Concert programme, 7 August 1969. 221

10.1 Stick positions from the 'Performance Notes' for Harrison Birtwistle's *For O, For O, The Hobby-Horse is Forgot* (1976). © Copyright 1976 by Universal Edition (London) Ltd., London. Used with the permission of Universal Edition (Vienna). 232

10.2 Performer positions in Erika Fox's *Round for Fourteen Strings* (1974). © Copyright Erika Fox. Used with the composer's permission. 233

10.3 Prayer Gestures for Stockhausen's *Inori* (1973–4), compiled by Nancy Wyle and reproduced in the published score. © Copyright 1979 Stockhausen-Verlag. Used by permission of the Stockhausen-Stiftung für Musik. 235

10.4 Roger Marsh, Archer (Tom) Endrich, and Bernard Rands performing Richard Orton's *Mug Grunt* (1972), at the Shaw Theatre, London in 1974, with the York University music theatre group 'Clap'. © Copyright Peter Harrap/Report-IFL Archive/reportdigital.co.uk; used with their permission. 236

10.5 Hans Keller, Peter Maxwell Davies, Harrison Birtwistle and Milein Cosman at the Dartington Summer School of Music, 1970. Photograph by Charles Davis. © Copyright Dartington Summer School of Music Archive; used with their permission. 239

10.6 Marc Wilkinson at the National Theatre, London, preparing the use of invented percussion instruments and rehearsing with actors and musicians for Peter Shaffer's production of *The Royal Hunt of the Sun*. Photographs taken at the Old Vic Theatre, London, *c.* 1963, by Angus McBean, stored at the National Theatre Archive, London. © Copyright Houghton Library, Harvard University; used with their permission. 246

Figures, tables, and music examples   ix

10.7 Actors Fred Warder and Morag Hood mime the
transformation of the Fair Sister into a harp, in Harrison
Birtwistle's *Bow Down* (1977), from the original performance
in London's National Theatre. Photograph by John Haynes.
© Copyright Lebrecht Music & Arts; used with their permission.   251

12.1 Dimension spaces illustrating the gestures of a musician
(left) and dancer (right), in Jensenius *et al.* (2010: 25).   282

12.2 The Bozzini Quartet during performance of Mauricio
Kagel's String Quartet II, around rehearsal number 13.   287

12.3 The Bozzini Quartet during performance of Mauricio
Kagel's String Quartet II, around rehearsal number 14.   288

13.1a Diagram from Salzman and Desi (2008: 322).   297
13.1b 1st variation.   298
13.1c 2nd variation.   298

13.2 Luigi Nono, preparatory sketch for a 'theatrical work 1961';
notebook 'Q.007', f. 5 *recto*, ref. cat. 23.06.01/05r
(*Intolleranza 1960*); courtesy of the Archivio Luigi Nono.   305

13.3 Luigi Nono, sketch in notebook 'B.017', f. 2 *recto*, ref.
cat. 26.05.01/18 (*Da un diario italiano*), with numbers added;
courtesy of the Archivio Luigi Nono.   306

13.4 Luigi Nono, sketch in notebook 'B.017', f. 3 *recto*, ref.
cat. 26.05.01/19 (*Da un diario italiano*), with numbers added;
courtesy of the Archivio Luigi Nono.   307

13.5 Luciano Berio, sketch for *Opera*, 1st version (*c.* 1969);
Luciano Berio Collection, Paul Sacher Foundation
(with kind permission).   309

13.6 Luciano Berio, *Esposizione*, 'temporal scores' sketch.
Paul Sacher Stiftung, Cathy Berberian Collection. By
kind permission.   314

Tables

10.1 Six kinds of relationship between mime(-dance) and music.   231
12.1 Amended table of movement types. The border between
performance and frame is the 'metaphysical divide'.   283

Music examples

2.1 Bernd Alois Zimmermann, *Die Soldaten*, Act 4, Scene 1, p. 428
from the full score. Zimmermann notates the simultaneous
musical events and strata as well as three film projections
which show elements of the narration. Reproduced by kind
permission of Schott Music GmbH.   40

x   *Figures, tables, and music examples*

3.1   First page of 'Conversation' from *Aventures* by György
      Ligeti. © Copyright by Henry Litolff's Verlag, Leipzig,
      for all countries of the world. Reproduced by kind permission
      of Peters Edition Limited, London.   57

3.2   Luciano Berio, *Air I*, from *Opera*, I Act,
      pp. 1–2. © Copyright 1977 by Universal Edition (London)
      Ltd, London, Copyright assigned to Universal Edition A.G.,
      Wien. By kind permission.   69

3.3   Luciano Berio, *Air I*, from *Opera*, I Act, p. 9. © Copyright
      1977 by Universal Edition (London) Ltd, London,
      Copyright assigned to Universal Edition A.G., Wien.
      By kind permission.   71

5.1   Karl-Birger Blomdahl, *Aniara*, piano-vocal score pp. 96–97
      ('The crowd sits down to look at and to listen to the Mima.' –
      'MIMABAND I' [8'37''] – 'Blue flash of lighting from the
      Mima. Earth is blown up into pieces. Panic in the
      Mima-hall.'). © SCHOTT MUSIC Ltd, London.   113

5.2   Giacomo Manzoni, *Atomtod*, first page of the score (detail).
      © Edizioni Suvini Zerboni – Sugarmusic S.p.A., Milano.   116

7.1   Leibowitz, *Todos caerán*, vocal score: Act I, Tableau 1,
      Scene 1, bars 1–2.   164

7.2   Leibowitz, *Todos caerán*, orchestral score: Act I, Premier
      Tableau, Scene 1, bars 44–6.   166

7.3   Leibowitz, *Todos caerán*, vocal score: Act II, Premier
      Tableau, Scene 1, bars 36–40.   167

7.4   Leibowitz, *Todos caerán*, vocal score: Act I, Premier Tableau,
      Scene 2, bars 193–8.   168

7.5   Leibowitz, *Todos caerán*, vocal score: Act I, Deuxième
      Tableau, Scene 6, bars 836–8.   170

7.6   Leibowitz, *Todos caerán*, vocal score: Act II, Deuxième
      Tableau, Scene 2, bars 629–34.   171

8.1   Domenico Guaccero, *Novitá assoluta*, autograph score, p. 8.
      Reproduced by courtesy of the Institute of Music of the
      Fondazione Giorgio Cini and Guaccero's heirs.   186

10.1 Page four of Michael Finnissy's *Bouffe (for a person alone
      on stage)* including a precisely notated vocal outburst for the
      actor-mime (1975). © Copyright Michael Finnissy. Used with
      the composer's permission.   238

12.1 Mauricio Kagel, String Quartet II, rehearsal number 13,
      by kind permission of Universal Edition. Translation of
      instructions: first violin – '1st violin covers the left hand

Figures, tables, and music examples xi

and fingerboard of the 2nd violin with a cloth (at least
50 × 50 cm)'; second violin – '1st violin lays a cloth on
LH and fingerboard [. . .] from here on the prescribed pitches
should be regarded as approximate. The performer goes on
playing, unperturbed, beneath the cloth'; cello – 'blow into
other sound hole [. . .] simile: breathe in several times'. 286

12.2 Mauricio Kagel, String Quartet II, rehearsal number 14,
by kind permission of Universal Edition. Translation of
instructions: viola – 'Having got to the nut of the bow,
the right hand grips the cloth. The upbow movement is then
vigorously continued with an upward thrust. The performer
'freezes', with arm raised (and the cloth in his [sic] hand).
Immediately afterwards: bring arm down slowly. [. . .]
let CLOTH drop.' 288

13.1 Luciano Berio, *Esposizione*, score previously deposited in the
archive of Universal Edition, Wien (now preserved in the
Paul Sacher Foundation, Luciano Berio Collection), p. 4.
By kind permission. 313

Contributors

Robert Adlington holds the Queen's Anniversary Prize Chair in Contemporary Music at the University of Huddersfield. He has written widely on various aspects of contemporary music, with a particular focus upon the relationship of avant-garde musicians to the political movements of the 1960s. He is author of the books *The Music of Harrison Birtwistle* (Cambridge University Press, 2000), *Louis Andriessen: De Staat* (Ashgate, 2004) and *Composing Dissent: Avant-garde Music in 1960s Amsterdam* (Oxford University Press, 2013). He edited the volumes *Sound Commitments: Avant-garde Music and the Sixties* (Oxford University Press, 2009) and *Red Strains: Music and Communism outside the Communist Bloc* (Oxford University Press, 2013). He has held editorial positions with the journals *Music Analysis* and *Twentieth-Century Music*.

David Beard is Reader in Musicology at the School of Music, Cardiff University, where he specialises in contemporary music, especially post-war British music. Recent publications include chapters in *The Music of Simon Holt* (Boydell & Brewer, 2017) and *Harrison Birtwistle Studies* (Cambridge University Press, 2015), which he co-edited. He is the author of *Harrison Birtwistle's Operas and Music Theatre* (Cambridge University Press, 2012), and co-author (with Kenneth Gloag) of *Musicology: The Key Concepts* (Routledge, 2005; revised second edition 2016). In 2016–17 he was awarded a Cardiff University Research Leave Fellowship to work on the music of Judith Weir. He is a Trustee and member of the Editorial Board of *Music & Letters* (Oxford University Press).

Stefania Bruno holds a PhD in the History of Modern and Contemporary Theatre. She is a dramaturg, and is responsible for the research of the Cooperative En Kai Pan in Naples, which she co-founded in 2014. She is also teacher of creative writing and dramaturgy at the Naples Lalineascritta Laboratori di Scrittura. Her main areas of subject expertise are theatre of the second half of the twentieth century, Luca Ronconi, and the relationships between theatre and music theatre. Publications include 'Luca Ronconi maestro d'attori: il Centro Teatrale Santacristina' (*Acting Archives Review*, 2013) and 'L'avanguardia teatrale e la definizione di un nuovo codice spettacolare. Questioni linguistiche e drammaturgiche nel solco di una periodizzazione problematica' (in *Teatro di avanguardia e composizione sperimentale per la scena in Italia: 1950–1975*, 2017).

Contributors xiii

Esteban Buch (b. Buenos Aires, 1963) is a professor of music history at the École des Hautes Études en Sciences Sociales (EHESS) in Paris. A specialist in the relationships between music and politics in the twentieth century, he is the author of *Trauermarsch. L'Orchestre de Paris dans l'Argentine de la dictature* (Seuil, 2016), *Le cas Schönberg. Naissance de l'avant-garde musicale* (Gallimard, 2006), and *Beethoven's Ninth: A Political History* (University of Chicago Press, 2003), among other books. He is also the co-editor of *Composing for the State: Music in Twentieth Century Dictatorships* (Ashgate, 2016) and other collective volumes. He has written opera librettos, including for Sebastian Rivas's *Aliados. Un opéra du temps réel* (2013).

Angela Ida De Benedictis holds a PhD in musicology (Pavia University) and undertook post-doctoral research in Berlin with a grant from the Alexander von Humboldt Foundation. She is a member of the Scientific Board of the Paul Sacher Foundation in Basel (appointed 2014), where she is curator of twenty-five manuscript collections (including Berio, Boulez, Lachenmann, Maderna and Sciarrino). She is Director of the Centro Studi Luciano Berio and member of the Scientific Committee of the Archivio Luigi Nono. Previously she worked as Assistant Professor at the University of Pavia. Her main research interests are theory and analysis relating to twentieth-century music; music theatre; music for radio; and music and technology. Publications include the writings of Nono (Ricordi-LIM, 2000; il Saggiatore, 2007; University of California Press, 2018) and Berio (Einaudi, 2013), books and essays on theory and analysis, and critical editions of works by Berio, Berberian, Maderna, Nono and Togni.

Björn Heile is Professor of Music (Post-1900) at the University of Glasgow. He is the author of *The Music of Mauricio Kagel* (2006), the editor of *The Modernist Legacy: Essays on New Music* (2009), co-editor (with Peter Elsdon and Jenny Doctor) of *Watching Jazz: Encountering Jazz Performance on Screen* (2016) and co-editor (with Charles Wilson) of *The Routledge Research Companion to Modernism in Music* (2018). He specialises in new music, experimental music theatre and jazz, with particular interests in embodied cognition, global modernism and cosmopolitanism. He has more projects than he cares to remember, most of which inhabit the twilight zone between the utopian and the doomed.

Harm Langenkamp lectures in Musicology at the University of Amsterdam. His research explores the intersections between music, international relations and cultural diplomacy, and has been supported by the Netherlands Organisation for Scientific Research, the Paul Sacher Foundation, the Harry Ransom Center (University of Texas at Austin), the Beinecke Library (Yale University) and the Rockefeller Archive Center. He is currently preparing a monograph based on his dissertation (tentatively titled *Cosmopolitan Counterpoint: Overt and Covert Musical Warfare and Diplomacy in the Early Cold War*), which analyses advocacies of musical cosmopolitanisms during the early Cold War, with a particular focus on the music festivals the Russian émigré composer Nicolas xiv *Contributors*

Nabokov organised on behalf of the CIA-sponsored Congress for Cultural Freedom in the 1950s and early 1960s.

Alessandro Mastropietro graduated in Composition, Electronic Music and Orchestral Conducting. He obtained his PhD in 2005 (dissertation title 'Nuovo Teatro Musicale tra Roma e Palermo, 1961–1973'; published – enlarged and updated – in 2019 by LIM, Lucca) from the University 'La Sapienza' in Rome. He is now Research Professor in Musicology at the University of Catania. His research primarily focuses on the music of the last 60 years, with emphasis on experimental music theatre in Italy; and instrumental music from the second half of the eighteenth century, especially Boccherini's works. He has edited the critical edition of Domenico Guaccero's writings in the 'Le Sfere' series, and published volumes on composers Paolo Renosto (LIM, 2013) and Francesco Pennisi (LIM, 2014).

Andreas Münzmay is professor of musicology at Paderborn University, Germany. He holds degrees in musicology, music and French studies. In 2008 he received a PhD from the University of Arts, Berlin, for his thesis on French librettist Eugène Scribe (*Musikdramaturgie und Kulturtransfer*, publ. Schliengen 2010). He taught musicology in Berlin, Stuttgart, Potsdam, Bayreuth and Frankfurt and has been working as an editor in the 'OPERA – Spektrum des europäischen Musiktheaters' historical-critical hybrid editions series of the Akademie der Wissenschaften Mainz. In addition to his editorial work in the Digital Humanities, he conducts research primarily on music theatre, music in the context of other media, improvisation and jazz. Andreas Münzmay was awarded the Hermann Abert Prize from the German Society for Music Research (GfM) in 2012.

Vincenzina C. Ottomano is currently postdoctoral research assistant and lecturer at the University of Berne as well as Assistant at the Centro Studi Luciano Berio (Florence). She received her PhD in Musicology at the University of Berne on *The Impact of Russian Opera in France and Italy*. Her research interests include: history and theory of music theatre (particularly of the nineteenth and twentieth century), Russian and Italian opera, reception studies, and music and politics. Her publications include *Claudio Abbado alla Scala* (with Angela Ida De Benedictis; Rizzoli, 2008), a special issue of the journal *Musiktheorie* on Russian opera's reception ('Kulturtransfer und transnationale Wechselbeziehungen: Russisches Musiktheater in Bewegung'; 2015) and the volume *Luciano Berio. Interviste e colloqui* (Einaudi, 2017). Since 2015 she has also been managing editor of the journal *verdiperspektiven*.

Francesca Placanica is a singer and artist-researcher currently holding a Visiting Research Fellowship at the University of Huddersfield. She lectured in Performance and Musicology at Maynooth University, where she also acted as project leader for the Irish Research Council-funded postdoctoral project 'En-Gendering Monodrama: Artistic Research and Experimental Production' (2015–17). Francesca is co-editor of *Cathy Berberian: Pioneer of*

Contemporary Vocality (Ashgate, 2014) and holds a PhD from the University of Southampton (2013). In 2017 she was granted an Irish Arts Council music commission award for a new vocal piece from composer Ryan Molloy and poet Martin Dyar, which she premiered in 2018. Her publications, spanning opera studies and twentieth-century vocality, have appeared and are forthcoming in numerous anthologies and journals. She has been invited as performer and speaker at international symposia and is the creator of the *Embodied Monologues* interdisciplinary research series and network.

Holly Rogers is reader in Music at Goldsmiths, University of London. Before this, she was the founding director of the Research Centre for Audio-Visual Media at the University of Liverpool, Fulbright Scholar at San Francisco's DocFilm Institute, and Research Fellow at the Humanities Institute of Ireland. Holly is the author of *Visualising Music: Audio-Visual Relationships in Avant-Garde Film and Video Art* (Lambert Academic Publishing, 2010) and *Sounding the Gallery: Video and the Rise of Art-Music* (Oxford University Press, 2013). She has also edited several books on audiovisual media: *Music and Sound in Documentary Film* (Routledge, 2014), *The Music and Sound of Experimental Film* (Oxford University Press, 2017) and *Transmedia Directors: Sound, Image and the Digital Swirl* (2019). She is a founding editor for the Bloomsbury book series New Approaches to Sound, Music and Media.

Julia H. Schröder (PhD) is a musicologist with research interests in contemporary music, experimental composition, electroacoustic music, sound art, music and dance, sound in theatre, and sound studies. Currently she holds a postdoctoral position as researcher at the Johannes Gutenberg-Universität Mainz and teaches on the Master's programme 'Sound Studies and Sonic Arts' at Berlin's University of the Arts. Her book publications include: *Zur Position der Musikhörenden. Konzeptionen ästhetischer Erfahrung im Konzert* [On the Position of the Listeners: Concepts of Aesthetic Experience in Concert Situations] (Hofheim, 2014); *Cage and Cunningham Collaboration. In- und Interdependenz von Musik und Tanz* [Cage & Cunningham Collaboration: In- and Interdependency of Music and Dance] (Hofheim, 2011).

Jean-François Trubert is Professor of Music, Head of Art Department, and Head of Programme for Music Education at the Université Côte d'Azur (Université Nice Sophia Antipolis). He has received grants from the Kurt Weill Foundation (New York) and the Paul Sacher Foundation (Switzerland). His main research interests are music dramaturgy and new music theatre, including Kurt Weill, Hanns Eisler, Luciano Berio, Mauricio Kagel and Georges Aperghis. He has given lectures internationally, and has been published in peer-reviewed books and journals (including *Contemporary Music Review*, *Brecht Yearbook*, *Loxias* and *Dissonance*). He is currently coordinator of the 'Avant-Gardes' collection at the French publisher Delatour.

Acknowledgements

In keeping with the guiding principles of the book series *Musical Cultures of the Twentieth Century*, this volume has its origin in a conference held in Venice in November 2016. The conference offered an opportunity to test new readings and analyses, which could subsequently be developed and refined in light of collective discussion. Thanks are due to the Fondazione Giorgio Cini, which hosted the 2016 event, and to the international advisory committee – comprising Gianmario Borio, Giordano Ferrari, Dörte Schmidt, Daniela Tortora, and the editor of this book – which determined both the themes of the conference and the line-up of speakers. In the early stages of preparation of this book, Dörte Schmidt undertook important editorial work on a number of the chapters and provided valuable advice to the editor. Thanks are also due to Professor Schmidt's student assistant at the Universität der Künste Berlin, Yorick Lohse, for fact-checking and copyediting of several chapters. Further helpful suggestions came from Routledge's anonymous reviewers. Routledge's music editors Heidi Bishop and Laura Sandford, and editorial assistant Annie Vaughan, have offered encouraging and patient support as the volume has come together. Finally, thanks are due to Sally Davis for the translation from Italian of the chapter by Stefania Bruno and to Marco Cosci for preparing the volume's index.

Acknowledgements for individual chapters, including permission to reproduce copyrighted material, are included within the chapters concerned.

Introduction

Why 'new music theatre' now?

Robert Adlington

This volume has its origin in a two-day conference, convened in November 2016 by the Institute of Music of the Giorgio Cini Foundation in Venice. An advisory committee comprising Gianmario Borio, Giordano Ferrari, Dörte Schmidt, Daniela Tortora and the editor of this volume assembled a list of speakers from across Europe, to address six crucial themes for the topic of experimentation in European music theatre between 1955 and 1975. The 2016 conference itself sprang out of a 2015 seminar at the Cini Foundation on 'Avant-garde Theatre and Experimental Music for the Stage in Italy 1950–1975'. The interest raised by that event, whose proceedings are now published online (Borio, Ferrari and Tortora (eds) 2017), cemented the view that a broadening of the enquiry to other parts of Europe was both timely and necessary, in order to grasp the transnational currents that were foundational to the development of European new music theatre during this period.

The present volume preserves the scope and structure of the 2016 conference, whilst permitting contributing authors to deepen their analysis in the light of the discussions that took place in Venice and subsequently. The six themes of the conference now form the basis for the main sections of the book. As described below in greater detail, these address: the influence upon new music theatre of new conceptions of drama from the spoken theatre; the engagement of composers, performers and producers with new technologies; the involvement of new music theatre with political issues; the role of non-conventional places and spaces; new music theatre's reconception of performance; and the questions that face today's musicologists and analysts when studying new music theatre. The aspiration is to offer a more sustained assessment of these key themes than is possible in the survey format adopted by a number of published studies (e.g. Mahling and Pfarr (eds) 2002; Reininghaus and Schneider (eds) 2004; Salzman and Desi 2008). The chronological period appraised within this volume offers a further point of difference with other publications (e.g. Danuser (ed.) 2003; Ferrari (ed.) 2006, 2007, 2008 and 2009; Rebstock and Roesner (eds) 2012); volume contributors are specifically interested in the 'transformations' that characterised new music theatre production during the social, cultural and political ferment of the long 1960s. The primary focus remains Western Europe, but a number of the chapters also recognise the centrality of kinds of influence and exchange from further afield, notably the United States.

2 *Introduction*

Each of the Venice speakers is represented in this volume, and a thirteenth contributor, Stefania Bruno, was added to fill out the delineation of new music theatre's relation to contemporaneous experimental spoken theatre. As a consequence, the book faithfully reproduces a key goal of the conference, namely to encompass multiple European perspectives on the subject, reflecting the different emphases and debates across national traditions of research and scholarly enquiry. This aspect can be perceived in the great diversity of repertoire assessed, including many practitioners and works that have remained little known outside their country of origin. It also manifests itself in the different approaches adopted by authors, which arise from a mix of archival, applied and theoretical methodologies, and scholarly perspectives that are variously empirical, systematic, hermeneutical and/or critical in nature.

A further consequence of the multi-perspectival nature of our project concerns the question of how the subject itself – new music theatre – is to be defined. As a number of authors observe, deciding what does and what does not belong to this genre – and even whether such a genre can be said to have existed at all – has long been a preoccupation of music historians, and indeed was present also within practitioners' contemplations at the time. Rather than adhering to a single conception across all chapters, authors have been encouraged to be alert to the ambiguities in existing terminology, and the lively debates that have existed for over sixty years about the boundaries between instrumental music, opera, and music theatre – and, one might add, dance, mime, spoken theatre, the popular musical, performance art, happenings, and installations as well. Contributors to this book adopt different positions on these questions, meaning that the volume's coverage includes a wide spectrum of creative endeavour, bridging institutions, art forms and audiences that are sometimes regarded as lying outside the bounds of avant-garde music. It may be said, however, that every chapter shares an interest in a remarkable facet of adventurous music-making in Europe (and indeed elsewhere) during the years 1955 to 1975: namely, the adoption of an acutely reflective or critical approach to the relation of music's sonic qualities to other aspects of its performance. It is here that one element of our project's timeliness resides.

Why new music theatre now?

In the first volume of this book series, *Musical Listening in the Age of Technological Reproduction*, Nicholas Cook argues that 'the idea of a purely acoustic music' – a music to which the appropriate audience response is solely auditory – held sway only 'as a sixty-year hiatus separating the regimes of the old and the new multimedia' (Cook 2015: 189). Before the advent of mass-produced sound recordings, musical experience was inherently multimodal (that is to say, involved multiple senses) because it took place in the physical presence of performers who were seen as well as heard. The public context and the characteristics of particular performance spaces added further to the multimedia spectacle. The significance for musical experience of such non-auditory stimuli was repressed, rather than eradicated, by the spread of aesthetic ideologies that sought to downplay the social dimension of music-making and elevated instead the 'ideal thought' of the composer-genius. Since the 1980s, Cook argues, the spread of video and digital technology has brought audiences back to an acceptance of music as a form speaking to multiple senses. Today, every song comes with a video, YouTube is the leading medium for discovering new music of all kinds, acts of musical creation are mostly mediated through a computer screen (and increasingly the multimediality of computer technology also informs the compositional process), and the silos separating distinct artistic genres are being steadily dismantled. During the 'hiatus' between these two eras, audiences may have thought they were 'just listening' – whether on record, over the radio, or in the formal and controlled environment of the modern concert hall – but (as Björn Heile notes in his chapter in this volume) modern cognitive psychology argues against a rigid separation of the different sensory modes, proposing instead that audition is invariably affected by visual perception, and that even 'blind' audition mobilises experiences that draw on the understanding and sensibilities of the entire human sensorium.

In all these respects, European new music theatre of the period 1955–1975 connected to larger continuities and conventions in human musicking. This is a point overlooked by Cook: he prefers to regard the post-1945 avant-garde as complicit in the policing of the notion of a purely acoustic music, the Romantic ideal of supra-social invention being taken up by a 'modernist cartel' (Cook's words) that consigned any musical practice that was overly dependent upon the 'non-musical' (often meaning: non-sonic) to the trash heap of kitsch and entertainment (ibid.: 194–5). But in the music theatre of composers including Birtwistle, Kagel, Ligeti, Nono and Stockhausen – figures that Cook would certainly align with what he disparagingly terms 'hardcore modernism' – we in fact find an array of vigorous interrogations of the idea of pure music. These interrogations may involve attempts to expand the category of music out to new 'parameters' of movement and space; the exploration of the permeable boundaries between sound and sense; the dissolution of the boundaries separating traditional artistic genres; or opening the floodgates to ideas, events and meanings from the wider world.

If the new music theatre of these decades amounts, in varied ways, to a rediscovery of music's historical multimediality, it also strikingly anticipates compositional directions of the present. A workshop at the 2016 Darmstadt International Summer Course entitled 'Music in the Expanded Field' sprang from the perception that 'today, many composers are working beyond the traditional boundaries of music, expanding into other media and/or practices, often drawing from the visual fields' (Cicilliani 2015). Earlier the same year, Jennifer Walshe proposed the term 'the New Discipline' 'as a way . . . to connect compositions which . . . share the common concern of being rooted in the physical, theatrical and visual, as well as musical; pieces which often invoke the extramusical, which activate the non-cochlear' (Walshe 2016). Such an expanded conception of the composer's activity is perhaps to be expected as a product of the transformative developments in digital technology. Walshe, for instance, has invoked the post-1970s phenomena of MTV and the internet as reasons for not wishing to resurrect the historically resonant category of 'music theatre' for her

4   *Introduction*

own unclassifiable practice: for her, 'the physical, theatrical and visual' are just properties of music. The emergence during the 1990s of what has been termed 'relational aesthetics' in the field of visual art, and of 'immersive' productions in the spoken theatre, form further contexts for recent composers' changing preoccupations (see Bourriaud 2002; Machon 2013).

Underpinning many composers' work in this area are motivations that were clearly presaged in the new music theatre of the 1950s and 1960s. For instance, the 2016 Darmstadt workshop call highlighted how 'music in the expanded field' concerned a *musical* practice for which sound was insufficient – in distinction to 'many more conventional combinations of media, where the respective boundaries – along with the different authors – can easily be detected' (Cicilliani 2015). This desire to move beyond conventional pairings of artistic practices, and to extend musical principles visually, were already familiar themes in 1960s music theatre, not least in works that made innovative use of mime and gesture (appraised in David Beard's chapter in the present volume). Walshe's work foregrounds the performing body in an effort to overcome what Alex Ross has termed 'the aggressive affectlessness of the average professional musician' (Ross, in Cook 2015: 195), and to recognise instead that (in Walshe's words) 'there are people on the stage, and that these people are/have bodies' (Walshe 2016). But this was a preoccupation already for figures such as Dieter Schnebel, whose series of 'visible music' works of the early 1960s arose from the perception that the composer controlled not just sounds but also 'actions' (see Jarzina 2005); and for Mauricio Kagel, whose classic works of instrumental theatre gleefully parody the physical manners of classical performance. Both Schnebel and Kagel played a prominent role in the congress 'Neue Musik – Neue Szene' ('New Music – New Stage') at the 1966 Darmstadt course – a clear precursor to the 'expanded field' meeting held half a century later (Decroupet and Kovács 1997).

Younger composers today are also drawn to the way that a foregrounding of the performing body tends to invoke the concrete worlds of first-person experience, social interaction and political action. The human body, Jessica Aszodi has recently argued, is inherently referential, offering a means of exploring 'the interior experience of music making, community kinetics, directionality, interpersonal relationships, sexual hierarchies' and so on (Aszodi 2017). For Walshe, the body is not just a referential site; it's a political one:

> Different people, with their different bodies, mean vastly different things, are read in vastly different ways. In the last year or two in particular, as movements such as Black Lives Matter gained traction, as discussions around non-binary gender and trans rights pushed to the fore, as elite composers discussed their BDSM [bondage, discipline and sadomasochism] lifestyle openly, it seemed that perhaps it might be possible for new music to dive into *people*.
> (Walshe 2016)

Of course, it could be argued that 'different people, with their different bodies' – interpreted (for instance) in terms of the perceived threat of strangers from afar, or the allure of a sexual 'other' – have been the mainstay of music drama since the birth of opera. Admittedly, it's a preoccupation that has been handled in diverse ways by successive generations. For many composers of new music theatre in the 1950s and 1960s, the domain of everyday interpersonal experience remained problematic as subject matter, the 'everyday' tending to serve as a dichotomous pole to progressive art-making. For these composers, the themes of colonialism and imperialism offered more reliably confrontational means of engaging with the wider world – one thinks of Nono's *Intolleranza 1960* (1961), discussed by a number of contributors to this volume, as well as Maderna's *Hyperion en het geweld* (1968) and the collaboratively composed *Reconstructie* (1969), discussed in this volume by Harm Langenkamp. European music theatre also engaged with kinds of sexual liberation, as in Bussotti's *Passion selon Sade* (1966) and Maxwell Davies' *Vesalii icons* (1969). Even closer to Walshe's focus on the physical attributes of musicians are the creative approaches taken by leading stage performers of new music theatre in the 1960s and 1970s, who, as Francesca Placanica discusses in her chapter on 'embodied commitments', sought to assert the body on stage as a textual figure in its own right.

A different route to the political within 'the expanded field' of our own time is explored by Ashley Fure's recent 'opera for objects' *The Force of Things* (2016). This work encourages reflection on the relationship of humanity to the environment, by placing things, rather than humans, centre stage. In Fure's words, the work's choreographed movement of an array of suspended objects (including melting ice) presents a 'continually transforming perceptual space' that places humans 'not above but amidst this web of things and force we call a world' (Fure, in Landa 2016). Fure's work may be regarded as a descendant of the anti-establishment critique of earlier new music theatre (explored in the present volume by Langenkamp and Esteban Buch), albeit that the focus of attention has shifted from the exploitation and control of humans, to that of the natural world on which we all depend. But Fure's work also brings back into focus a central concern for composers of the 1950s and 1960s, between the abstract and the representational. Her programme note encourages audiences to relate their experience of the work to wider environmental dangers, but the work itself contains no explicitly referential content and could be appraised purely in sonic-sculptural terms. For many composers of music theatre between 1955 and 1975, even as levels of extra-musical meaning were admitted back into their compositions, there remained a question as to how to forge a convincing relationship between those meanings and the autonomous structural devices of advanced compositional technique – a conundrum addressed in various ways in the chapters by Alessandro Mastropietro, David Beard and Björn Heile. That this remains an abiding concern for today's producers of music theatre is indicated by the workshop 'Sound and Story' convened in 2017 at Berlin's Wissenschaftskolleg, involving the composers Liza Lim, Isabel Mundry and Hans Thomalla alongside academics and dramaturgs, which aimed to assess 'the conflict between narration (representation of stories) and presence (autonomy of sound, image and movement) in contemporary opera' (Thomalla 2017).

6   *Introduction*

As was the case fifty years ago, composers' present-day exploration of an expanded practice has not occurred simply through a sense of inner aesthetic compulsion. Practicalities and logistical pressures have played their part – not least, the contraction of well-resourced opportunities that has accompanied our era of austerity, and the conservatism that this has encouraged amongst the established institutions. Admittedly, such practical factors are sometimes difficult to separate from a dislike on the part of young creatives for institutional entanglements and the formalities of conventional venues. A feature of the expanded practice of collectives such as Mocrep and Bastard Assignments has been the replacement of the grandiose 'total theatre' model – whose post-war revival is chronicled in this volume by Julia Schröder – with more intimate productions housed in unconventional spaces and animated by do-it-yourself technologies. These often encourage more flexible relationships between performer and audience, marking a departure from the segregation of the conventional concert hall and thus inevitably highlighting the individual bodies and acts of performance that underpin all presentation of music. They also draw attention to the physical setting for the production, and indeed may frequently make a virtue of the qualities of the space as part of the performance itself (as occurred also in late 1960s Rome and Avignon, scenes described here in chapters by Alessandro Mastropietro and Jean-François Trubert). In works such as Lia Kohl's *sorry, thanks* or Caitlin Rowley's *Aides memoire* the effect of these new orientations is truly to complicate the categories of music and theatre: sociality and place instead come to the fore.[1] In these regards too, the 'transformations' attempted in European new music theatre fifty years ago remain instructive for contemporary composition today, both for what has been retrieved or rediscovered, and for what has been left behind.

Overview of the volume

As mentioned above, the book, like the conference from which it developed, is structured according to six themes, determined by the conference advisory committee as representing areas particularly requiring fresh scholarly attention. Each theme is tackled by two (or in the first case, three) authors presenting complementary perspectives. Part I, 'Between the avant-gardes: new music theatre and new conceptions of drama', addresses the ways in which, in working towards a new music theatre, composers and their collaborators (including writers, stage directors, performers and others) drew upon and adapted theories of drama from both the so-called 'historical' and 'neo' avant-gardes. Stefania Bruno surveys the complex and sometimes dissonant counterpoint that existed between different artistic avant-gardes in late 1950s Europe; this counterpoint reflected diverse national histories and institutional affiliations, and manifested itself in varying attitudes to the very idea of an 'avant-garde'. She proceeds to show how the 1960s then

---

1 These works are documented at www.mocrep.org/#/bastards/ and http://caitlinrowley.com/music/aides-memoire-pov/ respectively (both accessed 4 October 2018).

Introduction 7

saw a measure of convergence take place amongst theatre practitioners, in which the decentring of the literary text and an embrace of openness played key roles. Paying particular attention to this story as it played out in Italy, Bruno traces the rise of 'scenic writing' as symptomatic of the 'new theatre' – a concept that, as Alessandro Mastropietro shows in a later chapter, had direct consequence for producers of music theatre.

Julia Schröder and Vincenzina Ottomano both focus upon composers' interest in leading figures of earlier European avant-garde theatre. Schröder grapples with a buzzword of the 1960s, 'total theatre', which for a while seemed to be the desired end of any composer embarking upon a theatrical project, but which had important precursors in the work of Erwin Piscator, Vsevolod Meyerhold and Antonin Artaud (amongst others). As Schröder recounts, in 1966 Mauricio Kagel raised the uncomfortable question of the proximity of pre-war 'total theatre' experimentation to the grand spectacles of twentieth-century totalitarian regimes; but as Schröder makes clear, composers such as Nono and Bernd Alois Zimmermann wished to retrieve the socially critical element of pre-war multimedia experiments, and the idea of total theatre also found expression in new small-scale works that sidestepped grandiosity and the grip of state institutions. Ottomano traces the influence of other leading figures of twentieth-century spoken theatre – specifically, Beckett, Ionesco and Brecht (the latter as filtered through the writings of Ernst Bloch and Lionel Abel) – on Ligeti, Berio and Pousseur. By so doing, she offers historical illumination of three important themes in much new music theatre: an interrogative approach to language; audience participation; and the self-consciousness of the theatrical act. Both Schröder and Ottomano highlight the important role played in the cross-European reception of such theatrical ideas by new translations of key works and international tours by leading practitioners.

Part II addresses 'Expansions of technology'. From the mid-1950s, music theatre was created in a context of rapidly developing new entertainment and media technologies. This context could be the source both of anxiety and inspiration. New music theatre increasingly incorporated visual and light projections, electronics, sound diffusion, and video and sound recordings. Radio and television were also seen as having potential for music-theatrical experiment, carrying the appeal of unprecedentedly large potential audiences. At stake in this relationship was the degree to which new music theatre accommodated itself to the modes of production and reception characteristic of the new media, or instead subverted these technologies and utilised them to quite new ends. Holly Rogers considers the latter dilemma in her discussion of moving-image technology in the 1965 Boston production of Nono's *Intolleranza*. Noting the tendency for today's opera productions to utilise film in order to heighten a sense of immersion and hyperreality, Rogers analyses Josef Svoboda's deployment of 'Laterna Magika' technology as serving very different ends, which register both the Brechtian tradition of the *V-effekt*, but also an emerging consciousness amongst the American public about the way in which television technology mediated and even misrepresented global events. Andreas Münzmay's discussion of the use of electronic tape sound in music theatre works also draws substantially on contemporaneous debate about

8 *Introduction*

the new media. Taking Marshall McLuhan's theorisation of a medium as something that 'extends man', Münzmay proposes a typography of kinds of 'extension' of the theatre through electronic sound, highlighting in the process the variety of theatrical functions that may be served by electronic means.

The appeal of music theatre to composers in the 1960s must be attributed in part to the way in which theatrical ventures enabled overt engagement with the political and cultural debates of the time. New music theatre resonated with the subversive and antagonistic spirit of the long 1960s at multiple levels. Many works featured explicitly political subject matter. Others offered more implicit kinds of critique in their restructuring of theatrical behaviours and modes of expression. The rejection of the traditional theatrical space was considered part of a general critique of established institutions, with formal as well as institutional consequences. Our volume contains two chapters assessing different aspects of the use of music theatre for 'the critique of established power' (Part III). Harm Langenkamp takes as his point of departure the cultural congress hosted by Fidel Castro in Havana in January 1968. A number of prominent European composers and writers who attended subsequently turned to music theatre as a means to continue their struggle for alternative social models. Langenkamp's discussion of two such works, staged in Belgium and the Netherlands, is instructive in pointing to the problems that regularly arose with such aspirations: first, the tension between individual artists' strongly held ideological commitments and the collective collaboration (and therefore compromise) intrinsic to most music theatre works; second, the troubling relationship with European 'establishment' institutions – such as national arts councils, festivals and opera companies – who increasingly found their purposes served by association with 'progressive' politics and ideals. The paradoxes of the situation are underlined by the case-study work examined by Esteban Buch: the 'grand opera' *Todos caerán* ('Everyone must fall', 1972) by a representative of an older generation, René Leibowitz. This work, through its reliance upon the traditional forms and theatrical devices of the opera house, represented an implicit critique of the more aesthetically adventurous work of younger composers, and its libretto additionally presented ostensibly revolutionary movements as themselves having become a kind of 'established power'; yet the work was never performed. Buch approaches the work as a revealing negative image of the new music theatre of the time.

The concern with the critique of established power spills over into Part IV, which examines 'New venues and environments'. This section explores institutional and geographical contexts for the production of new music theatre, including the role of fringe (or 'off') theatre, alternative cultural festivals, and newly prominent centres of artistic production. Relevant considerations include the different conceptualisations of marginality and difference characterising such contexts, and the place of local and regional networks – both artistic and institutional – in giving shape to music theatre activity. The authors addressing this theme concentrate on two exemplary situations: the complex network of artists and initiatives that made Rome a stimulating site for theatrical experimentation; and the emergence of music theatre as a primary strand of the programming at the Festival d'Avignon

Introduction 9

in southern France. Alessandro Mastropietro, writing on Rome, reveals a scene of great creative ferment during the 1960s, characterised by adventurous collaborations between different artistic practices, and the participation of both 'fringe' and established venues. The events and works chronicled here are little known outside of Italy, a fact that reminds us of the limited international mobility of significant works of music theatre, perhaps in part because of their intense engagement with local languages and theatrical traditions. Jean-François Trubert places the emphasis upon key personal relationships in order to explain the sudden flowering of music theatre activity at the Festival d'Avignon. Essential to this development, which kickstarted the rather delayed inception of new music theatre composition in France, were the relationships of festival director Jean Vilar with choreographer Maurice Béjart and radio producer Guy Erismann. A further central role in Trubert's story is played by the American theatre troupe The Living Theatre, whose itinerant productions, staged around Europe, made an impact on many of the musicians surveyed in this book.

Amongst the lessons learnt from groups such as The Living Theatre was the availability and potential of a quite new conception of the performer, one who, far from being limited to the role of faithful executant, was instead a full participant in the creation of new work – and moreover, for whom artistic practice was not always to be separated from other domains of life. In Part V, 'Reconceiving the performer', two chapters address different manifestations of the co-creative role taken by performers in new music theatre. David Beard looks specifically at mime, which was especially (although not exclusively) influential in British music theatre during the 1960s and early 1970s. Mime, by dispensing with language, appealed as a kind of neutral meeting ground for musical performance and spoken theatre, and it reflected a growing awareness of the potential of the performing human body within theatre practice at large (Beard talks of a 'musicalisation' of the theatre world at this time). In the case of British music theatre, the interest in mime also reflected specifically upon the particular talents of an individual performer, Mark Furneaux, who worked with Birtwistle, Goehr, Maxwell Davies and other leading composers. The role of extraordinary talents is also central to Francesca Placanica's discussion of new vocal practices in music theatre, which pays particular attention to the part played by Roy Hart and Cathy Berberian in the creation of music theatre works that are today often attached to the name of only one composer. Placanica's wider argument concerns the relationship between a view of new music theatre that foregrounds the embodiment of works in performance, with a historiographical recognition of the collaborative authorship at play in the workshop situations where works were often developed: to speak of a single author is often a grave misconception.

Part VI, finally, turns to the challenges of 'Analyzing new music theatre'. Some of these challenges are already evident from the discussions in the preceding section: the centrality to a work's original conception of actors' movements, even their personal physiognomy, not to mention other aspects of the *mise-en-scene* devised for a premiere production, are rarely reflected in composers' scores. From this arises fundamental questions regarding the identity of the work, and the

10 *Introduction*

status (and incompleteness) of different kinds of documentation. Björn Heile's approach to these challenges is to foreground an element of cognition mentioned earlier in this introduction: namely, that no experience of sound takes place without some kind of 'embodied' (if imagined) experience of movement. Heile lays out some of the possible consequences of this for our understanding of musical experience, proposing that a highly salient aspect of our response to experimental music theatre concerns the degree of congruency 'between the movements we imagine in response to the sounds we hear and the actual movements' made by musicians. What results from this is a scheme for interrelating both sound and gesture that moves us beyond the purely sonic focus of most music analysis. Angela Ida De Benedictis throws the spotlight onto the question of what documentation is considered to be significant for an adequate analytical account. Noting the tendency of accounts of music theatre to concentrate upon just one element of what is inherently a multimedia phenomenon, De Benedictis argues that 'in new music theatre the music gradually stops being the structural element *par excellence*', with the consequent necessity of 'giving priority to analytical instruments that do not take off only from the score, but above all from the performance documentation'. This includes materials left by collaborators other than the (named) composer, and, often most valuably, surviving audiovisual records of original productions – although De Benedictis notes that these are sadly often either fragmentary or non-existent. If this represents a pessimistic point of conclusion for music analysts and historians, it nonetheless serves as an important reminder of what tended to bring composers to theatrical experimentation in the first place (and has continued to do in the present day): namely, how to seize upon the ways in which music is always more than just itself.

References

Aszodi, Jessica (2017), 'Undisciplined music', *New Music Box*, https://nmbx.newmusicusa.org/undisciplined-music/ (accessed 14 May 2018).

Borio, Gianmario, Giordano Ferrari and Daniela Tortora (eds) (2017), *Teatro d'avanguardia e composizione sperimentale per la scena*, Venezia: Fondazione Giorgio Cini Onlus, http://omp.cini.it/index.php/FGCOP/catalog/book/3 (accessed 14 May 2018).

Bourriaud, Nicolas (2002), *Relational Aesthetics*, trans. Matthew Copeland, Paris: Les Presses du reel.

Cicilliani, Marko (2015), 'Call for projects "Music in the Expanded Field" – workshop on audiovisuality, 48th International Summer Course for New Music Darmstadt 2016', email call for proposals, online at www.degem.de/call-call-for-projects-music-in-the-expanded-field-marko-ciciliani/ (accessed 14 May 2018).

Cook, Nicholas (2015), 'Hearing images, seeing sounds: listening outside the modernist box', in Gianmario Borio (ed.), *Musical Listening in the Age of Technological Reproduction*, Farnham, UK: Ashgate, pp. 185–202.

Danuser, Hermann (ed.) (2003), *Musiktheater heute: Internationales Symposion der Paul Sacher Stiftung Basel 2001*, Mainz: Schott.

Decroupet, Pascal and Inge Kovács (1997), 'Musik und Szene', in Gianmario Borio and Hermann Danuser (eds), *Im Zenit der Moderne: Die Internationalen Feienkurse für Neue Musik Darmstadt 1946–1966*, volume 2, Freiburg: Rombach, pp. 311–32.

Ferrari, Giordano (ed.) (2006), *L'opéra éclaté. La dramaturgie musicale entre 1969 et 1984*, Paris: L'Harmattan.

Ferrari, Giordano (ed.) (2007), *La musique et la scène. L'écriture musicale et son expression scénique au XXe siècle*, Paris: L'Harmattan.

Ferrari, Giordano (ed.) (2008), *La parole sur scène. Voix, texte, signifié*, Paris: L'Harmattan.

Ferrari, Giordano (ed.) (2009), *Pour une scène actuelle*, Paris: L'Harmattan.

Jarzina, Asja (2005), *Gestische Musik und musikalische Gesten. Dieter Schnebels 'visible music'*, Berlin: Weidler.

Landa, Carla A. (2016), *Selected Works 2010–2016*, online at https://issuu.com/carla-landa/docs/2016landa (accessed 14 May 2018).

Machon, Josephine (2013), *Immersive Theatres: Intimacy and Immediacy in Contemporary Performance*, Basingstoke, UK: Palgrave Macmillan.

Mahling, Christoph-Hellmut and Kristina Pfarr (eds) (2002), *Musiktheater im Spannungsfeld zwischen Tradition und Experiment (1960 bis 1980)*, Tutzing: Schneider.

Rebstock, Matthias and David Roesner (eds) (2012), *Composed Theatre: Aesthetics, Practices, Processes*, Chicago, IL: University of Chicago Press.

Reininghaus, Frieder and Katja Schneider (eds) (2004), *Experimentelles Musik- und Tanztheater*, Laaber: Laaber-Verlag.

Salzman, Eric and Thomas Desi (2008), *The New Music Theater: Seeing the Voice, Hearing the Body*, New York: Oxford University Press.

Thomalla, Hans (2017), 'Sound and Story', workshop synopsis, Wissenschaftskolleg zu Berlin website, www.wiko-berlin.de/veranstaltungen/workshop//sound-and-story/home/ (accessed 14 May 2018).

Walshe, Jennifer (2016), 'Die Neue Disziplin', *MusikTexte*, 149, pp. 4–5. English version: 'The new discipline', online at http://musiktexte.de/WebRoot/Store22/Shops/dc91cfee-4fdc-41fe-82da-0c2b88528c1e/MediaGallery/The_New_Discipline.pdf (accessed 14 May 2018).

Part I

Between the avant-gardes

New music theatre and new
conceptions of drama

1 The definition of a new performance code

From the avant-garde to 'new theatre'

Stefania Bruno

'What is the avant-garde?' wondered Roland Barthes in his famous article of 1961 (1961: 10). For over a decade numerous events had been taking place in the theatre and more generally in the world of art under the aegis of the avant-garde, but even so, what could or could not be labelled as such still eluded clarification in the early sixties. Indeed, the term appeared so often in contemporary accounts that the so-called avant-garde theatre had become the necessary counterpart of the so-called traditional theatre, with a resulting inevitable and continuous shift in meaning that blurred the lines between these categories even more. To use Barthes' words again, if the avant-garde was everything new, if it was everything that challenged the typical literary conventions of the time, creating unease in the audience, then one must deduce that the avant-garde was a recurring phenomenon that allowed forms and codes minus all their novelty and elements of protest to be assimilated within the repertoire, in a potentially infinite dialectic.

Such a vision is now partly outdated and the story of the avant-garde cannot be separated from a widening of the interpretative horizon. In fact, while certain aspects link the second avant-garde of the twentieth century to the historical avant-gardes and to the partial revival of their aesthetics, they also play a role in making it profoundly different. The first of these is the time it lasted. It is extremely difficult to circumscribe the time span that marks the birth and the development of the avant-garde. Numerous exhaustive attempts have been made to historicize the avant-garde, so as to produce a timeline of its crucial events and defining moments. However, if and when these studies did manage to fix the fundamental dates, the intrinsic problems in trying to summarize a phenomenon whose effects extend well beyond the conventionally assigned temporal limits became blatantly obvious. The second aspect is the strong discontinuity between the ideas and the practices of the various artists involved in the avant-garde and the birth of a 'new theatre', both in Europe and in the United States, between 1950 and 1975. This was due not only to the different cultural situations in each of the countries involved, but also to the reluctance of the various protagonists of this era to recognize themselves as part of a movement or to establish a shared ideology. The third aspect is the lasting effect of the trends and linguistic and aesthetic codes that developed during the avant-garde. These were not simply assimilated by traditional theatre, but played a role in opening up an autonomous

16 *Stefania Bruno*

theatrical field in which experimentation and research were no longer perceived as disruptive elements, but as recognized practices for stage writing.

This chapter aims to highlight some of the key events and theoretical discussions that marked not only the birth of the post-war avant-gardes but also the definition of the concept of 'new theatre'. The analysis will be conducted first by taking into consideration the wider European scenario in which the avant-garde phenomenon spread, and then by paying particular attention to the peculiarity of the Italian case. This point of view is useful to bring into focus the discontinuity between the main events of the avant-garde movements in different countries, above all during the 1950s, followed by the 'cultural alignment' (Visone 2010) that took place from 1961 onward between Italy, Europe and the United States, thanks to which the new theatre was finally recognized as the field where different artists with different visions could coexist and collaborate. Consideration will be given to the events that made this cultural alignment possible: the direct influences of the American avant-gardes and of the French new dramaturgy; the diffusion of the thought of Antonin Artaud and Bertolt Brecht and the recovery of the aesthetics of the historical avant-gardes; the attempts to build an independent circuit for experimentation; and, finally, the increasing hybridization between different artistic languages.

The analysis will focus on the Italian critical debate of the second half of the sixties, when a new generation of critics read the performances of avant-garde artists as the manifestation of a widespread desire to emancipate the languages of theatre from subordination to the written text, and to build a new relationship with the audience. The category of 'scenic writing', coined at this time by Giuseppe Bartolucci, will be used here as an encapsulation of the radical change in approach to the performative event that occurred during the spread of the avant-garde, and a necessary key to understanding why the concept of new theatre has been and still is fundamental for the historicization of Western performing arts of the twentieth century (Mango 2003). Finally, the discussion will focus on some of the main trends that developed immediately after 1968 and that became independent fields of research within the new theatre, such as theatre laboratory, theatre anthropology, third theatre and animation theatre, to show why we must consider new theatre a central twentieth-century tradition.

The rise of the avant-garde and the European scenario

Let us consider a few important dates. A key moment for the post-war American avant-garde occurred in 1952, with the happening conducted by John Cage at Black Mountain College in North Carolina. The event largely upended Western theatrical conventions. In fact, Cage's happening consisted of a series of independent actions that took place in a setting, the college dining hall, where there was no structural division between audience and performer space. The spoken text made use of all kinds of materials and its performance did not aim in any way either to construct or transmit meaning. The different languages that interacted in this environment, from music to visual arts, were all placed on the same

The definition of a new performance code 17

plane, treated as independent semantic units, and assembled in a random manner, thereby eliminating the rigid causality so typical of Western theatre. The final outcome was a completely random and unrepeatable performance, in which the dramatic action was whatever happened (Kirby 1965).

Cage's happening contributed to the foundation of a new performance genre. It was a foretaste of the long season of happenings that were yet to come, and also one of the first manifestations of that 'power of performance' (Fisher-Lichte 2004) which in the next twenty years would affect all the arts, radically transforming them in intent and form. Both Cage and the Living Theatre, founded in New York in 1947 by Julian Beck and Judith Malina, also had a direct influence on the European avant-garde (De Marinis 1987). Cage came to Europe in 1958 to participate in Darmstadt's Internationale Ferienkurse für Neue Musik. The Living Theatre began their European diaspora in 1964, which culminated in the performance of *Paradise Now* at the Avignon Festival in July 1968. Cage, along with Malina and Beck, were connected to the European avant-gardes of the early twentieth century. Malina attended Erwin Piscator's Dramatic Workshop at the New School for Social Research in New York, where she met European artists, such as Bertolt Brecht and Max Ernst, who influenced the way in which the group was organized in its first ten years of activity. Beck had strengthened his ties to the world of action painting and artists such as Jackson Pollock and Willem De Kooning, and assimilated the aesthetics of Duchamp and Picasso (Biner 1968). In the long period Cage spent in post-war Europe, he collaborated with Marcel Duchamp, came across the surrealists, and read the writings of Antonin Artaud, experiences that proved essential in his elaboration of the theory and practice of aleatory music (Cage 1981). The avantgarde style that came to Europe from the United States thus seems to come full circle, the drive for innovation arising from the revival of the past.

The European scenario in the fifties is however far more complex. The generation that had lived through World War Two was grappling with reconstruction and the need to spread the values of Liberation. The myth of the people's theatre was revived by the post-war need to transmit historical memory and civil values by striking a cultural deal with the audience, according to which aesthetic and formal concerns were linked to civil, educational and political ones. Such a vision lay behind innovations in the language of theatre in both France and Italy, albeit with differences in form and nature. In France, these innovations found embodiment in the Théâtre National Populaire (TNP) and in the Festival of Avignon, whose founder and organizer was Jean Vilar.[1] In Italy, they materialized with the establishment of the Stabili (i.e. permanent regional) theatres, starting with the foundation of Milan's Piccolo Teatro by Giorgio Strehler and Paolo Grassi in 1947. In Germany, Brecht had chosen to transfer the Berliner Ensemble to the Soviet bloc, which would not be an easy place for him and his group to leave on tour. The Berliner Ensemble performed in France on 29 June 1954 as part of the First International Paris Festival, presenting *Mutter Courage*

1 See the chapter by Jean-François Trubert in this volume.

18   *Stefania Bruno*

und ihre Kinder, but the performance scheduled during Venice's 1951 Biennale Teatro had to be cancelled because the Ensemble's members were denied visas. Despite these difficulties, one of the fundamental events of this decade was certainly the spread of Brechtian theatre, promoted in France by critics, from Barthes to Bernard Dort, who already supported the TNP. In Italy the Piccolo had officially taken over the transmission of Brecht's legacy since 1956, with the staging of *Die Dreigroschenoper* directed by Strehler.

The year 1956 marked a turning point in the decade. This was the year of Brecht's death, and of Peter Szondi's *Theorie des modernen Dramas* (Szondi 1956). Szondi's work was the first and most comprehensive attempt to analyse European dramaturgy in the years stretching from 1880 to 1950. At a time when a precise definition of the categories of tradition and avant-garde was still missing, Szondi read the history of European dramaturgy as a dichotomy between Renaissance and modern drama: whilst the first is absolute, essential and autonomous, the second arises from the rupture of dramatic unity through the introduction of an epic ego. The progressive epicization of dramatic works, from Ibsen onwards, reaches its climax in Brecht's dramaturgy, where the structure of the text is now discontinuous and the typical causal and consequential relationships of Renaissance drama have collapsed. Moreover, the way in which the sequences of syntactic elements forming the scene are assembled means that the presence of the author-director is continually visible in the dramaturgical writing. Szondi's essay was based on one of Hegel's pervading principles, namely that a work of art is a synthesis of form and content. Szondi therefore assumed that any formal change within European dramaturgy was determined by the need to express new content. He dedicated a whole chapter to Piscator, recognizing that his approach to the *mise-en-scène* was similar to a dramaturgical act. This is the only mention of direction: his analysis was still based on the conceptual identification between dramatic text and theatre. Thus, his theory continued to assume that every aspect of the performance overseen by the director is subordinate to the text and, consequently, confirmed the strong belief, still popular in Europe at that time, that any renewal of theatre had to originate from the written page.

Szondi's review did not go beyond 1950 and did not deal with the dramaturgy that had already spread throughout Europe in the period in which he was writing. In 1950 Eugène Ionesco made his début in France with *La Cantatrice chauve* at the Théâtre des Noctambules, while Roger Blin performed Beckett's *En attendant Godot* in 1953 at the Théâtre de Babylone. Arthur Adamov, whose name has traditionally been associated with the former two, began writing for the theatre in 1947. This new dramaturgy, which Barthes in 1961 had no hesitation in defining as avant-garde, stood out precisely because it questioned the supremacy of content over the form of a work of art. In this 'theatre of language' (Barthes 1961), the word is freed from a need to produce meanings. On the contrary, the impoverished setting produces an empty but strongly symbolic space in which the few objects are dulled into totems. Thus, we witness the deconstruction of the synthesis of persona and action that runs through the plot, one of the real cornerstones of Western dramaturgy from 1500 onwards. A process of dehumanization reduces the personas to objects among objects. Finally, there is no longer a relationship between word and action, the word does not act, and the action seems to have no meaning.

The Italian case

The publication in 1956 of Eduardo Sanguineti's collection of poems *Laborintus* marked the debut of the literary neo-avant-garde in Italy. The movement gained momentum over the years through numerous articles published in *Il Verri* magazine, and eventually established itself as the so-called Gruppo 63 (Group 63) during the conference held in Palermo, from 3–8 October 1963, within the Settimane Internazionali Nuova Musica (International New Music Weeks). However, it exerted little influence on the theatrical avant-garde which came to prominence in 1959. The theatrical avant-garde's origins lay instead in the crisis affecting the Stabili system and in the need expressed by the new generation of directors to question the function of the theatre itself. The opening of the Accademia Nazionale d'Arte Drammatica in 1936 and the establishment of the Stabili theatres from 1947 onwards had marked the beginning and end of a period of reform to theatrical practice, in which stage direction finally became regularly employed in Italy – far later than in the rest of Europe. Yet this reform was unable to supplant the vision of the theatre as a perfect synthesis of written word and actor's voice, in which the director question is of marginal importance. The very pact with the audience that underlies such theatres is based on the link between the State, which subsidizes and manages the theatre, and the audience. Such a relationship is consolidated in the first instance by the repertoire of texts, whose compilation usually falls to the director. The first directors in Italy were both critics and interpreters (Meldolesi 1984). Such a perspective sees the director-interpreter as the essential go-between in the author–audience relationship. The director is required to manage an ensemble of actors in order to obtain an integral and faithful representation of the text, but he/she is all too easily reprimanded when he/she prevails over the author or the actors by imprinting his/her own personal ideas onto the performance. And this opinion was shared by the first generation of directors themselves. Strehler wrote: 'There is only one artist in the theatre: the author of the dramatic text. There is only one vocation: that of the poet. There is only one dramatic reality: the text' (Strehler 1974: 162).

The new generation of directors that gained prominence from 1959 – Carlo Quartucci, Carmelo Bene and Claudio Remondi – immediately declared their need to break with interpretative practice in the light of the autonomy of theatre. Quartucci was inspired by Beckett's dramaturgy to carry out his first experiments in this sense, staging *En attendant Godot* twice, in 1959 with the Latino-Metronio university company, and in 1964 at the Duse Theatre in Genoa with the production by the Genoa Stabile theatre. The young director, who had studied architecture, read *En attendant Godot* as an abstract painting, treating every textual element – characters, gestures, words – as material from which the scene could be composed (Quartucci 1968: 216–18). By working mainly on the stage directions, he was

20   *Stefania Bruno*

able to produce a complex phonetic-gestural score from Beckett's play: since the personas' actions and their movements delineated the geometric design of the set, this score shaped both the temporal dimension of the performance (its rhythm) and the spatial one.

During the same period, Bene was deconstructing the repertoire of texts by making flamboyant use of his own expressive instruments, particularly his voice, establishing him as the sole author and interpreter of his own shows. An emblematic case in this respect is his *Hamlet*, on which he worked for many years and staged three times between 1962 and 1967 (Petrini 2004). In his first *Hamlet* of 1962, he dismantled and reassembled his new translation of Shakespeare's play in such a way that the different scenes happened simultaneously and overlapped each other, also thanks to a stage set which was built on three different levels (Bene 1995: 629–34). Any dramatic continuity was thereby interrupted and all meaning lost. In his second version of 1965 – *Basta con un 'Vi amo' mi ero quasi promesso. Amleto o le conseguenze della pietà filiale* ('Enough with the "I love you" I had almost promised: Hamlet or the consequences of filial remorse') – Bene interpolated the Shakespearean tragedy with Jules Laforgue's parody *Hamlet, ou les suites de la piété filiale*. His parodic intention went even further in 1967 with his *Amleto o le conseguenze della pietà filiale da Laforgue secondo Carmelo Bene* ('Hamlet or the consequences of filial remorse after Laforge according to Carmelo Bene'), in which the Shakespearean tragedy was reduced to nothing more than a few quotes. Stage performances in the 1960s were characterized by deconstruction, abstraction and intertextuality, forming a close link between prose and musical theatre.[2]

Within this scene, the new artists were extremely uncomfortable about the historical avant-garde: the association between the avant-garde and fascism led to the perception of it being at odds with the values imposed after the Liberation. This denied relationship was one of the causes of the paradoxical situation that came about in Italy in the following decade, with the birth and diffusion of an avant-garde that refused to acknowledge itself as such. On the one hand, the theatrical avant-garde oscillated between the search for autonomy and an attempt at integration within the Stabili theatre system; its members did not take part in the development of theories or ideologies, nor did they manage to imagine or make the most of any kind of common path. On the other hand, although the literary avant-garde was seemingly more enlightened and organized, many years would pass before their first official meeting in Palermo. Moreover, even at this meeting, their difficulty in coming to terms with the legacy of the historical avant-gardes led them to suggest the use of the term *experimentalism* rather than avant-garde in order to describe the aesthetics and linguistic practices that would be developed in the next few years (Guglielmi 1963: 15–24).

---

2 Mario Ricci also deserves mention for his intentionally abstract performance that opened in 1962: *Movimento n.1 per marionetta sola* (Rome, at the home of critic and art historian Nello Ponente).

The definition of a new performance code 21

In the field of musical theatre, however, the avant-garde made its debut precisely in the spirit of a revival of the past (Molina 1961: 4–9). Luigi Nono presented *Intolleranza 1960* at La Fenice in Venice in 1961, based on an idea of Angelo Maria Ripellino and with stage design by Emilio Vedova. The performance was a montage of sounds, images and gestures and took place in a polycentric space. It resulted in a rich interaction between music, text, the visual arts and the performance space. The images projected on nine moveable screens, and the music, sounds and choirs coming from different sound sources were all treated as autonomous units and superimposed on one another, enveloping the public in a sonorous and visual blanket. Nono aimed to establish a new relationship between stage action and audience, inspired by the Bauhaus architects and Piscator's and Meyerhold's theatre. He imagined 'building new theatres with moveable stages allowing the place for the action to be decided each time, which could even happen simultaneously on different planes and in different places' (cited in Molina 1961: 5).

In the same year the composer Aldo Clementi and the painter Achille Perilli presented *Collage* at the Teatro Eliseo in Rome. This abstract ballet had an extremely meagre plot which made use of moving silhouettes, movable sculptures, lighting effects and magic lantern projections (Lux and Tortora: 2005).[3] Perilli championed the idea of putting art and theatre together in the attempt to establish a new collaborative relationship with the audience, and he openly declared the connection with the early twentieth-century pictorial avant-gardes. 'The performance space', he proposed, 'is no longer an opening onto reality, or let us say a debate about the problem of reality, but it springs into action through its audience and it can never do without their mind and imagination' (cited in Molina 1961: 8). A search was under way, in other words, to find a new role for the audience within a musical performance and within a new theatricalization of music, combined with a reflection and revival of the theory and practice of the historical avant-gardes. The ideal space for composers to weave new relationships between the arts was precisely the theatre.

Cultural alignment and new theatre

Around 1961, the avant-garde movements in Europe were still quite inconsistent. Despite their essentially syntonic goals, the various moments of revival that came about within the literary, theatrical, musical and artistic circles were isolated happenings. Meanwhile the critics were still not working on elaborating new interpretative categories and thus failed to acknowledge the status of the avant-garde.

This lack of cohesion diminishes noticeably in the years between 1961 and 1967. A great number of events took place in this period, giving increasing visibility to the avant-garde phenomenon and to the cultural alignment between Italy, Europe and the United States (Visone 2010). Fluxus arrived in Europe between

---

3 See also the chapter by Alessandro Mastropietro in this volume.

22   *Stefania Bruno*

1961 and 1963. The network had been founded by a group of young artists, Jackson Mac Low, La Monte Young, George Brecht, Al Hansen, Dick Higgins and George Maciunas, who had soaked up Cage's lessons at the New School for Social Research in New York from 1957 to 1959. Numerous other members joined the group over the years, from the Italians Sylvano Bussotti and Giuseppe Chiari to the German Joseph Beuys, in the name of experimentation and hybridization of the arts through the performative event (Higgins 2002). The Living Theatre first came to Europe as early as 1961, invited by Rome's Teatro Club, and performing Jack Gelber's *The Connection* and William Carlos Williams' *Many Loves*. In 1964 they began a long period of wanderings around Europe, during which they produced some of the most significant performances of the decade. Amongst these later productions, let us just cite: *Mysteries and Smaller Pieces* (Paris, 1964); *Frankenstein* (Venice, 1965); *Antigone* (Krefeld, Germany, 1967); *Paradise Now* (Avignon, 1968). Living Theatre was at the peak of its Artaudian phase when it arrived in Europe, inspired by the translation of *Le théatre et son double* that had come out in the United States in 1958. For Beck and Malina, the Artaudian writings and the Theatre of Cruelty represented the synthesis of art and life that they had previously tried to produce on stage, with their meta-theatrical expedients of a Pirandellian mould. During their time in Europe, they deepened their vision of the theatre as a force for change and action in the world, by creating collective plays and progressively involving the audience in the performance action (Beck and Malina 1970: 65–7).

Peter Brook's experimentation was also influenced by Artaud and the Theatre of Cruelty. In 1963 he set up an experimental workshop with a group of thirteen actors chosen from the Royal Shakespeare Company of which he was director. The workshop culminated in the performance of *Marat/Sade*, taken from Peter Weiss's *Die Verfolgung und Ermordung Jean Paul Marats dargestellt durch die Schauspielgruppe des Hospizes zu Charenton unter Anleitung des Herrn de Sade* ('The Persecution and Assassination of Jean-Paul Marat as Performed by the Inmates of the Asylum of Charenton Under the Direction of the Marquis de Sade'), published the same year. Brook's project was the first successful attempt to include such experimentation within a traditional theatre and had a resonance across Europe, becoming one of the crucial events of the late twentieth century. Weiss's drama was structured so that Brechtian elements, such as the montage of opposing scenes, the alternation of comedy, tragedy and farce, along with recitatives and songs, are accompanied by Artaudian elements, such as violence and a meta-theatricality that teeters on the brink of confusion between art and life. Brook developed the original structure of the work by focusing on corporcality and the search for a direct and immediate relationship with the audience (Marowitz 1966).[4] This is also the period when Hermann Nitsch's Orgyen Mysterien Theater was staging performances in Austria and Germany, after its conception in Vienna

---

4   For more on Brook's relationship to developments in music theatre, see the chapter by Francesca Placanica in this volume.

The definition of a new performance code 23

in 1957. The artist's aesthetic concept subsumed Artaudian and Wagnerian influences, and was based on the dream of rekindling the spirit of Greek tragedy. The combination of art and life was translated into a performance in which the participants took part in bloody rituals, dismemberment of animals and orgies, whilst mythological and religious symbols, such as Dionysus and Jesus Christ, overlapped each other (Nitsch 1969).

In June 1965 the translation followed by the dissemination of Artaud's works in a monographic issue of the *Sipario* magazine finally brought the debate about the French visionary to Italy too. In the same year Bussotti presented *La Passion selon Sade, mystére de chambre* in Palermo during the Settimane Internazionali Nuova Musica. In this self-declared rewriting of Bach, the composer intertwined Artaudian influences with situations and characters taken from the Marquis de Sade's novels. Most importantly though, he managed to combine musical and theatrical language within a dense performative score made of drawings, notes and gestures. Far from being a mere container for a complicated visual transcription of the music, the stage becomes the space in which to experiment with a new total theatre, in the name of a common performative thrust between the artistic languages involved in constructing the performance-event (Tortora 2013). Bussotti's compatriot Egisto Macchi, in *A(lter)A(ction)* on Mario Diacono's text (Rome, 1966), not only drew direct inspiration from the letters Artaud wrote during his stay at the psychiatric asylum, but also used Artaud as the main character of the action. He becomes part of a performance structure that includes both music and theatre but also cinema – thanks to the participation of Sergio Tau and Franco Valobra – and art – thanks to the intervention of Jannis Kounellis. Once again the Artaudian influences are felt within a total theatre project in which there are no longer any subordinate relationships between the various languages that dialogue on stage (Tortora 1998; Cosci 2017).[5]

The autumn of 1965 saw the first Italian performance of a work openly inspired by the need to experiment with a new model of dramaturgical production not based on a literary text. Giuliano Scabia and Carlo Quartucci's *Zip-Lap-Lip-Vap-Mam-Crep-Scap-Plip-Trip-Scrap e la Grand Mam alle prese con la società contemporanea* ('Zip-Lap-Lip-Vap-Mam-Crep-Scap-Plip-Trip-Scrap and the Grand Mam Struggling with Contemporary Society') was produced by the Genoa Stabile and the Venice Biennale. They had worked on the production within the Studio theatre which Quartucci had directed since 1964 (Visone 2010: 77–92). Scabia, a young poet linked to Gruppo 63, had previously collaborated with Nono, writing the text for *Un diario italiano* in 1964. Openly stating their connection to the historical avant-garde and drawing inspiration from, among others, Artaud, Meyerhold, Prampolini and Pollock, Scabia and Quartucci came up with a performance whose dramatic composition was constructed directly on the stage (Quartucci and Scabia 1965: 11–13). Scabia was inspired by *Intolleranza 1960* to imagine an acentric structure, with several

---

5 For more on Macchi's *A(lter)A(ction)* see the chapter by Alessandro Mastropietro in this volume.

24   *Stefania Bruno*

actions taking place in the same space involving the audience. The dramaturgy does not include characters in the literary sense; rather, masks are employed, halfway between puppets and clowns. Scabia gradually composed the text as the actors improvised the various scenes during the rehearsals directed by Quartucci. Scabia's and Quartucci's aim was to completely objectify the performance: the stage was no longer used as a container, but as a producer of signs. The Living Theatre's production of *Frankenstein* on the same dates in Venice was in perfect alignment. In this group creation, Mary Shelley's novel only served as the pre-text, while the dramaturgical elaboration and the stage action came about within the event itself (Beck and Malina 1982). *Zip*'s poor critical reception did not repay the great effort lavished on its production. However, the lesson learned from this experience taught that the avant-garde had no place within the system of Stabili theatres; the new performance codes necessitated the application of new interpretative categories.

This theoretical impasse was resolved by a new generation of critics, who had come into being in the early years of the post-war avant-garde. They fuelled the debate on Artaud, Brecht and the new dramaturgy, within the broader context of a more general reflection on theatrical autonomy. This finally led to the revival of the historical avant-gardes (Bartolucci 1968). Indeed, the figure of the critic was behind the first attempt to unify the different artistic paths that had been present in Italy for almost ten years. The critics Giuseppe Bartolucci, Ettore Capriolo, Edoardo Fadini and Franco Quadri drew up the manifesto *Per un convegno sul nuovo teatro*, which was signed by directors, actors, writers, musicians, dancers, set designers, singers and stage technicians and published in *Sipario* in 1966.[6] The manifesto was the official call to a conference aimed at opening the debate on the avant-garde and formulating the status of a new theatre, which would be innovative not only at the aesthetic and technical-formal levels but also in terms of its production and organization. This would allow the codes of representation and production to be redefined so that an alternative to the Stabili theatre system could be set up (Bartolucci, Capriolo, Fadini and Quadri 1966: 2–3).

While Italy was trying to give a theoretical structure to the theatrical avant-garde, performances were taking place throughout Europe that broadened the scenario even further. In 1966 and 1967, Jerzy Grotowski's Teatr Laboratorium left Poland to perform in France, Italy and Scandinavia. It provocatively labelled itself 'rearguard' (Flaszen 1980: 60–1) and followed a path that led backwards towards theatre's anthropological roots, rather than attempting to search for what was new as an end in itself. Grotowski had been living and working with his actors in a

---

6 The signatories in alphabetical order were: Corrado Augias, Giuseppe Bartolucci, Marco Bellocchio, Carmelo Bene, Cathy Berberian, Sylvano Bussotti, Antonio Calenda and Virginio Gazzolo, Ettore Capriolo, Liliana Cavani, Leo De Berardinis, Massimo De Vita and Nuccio Ambrosino, Edoardo Fadini, Roberto Guicciardini, Roberto Lerici, Sergio Liberovici, Emanuele Luzzati, Franco Nonnis, Franco Quadri, Carlo Quartucci and the Teatrogruppo, Luca Ronconi, Giuliano Scabia and Aldo Trionfo.

The definition of a new performance code   25

monastic regime since 1959. His work was inspired by an integral humanism, which compelled him to strip away everything that was inessential, leaving behind just the relationship between actor and spectator (Grotowski 1968). Experiences like Grotowski's were the model for Eugenio Barba's Odin Teatret which sprang to life in Oslo in 1964, and underscored the essential nature of the question of the actor in the establishment of the new theatre. In fact, a fundamental line of performing arts research would develop around the central role of the actor's body and voice, as instruments of writing, action and relationships (Barba and Savarese 1991).[7]

Back in Italy, the *Per un nuovo teatro* conference was finally held in Ivrea from 10 to 12 June 1967. The various discussions brought to light all the problems related to the attempt to unite the different 'souls' of the Italian avant-garde. On the one hand some participants strongly supported the necessity to establish norms. They were above all suspicious of anyone expressing a different view from their own. Others rejected any kind of codification and expressed the need to enter a new phase of their experience (Visone 2010: 227–55). However, notwithstanding the drama of these discussions, the conference did result in the theoretical overcoming of the idea of the 'avant-garde', which was now replaced definitively by the category of new theatre. And the latter was destined to last much longer, indeed even right up to the present day (Valentini 2016).

Open work and scenic writing

A substantial change in the approach to theatre and its expressive codes came about in the period that started in the early 1950s and reached its peak in the 1960s. A definition was needed for new theatre, a category that can embrace multiple and extremely discontinuous experiences and at the same time overcome the dialectics of traditional and avant-garde theatre.

The concept of 'truth' now turned up in all the dyads used to talk about theatre in these years: reality-artwork, art-life, form-content, artwork-audience. Brook defined Deadly Theatre as the tendency for any genre, including avant-garde performances, to repeat schemes that deny the truth of the theatrical experience. He contrasted this with Immediate Theatre, which can become a unique and unrepeatable event that takes shape within its relationship with the members of the audience (Brook 1968). Grotowski searched for theatrical truth by re-establishing the relationship between actor and public, formulating the category of Poor Theatre (Grotowski 1968). In Italy the signatories of the *Per un convegno sul nuovo teatro* manifesto asserted the importance of experimentation, which has 'wide margins of error' and is intent on making an 'unconditional total protest' (Bartolucci, Capriolo, Fadini and Quadri 1966: 3). Some of these reflections occurred posthumously to the experiences to which they relate, confirming the experimental nature of the theatrical avant-garde of the late twentieth century.

---

7 See the chapter by Francesca Placanica in this volume.

26 *Stefania Bruno*

However, even at the time of these artists' first experimentations, it was becoming apparent that the avant-garde had brought a third dimension to the framework of binary relationships, which governed both the approach to artistic creation and the production and interpretation of each work. In 1953, just after the new dramaturgy had made its debut, Roland Barthes published *Le degré zéro de l'écriture*. This work added the category of writing to the interpretative framework, highlighting how the literary work is the product of the intersection of the horizontal and vertical axes of language and style respectively. Writing is the 'meaningful gesture of the writer' (Barthes 1953: 20), and it is absolutely random and unrepeatable; in short, it is free. The consequences of adding this third formal reality to the dualistic relationship on which the literary work was believed to be founded were significant. First, it is not always correct to assume that the changes occurring within the writing codes of a literary work only occur at the historical and social levels of language or style; they may also originate in an imbalance in the system of relationships with the formal sphere of writing. Second, the nature of writing is gestural, the manifestation of an action within the work.

Barthes made it clear from the outset that the avant-garde would operate not just on form, but also on language. The latter is considered not only as the system of signs that compose the work, but also as the artist's attitude in composing these signs to produce meanings and more. This change of focus from the work, as a complete synthesis of form and content, to writing, as a gesture that gives substance to the composition and connects the audience directly with the author, summarized in a nutshell the changes that were to come: the work of art would no longer be conceived as a product, but as a process.

If we broaden our horizon, we find that the events organized by the American avant-garde were also inspired by the same desire on the part of the artists to break with the duality of the art–audience relationship. They wanted to become part of this relationship, not delivering a finished product from which they had previously distanced themselves, but a lively and open structure, in which the work is composed at the same time as it is enjoyed, and the members of the audience become participants and co-authors of an event that will therefore be unique and unrepeatable. This fundamental opening in the art–audience loop was the catalyst for the performative thrust that runs through the period of time in which the post-war avant-gardes came to life (Fischer-Lichte 2004). In the theatrical field, this timeline reaches from the first happenings to Richard Schechner's definition in 1968 of six axioms for the environmental theatre (Schechner 1968: 41–64). A key landmark is the publication in 1962, a year before the Gruppo 63 conference in Palermo, of Umberto Eco's collection of essays *Opera aperta*. Inspired by the works of the experimental composers, Eco reinterpreted the history of literature from the Baroque to James Joyce as a progressive opening of literary work, which increasingly includes the reader within the meaning-making process. The work becomes a multiplied universe, which is not subject to a single ordering principle, but where continuous integrations, interpolations and hybridizations can take place (Eco 1962). Thus, the theoretical grounds were laid for the interpretation of a work that is composed of more than just literary materials,

The definition of a new performance code   27

which are not necessarily linked by relationships of consequentiality but only by coexistence. The author assigns the reader with the complete responsibility of composing not only the meaning, but also the definitive structure of the work.

The opening of the work entailed the irruption of subjectivity into the performance: every theatrical event was conceived as a subjective experience, both for the actors and the spectators, meaning that perception and kinds of relation became the main vehicles for composing the work. The subjectivity in the work could assume different forms. For example, the Living Theatre tried to encourage the audience to take an increasingly active part in the composition of the work, to such an extent that the selfsame theatrical event is dismembered. Other artists entered into their work both physically and vocally: they were the material manifestation of the gesture of creation, the prime mover of the totality in which the audience is involved, or, on the contrary, they offered themselves as an object of that creation, to be annihilated in the relationship with the participants in the event. Carmelo Bene and Sylvano Bussotti were two of these artist-creators, essential presences on the stage in their performances, while Hermann Nitsch could be either rite officiant or sacrificial victim.

This admission of subjectivity into the work of art presupposed a new attitude to performance as autonomous of, rather than at the service of, the written text. In fact, it is difficult to imagine how avant-garde experiments could take place in a theatrical field whose system of thought did not consider the performance as itself the work of art, but merely as the transcodification of the real work, the literary text, to a container, namely, the stage. This subordination of the stage action to the text was still very widespread in Europe in the mid-sixties and as a consequence, all the languages that coexist on the stage, be they verbal, visual or musical, were also considered as tools at the service of the text, which remained the main object of critical analysis.

The problem of theatrical autonomy became a central issue in Italy, where the vision of directing as a language and of the director as the author of the performance was slow to catch on. The year 1959 marked the start of a radical change, uniting experiences that had come into being in different ways and with different purposes. From this moment on, the interpretative practice that had set Italian directing apart was put aside and the performative space as the place where the theatrical action occurs was now recognized as a theatrical element of primary importance. The critic Giuseppe Bartolucci coined the term 'scenic writing' to describe both the way in which modern directors approached the action, and the underlying vision: 'Does dramaturgy, scenic writing exist? And what is it, what is it about: does it associate word to action, or does it associate image to action? Or is it simply just a case of word-action or image-action?'(Bartolucci 1968: 8). If the performative space is such a primary element, then it follows that all the different objects incorporated therein do not constitute a system of hierarchically organized signs that are subordinate to the literary text, but that each and every one of them is a system in itself. The prerequisite for the relationship with the other sign systems is the coexistence of these verbal, visual, musical or performative elements within the performative space. When scenic writing enters into the

28 *Stefania Bruno*

relationship between text and performative space, it finally liberates directing: on the one hand, the latter is recognized as a language, while, on the other, the distinction between directing and dramaturgy is overcome, because scenic writing is nothing else than 'dramatic writing (i.e. writing the action) itself' (Mango 2003: 37). The new interpretative model that emerged in Italy at the turn of the seventies was one that coupled scenic writing (Bartolucci 1963: 61–72) with new theatre: a new codification of performance, through the multiplication of genres, forms and movements.

New theatre's tradition and permanency

In the period from the late 1960s to 1975 a series of trends were born within the field of new theatre. The permanency of these trends in subsequent contemporary arts makes it impossible to consider new theatre a historical phenomenon, such as the avant-garde. It is rather a twentieth-century tradition, a territory of theatre characterized by the drive towards innovation and research both in the fields of languages and techniques, and in those of production, organization and the relationship with the public.

An important catalyst to these developments was the 1968 protest movements which swept the theatre world, accelerating the changes that had been pursued for many years by the avant-garde protagonists. The main question for the artists who fought for the autonomy of theatre and the renewal of its language became: 'what is theatre?' (Brook 1968). Many of them were infected by the desire to overcome theatre understood as a fictitious representation of life, in favour of a widespread event capable to involve whole communities of people and to trigger real change in society. In Italy, after the *Per un nuovo teatro* conference, Quartucci started the *Camion* project, with the objective of working with people living in poorer suburbs, where theatre had no presence (Quartucci and Fadini 1976). In 1969–70 Giuliano Scabia lead the 'decentralizing' project for Turin's Teatro Stabile, working in four suburban districts of the city inhabited by workers and immigrants (Casi 2012). Then, from 1972 he started the project *Teatro Vagante* (Wandering Theatre), that became the name for his entire work as a poet, storyteller and man of theatre. *Teatro Vagante* consisted of a series of theatrical and poetic actions conducted throughout Italy: in mental hospitals, involving the patients (Scabia 2011); in small communities, where they could last days; and on the mountains, where Scabia walked and acted, followed by anyone who wanted to do so (Marchiori 2005).

One of the major changes that marked the advent of the new theatre and united the experiences of artists working in different countries and holding different visions of theatre was the diffusion of the model of the laboratory, conceived as a system of rehearsal and experiment based on research and group creation. From 1969, the desire to work in a permanent research dimension drove Jerzy Grotowski to withdraw from the preparation of further performances. Through four main phases (Paratheatre, 1969–75; Theatre of Sources, 1976–82; Objective Drama, 1982–86; Art as Vehicle; 1986–99), Grotowski's work was directed at a constant exploration of human expressiveness (Schechner and Walford 1997).

The definition of a new performance code 29

Eugenio Barba, following in the steps of his master Grotowski and also the studies begun by Schechner and the anthropologist Victor Turner, promoted the spread of theatre anthropology: a discipline that studies human pre-expressivity through the comparison between Western and Eastern performative and ritual traditions (Barba 1993). In the long wandering of Odin Teatret through Europe, South America and Asia, Barba gathered around him the so-called third theatre, made of all the groups not recognized by the establishment. Third theatre is not a movement, but a vision of theatre in an ethic, political and social sense, that Barba often used in reference to artists of the past, such as Artaud, and that still inspires the constitution of new groups (Barba 1977). In 1970 Peter Brook founded the CIRT (Centre Internationale de Recherche Théâtrale) in Paris, where he extended the laboratory model of research, undertaken since the early sixties, to embrace an intercultural perspective. *Orghast*, the first international performance of CIRT, which debuted in 1971 in Persepolis (Iran), was the result of a study of voice that developed into the invention of a new language (Bablet 1973).[8]

In Italy, the phenomenon of 'cellars' (basements, warehouses and garages converted into small theatres) that had begun to emerge as early as 1964 (Visone 2010) developed so extensively and had such a deep impact on the audience between 1968 and 1975 that it became impossible for the theatre establishment and the press to ignore the existence of an alternative circuit. The cellars were the places where the avant-garde principles of the sixties, encapsulated in the discussion of the *Per un nuovo teatro* congress (Bartolucci, Capriolo, Fadini and Quadri 1966), established roots, and where the artists found a stronger identity. The main objective of the new ideology was to change the dramaturgical paradigm from the staging of a written text to the multiple aspirations of collective creation, the laboratory as a new productive tool, and the search for a new relationship with the audience. The cellars were also the ideal space for the practice of scenic writing. As structures not built for theatre, they became the perfect 'empty space' (Brook 1968): an infinitely adaptable space, where the form and the sense of different performances originated in the relationship that the group of actors established with the audience (Margiotta 2013).

In the same years, there arose a considerable continuity between the ideas and the experimental practices of actors, directors and composers. The foundation in 1965 of Compagnia del Teatro Musicale di Roma (Music Theatre Company of Rome) by Domenico Guaccero, Egisto Macchi and Sylvano Bussotti (who left the project in 1966) was the most important attempt made by Italian composers to build a private company that would work as an independent experimental theatre.[9] In the intentions of its creators, the Compagnia was supposed to bring together artists and technicians, to produce original works and to organize festivals, soirées and events. The most innovative aspect of the project was the vision of music theatre performance as the product of collaboration between different

8 For more on Brook's work with CIRT see the chapter by Francesca Placanica in this volume.
9 For further discussion see the chapter by Alessandro Mastropietro in this volume.

30 *Stefania Bruno*

artists and different languages, each of them possessing autonomy in the process (Mastropietro 2017). Guaccero's *Scene del potere* (Palermo, 1968), an ambitious project of total theatre developed from 1962, was the last production of the Compagnia and a synthesis of its vision. The performance was a montage of different actions that took place simultaneously in different points of the entire space of the Teatro Biondo, surrounding and involving the audience. The music, the song, the dance and the acrobatics were entrusted to different performers, each with its own assigned space (Caputo 2017).

The year 1975 is not an end date: new artists, groups and trends arose throughout the 1970s, 1980s and 1990s. The research of Quartucci and Scabia inspired the development in Italy of animation theatre, social theatre and children's theatre. The third theatre now counts numerous groups around the world. The field of anthropological, intercultural and cross-cultural research has considerably grown. Bob Wilson's *Deafman Glance* in 1970 opened a new perspective on experimentation, introducing questions about storytelling, action, and the temporal and spatial dimension of the performance. In Italy, in 1973, the first groups of the so-called teatro immagine started to work, proposing an aesthetic based on the visual aspects of performance. Since then, multimediality, new technologies, and the hybridization of languages have become autonomous fields of experimentation.

Today's contemporary art is characterized by a constant quest for the new, a specific trend towards innovation. Thus the categories for analysing the performative event must be developed very quickly and it is necessary to take account of the specific collaboration between different disciplines. However it is certain that the epochal overturning in the approach to performance occurred in the period 1955 to 1975. The major changes that occurred when new theatre made its debut were threefold. First, there was the overcoming of the dichotomy of text and performance by considering the performance as the text. In this conception, every element involved is at the same time both writing material and a sign to be interpreted, allowing new relationships between languages to be set up. Second, there was the open performance-form, in which the members of the audience are not simply there to enjoy the product, but actually take part in a dramaturgical process. Third there is the increased focus on action as a basic element of theatrical vocabulary in the verbal, visual and musical languages, which contributes to constructing works that thereby become highly performative. Over the decades, the selfsame category of scenic writing has developed into a real performance code, which foresees the continuous redefinition of the relationship between languages within an environment that is both semiotic (as it produces meanings) and performative (in so far as actions take place therein). As a result, the very concept of performance has been extended beyond the traditional system of genres.

References

[Various] (1952), 'Della scissione tra la cultura e il teatro', *Sipario*, 73, pp. 14–16; 74, pp. 15–16; 75, pp. 3–4.
[Various] (1965), 'Il Teatro della crudeltà (speciale)', *Sipario*, 231.

The definition of a new performance code 31

Bablet, Denis (1973), 'Rencontre avec Peter Brook', *Travail théatral*, 10, pp. 3–29.

Barba, Eugenio (1977), 'Il Terzo Teatro', *Ridotto rivista mensile di cultura e di vita teatrale*, 1/2, pp. 3–4.

Barba, Eugenio (1993), *La canoa di carta. Trattato di antropologia teatrale*, Bologna: Il Mulino.

Barba, Eugenio and Nicola Savarese (1991), *A Dictionary of Theatre Anthropology: The Secret Art of the Performer*, London: Routledge.

Barthes, Roland (1953), *Le degré zéro de l'écriture*, Paris: Seuil.

Barthes, Roland (1961), 'Le théâtre français d'avant-garde', *Le Français dans le monde*, 12, pp. 10–15.

Bartolucci, Giuseppe (1963), 'Tradizione e rottura nel teatro italiano', in Renato Barilli and Angelo Guglielmi (eds), *Gruppo 63. Critica e teoria*, Milan: Feltrinelli, pp. 61–72.

Bartolucci, Giuseppe (1968), *La scrittura scenica*, Rome: Lerici.

Bartolucci, Giuseppe, Ettore Capriolo, Edoardo Fadini and Franco Quadri (1966), 'Per un convegno sul nuovo teatro', *Sipario*, 247, pp. 2–3.

Bartolucci Giuseppe, Ettore Capriolo, Edoardo Fadini and Franco Quadri (1967/68). 'Elementi di discussione', *Teatro*, 2, pp. 18–25.

Beck, Giuseppe and Judith Malina (1982), *Il lavoro del Living Theatre (materiali 1952–1969)*, Milan: Ubulibri.

Beck, Julian and Judith Malina (1970), *Paradise Now*, Turin: Einaudi.

Bene, Carmelo (1995), *Opere*, Milan: Bompiani.

Biner, Pierre (1968), *Il Living Theatre*, Bari: De Donato.

Brook, Peter (1968), *The Empty Space*, London: McGibbon & Kee.

Cage, John (1981), *For the Birds: John Cage in Conversation with Daniel Charles*, Boston, MA: Marion Boyaes.

Caputo, Simone (2017), 'Musica, parlato, azione, scena, film: teatro lirico con film: *Scene dal potere* di Domenico Guaccero', in Gianmario Borio, Giordano Ferrari and Daniela Tortora (eds), *Teatro d'avanguardia e composizione sperimentale per la scena*, Venezia: Fondazione Giorgio Cini Onlus.

Casi, Stefano (2012), *600.000 e altre azioni teatrali per Giuliano Scabia*, Pisa: ETS.

Cosci, Marco (2017), 'La scena media(tizza)ta: teatro, cinema e televisione in *A(lter)A(ction)*', in Gianmario Borio, Giordano Ferrari and Daniela Tortora (eds), *Teatro d'avanguardia e composizione sperimentale per la scena*, Venezia: Fondazione Giorgio Cini Onlus.

De Marinis, Marco (1987), *Il Nuovo Teatro. 1947–1970*, Milan: Bompiani.

Eco, Umberto (1962), *Opera aperta*, Milan: Garzanti.

Flaszen, Ludvig (1980), 'Dopo l'avanguardia', *Sipario*, 104, pp. 60–1.

Grotowski, Jerzy (1968), *Towards a Poor Theatre*, Odin Teatrets Forlag.

Guglielmi, Angelo (1963), 'Avanguardia e sperimentalismo', in Renato Barilli and Angelo Guglielmi (eds), *Gruppo 63. Critica e teoria*, Milan: Feltrinelli, pp. 15–24.

Fisher-Lichte, Erika (2004), *Ästhetik des Performativen*, Frankfurt am Main: Suhrkamp Verlag.

Higgins, Hannah (2002), *Fluxus Experience*, Berkeley, CA: University of California Press.

Kirby, Michael (1965), *Happenings: an Illustrated Anthology*, New York: Dutton.

Lux, Simonetta and Daniela Tortora (2005), *Collage 1961. Un'azione dell'arte di Achille Perilli e Aldo Clementi*, Rome: Gangemi.

Mango, Lorenzo (2003), *La scrittura scenica*, Rome: Bulzoni.

Marchiori, Ferdinando (2005), *Il Teatro Vagante di Giuliano Scabia*, Milan: Ubulibri.

Margiotta, Salvatore (2013), *Il Nuovo Teatro in Italia 1968–1975*, Pisa: Titivillus.

32 Stefania Bruno

Marowitz, Carl (1966), 'Storia e tecniche del Lamda Theatre of Cruelty', *Sipario*, pp. 244–5.

Mastropietro, Alessandro (2017), 'Intorno alla Compagnia del Teatro Musicale di Roma: un nuovo modello operativo, tra sperimentazione e utopia', in Gianmario Borio, Giordano Ferrari and Daniela Tortora (eds), *Teatro d'avanguardia e composizione sperimentale per la scena*, Venezia: Fondazione Giorgio Cini Onlus.

Meldolesi, Claudio (1984), *Fondamenti del teatro italiano*, Florence: Sansoni.

Molina, Franco (1961), 'Tre spettacoli astratti, Intolleranza 1960. Collage. Scatola Magica', *Sipario*, 183, pp. 4–9.

Nitsch, Hermann (1969), *Orgyen Mysterien Theater*, Darmstadt: März.

Petrini, Armando (2004), *Amleto da Shakespeare a Laforgue per Carmelo Bene*, Pisa: ETS.

Quartucci, Carlo (1968), 'L'occhio di Beckett', in Giuseppe Bartolucci (ed.), *La scrittura scenica*, Rome: Lerici, pp. 216–18.

Quartucci, Carlo and Giuliano Scabia (1965), 'Per un'avanguardia italiana', in *Sipario*, 235, pp. 11–12.

Quartucci, Carlo and Edoardo Fadini (1976), *Viaggio nel Camion dentro l'avanguardia ovvero la lunga cinematografia teatrale (1960–1976)*, Turin: Cooperativa Editoriale Studio Forma.

Scabia, Giuliano (2011), *Marco Cavallo. Da un ospedale psichiatrico la vera storia che ha cambiato il modo di essere del teatro e della cura*, Meran: Edizioni Alpha Beta Verlag

Schechner, Richard (1968), '6 axioms for the environmental theatre', *Tulane Drama Review*, 12/3, pp. 41–64.

Schechner, Richard and Lisa Walford (1997), *The Grotowski Sourcebook*, London: Routledge.

Strehler, Giorgio (1974), *Per un teatro umano*, Milan: Feltrinelli.

Szondi, Peter (1956), *Theorie des modernen Dramas*, Frankfürt am Main, Suhrkamp Verlag.

Tortora, Daniela (1998), 'A(lter) A(ction), un tentativo di teatro musicale d'avanguarda', *Il Saggiatore Musicale*, 5/2, pp. 327–44.

Tortora, Daniela (2013), 'Da * selon Sade a La Passion selon X. Intorno alla Passion selon Sade di Sylvano Bussotti', *Studi Musicali*, new series, 4/1, pp. 203–35.

Valentini, Valentina (2016), *Nuovo Teatro made in Italy. 1963–2013*, Rome: Bulzoni.

Visone, Daniela (2010), *La nascita del Nuovo Teatro in Italia.1959–1967*, Pisa: Titivillus.

2 Total theatre and music theatre

Tracing influences from pre- to post-war avant-gardes

Julia H. Schröder

The best known *Gesamtkunstwerke*, i.e. total works of art, are undoubtedly Karlheinz Stockhausen's cycle *Licht* (1977–2003), consisting of seven operas, and Richard Wagner's *Der Ring des Nibelungen* (1848–1874) with four operas. Stockhausen's cycle lasts approximately twice the total duration of Wagner's. Both share an interest in syncretism, and an *auteur* perspective, in the sense commonly applied to the image of a French filmmaker who controls all aspects of film (as opposed to the collaborative working of Hollywood with its influential studios). In the theatrical context, the *auteur* seeks control over every aspect of a production, and thus qualifies as the creator of what has become known as 'total theatre'. In several ways the term 'total theatre' is apt for Wagner's *Ring* as well as for Stockhausen's *Licht*; both composers not only composed the music but also wrote the libretto, and extended their control from costumes to the choice of the performance venue. In Wagner's case a new opera house was designed and built in Bayreuth. In Stockhausen's case the performance space is extended through live transmission, for example of a string quartet playing in four helicopters. Eclecticism and reception of other cultures – in Wagner's case Northern mythology; in Stockhausen's case Asian theatre such as Japanese Nô and Kabuki, Indian Kathakali, Balinese Legong to mention but a few[1] – can be viewed as a positive widening of cultural influence. Yet, these opera cycles can also be interpreted as examples of the dangerous proximity between concepts of totality and 'totalitarian aesthetics'.

The following discussion aims to establish links between notions of 'total theatre' in pre-war spoken theatre and post-war music theatre. The term 'total theatre' was quite present in the post-war discourse on music theatre, without being defined in a definite way: for instance, in the Editorial to the English and French Magazine *World Theatre* from 1965, 'total theatre' is defined provisionally as

> a performance that combines several types of performance. It unites drama, song, dance, mime etc. In order to integrate text, pictures, sound and movement, its producer may use various technical devices, i.e. improved theatrical machinery, but also cinematographical and electro-acoustical equipment etc.
>
> (Hainaux 1965: 540)

---

1 Stockhausen refers to these influences in his letters to Albrecht Riethmüller, which will be published in the near future.

34   *Julia H. Schröder*

Symptomatic of the ubiquity of the term is that the next paragraph of the quoted text already questions this definition: here, the term 'total theatre' is also used to speak about involvement of the spectator, today's audience participation. The assembled articles and questionnaires for two issues of the magazine on the topic of total theatre show the term to have become especially fashionable in the mid-1960s. As an indication of the term's reception, the list below shows prominent uses of the term 'total theatre' from the 1920s and 1930s, followed by examples from the 1960s, and – shortly afterwards – their musicological acknowledgement.

Theatre:

László Moholy-Nagy: 'Theater der Totalität' (1925)[2]

Walter Gropius (Erwin Piscator): 'Totaltheater' (1927)[3]

Antonin Artaud: 'Théâtre total' (1933)[4]

Jean-Louis Barrault: 'le Théâtre total' (1938)[5]

Composers:

Luigi Nono, 'Teatro totalmente *engagé*' (1963)[6]

Bernd Alois Zimmermann: 'Oper als totales Theater' (1965)[7]

Iannis Xenakis: 'Total Theatre' (1966)[8]

Mauricio Kagel: 'Wollt Ihr das totale Theater?' (1966)[9]

Music theory:

Hans Heinz Stuckenschmidt: 'Total Theatre' (1967)

Milko Kelemen: 'Sehnsucht nach dem totalen Theater' (1968)[10]

---

2 See Moholy-Nagy (1975 [1925]).
3 See Piscator (1986b [1929]). Piscator wrote in retrospect: '[W]hile Gropius and I applied Theatre-of-Totality to a concrete form of architecture, Total Theatre involves a dramatico-aesthetic concept, the somewhat vague notion of a collective liberation of the figurative arts' (1966: 5).
4 See Artaud (2010 [1938]: 61): 'Practically speaking we want to bring back the idea of total theatre, where theatre will recapture from cinema, music hall, the circus and life itself those things that always belonged to it.' Antonin Artaud's text 'Theatre and Cruelty' was written in May 1933 and published in 1938; see also Artaud 1978: 104.
5 See Barrault (1967 [1949]).
6 See Nono (2001 [1963]: 121). My translation of this term would be 'totally committed theatre' in a political sense; see Nono 2001 [1963]: 121. According to the editors of the critical edition of Nono's writings, this text originated as a lecture for the *Corso internazionale di alta cultura contemporanea* (27 Septembre 1962) at Fondazione Cini, S. Giorgio (Nono 2001: 567).
7 See Zimmermann (1966).
8 See Matossian (2005: 246).
9 See Kagel (1997 [1966]).
10 Although the composer Milko Kelemen (1968) writes in his article for *Melos* about his own compositions, the text is historically informed and may also be considered a music-historical contribution.

Gilbert Chase: 'Toward a total musical theatre' (1969)

E. T. Kirby (ed.): *Total Theatre: A Critical Anthology* (1969)

Parameters and totality in experimental music theatre

During the late 1920s, an all-encompassing concept of theatre came about wherein the outstanding innovations belonged to formerly accessory realms, particularly the staging. Theatre directors such as Vsevolod Meyerhold[11] and Erwin Piscator are therefore primary subjects of this research, even though they wrote neither a dramatic text nor a musical composition. The interpretation and staging of a play – in German, the 'Inszenierung' – usually involves the forming of aspects of theatre that are ephemeral. In total theatre, these aspects are no longer accidental but integrated into the total concept. In later music theatre works they were to be transformed into parameters to be notated in a score, as in Mauricio Kagel's *Himmelsmechanik* (1965).[12] *Himmelsmechanik* was composed for the traditional stage effects of a theatre. The score resembles a storyboard, of the kind used in a visual planning of a film. Sketches show the movement of clouds over the stage-screen, the rising of a sun, later also sounds of rain and thunder. Although Kagel called it a composition, it can be described as choreography for the theatre machinery. Kagel's *Himmelsmechanik* not only extends the parametrization of music to other stage aspects, it also serves as an example of the post-war avant-garde being influenced by the pre-war avant-garde. A similar 'score' for the organization of all theatrical elements, or rather the stage's technical parts, had already been developed by László Moholy-Nagy for his Bauhaus experiments in the 1920s. However, this technical theatre form of his 'mechanische Exzentrik' with mechanical music instruments still excluded the human actor, who was a part of Moholy-Nagy's 'total theatre' concept (see Scheper 1988).

In other compositions from the 1960s, Mauricio Kagel also organized stage actions by instrumentalists. On the one hand these 'compositions' cannot be called 'total theatre' because they follow a reduced aesthetic and work with limited means: for example, only with the stage-effect machinery. Matthias Rebstock (2007: 86) calls the 'de-composition' he finds in both Dada and Kagel's works a 'negative total theatre'. An example would be the decomposition of the rituals of a concert into an instrumental theatre piece in Kagel's composition *Sur scène*.[13] One can equally argue that Kagel shows how total theatre works, namely,

---

11 Notably, Meyerhold was a very musical director (Meyerhold 1979: 58ff.). He re-worked one play, *The Revisor* by Gogol, in such a way that the order was re-arranged and followed a musical formal logic (Schmidt 1994: 353ff.; see also Picon-Vallin 2003).

12 Mauricio Kagel: *Die Himmelsmechanik. Komposition mit Bühnenbildern* (1965) [score], London: Universal Edition, 1967. Interestingly, Rebstock found sketches that point to a serial organization of this composition, at least in an early stage (Rebstock 2007: 207–14).

13 One is reminded of the reading of the stage directions in Barrault's version of Paul Claudel (see Kapp 1994). Kapp relates this to Alfred Jarry, as well as the change of scenery without curtain, which Claudel suggests in the foreword to his play (ibid.: 260). We also find this in some phases of Meyerhold's theatre.

36   *Julia H. Schröder*

by employing *all* the theatrical means and media – albeit in various pieces. Christa Brüstle (2013: 134ff.) has even claimed that Kagel's 'instrumental theatre' is 'total theatre' in the sense of Jean-Louis Barrault, whose theatre Kagel knew from the company's South American tour in the early 1950s. Brüstle's linking of Barrault's actor-based total theatre concept with the instrumentalist-based experimental music theatre of Kagel is convincing: the totality of the performer's actions are composed in their respective theatres. Barrault dated his first 'total theatre' piece to the staging of Knut Hamsun's *Hunger* in 1938, explaining that a total scale of human expression should be part of the theatre, including singing, lyrical declamation, crying, breathing, being still, and all types of gestures and dance (1967 [1949]: 99, 101–3). Under the influence of Antonin Artaud, Barrault even wrote a conceptual sketch entitled 'On Total Theatre: Concert for a Man' (ibid.: 83).

A similar totality of vocal expressions is the theme of another work of experimental music theatre: Dieter Schnebel's *Maulwerke* for articulatory organs and reproductive equipment (i.e. microphones, projection, film and video), written between 1968 and 1974. This vocal composition can be described as different etudes on articulation. The score provides formal sketches, and indicates also the positions of articulatory organs such as lips, mouth and throat to explain the non-verbal experimental articulations. Schnebel asks for microphones and contact microphones to amplify the soft breathing sounds and to be used as instruments, as well as possible live-video for close-up of the movements of the mouths. The composer also suggests slide projections to accompany the different movements, possibly harking back to the use of projections in 1920s theatre. In his list of subjects to be projected a distinct idea of totality can be found, for Schnebel requests images from various demographical strata, emotions, communicative situations, and so on. Typically for the 1960s, Schnebel's score is an open score, consisting of performance materials that take no definitive form, and which expect of the performer a process of self-discovery through which these new articulations are to be developed. The work coincides with what Gianmario Borio has demarcated as a shift, taking place around 1968, from the object character of art to the notion of art as a performative act and a form of social communication, with an aim for 'total experience' (2007: 31). Schnebel's composition is an example of experimental music theatre to be performed in art galleries and on small concert stages, not in the opera house.

Totalitarian aesthetics? Opera discourse and experimental music theatre

It was Mauricio Kagel (1997 [1966]: 245; see also Kovács and Decroupet 1997: 317) who provocatively asked in 1966 'Do you want total theatre?', paraphrasing the National Socialists' propaganda minister Joseph Goebbels' question to the German people in 1943: 'Do you want total war?' In fact, after Walter Gropius' *Totaltheater* there was another plan for a total theatre building, Wilhelm Käb's *Totalbühne* of 1938 (Käb 1941), which adhered to a fascist monumental aesthetics (Woll 1984: 188). Although Käb held a patent on his 'Totalbühne' it is clearly a copy of the earlier models by Andor Weininger, Friedrich (Frederick) Kiesler, Gropius, and others. The inclusion of open-air stage spaces made this 'Nationalsozialistische Kulturfeierstätte' (National Socialist festival site) attractive for mass spectacles and military shows of the regime. The term 'Totalbühne' hints at the ritual quality of Wagner's 'Bühnenweihfestspiel' *Parsifal* and other works that were not only admired by the National Socialists but could easily be incorporated into their ideology. The proximity of totalitarian politics and some concepts of total theatre has also been noted by Hans Heinz Stuckenschmidt (1967: 5).

Kagel asked his question in a lecture at the symposium 'Neue Musik – Neue Szene' in Darmstadt in 1966, where several composers spoke about their new music-theatre works and concepts. The term 'total theatre' was used frequently. Inge Kovács has analysed how Kagel's lecture was offered as a direct critique of Bernd Alois Zimmermann's 1965 essay 'Opera as total theatre', which was reprinted in 1966 by the newspaper *Darmstädter Echo* under the title 'The future of opera'; the reprint was distributed and discussed as part of the Darmstadt course's lecture series (see Kovács and Decroupet 1997: 317ff; Kovács 2002). Kagel's rhetorical question 'Do you want a totally organised, serially sterilized theatre?' seemed to be directed against Zimmermann's contemporary opera *Die Soldaten*, about which Zimmermann had stated, 'The whole opera is based on one symmetrical all-interval-series' (1974: 95). But Zimmermann's 'pluralistic technique' also included quotations: stylistic quotations 'quasi jazz', direct citations from compositions, and recorded material from 'real life'. It is not at all 'pure' or 'clean' – and perhaps Kagel attacked an ideal rather than Zimmermann's opera itself. But Kagel certainly distanced his own reduced instrumental theatre from the technically optimized stage of the opera house as envisioned by Zimmermann.

Hidden references: Zimmermann's opera as total theatre

In his essay, whose reprint was given the Wagnerian title 'The Future of Opera', Zimmermann asked for 'opera as total theatre!' (1986 [1965]: 60).[14] He proposed that all theatrical media, i.e., architecture, sculpture, painting, music theatre, spoken theatre, ballet, film, microphones, television, magnetic tape and audio technology, electronic music, *musique concrète*, circus, musical theatre shows, and all forms of movement theatre, should be combined in a pluralistic opera. One step in that direction had been taken in his opera *Die Soldaten*, where Zimmermann employed in some scenes the spoken word, singing, crying, whispering, jazz, Gregorian chant, dance, film, and the complete technical resources of the modern theatre to create a pluralistic form of music theatre. For instance, the 'Casino' scene of Act 4, Scene 1 makes use of orchestra and organ music, ensemble and solo singing, rhythmical speaking, tap-dancing, and doubles of the characters. Film stills are precisely described in the score and their projection is synchronized with the music. The different groups of singers and dancers on stage

---

14 I am grateful to Lydia Rilling for pointing out important sources on Bernd Alois Zimmermann.

38 *Julia H. Schröder*

are spatially organized by the scoring. Even the light is rhythmicized and fully notated, to illuminate changing speakers. As Zimmermann commented,

> For me, 'total theatre' means the concentration of all artistic media in an adequately equipped auditorium for the purpose of communication. The first and last scenes [of Act 4] of my opera [*Die Soldaten*] require the interplay of musical, vocal, spoken, danced, mimed, cinematographical and spatial factors.
>
> (Zimmermann 1966: 45)

Zimmermann's idea of simultaneous actions on stage that are extended into simultaneous presentation of different times (past – present – future) is realized in some parts of *Die Soldaten*. He refers to the idea of 'virtual simultaneity' (Seipt 1989: 148) found in various scenes of the source for his libretto, a 1776 drama by Jacob Lenz.[15] The staging of several scenes on different parts or levels of one stage, the *Simultanbühne* (simultaneous stage), was already employed in the early avant-garde theatre of Meyerhold and Piscator amongst others, as the latter described retrospectively:

> Theatre-of-Totality [. . .] refers to a building 'totally' conceived for acting, and in which the spectator, as spatial centre, is surrounded by, and 'totally' confronted with a 'total' stage. On this stage, or rather on these multiple stages, the precise interplay of historical events, the synchronization of social and political action and reaction can be presented simultaneously.
>
> (Piscator 1966: 9)

The idea to use film as a narrative means parallel to the stage action was similarly anticipated in the 1920s. There are several examples of film projection as narrative device in experimental art around 1927.[16] László Moholy-Nagy, for instance, envisioned a form of narration involving several film-projections, for which he coined the term 'polycinema'. Using a diagrammatic representation of two film-strips crossing, Moholy-Nagy explained how two simultaneous film projections could tell a story about the intersecting lives of two people: the first film shows the life of Mr A, the second film shows the life of Ms B, and both films cross at the moment that their lives cross in the form of love, marriage, and so on (1986 [1927]: 39ff.).

In the theatre a film can similarly comment on the stage action. Erwin Piscator related his narrative strategy towards film projection in his 1927 production of *Rasputin* (see Figure 2.1) as follows: on the right side a chronology of

---

15 Zimmermann had planned the simultaneity of various scenes in the last act from the beginning; see the letter to his publisher dated 21 August 1958, quoted in Ebbeke (1998: 63). Dörte Schmidt (1993: 86–99) has analysed this simultaneity and also its extension from the libretto into the music.

16 Here a parallel opens up to the happenings of the American theatre scene in the 1960s. Gilbert Chase (1969: 27) writes of 'the "total theater" of intermedia, crossing all boundaries, transcending all categories'; see also Kirby 1966.

important events is projected as scrolling text; on stage Rasputin predicts the Tsarina's good fortune, while the audience can see the opposite in a film projection (above the stage), namely the execution of the tsar and his family (Piscator 1959: 12; reprinted in Pörtner (ed.) 1960: 151). Her future is the audience's past, and stage and film can give contradictory information in the course of the performance, leading Birri to talk of a new type of simultaneous stage (1982: 143). According to Klaus Ebbeke, Zimmermann was familiar with the anthology on experimental theatre by Paul Pörtner in which Piscator's lecture was reprinted (1998: 65).[17]

Figure 2.1 Erwin Piscator's staging of *Rasputin* (1927): On stage the actors play an event from the historical past; over the stage a film shows the historical future; and on the side of the stage, a text-projection gives chronological data to contextualize the two represented events. The collage, consisting of a stage photograph and a film still, was published in Erwin Piscator's book *Das politische Theater* (1929).

---

17 Ebbeke assumes that Zimmermann read about Jacques Polieri's 'surround theatre' concepts in Pörtner's anthology. In fact, Pörtner (1960) includes a text by Polieri but in this document he does not describe his spherical theatre ideas or his 'Théâtre du mouvement total'. This leads me to presume that Zimmermann read in Pörtner's anthology texts and commentaries on total theatre by Moholy-Nagy, Piscator and others.

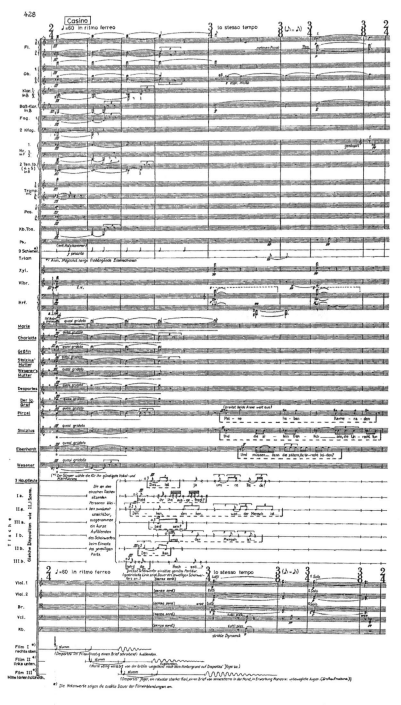

Example 2.1 Bernd Alois Zimmermann, *Die Soldaten*, Act 4, Scene 1, p. 428 from the full score. Zimmermann notates the simultaneous musical events and strata as well as three film projections that show elements of the narration. Reproduced by kind permission of Schott Music GmbH.

Total theatre and music theatre   41

Zimmermann's inclusion of film in *Die Soldaten* certainly bears a resemblance to Piscator's approach. In the score of Zimmermann's *Soldaten* staves are included that show the content and timing of three film projections on stage. The score prescribes which scenes the films shall show and their synchronization with the music (see Example 2.1). With the film images the composer added a layer of storytelling, as suggested by the examples from the 1920s. Dörte Schmidt has argued that Zimmermann probably also knew that Alban Berg had planned to include film projection in his unfinished opera *Lulu*, for the film projections are specified in the work's libretto, published in 1936 (1993: 94, 96).

Overwhelming: the immersion of the spectator-listener

When Zimmermann wrote about 'total theatre' in the context of *Die Soldaten*, he did not relate this term to Piscator's 'Totaltheater', although as we have seen we can find similarities, such as the film projections. Zimmermann also states that the opera house for a pluralistic music theatre would need to have a specific architecture: it would have to be 'omni-mobile', an absolutely available architectural space (1986 [1965]: 62). This closely resembles the new theatre building planned by Bauhaus director Walter Gropius for Erwin Piscator in 1927 – the 'Totaltheater' as it was called (Scheper 1988: 260ff.; Piscator 1986a). It was never built. In this 'Totaltheater' the auditorium could be changed between arena form and circus form, with the stage in the centre. These changes could be done in the midst of a performance so that the audience's view and involvement was changed, as a part of the theatre experience. Gropius and Piscator wanted to involve the individual audience member, to give him or her an experience that today would be called 'immersive'. As Gropius declared, 'Word, light and music have no fixed place anymore. . . . Overwhelming of the spectator is the goal of this "Totaltheater", and all technical means have to submit to this goal' (Gropius 1934: 169).

Why did Zimmermann not mention his predecessors who had similar visions for a new theatre architecture and used not only the same term – Walter Gropius' 'Totaltheater' in 1927 and Moholy-Nagy's 'Theater der Totalität' (theatre of totality) in 1925 – but also similar means?[18] It would certainly have been difficult for a composer such as Bernd Alois Zimmermann, born in 1918, to have access to early avant-garde documentation. Manfred Schuler states that Zimmermann thought he had invented the term 'total theatre', since the National Socialists' regime had erased the knowledge about earlier left-wing theatre (2002: 118, 121). Contrary to this assertion, however, I assume that Zimmermann was aware of the historic predecessors.[19] Erwin Piscator returned to Berlin in 1951, staged plays with simultaneous scenes in Hamburg in 1959, and became head of the newly

18 Zimmermann does however mention Meyerhold's name in reference to biomechanics (1986 [1965]: 63).

19 Elzenheimer shares this assumption (2017: 113). I am grateful to Dörte Schmidt for pointing out this essay, which addresses Zimmermann from a similar perspective to that taken in this chapter.

built *Freie Volksbühne* in 1963. These were events well covered in the press. They must have drawn Zimmermann's attention to the earlier achievements of Piscator, some years before his *Soldaten* was premiered in 1965.

There were further influences. Zimmermann writes that, in his ideal opera house for a pluralistic music theatre, it should be possible to rotate and recline the listeners' seats ('Einrichtung von Kipp-, Dreh- und Liegesitzen'; 1986 [1965]: 63), an idea one can already find in Antonin Artaud's *Theatre of Cruelty* in 1932. Since Zimmermann was interested in Alfred Jarry's *Père Ubu* and read French, it is probable that he also read Artaud in the original. Artaud deems the division of stage and auditorium to be obsolete. The action should take place around the spectators, as well as on galleries over their heads. The audience would sit 'on swivelling chairs allowing them to follow the show taking place around them' (Artaud 2010 [1938]: 68).[20] The surround sound, the famous cry at the end, and the cruelty of the rape scene in Zimmermann's *Soldaten*, all have a specific predecessor in Antonin Artaud's theatre, namely *Les Cenci* (1935), where Artaud with the help of his sound engineer and composer Roger Désormière placed four loudspeakers in the corners of the auditorium to surround the spectators and overwhelm them, matching the cruelty of his play which stages scenes of rape and torture (Artaud 1979: 46; see also Blüher 1991: 128; Curtin 2014; Boisson 2016; Brangé 2016). Artaud had employed the term 'total theatre' since the 1930s. In 1938 he wrote:

> And in order to affect every facet of the spectator's sensibility, we advocate a revolving show, which, instead of making stage and auditorium into two closed worlds without any possible communication between them, will extend its visual and oral outbursts over the whole mass of spectators. [. . .] Practically speaking we want to bring back the idea of total theatre, where theatre will recapture from cinema, music hall, the circus and life itself those things that always belonged to it.
>
> (Artaud 2010 [1938]: 61)

Theatre music – music as part of the total theatre?

Zimmermann may have been introduced to Artaud's writings by his colleague Pierre Boulez. Between 1946 and 1955 Boulez worked as a theatre musician with the Compagnie Madeleine Renaud–Jean-Louis Barrault. There he became familiar with Artaud, as well as the notion of *théâtre total*, and he also wrote music for the stage, which Martin Zenck has likened to a lost opera by the famous opera conductor (Boulez) who never composed an opera (2004: 58; 2014). In Boulez's music for Barrault's staging of *L'Orestie* (1955) by Aeschylus, the actors have to sing and there are extended choir passages. For the performance the long score was severely cut. The singing parts for the main

---

20 Artaud probably knew about Piscator's and Gropius' *Totaltheater* plans (Blüher 1991: 60).

Total theatre and music theatre 43

actors had apparently been too difficult and were cut as well (O'Hagan 2007). The cut material was re-used in various later concert works, including *Pli selon pli* and *Le marteau sans maître*. Zenck assumes that Barrault's *théâtre total* was not one that integrates all of the theatrical means (including music), but rather one that allows them mutual distance (2004: 56). Otherwise the collaboration with Boulez might have proven difficult.

It is interesting to note that Iannis Xenakis set the *Oresteia* to music in 1966, and apparently referred to it as 'total theatre' as well (Matossian 2005: 246).[21] Therein the audience is supposed to join the rites, playing on metal simantras (percussion instruments). Such audience participation and the ritual quality are markers of another strand of total theatre. A historical predecessor is the re-enactment of the October revolution, *The Storming of the Winter Palace* (1920) in Russia, with thousands of actors and hundreds of musicians at the original sites in the city where the observers became part of the action (Leach 1994: 46). Later music theatre works that involve the audience include Henri Pousseur's *Votre Faust* (1961/68), where the audience decides which turns the narrative takes. Giacomo Manzoni's opera *Atomtod* (1965) involved the audience from the moment they entered the auditorium (Manzoni 1997 [1966]). The work begins

> when the lights in the auditorium are still on, when the spectators are still looking for their seats. While the lights are dimming film strips are projected onto four squares on the curtain, and electronic sounds are emitted from loudspeakers. All musical and dramatic action is combined and integrated into the action.
>
> (Stuckenschmidt 1967: 12)

Similarly, the Dutch opera *Labyrint* (1966) by Peter Schat began when the audience members entered: 'the murmur of their voices mingled with sounds of whispering from the loudspeakers' (ibid.). Such strategies aimed to achieve the total experience of the audience. At the same time, in 1965 Luigi Nono composed music for Erwin Piscator's staging of Peter Weiss' documentary theatre *Die Ermittlung*, a play that was assembled from testimonies at the Frankfurt Nazi trials. Nono composed tape music for the theatre performance, which was played through loudspeakers in all corners of the auditorium, as well as from above and below (Riede 1986: 81; De Benedictis and Schomerus 1999/2000; Kontarsky 2001: 70; Nono 2004 [1987]: 61).

---

21 In her book on Xenakis, Nouritza Matossian writes the following about his music for the theatre (mainly Greek drama): '[Xenakis] later coined the term *Total Theatre*, combining speech, poetry, chant, song, dance, instrumental music and visual spectacle with masks, costumes and sets. [. . .] Xenakis' fundamental concern was to redress the balance of music and dance in a generous framework which would revive what he considered to be a total theatre. Far from regarding the drama as a libretto in need of a musical setting he considered it in its archaic historical and social context' (Matossian 2005: 246).

44   *Julia H. Schröder*

Politically committed music theatre: using the total theatre space[22]

In his music theatre works, Nono aimed at a continuation of the avant-garde theatre traditions that had been cut off by World War Two; Piscator, Brecht and the Bauhaus-masters had had to emigrate from Nazi Germany, and Meyerhold had been executed in Stalinist Russia in 1938. Nono owned René Fülöp-Miller's book on Russian theatre from 1928, which boasts many photographs from the original productions (Fülöp-Miller and Gregor 1928); Nono quoted from it in a 1961 article (2001 [1961]: 566).[23] Nono's knowledge of contemporary sources on the pre-war theatrical avant-gardes clearly influenced his works. On a sketch made in preparation for his opera *Intolleranza 1960* (reproduced in Jansen and Wagner 2004: 25), Nono notes the names of key predecessors: first, the Russian triumvirate of political theatre 'Meyerhold, Tairov, Vachtangov'; followed by luminaries from German theatre of the 1920s, Piscator, Toller, Grosz and Brecht;[24] and then the name of Oskar Schlemmer, who was head of the Bauhaus-Stage.[25] *Intolleranza 1960* combined ideas and texts from the mentioned artists and was originally to be based on a libretto by historian Angelo Maria Ripellino, whose book on Russian avant-garde theatre (1959) was very important for Nono,[26] and who gave Nono material on Meyerhold and others (see Nono 2004 [1987]: 42). Nono learnt about Erwin Piscator's theatre from Hermann Scherchen and from Piscator himself, after meeting Piscator in 1952 (ibid.: 42, 138).[27] *Intolleranza 1960* was originally planned as a 'spatial theatre piece in the sense of Meyerhold and Piscator' but ended up as something different, for which Nono rejected the description 'opera' and coined the term 'azione scenica' (2004 [1987]: 58–60). The whole conception of this form of music theatre was meant to use the sound space and the stage space at the same time (Nono in Cadieu 1975 [1961]: 183). In addition to loudspeakers surrounding the auditorium, Nono had originally planned to have parallel action of film images and to develop the lighting as a functional part of the music. The latter can still be seen in the score (see Nono 1962, bars 556–558) where the light gets brighter at the same time as a *crescendo* in the music, leading to the entry of the

---

22 Luigi Nono: 'L'uso dello spazio totale' (Nono 1987: 504).
23 Fülöp-Miller had co-authored this volume of pictures and photographs with the musicologist Joseph Gregor. The German edition is contained in Nono's library (ALN signature E46) as well as the Italian one; the latter erroneously omitted the book's co-author, Joseph Gregor, a mistake reproduced in Nono's quotation from it (but corrected in the critical edition of Nono's writings).
24 In 1927 Piscator staged Toller's play *Hoppla, wir leben!*; he also used an animated film by Grosz in his production of *Der brave Soldat Schwejk*, for which Brecht was part of the dramaturgical team.
25 Another name on this sketch was 'Flanagan', which might refer to the following book: Hallie Flanagan, *Shifting Scenes of the Modern European Theatre*, London: Harrap, 1929.
26 Ripellino's book *Majakovskij e il teatro russo d'avanguardia* is contained in Nono's library at the Archivio Luigi Nono in Venice: ALN signature B 1342.
27 1953 is the date given by the editors of Nono 2004 [1987]: 153. Nono himself remembered meeting Piscator in 1954 (ibid.: 60). De Benedictis has published an Italian translation of their exchange of letters from 1952 (De Benedictis and Schomerus 2000: 171ff.).

choir at *ff* with full illumination. Nono had a multifaceted approach to and knowledge of theatre theories and theatre history, but was concerned also to develop new ideas, which express themselves in his rejection of the term 'opera'.[28] This development of new music-theatre poetics resulted in new generic terms, which rendered the catchword 'total theatre' superfluous.

Conclusion: no need to re-establish the term 'total theatre'

In the mid-1960s the reception of the pre-war theatrical avant-garde had reached a new height, manifesting itself in reprints and publications of the texts from the 1920s and 1930s, as well as new discussions. Histories, anthologies and reprints include (to name just a few examples) Angelo Maria Ripellino's *Majakovskij e il teatro russo d'avantguardia* of 1959, with a German translation in 1964; Paul Pörtner's anthology *Experiment Theater* of 1960; and a 1965 reprint of *Die Bühne im Bauhaus*, which had been edited in 1925 by Oskar Schlemmer, László Moholy-Nagy and Farkas Molnar. The severed tradition of avant-garde art was rediscovered after its disruption by the cultural politics and genocide of the National Socialists.

A cursory glance at the contemporary music-theatre discourse of the 1960s has shown that composers were aware of those ideas, concepts and innovations, as we can see in the contributions to the 1966 Darmstadt symposium on music theatre, or in the writings of composers such as Luigi Nono. In fact, the discussion of 'total theatre' was so central in 1965 that we can question the contention that Bernd Alois Zimmermann was not aware of the pre-war theatrical avant-garde when he developed his ideas on total theatre and the new dramaturgical means used in his opera *Die Soldaten*.

As the reception of pre-war theatre by post-war music-theatre composers showed, the discourse on total theatre did not bring about a fixed definition of that term. It could either refer to a totality of human expression ordered in a parameterized, serialized way, or to use of the totality of theatrical media, including the theatre building and other technical possibilities. A third option included improvisation, open form and inclusion of the audience. Many composers distanced themselves from the term because of its ubiquity and vagueness. Mauricio Kagel even criticized the term by juxtaposing it with totalitarian politics. It is not by accident that the term 'total theatre' vanished: the development of different music-theatre concepts was accompanied by forms of institutional critique that manifested themselves in experiments with new genre names: 'experimental music theatre'; 'pluralistic music theatre' (Zimmermann); 'azione scenica' (Nono). There was no need to revive the term 'total theatre', but its reception history nonetheless shows lines of influence that have been disregarded in other historical accounts.

In this survey of the (primarily) German-language discourse around the idea of 'total theatre', the relations to North American developments have been neglected.

---

28 A recent study of Nono's music theatre works from the perspective of a contemporary theatre historian carries the title 'In search of a new music theatre: Luigi Nono's political-aesthetic experiments between 1960 and 1975' (Lehmann 2019).

46   *Julia H. Schröder*

By way of conclusion, it is worth noting that happenings, environmental theatre and performance art – practices that operate beyond the traditional genre boundaries – have often been linked to the term 'total theatre'. One can mention a few examples of relevant connections between American and European artists. As early as 1958 the poet M. C. Richards published her translation of Antonin Artaud's *The Theatre and its Double* (1938) into English, a project that originated in David Tudor's and John Cage's connections to Pierre Boulez, and which accelerated the reception of Artaud. M. C. Richards had read Barrault's *Reflections on the Theater* in 1951, in which *The Theater and its Double* is mentioned (Harris 1987: 228). Following that, she probably borrowed David Tudor's copy of Artaud's book (Smigel 2007: 183ff). Tudor had studied Artaud to prepare for his performance of Pierre Boulez's *Second Piano Sonata*, having been introduced to it by John Cage who knew Boulez. In 1950 Cage wrote to Boulez that

> Tudor had spontaneously devoted himself to the labor of understanding and playing the Sonata [by Boulez] . . . . He studied French in order to read your articles in *Contrepoint* and *Polyphonie* [. . .] and he has made a collection and study of Artaud.
>
> (cited in Nattiez 1990: 122)

The following year Cage related to Boulez that 'I have been reading a great deal of Artaud. (This because of you and through Tudor who read Artaud because of you.)' (ibid.: 154). M. C. Richards commenced her translation project in 1952.

American dancers and experimental theatre companies also worked with European composers. Anna Halprin's dance group of 'totally trained' performers performed acrobatics and sang in Berio's *Esposizione* (Venice, 1963).[29] Although Stuckenschmidt considers *Esposizione* the first 'total music theatre' (1967: 8), Berio himself was more than doubtful of the value of this term. In 1967 he wrote the following to Cathy Berberian, who was preparing a conference talk:

> However, do not talk about 'total theater': it's a load of nonsense. Total theatre *does not exist* in practice: it is a utopia. But there is a virtual 'theatricality' in all things. It is about establishing and discovering deeper and more 'total' (non-exclusive) relationships in the 'theatricalizable' elements: the voice is one of the most important.[30]

---

29 For more on this performance, see the chapter by Angela Ida De Benedictis in the present volume.
30 'Tu comunque, non parlare di "total theater": è una grossa balla. Il total theater *non esiste* in pratica: è un'utopia. Esiste però una virtualità "teatrale" in tutte le cose. Si tratta di istituire e scoprire relazioni più profonde e "totali" (non esclusive) negli elementi "teatralizzabili": la voce è uno dei più importanti.' Luciano Berio in a letter to Cathy Berberian (20 May 1967), Paul Sacher Foundation, Basel, Cathy Berberian Collection; translation by Robert Adlington. With kind permission of the Paul Sacher Foundation, and the estates of Cathy Berberian and Luciano Berio. I am most grateful to Angela Ida De Benedictis who showed this passage to me at the 'New Music Theatre' symposium in Venice and was so kind to make its publication here possible. For the genre questions around *Esposizione* see De Benedictis 2016.

Total theatre and music theatre 47

Also important to mention here is Luigi Nono's collaboration with the Living Theatre on *A floresta é jovem e cheja de vida* (1965/66); recordings of rehearsals and discussion involving Nono, Judith Malina, Julian Beck and others have recently been transcribed and published (Jozefowicz 2012). In 1969 E. T. Kirby edited *Total Theatre: A Critical Anthology* where the term was understood to include a range of theatre concepts from Wagner's ideas to happenings and environmental theatre, as well as the reception of non-European theatre; Japanese Kabuki, for instance, is deemed to be 'perhaps the highest development of total theatre' (Kirby 1969: 176). Totality seems to have been a motive for the inclusive approach of Kirby's book, which placed it in accordance with the *Zeitgeist*.

References

Artaud, Antonin (2010 [1938]), *The Theatre and Its Double*, translated by Vicor Corti, Richmond: One World Classics.

Artaud, Antonin (1978), *Œuvres complètes*, volume 4, Paris: Gallimard.

Artaud, Antonin (1979), *Œuvres complètes*, volume 5, Paris: Gallimard.

Barrault, Jean-Louis (1967 [1949]), *Mein Leben mit dem Theater* (*Reflexions sur le théâtre*), translated by Robert Picht, Cologne: Kiepenheuer & Witsch.

Birri, Ursula (1982), 'Totaltheater bei Meyerhold und Piscator. Analyse der Inszenierungen "Mysterium buffo" von Wladimir Majakowski und "Rasputin" nach Alexej N. Tolstoi und P. E. Schtschegolew' (Ph. Diss., Universität Zürich).

Blüher, Karl Alfred (1991), *Antonin Artaud und das 'Nouveau Théâtre' in Frankreich*, Tübingen: Günter Narr.

Boisson, Bénédicte (2016), 'Une "bande-son" trop peu écoutée: la musique de scène des *Cenci* d'Antonin Artaud', in Jean-Marc Larrue and Marie-Madeleine Mervant-Roux (eds), *Le son du théâtre, XIXe–XXIe siècle. Histoire intermédiale d'un lieu d'écoute moderne*, Paris: CNRE Éditions, pp. 247–60.

Borio, Gianmario (2007), 'Avantgarde als pluralistisches Konzept: Musik um 1968', in Arnold Jacobshagen and Markus Leniger (eds), *Rebellische Musik. Gesellschaftlicher Protest und kultureller Wandel um 1968*, Cologne: Dohr, pp. 15–33.

Borio, Gianmario and Hermann Danuser (eds) (1997), *Im Zenit der Moderne. Die Internationalen Ferienkurse für Neue Musik, Darmstadt 1946–1966*, 4 vols., Freiburg im Breisgau: Rombach.

Brangé, Mireille (2016), 'Les dispositifs de reproduction sonore dans le théâtre d'Artaud', in Jean-Marc Larrue and Marie-Madeleine Mervant-Roux (eds), *Le son du théâtre, XIXe–XXIe siècle. Histoire intermédiale d'un lieu d'écoute moderne*, Paris: CNRE Éditions, pp. 235–45.

Brauneck, Manfred (2001 [1983]), *Theater im 20. Jahrhundert. Programmschriften, Stilperioden, Reformmodelle*, Reinbek: Rowohlt.

Brüstle, Christa (2013), *Konzert-Szenen. Bewegung, Performance, Medien. Musik zwischen performativer Expansion und medialer Integration 1950–2000*, Stuttgart: Franz Steiner.

Cadieu, Martine (1975 [1961]), 'Duo avec Luigi Nono', in *Nouvelles littéraires* No. 1754 (13 April 1961), p. 1 and 9, published in German in Luigi Nono, *Texte. Studien zu seiner Musik*, ed. Jürg Stenzl, Zurich: Atlantis, pp. 179–183.

Chase, Gilbert (1969), 'Toward a total musical theatre', *Arts in Society*, 6/1, pp. 26–37.

Curtin, Adrian (2014), *Avant-Garde Theatre Sound: Staging Sonic Modernity*, Basingstoke, UK: Palgrave Macmillan.

48   *Julia H. Schröder*

De Benedictis, Angela Ida (2016), 'From *Esposizione* to *Laborintus II*: transitions and mutations of "a desire for theatre"', in Giordano Ferrari (ed.), *Le theatre musical de Luciano Berio*, vol. I: *De Passaggio à La vera storia*, Paris: L'Harmattan, pp. 177–246.

De Benedictis, Angela Ida and Ute Schomerus (1999/2000), 'La lotta "con le armi dell'arte": Erwin Piscator e Luigi Nono. Riflessioni e documenti', *Musica/Realtà. Rivista quadrimestrale*, 60/1, pp. 189–205; and 61/2, pp. 151–84.

Ebbeke, Klaus (1998), 'Zur Entstehungsgeschichte der Soldaten. Wiener Fassung', in Heribert Henrich (ed.), *Zeitschichten. Gesammelte Aufsätze zum Werk von Bernd Alois Zimmermann*, Mainz: Schott, pp. 58–71.

Elzenheimer, Regine (2017), '"Theater als internationaler Freistaat des Geistes": Bernd Alois Zimmermanns Utopie eines "totalen Theaters"', in Oliver Korte (ed.), *Welt – Zeit – Theater: Neun Untersuchungen zum Werk von Bernd Alois Zimmermann*, Hildesheim: Olms, 111–30.

Ferneyrou, Laurent (ed.) (2003), *Musique et dramaturgie. Esthétique de la représentation au XXe siècle*, Paris: Sorbonne.

Fülöp-Miller, René and Joseph Gregor (1928), *Das russische Theater. Sein Wesen und seine Geschichte mit besonderer Berücksichtigung der Revolutionsperiode*, Wien: Amalthea. English Edition: René Fülöp-Miller and Joseph Gregor (1930), *The Russian Theatre, Its Character and History, with Special Reference to the Revolutionary Period*, translated by P. England, Philadelphia: Lippincott.

Gropius, Walter (1934), 'Theaterbau', in *Apollo in der Demokratie*, Mainz/Berlin: Kupferberg, pp. 115–21; reprinted in Manfred Brauneck (1983/2001), *Theater im 20. Jahrhundert. Programmschriften, Stilperioden, Reformmodelle*, Reinbek: Rowohlt, pp. 161–69.

Hainaux, René (1965), 'Editorial', *Le Théâtre dans le monde / World Theatre*, 14, p. 540.

Harris, Mary Emma (1987), *The Arts at Black Mountain College*, Cambridge, MA: MIT Press.

Jansen, Alexander and Andreas Wagner (eds) (2004), *Luigi Nono – Intolleranza 1960. Materialien, Skizzen, Hintergründe. Zur Inszenierung des Saarländischen Staatstheaters*, Saarbrücken: Pfau.

Jozefowicz, Nina (2012), *Das alltägliche Drama. Luigi Nonos Vokalkompositionen mit Tonband* La fabbrica illuminata *und* A floresta é jovem e cheja de vida *im Kontext der unvollendeten Musiktheaterprojekte*, 2 vols, Hofheim: Wolke.

Käb, Wilhelm (1941), 'Nationalsozialistische Kulturfeierstätte – Anregungen für eine "Totalbühne", von Oberbaurat W. Käb/München', in *Der Baumeister. Monatshefte für Baukultur und Baupraxis*, 39/9, plates 65–71.

Kagel, Mauricio (1997 [1966]), 'Neuer Raum – Neue Musik. Gedanken zum Instrumentalen Theater', in Gianmario Borio and Hermann Danuser (eds), *Im Zenit der Moderne. Die Internationalen Ferienkurse für Neue Musik, Darmstadt 1946–1966*, 4 vols, Freiburg im Briesgau: Rombach, vol. 2, pp. 245–66.

Kagel, Mauricio (1967), *Die Himmelsmechanik. Komposition mit Bühnenbildern* [score], London: Universal Edition.

Kapp, Volker (1994), 'Totales Theater als Herausforderung an die Interpreten: literaturwissenschaftliche Bemerkungen zu den Inszenierungen von Claudels *Soulier de satin* durch Jean-Louis Barrault und Antoine Vitez', in Franz Norbert Mennemeier and Erika Fischer-Lichte (eds), *Drama und Theater der europäischen Avantgarde*, Tübingen, Basel: Francke, pp. 255–70.

Kelemen, Milko (1968), 'Sehnsucht nach dem totalen Theater', *Melos*, 35/7–8, pp. 287–90.

Kirby, E. T. (ed.) (1969), *Total Theatre: A Critical Anthology*, New York: Dutton.

Kirby, Michael (1966), 'The Uses of Film in the New Theatre', *The Tulane Drama*, 11/1 (Autumn 1966), pp. 49–61.

Kontarsky, Matthias (2001), *Trauma Auschwitz. Zu Verarbeitungen des Nichtverarbeitbaren bei Peter Weiss, Luigi Nono und Paul Dessau*, Saarbrücken: Pfau.

Kovács, Inge (2002), 'Der Darmstädter Kongreß "Neue Musik – Neue Szene" 1966', in: Christoph-Hellmut Mahling and Kristina Pfarr (eds), *Musiktheater im Spannungsfeld zwischen Tradition und Experiment (1960 bis 1980)*, Tutzing: Hans Schneider, pp. 25–34.

Kovács, Inge and Pascal Decroupet (1997), 'Musik und Szene', in Gianmario Borio and Hermann Danuser (eds), *Im Zenit der Moderne. Die Internationalen Ferienkurse für Neue Musik, Darmstadt 1946–1966*, Freiburg im Breisgau: Rombach, vol. 2, pp. 311–32.

Leach, Robert (1994), *Revolutionary Theatre*, London: Routledge.

Lehmann, Irene (2019), *Auf der Suche nach einem neuen Musiktheater. Politik und Ästhetik in Luigi Nonos musiktheatralen Arbeiten zwischen 1960 und 1975*, Hofheim: Wolke.

Manzoni, Giacomo (1997[1966]), 'Neue Musik – Neue Szene' (1966), in Gianmario Borio and Hermann Danuser (eds), *Im Zenit der Moderne. Die Internationalen Ferienkurse für Neue Musik, Darmstadt 1946–1966*, 4 vols, Freiburg im Breisgau: Rombach, vol. 3, pp. 235–44.

Matossian, Nouritza (2005 [1981]), *Xenakis*, Lefkosia: Moufflon Publications.

Meyerhold, Wsewolod E. (1979), *Schriften. Erster Band 1891–1917*, Berlin: Henschelverlag.

Moholy-Nagy, László (1975 [1925]), 'Theater, Zirkus, Varieté', in Oskar Schlemmer, László Moholy-Nagy and Farkas Molnar (eds), *Die Bühne im Bauhaus* (*Bauhausbücher*, vol. 4) reprinted in facsimile as *Neue Bauhausbücher*, ed. Hans M. Wingler, Mainz: Florian Kupferberg, pp. 45–56.

Moholy-Nagy, László (1986 [1927]), *Malerei, Fotografie, Film*, Berlin: Gebrüder Mann.

Nattiez, Jean-Jacques (ed.) (1990), *Pierre Boulez, John Cage. Correspondance et Documents*, Winterthur: Amadeus.

Nono, Luigi (2001 [1961]), 'Appunti per un teatro musicale attuale', in Angela Ida De Benedictis and Veniero Rizzardi (eds), *Scritti e colloqui*, volume 1, Lucca: Ricordi, pp. 86–93 and 566.

Nono, Luigi (1962), *Intolleranza* [score], AV 75, Mainz: Ars Viva.

Nono, Luigi (2001 [1963]), 'Possibilità e necessità di un nuovo teatro musicale', in Angela Ida De Benedictis and Veniero Rizzardi (eds), *Scritti e colloqui*, volume 1, Lucca: Ricordi, pp. 118–32.

Nono, Luigi (1975), *Texte. Studien zu seiner Musik*, ed. Jürg Stenzl, Zurich: Atlantis.

Nono, Luigi (2001 [1987]), 'Un'autobiografia dell'autore raccontata da Enzo Restagno', in Angela Ida De Benedictis and Veniero Rizzardi (eds), *Scritti e colloqui*, volume 2, Lucca: Ricordi, pp. 477–568.

Nono, Luigi (2004 [1987]), *Incontri. Luigi Nono im Gespräch mit Enzo Restagno*, translated into German and edited by Matteo Nanni and Rainer Schmusch, Hofheim: Wolke.

Nono, Luigi (2001), *Scritti e colloqui*, ed. Angela Ida De Benedictis and Veniero Rizzardi, Lucca: Ricordi, 2 vols.

O'Hagan, Peter (2007), 'Pierre Boulez and the Project of *L'Orestie*', *Tempo*, 241, pp. 34–52.

Picon-Vallin, Béatrice (2003), 'Vers un théâtre musical. Les Propositions de Vsevolod Meyerhold', in Laurent Ferneyrou (ed.), *Musique et dramaturgie. Esthétique de la représentation au XXe siècle*, Paris: Sorbonne, pp. 45–64.

50 *Julia H. Schröder*

Piscator, Erwin (1959), 'Technik – Eine künstlerische Notwendigkeit des modernen Theaters. Vortrag für die 32. Bühnentechnische Tagung am 28. Juli 1959 in Mannheim', *Bühnentechnische Rundschau* (October, no. 5), pp. 10–14.

Piscator, Erwin (1966), '"Totaltheater" (theatre of totality) and "totales Theater" (total theatre)', *Le Théâtre dans le monde / World Theatre*, 15/1, pp. 5–9.

Piscator, Erwin (1986a), *Eine Arbeitsbiographie in 2 Bänden: Band 1, Berlin 1916–1931; Band 2, Moskau – Paris – New York – Berlin 1931–1966*, ed. Knut Boeser and Renata Vatková, Berlin: Fröhlich & Kaufmann.

Piscator, Erwin (1986b), *Zeittheater. 'Das politische Theater'* [1929] *und weitere Schriften von 1915 bis 1966*, selected and edited by Manfred Brauneck and Peter Stertz, Reinbek: Rowohlt.

Pörtner, Paul (ed.) (1960), *Experiment Theater. Chronik und Dokumente*, Zürich: Die Arche.

Rebstock, Matthias (2007), *Komposition zwischen Musik und Theater. Das instrumentale Theater von Mauricio Kagel zwischen 1959 und 1965*, Hofheim: Wolke.

Riede, Bernd (1986), *Luigi Nonos Kompositionen mit Tonband. Ästhetik des musikalischen Materials – Werkanalysen – Werkverzeichnis*, München, Salzburg.

Ripellino, Angelo Maria (1959), *Majakovskij e il teatro russo d'avantguardia*, Torino: Einaudi.

Ripellino, Angelo Maria (1964), *Majakowskij und das russische Theater der Avantgarde*, translated into German by Marlis Ingenmey, Cologne: Kiepenheuer & Witsch.

Scheper, Dirk (1988), *Oskar Schlemmer. Das Triadische Ballett und die Bauhausbühne*, Berlin: Akademie der Künste.

Schmidt, Dörte (1993), *Lenz im zeitgenössischen Musiktheater. Literaturoper als kompositorisches Projekt bei Bernd Alois Zimmermann, Friedrich Goldmann, Wolfgang Rihm und Michèle Reverdy*, Stuttgart: Metzler.

Schmidt, Herta (1994), 'Mejerchol'ds Regiearbeit an Puskins Drama *Boris Gudonov*', in Franz Norbert Mennemeier and Erika Fischer-Lichte (eds), *Drama und Theater der europäischen Avantgarde*, Tübingen, Basel: Francke, pp. 341–64.

Schnebel, Dieter (1971), *Maulwerke* [score], ED 7083, Mainz: Schott.

Schuler, Manfred (2002), 'Zu Bernd Alois Zimmermanns Oper als "totalem Theater"', in Christoph-Hellmut Mahling and Kristina Pfarr (eds), *Musiktheater im Spannungsfeld zwischen Tradition und Experiment (1960 bis 1980)*, Tutzing: Hans Schneider, pp. 117–22.

Seipt, Angelus (1989), 'Polyphonie und Collage. Die Simultanszene in Zimmermanns *Soldaten* und das Musiktheater der Gegenwart', in Klaus Wolfgang Niemöller and Wulf Konold (eds), *Zwischen den Generationen. Bericht über das Bernd-Alois-Zimmermann-Symposion Köln 1987*, Regensburg: Gustav Bosse, pp. 145–61.

Smigel, Eric (2007), 'Recital Hall of Cruelty: Antonin Artaud, David Tudor, and the 1950s Avant-Garde', *Perspectives of New Music*, 45/2, pp. 171–202.

Stuckenschmidt, Hans Heinz (1967), 'Total theatre', in *The World of Music / Die Welt der Musik / Le monde de la musique*, 9/1, pp. 5–16.

Woll, Stefan (1984), *Das Totaltheater. Ein Projekt von Walter Gropius und Erwin Piscator*, Berlin: Gesellschaft für Theatergeschichte.

Zenck, Martin (2004), 'Pierre Boulez' Oper *Orestie*. Die Bühnenmusik von Pierre Boulez zu einer *Orestie* (1955) und das Opernprojekt einer *Orestie* (1995) von Heiner Müller und Pierre Boulez', *Musik und Ästhetik*, 29, pp. 50–73.

Zenck, Martin (2014), 'Pierre Boulez und seine Arbeiten für die Compagnie Renaud-Barrault. Zur Bühnenmusik der *Orestie* (1955)', in Ursula Kramer (ed.), *Theater mit Musik*, Bielefeld: Transcript, pp. 355–94.

Zimmermann, Bernd Alois (1986 [1965]), 'Zukunft der Oper. Einige Gedanken über die Notwendigkeit eines neuen Begriffes von Oper als Theater der Zukunft', in Wulf Konold (ed.), *Dokumente und Interpretationen*, Cologne: Wienand, pp. 57–64.

Zimmermann, Bernd Alois (1966), 'Theatre people are replying to our inquiry [regarding total theatre]', *Le Théâtre dans le monde / World theatre*, 15, p. 45.

Zimmermann, Bernd Alois (1974), 'Drei Szenen aus der Oper *Die Soldaten*', in Christof Bitter (ed.), *Intervall und Zeit. Aufsätze und Schriften zum Werk*, Mainz: Schott, pp. 93–5.

Zimmermann, Bernd Alois (1975), *Die Soldaten*. Oper in vier Akten nach dem gleichnamigen Schauspiel von Jakob Michael Reinhold Lenz [score], Mainz: Schott.

3 Theatre as problem

Modern drama and its influence in Ligeti, Pousseur and Berio

Vincenzina C. Ottomano

In an interview he gave to Zoltán Peskó in April 1972, focusing on the issues of contemporary music theatre, Pierre Boulez stated:

> We must also remember that the evolution of music has been strongly influenced by that of the theatre, whose stage styles are always much ahead. The epoch of experimentation began rather early in theatre – not only in the spoken theatre, but also in the mime and ballet theatres. This is why in today's spoken theatre the text has obviously lost its former pre-eminence. If we examine the work of advanced theatrical groups, such as Grotowsky or the Living Theatre, as well as their followers, we can easily note that they prefer to use a combination of stage, gestures, vocal techniques etc. – i.e., something sublimated, partly still subconscious. Musical theatre simply follows this trend – with a few years' delay: therefore, it is not based on a logical, coherent language any more, but rather on gestures, the semantic aspect having lost its pre-eminence.
>
> (Boulez and Peskó 1978: 2)

In hindsight, with a more holistic view of the historical period from the late 1950s through to the early 1970s, we can use Boulez's statement as a starting point to highlight trends and common points between spoken and musical theatre. But we can also question Boulez's claim that music theatre followed the lead of spoken theatre, and enquire whether we may instead perceive mutual influences and exchanges.

The approach in this chapter is twofold: first, I scan the writings, interviews and statements of some major composers for evidence of their reflections on theories of drama; second, I examine these reflections in the wider context of the issues that composers, from different individual perspectives, confronted in trying to rethink the very concept of theatre. Of course, from a methodological point of view, the composers' testimony does not by itself conclusively prove an influence of spoken theatre upon music theatre. Indeed, often the words of composers offer a partial, if not misleading, vision of their works. Elsewhere, more or less direct derivations, allusions, or references are best understood as retrospective 'labelling', a justification of a theatrical poetics to which the compositional work

Theatre as problem 53

might or might not actually adhere. Nonetheless, the composers' statements with which this paper is concerned bear witness to a common aspiration that emerged between the end of the 1950s and the beginning of the next decade, namely, that of reconsidering all the components of music theatre: the relationship with the theatrical tradition; the stage space; and the relationship between music and text.[1] The very nature of this aspiration reflects the broader issue of navigating 'music theatre' in its various manifestations; the inherent ambiguity of its definition is itself a consequence of composers' openness to new approaches and to the new possibilities of dramaturgical expression afforded by different media (such as radio broadcast, dance, and mime).

Therefore, rethinking musical theatre in the 1960s meant, above all, reflecting in the first place on theatre as a 'genre', by means of new research, new theoretical bases that each composer adapted according to his needs and interests (e.g. political theatre, epic theatre), while building, among other things, on the experiences of avant-garde spoken theatre. But it also meant deep reflection on the understanding of the value of theatre as an institution, and whether this institution might renew itself. That is to say, composers were required to assess the chances for the 'implicit' theatrical tension that they envisaged to find form and content within the space of an actual stage.

Back to Boulez: in the opening quote he talked about spoken theatre as a site of experimentation, and, in particular, he named Grotowski and the Living Theatre. Cage's and Nono's experiences with the Living Theatre, that of Berio with the group Open Theater, and the direct collaborations between composers and avant-garde playwrights – examples of which include *The Last Tape* (1961) by Marcel Mihalovici after Samuel Beckett's play of the same name, and *The Photo of the Colonel* (1964) by Humphrey Searle on a text by Eugène Ionesco – can all be considered as part of a single strand in which the two spheres of spoken and musical theatre were brought into contact. Besides these experiences of direct collaboration with theatre companies or with individual playwrights, however, the reflections of some composers suggest a totally different approach to the theories of drama. This approach arose in dialectical relation to the spoken theatre. It materialized in the challenge that spoken theatre posed to personal ideas on musical dramaturgy, and in the implicit or explicit relation of these ideas to broader dramatic theories, but it also started from the premise that musical theatre deals with a different medium (music), which is not only *one* of the components but often the main component, coordinating and sometimes governing the other elements of the stage and of the drama. In short, for some composers, the experience of spoken theatre (in particular contemporary spoken theatre) was not used as a direct model (textual source) or as an active component of the performing act, but rather as a reference, a point of comparison, or as a context for a personal theory of theatre.

---

1 For more general discussion on this topic see: Salzman and Desi 2008; Rozic 2008; Rebstock and Roesner (eds) 2012; Schwartz (ed.) 2014; Heile 2016; Borio, Ferrari and Tortora (eds) 2017.

54 *Vincenzina C. Ottomano*

Because of the breadth of this topic, I will illustrate this process of reception of dramatic theory through three examples only: the experiences of the composers György Ligeti, Henri Pousseur and Luciano Berio. Each of these composers reflects in a different way on the theories and practices of spoken theatre, and these reflections had correspondingly different consequences for compositions written during the 1960s and early 1970s. Choosing these three composers cannot be considered exhaustive of all the tendencies and responses by composers to spoken theatre in the second half of the twentieth century. However, my research intends to be a point of departure from which to trace some lines of continuity and discontinuity, and to offer insights that could open up a wider discussion into the theory of drama and the reciprocal influences between musical and spoken theatre.

Ligeti and the desire for the absurd

In 1981, in an interview with Claude Samuel, Ligeti explicitly referenced Antonin Artaud's 'théâtre de la cruauté' and the theatre of the absurd of Jarry and Ionesco: 'I may add that it [*Le Grand Macabre*] is not a literary opera, and yet it's closely related to the theatrical conceptions of Jarry, Artaud and Ionesco' (Ligeti 1983: 118). However, the seeds of a more direct engagement by Ligeti with contemporary theories of spoken theatre can be traced back to his first experiments for the stage.

In a lecture titled 'On Music Theatre', presented on 29 March 1979 during a Finnish radio broadcast for the performance of *Artikulation, Aventures* and *Nouvelles Aventures*, Ligeti outlined his views on avant-garde theatre. The starting point was the intrinsic influence of the electronic work *Artikulation* on his own approach to music theatre, and how this work deeply changed his relationship with text. Ligeti then proceeded to explain how at the core of *Aventures* and *Nouvelles Aventures*, composed between 1962 and 1965, there is a profound reflection by the composer on the relationships between both music and poetry, and music and language. The works' text is explored in its phonetic dimension as 'composed' material, rather than material 'to be composed':

> [in *Aventures* and *Nouvelles Aventures*] there is no specific text to be set to music, rather the text itself is composition, it is music. In both compositions I started from the basic idea of eliminating the meaning, the semantic level of language, working only with the musical and emotional level of language.
> (Ligeti 2007 [1979]: 78)[2]

The models referenced by Ligeti were manifold. He referred to Verlaine's poems, where the phonetic effects of the sounds of words prevails; to Joyce's language permutations in both *Ulysses* and in *Finnegan's Wake*; and, finally he referred to

---

2 All translations by the present author except where otherwise stated.

Theatre as problem   55

the subversion of the semantic aspects by Dadaists, in particular by Hugo Ball and in the *Ursonate* by Kurt Schwitters. At the same time, Ligeti acknowledged his own musical 'debt' towards composers that already explored these possibilities: in particular, *Gesang der Jünglinge* by Stockhausen, *Anagramma* by Kagel and *Omaggio a Joyce* and *Visage* by Berio (ibid.: 79; see also Levy 2017: 142–4).

The idea of the implicit theatricality of language evolved into research towards a more explicit, associative and imaginary theatricality. Hence, the stage version of these two compositions was conceived as an *anti-opera*, meaning a rejection of a traditional genre and of a traditional space: 'There are two versions of the *Aventures* works: one for concert performance and another that is visually staged, a staging that is already present in embryo in the music and that unravels a mysterious, ambiguous theatre of the absurd' (Ligeti 2007 [1979]: 84). Ligeti's theatrical poetics here drew in part on the avant-garde explorations of language and the relationship with the text undertaken by the theatrical and musical pioneers mentioned above. However, Ligeti's poetics also had deeper roots in a more complex reflection about codes of theatrical communication: in particular, the progressive reduction of both linguistic and scenic means introduced by Beckett since *Acte sans paroles I* (1957), and the discovery of an imaginary and asemantic space introduced by Ionesco.

The allusion to the 'theatre of the absurd' in the last quotation is particularly noteworthy. In 1957 in Paris, Ligeti witnessed performances of *La Cantatrice chauve* [The Bald Soprano] and *La Leçon* [The Lesson] by Ionesco (Steinitz 2003: 134; Beffa 2016: 153). Both works eventually became points of reference in Ligeti's approach to the question of music theatre. I am referring in particular to the introductory text by Ionesco to the play *The Bald Soprano*, emblematically titled 'The Tragedy of Language: How an English Primer Became My First Play' (Ionesco 1960). Ionesco's inspiration stemmed from his own experience of working with a language manual in order to learn English. In 'The Tragedy of Language' Ionesco writes about how the axiomatic forms of the manual dialogue (for instance, Mrs. Smith explains to her husband, Mr. Smith, that they have four children, and that the days of the week are seven) produced a kind of nonsense that transformed his perception of language: 'The very simple, luminously clear statements I had copied diligently into my schoolboy's exercise books, left to themselves, fermented after a while, became denatured, expanded and overflowed.' In *The Bald Soprano*, Ionesco attempted to transpose this 'meaningless' use of language onto the dramatic stage. The work, in its author's words, 'becomes a kind of play or anti-play, [the prefix anti- should be stressed] that is, a parody of a play, a comedy of comedy':

> Alas! the wise and fundamental truths [the characters] exchanged, each carefully linked to the next, had gone wild, their language had become disjointed; the characters disintegrated: their words became meaningless absurdities; the entire cast ended up quarrelling. It was impossible to grasp my heroes' motives in this quarrel. They didn't fling retorts at one another, not even sentence fragments, words; all they spoke were syllables, consonants and

56 *Vincenzina C. Ottomano*

vowels! . . . It represented, for me, a kind of collapse of reality. Words had become empty, noisy shells without meaning; the characters as well, of course, had become psychologically empty. Everything appeared to me in an unfamiliar light, people moving in a timeless time, in a spaceless space.

(ibid.: 178)

The analogy, the common thread that seems to connect Ligeti's theatrical poetics to the experience of the theatre of the absurd is even more evident when one considers the structure of works such as *Aventures* and *Nouvelles Aventures*. Ligeti often defines a few conventional situations ('Conversation', 'Commérages', 'Communikation'), or those that are distinctly theatrical ('Die grosse hysterische Szene', 'La serenata'), distorting, however, the code of communication. He refuses to consider language as the principal vehicle of the dramatic action; on the contrary, he attempts to penetrate into deeper layers of meaning, those which, in brief, he himself defines as 'eine rein affektive Sprache' ('a pure affective language') (Ligeti 2007 [1979]: 80). If, in conventional drama 'every word means what it says, the situations are clearcut, and at the end all conflicts are tidily resolved', in Ligeti as much as in the major authors of the so-called theatre of the absurd, the starting point is that

reality is never like that; it is multiple, complex, many-dimensional and exists on a number of different levels at one and the same time. Language is far too straightforward an instrument to express all this by itself. Reality can only be conveyed by being *acted out* in all its complexity.

(Esslin 1960: 12–13)

An obvious example of this way of acting with a transfigured, 'affective' language is that of 'Conversation' in *Aventures*. In the libretto written for the stage version, Ligeti imagined a scene in which the singers mime and 'exaggerate' gestures that refer to a conventional social situation: they bow to each other, offer cigarettes, exchange civilities, offer seats on imaginary chairs, make themselves comfortable. The result is the caricature of etiquette. The fracture, the short-circuit between the represented convention and the conception of the vocal material gives rise to the complexity and multiplicity of the theatrical expression: the communication between the three singers, in fact, is created starting from archetypal expressions of human communication, delineating an artificial, bewildered language capable of instituting new sense relationships that are different from and contrary to the given situation (see Example 3.1). This procedure is similar to that of the last scene of *The Bald Soprano* by Ionesco, which the playwright stages in a way that is just as evidently a typical 'middle-class' situation with all its rituals, gradually achieving, however, a real and true disintegration and atrophy of the language and communication between the protagonists, finally reducing it to a non-sense of phonemes, exclamations, single vowels and consonants (see Figure 3.1). In a certain sense, for Ligeti as much as for Ionesco, dialogue and language separate themselves from the 'true' events of the scene and are even put in direct contradiction with the action itself.

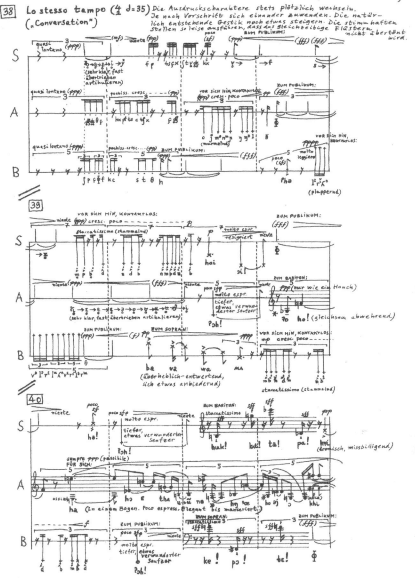

Example 3.1 First page of 'Conversation' from *Aventures* by György Ligeti. © Copyright by Henry Litolff's Verlag, Leipzig, for all countries of the world. Reproduced by kind permission of Peters Edition Limited, London.

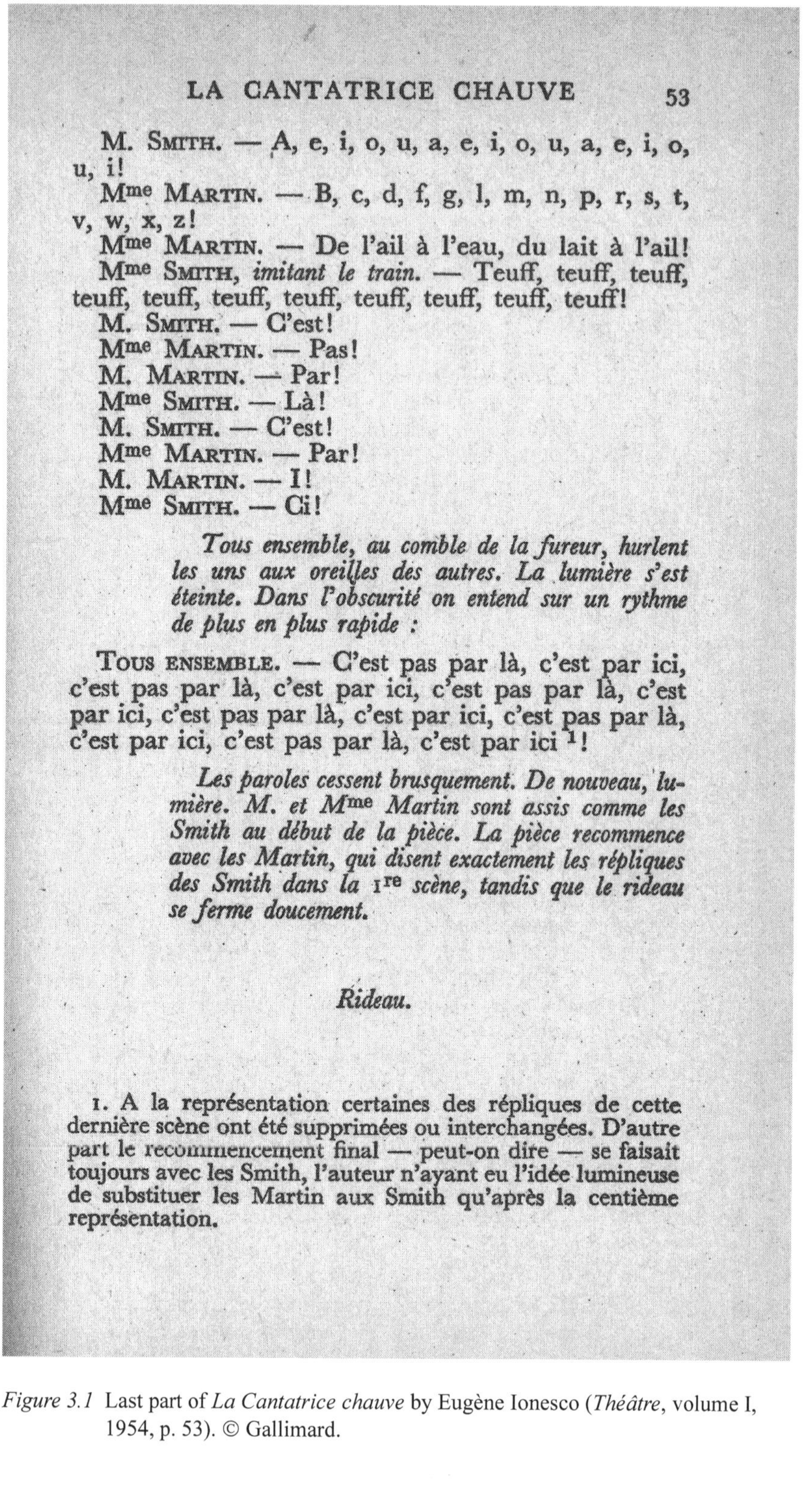

LA CANTATRICE CHAUVE   53

M. Smith. — A, e, i, o, u, a, e, i, o, u, a, e, i, o, u, i!

Mme Martin. — B, c, d, f, g, l, m, n, p, r, s, t, v, w, x, z!

Mme Martin. — De l'ail à l'eau, du lait à l'ail!

Mme Smith, *imitant le train.* — Teuff, teuff, teuff, teuff, teuff, teuff, teuff, teuff, teuff!

M. Smith. — C'est!

Mme Martin. — Pas!

M. Martin. — Par!

Mme Smith. — Là!

M. Smith. — C'est!

Mme Martin. — Par!

M. Martin. — I!

Mme Smith. — Ci!

> *Tous ensemble, au comble de la fureur, hurlent les uns aux oreilles des autres. La lumière s'est éteinte. Dans l'obscurité on entend sur un rythme de plus en plus rapide :*

Tous ensemble. — C'est pas par là, c'est par ici, c'est pas par là, c'est par ici, c'est pas par là, c'est par ici, c'est pas par là, c'est par ici, c'est pas par là, c'est par ici, c'est pas par là, c'est par ici [1]!

> *Les paroles cessent brusquement. De nouveau, lumière. M. et Mme Martin sont assis comme les Smith au début de la pièce. La pièce recommence avec les Martin, qui disent exactement les répliques des Smith dans la 1re scène, tandis que le rideau se ferme doucement.*

> *Rideau.*

1. A la représentation certaines des répliques de cette dernière scène ont été supprimées ou interchangées. D'autre part le recommencement final — peut-on dire — se faisait toujours avec les Smith, l'auteur n'ayant eu l'idée lumineuse de substituer les Martin aux Smith qu'après la centième représentation.

Figure 3.1 Last part of *La Cantatrice chauve* by Eugène Ionesco (*Théâtre*, volume I, 1954, p. 53). © Gallimard.

Theatre as problem 59

The tie between Ligeti and the theatre of the absurd remained a constant, albeit with very different premises and consequences, as the composer prepared himself for his second theatrical project, *Le Grand Macabre* (1974–77). The long genesis of the work, the first ideas of which date back roughly to the period of *Aventures* and *Nouvelles Aventures*, vouches for Ligeti's quest for a new aesthetical horizon, and specifically for a radical rethinking of his conception of theatre. Initially, the project – commissioned by Göran Gentele, director of the Stockholm Opera House – included a reference to the myth of Oedipus and to Kylwiria, an imaginary city mirroring the composer's childhood fantasies. Later, Ligeti considered as subjects Alfred Jarry's *Ubu Roi* or Ionesco's *Macbett*.[3] The composer's letters from this period to Ove Nordwall on the long search for a subject matter, and his reservations about using a 'pre-existent' text, testify to a need that was both continuous with and exceeded previous experiences. More than once, in fact, Ligeti even lingered on the possibility of a direct collaboration with playwrights such as Ionesco or Peter Weiss for the writing of the text; each time, however, the composer was confronted with the difficulty of putting to music, of 'seizing', a text born for prose theatre.[4] The search for a subject matter for the new opera also revealed a 'desire' for approaching the theatre of the absurd, understood, however, as an indirect, implicit assimilation, one tied more to its theoretical and aesthetic foundations than to its concrete elements (text/staging). In an interview from 1970 with Imre Fabian, Ligeti clarified just this position with regard to the theatre of the absurd:

> I drew near the theatre of the absurd through Ionesco. But I would never put to music a text by Ionesco, because for him as for Beckett and Pinter that which is dramatic operates at the purely linguistic level. They do not need music. I was looking for a piece in which the theatricality could come out through the music as with the great models of Da Ponte or Boito, a literature that needs music.
>
> (Ligeti and Fabian 1978: 30)

Finally, the meeting with puppeteer Michel Meschke marked a change of direction for both the choice of the text and the dramaturgy of the opera. *La Balade du Grand Macabre* (1934) by the Belgian writer Michel Ghelgerode appealed to Ligeti, although he explicitly asked Meschke to work on the prose of the play in the attempt to make it clearer, more direct, similar to Jarry's *Ubu Roi* (Ligeti literally asked Meschke to 'jarrify' the text):

---

3 For more detailed information about the genesis of *Le Grand Macabre* see Edwards 2017 and Searby 2010.

4 See especially the letter from Ligeti to Nordwall of 13 May 1964: 'I cannot, and I do not wish to compose music for a text; on the contrary, I would like a text for the specific nature of my music. [. . .] Ionesco, my favourite author, cannot be set to music. Only action, not words, must be set to music' (original in German, cited in Burde 1993: 272). For similar formulations see also Pustijanac 2013: 68–75.

60 *Vincenzina C. Ottomano*

Finally I found a theatre piece of Michel de Ghelderode. He died in the fifties, I think. The pieces are from the twenties or thirties. He was Flemish, but he wrote in French. This play was called *Ballade de Grand Macabre*. He is I think a very important precursor of Beckett and Ionesco, and very close to Artaud—of this kind, not exactly surrealistic, but this kind of theatre.

(Ligeti and Jack 1974: 28)

The theme of the end of the world described by Ghelderode seems to condense in itself all the ingredients that Ligeti was looking for, on a theoretical plane, in the plays of Artaud, Ionesco or Beckett: 'a play about the end of the world, a bizarre, demoniacal, cruel and also very comic piece, to which I wanted to give an additional dimension, that of ambiguity' (Ligeti 1983: 115).

Moreover, the inspiration sparked by *La Balade du Grand Macabre* resulted in a radical change in the composer's approach to the text – this time not only valued for its phonetic qualities but also treated as dramatic material – as well as in his approach to the concept of 'genre':

It gradually became clear to me that the idea of a non-conceptual text could not be pursued any further: this kind of text composition was worn out during the 1960s. I not only needed a clearly understandable plot, but also an equally clear and understandable sung and spoken text: from the 'anti-opera' emerged the 'anti-anti-opera', then on another level, once again, the 'opera'.

(Ligeti 2007 [1978]: 267)

Hence, for Ligeti, the starting point came from the opportunity to 'play' with a traditional structure (that of a more or less linear story organized in a traditional libretto) by alienating its elements. The opera as a genre was treated as an archetype, a ritual.

With respect to the premises that had characterized the composition of *Aventures*, Ligeti's approach to the theatre of the absurd also changed substantially: Ionesco clearly remained an important reference point in Ligeti's comments, but the composer's interest no longer (or not only) centred on non-conceptual uses of language, but now encompassed the construction of the drama in Ionesco and his predecessors Jarry and Ghelgerode. Filtering the ideas in the theatre of the absurd and adapting them to his own needs, Ligeti conceived of an opera based on entirely traditional elements (an apparently traditional libretto, a plot with a narrative structure, reference to vocal styles and instruments of the past) but which become progressively exaggerated and deformed to the point where they lose their own identity and become deeply ambiguous (see Pustijanac 2013: 69–71). In other words, in *Le Grand Macabre* Ligeti condensed some of the principles elicited from the reading of theatrical texts from the theatre of the absurd with his own perceptions about how these might function in the opera house. To summarize, in *Le Grand Macabre*, we can find two levels of the reception of spoken theatre: on the one hand, a level that affects the material of the work itself (the textual and semantic levels, represented by Ghelderode's play); on the other hand, a level that

Theatre as problem 61

concerns the structures of the composition, that is, the attempt to reinterpret and apply the theories of contemporary theatre.

Pousseur and the 'call to participation'

Substantially different were Henri Pousseur and Michel Butor's premises and goals in creating *Votre Faust*, subtitled by the authors a 'fantaisie variable genre opera' ('opera-like variable fantasia'). The work's title and subtitle are utterly revealing: each and every word contains in itself signals of the theoretical issues addressed by Pousseur and Butor. First, the myth of Faust as a literary and theatrical archetype from Goethe to Mann (see Hedges 2005: 147–55); second, the noun *fantaisie*, indicating the integration of seemingly incompatible materials, both on the textual level (where the language is at once descriptive and intelligible, and fragmented, reduced to sound material), and musically (where music is both sonic ornament of a given situation but also synthesis of heterogeneous objects such as citations, noise and pre-recorded sounds); third, the expression *genre opéra* questions the opera genre as an institution and in its historical continuity; finally, the two adjectives *Votre* and *variable* indicate the willingness of the two authors to create a certain mobility of the work, and to involve the very audience ('your') within this mobility.

Even before the premiere of *Votre Faust*, in his lecture on the work held in 1966 at the conference 'Neue Musik – Neue Szene' of the Darmstadt Ferienkurse, Pousseur stated that the idea of working with Butor was born from the deep fascination he experienced reading Butor's essay 'La musique, art réaliste' (Butor 1960), and from his fascination with a few critical writings of Butor on the nature of the novel and on its latent or more manifest 'mobility' (Pousseur 1997 [1967]; see also Decroupet and Kovács 1997). The premises of *Votre Faust* reflected, therefore, a need to explore new possibilities of narrative through the theatre, building upon Pousseur's and Butor's separate investigations of the issue in musical structure and literary texts. However, what I would like to pursue here is not so much the close relationship between Butor and Pousseur and the consequent implications for the genesis of the composition; rather I wish to investigate the dramatic roots of *Votre Faust* in order to show how, alongside the operatic genre, the concept of drama and theatre in its broadest theoretical and practical meaning stands as a basic element of the work's conception.

I refer, in particular, to an intense exchange between Pousseur and Berio that unfolded over a period of time and testified to an articulated process of thought and reflection surrounding *Votre Faust* and theatre in general. In 1969, Berio wrote an essay that sought to examine the reasons for the fiasco of the premiere of the opera at the Piccola Scala that had taken place in January of that year, and to analyse the complex relationship of heterogeneous elements and structures within the piece (text-music-scene) (Berio 2013 [1969]). Pousseur's reply to Berio's essay followed in the same journal issue (Pousseur 1969). It attributed the lack of success of *Votre Faust* to organizational and managerial problems at the Scala, and at the same time, as has been argued by Angela Ida De Benedictis, reiterated the permanent nature of the relationship between text and music within opera

62   *Vincenzina C. Ottomano*

(see De Benedictis's editorial note in Berio 2013: 540). But what is more interesting for our discussion is that, at a distance of more than ten years from the premiere of the opera, the aesthetic and compositional principles of *Votre Faust* were in fact radically called into question again. At the time of the French reprint (in 1983) of Berio's essay, Pousseur published a second open letter to Berio, entitled 'Les mésaventures de Notre Faust (lettre ouverte à Luciano Berio)' (Pousseur 1985). In this second reply Pousseur undertook an *a posteriori* self-reflection that is therefore doubly 'mediated': on the one hand the composer reflected on his experience of theatre with a retrospective view on the opera; on the other hand this very reflection, solicited by the confrontation with Berio, 'forced' Pousseur to call back into question the work and to investigate theoretically its theatrical objectives.

The fundamental starting point was the acknowledgement of the continuity between spoken theatre and musical theatre in *Votre Faust*, which was thus categorized as belonging to a hybrid genre:

> [O]ur intention was to combine in a quite original genre, not yet existent, the specific properties of the spoken theatre [. . .] and on the other hand, those of the musical show [. . .]; also, we took care from the very beginning that one field should not be hierarchically inferior to, subordinated to, or absorbed by the other. Fully aware of the problems of their integration into a new unit, we did not want to limit ourselves to only one possibility, be it a merger or a competition [. . .], but we wanted to study a variety of solutions and work specifically on variation that allowed this scale or palette.
>
> (ibid.: 112)

In the first place, therefore, Pousseur and Butor were interested in coordinating different elements (spoken theatre, musical show); but above all they were concerned to extrapolate some specific properties of theatrical communication which could allow continuous variation in the possibility of verbal expression to be created:

> We therefore started by imagining a whole range, a whole 'field' of possibilities of elocution and levels of comprehension, some of which I mention, with enormous simplification of their order, which is in continuous movement:
>
> – addressing (speech by the theatre director) the public
> – dialogue among the actors
> – inner monologue (recorded on magnetic tape and whose modulation would emerge from the general 'acoustic wash' or would blend into it), first in a single voice and then in a more or less dense polyphony, up to masses of shouts and other altogether indistinct crowd noises.
>
> (ibid.: 113)

The modes of communication of spoken theatre, and the very recited word of the actors, thus had a structural value within the work, a value that allowed it 'to

Theatre as problem   63

preserve for as long as possible the clarity of at least one or more layers of verbal flow', as Pousseur put it (ibid.: 114).

However, in his analysis, Pousseur pays less attention to spoken theatre as 'technique' of elocution than he does to the dramatic theories underlying the composition *Votre Faust*. The starting point is the idea of a theatre understood as a 'plea for participation', with its audience involved in determining, albeit in a controlled way, some developments of the plot:

> After an exciting quest for 'open forms' in the purely musical field, which in practice is synonymous with instrumental music [. . .], we thought possible and desirable to begin to also eliminate the barriers 'between the stage and the hall', between the artists and their audience, offering to the latter a form of limited, regulated, yet attractive participation.
>
> (ibid.: 118)

The reasons for including the mobility of the work were dictated primarily by the search for a compositional continuity with Pousseur's previous experiences, as well as those of other composers of the same generation (Pousseur explicitly mentions his *Scambi* and *Répons* as well as Stockhausen's and Boulez's compositions), and with Umberto Eco's theorization (from the standpoint of linguistics/ semiotics) of semantic openness (Eco 1962).[5] However, mobility also found its 'justification' in specific dramatic theories.

Pousseur therefore returned to Brecht's postulation of the idea of theatre as a 'transformation' of the audience. More specifically, Pousseur referred to the interpretation of Brecht's plays advanced by the philosopher Ernst Bloch. In reality, as a letter by Pousseur to Butor of 13 April 1965 testifies, the composer's fascination with Bloch's theories emerged at an already advanced phase of work on *Votre Faust*.[6] Nevertheless, in 1983 they were restrospectively offered by the composer as the foundational principle behind the mobility of an opera such as *Votre Faust*. 'In *The Principle of Hope*', Pousseur wrote,

> Bloch emphasizes the pedagogical nature of theatre, considered as a 'paradigmatic institution' (where the audience participates in, witnesses, and is complicit in an activity of 'putting to the test', whose conclusions might eventually be carried over on a larger scale by the audience in their daily life).
>
> (Pousseur 1985: 119)

Written between 1954 and 1959, the monumental three-volume *The Principle of Hope* devoted an entire chapter to the problem of theatre. Bloch began his

---

5 For a broader discussion of this issue see De Benedictis 2007 and Dack 2009.

6 Letter from Pousseur to Butor, 13 April 1965: 'Also another discovery was made: *Das Prinzip Hoffnung*, by Ernst Bloch. A magnificent book with which comes the will to fight like Jacob with the angel (for example, by writing an answer-echo-prolungation-polemic: 'Das Prinzip Glaube')'. Original in French. Paul Sacher Foundation, Henri Pousseur Collection, Korrespondenz, reproduced with kind permission.

64 *Vincenzina C. Ottomano*

discussion by examining the public's expectations when they go to the theatre and in particular the need for mimesis and for getting involved in the representation:

> These visitors want to be entertained in the performance, that is, to be released and become free, not automatically or simply free from something, but free to do something. There is, however, driving in all of them, what we may call mimic need. This need is more widespread than the poetic, it is connected positively not only with the submissive or hypocritical, but tempting desire to transform oneself. It shares this desire with the actor himself, seeks to satisfy it through him, that is, in all better cases, through what he respectively represents.
>
> (Bloch 1986 [1959]: 412–13)[7]

However, what was most interesting for Pousseur's argument was the principle expressed by Bloch that there are already pre-existing openings in drama:

> He [Bloch] then suggests – as a logical consequence of the fundamental questions raised by 'great drama', that is by the most significant works, in which, in his opinion, questions are always unsolved so that one has to continue digging – the invention of pieces in which the outcome will not be strictly fixed and that, through an organized system of returns, of bifurcations and other types of intervention, [. . .] would allow viewers to act to influence the evolution of the plot.
>
> (Pousseur 1985: 119)

If, then, in Bloch's theories the concept of 'openness' of the drama (in particular, Brecht's drama) represented a theoretical postulate, in Pousseur the mobility of *Votre Faust* was an empirical experiment into the involvement of the audience. As observed by Pascal Decroupet and Inge Kovács (1997), in *Votre Faust* there is an attempt to consider the public themselves as 'material' of the composition, material that can act, albeit along lines that are entirely controlled by the composer.

Berio and the (infinite) possibilities of representation

Browsing through the interviews, writings and other statements by Luciano Berio, one quickly realizes the composer's multifarious interests in the spoken theatre: from Brecht to Genet, from Beckett to Pirandello. The heterogeneity of these names not only shows his breadth of interests, but also makes it difficult to ascribe Berio's thinking to a specific poetics or theory of theatre.

For these reasons, I wish to focus on an essay by Berio that has only recently been published in Italian, in Angela Ida De Benedictis's edition of the composer's writings. The text is 'Problems of Musical Theater', the first of two lectures held

---

7 On Bloch's reading, see also Lehmann 2016: 125–7.

by the composer at Harvard University on 11 and 18 January 1967 (Berio 1967). Tackling a complex issue such as music theatre, Berio had first to deal with his own variegated theatrical experience. Strictly speaking, Berio started engaging with theatre in the 1960s with *Passaggio* (1963), but by that time he had already explored theatricality outside of traditional norms: spatially (radio plays), with dramatized performances (a kind of 'theatre for the ears': see, for instance, *Circles*), and by questioning some of the crucial functions of theatre (*Mimusique No. 2, Allez-hop*). In this sense, the nature of this text is profoundly different from the texts analysed in the previous sections: this text only partially engages with the 'actual' experience of music theatre, and instead proposes a broader reflection that seeks to investigate the historical reasons leading to the questioning of a genre. Eventually this text leads to a clear definition of the discrepancy between 'opera' and 'musical theatre'.

Echoing Brecht's considerations in 'Notes on *Rise and Fall of the City of Mahagonny*' regarding the impossibility of opera updating its content and technically modernizing its form without losing its 'culinary' character, Berio reflected on the impossibility of considering the genre of opera (understood in the most traditional sense of the term) as an actual genre, at least after Richard Strauss's *Rosenkavalier*, Berg's *Wozzeck* and *Lulu*, and Schoenberg's unfinished *Moses und Aron*. 'In those same years', Berio wrote, 'it was already clear that opera was no longer a meaningful form, but a manner, and, as such, bore on its body the signs of its inability to renew itself' (Berio 1967: 1). If this statement about the 'death' of traditional theatre seems to be a requirement inherent in the very concept of the avant-garde, which demands the transformation not only of an institution but, above all, of attitudes towards art, the structural opposition between opera and music theatre was more specifically located by Berio in the question of representation. In opera, representation was well defined and fixed; music theatre, on the other hand, repudiated exclusive views of representation:

> One: musical theater, seen as the general attitude towards the discovery or re-evaluation, through music, of the dramaturgy inherent in symbolic behavior [. . .]; the other, opera, seen as a form, or, at least in reference to an ideal formal model, an Aristotelian type of model, equally valid for the narration and for the music.
>
> (Ibid.: 4)

To a 'contemplative' model of opera (with a reference to the Brechtian metaphor of the 'bourgeois ritual') where the public is invited to witness the resolution of the plot established from the very beginning, Berio opposes a model of theatre that acts rather on meanings, where the participating audience is called to take decisions on a problem that is posed but not solved.

If the rejection of fixed modes of representation and the opening up of discussion into ritualism are essential points that determine a structural difference between opera and contemporary musical theatre, Berio also highlights the need to consider the experience of musical theatre not only in terms of a clear contrast

66   *Vincenzina C. Ottomano*

with opera. Contemporary musical theatre does not negate the opera experience, but if anything brings into discussion its principles and reflects upon its conventions and its history (ibid.: 10–11).

In the definition of self-reflexivity (a theatre that reflects on itself and therefore transforms itself), a key role in Berio's discussion was played by the famous essay by Lionel Abel 'Tragedy – or Metatheater?', which appeared in 1964 in the collection entitled *Essays in the Modern Drama* (Abel 1964).[8] Reflecting on Abel's theory, Berio not only explained the meaning of 'death of opera', but also the death of classic tragedy, in which man – thus, the characters – lives according to unchangeable and already set principles. Contrary to this is the self-aware character, a character who has a story and who contributes to his own dramatic realization:

> Opera is based on the ideals of classical tragedy. Now tragedy is dead. If we are interested in giving a meaning to our thoughts and actions, among our fellow men, we will never represent these thoughts and actions through the mechanics and implications of tragedy, that same idea of tragedy that supported and made possible most of [the] development of opera. Paraphrasing Lionel Abel, the author of an excellent book on meta-theater, we can say that tragedy glorifies the structure of the world, which it supposedly reflects in its own form, while today's theater glorifies the unwillingness of the imagination to regard any image of the world as ultimate. Tragedy makes human existence more vivid by showing its vulnerability to fate, while our theater makes human existence more dream-like by showing fate can be overcome [. . .] Tragedy cannot operate without the assumption of an ultimate order, while in the theater of our time, order is continually invented and improvised by man.
>
> (Berio 1967: 10)

These reflections already announce a theatrical poetics that would bear its mature fruits in Berio's theatrical output of a later period (see for example his relationship with the legacy of Verdi in *La vera storia*, or the play within a play in *Un re in ascolto*, through to the last compositions for music theatre *Outis* and *Cronaca del Luogo*). The grounds for this poetics was laid as early as the late 1960s, however, when Berio started work on his *Opera*, a composition in which the deformation of convention and the multiplication of meanings actualize his idea of a meta-semantic theatre. The title of this work, purposefully provocative, must be read at the same time as an 'exorcism of opera' (in Berio's own definition; see the letter quoted in Di Luzio 2014: 463), and also through the etymology of its Latin root as the plural of *opus*. The work correspondingly superimposes three apparently divergent subjects: the myth of Orpheus; the episode of the sinking of the *Titanic*; and a few parts of *Terminal*, a theatrical text by Susan Yankowitz, first staged in 1969 at Bordeaux's Théâtre Alhambra by the Open Theater of

---

8 On the role of Abel, see also Brüdermann 2007: 219–28.

New York, which styled itself as 'a collective investigation into mortality and a consideration of both personal and social responses to the fact of death' (Yankowitz 1998: 8). Berio's collaboration with the Open Theater placed itself in continuity with his earlier theatrical experiences (as he mentioned at the outset of his lecture, The Dancers' Workshop Company of San Francisco under the direction of Ann Halprin had placed a role of great importance in the realization of *Esposizione*; on this see De Benedictis 2016 and De Benedictis' chapter in the present volume), and at the same time it revealed Berio's curiosity and interest in the more contemporaneous forms of scenic experimentation (Maurin 2016).

As Berio himself stated in an interview of 1969, one of his first encounters with the Open Theater (which had been founded in 1963 by actor and former Living Theatre member Joseph Chaikin) occurred in Italy, precisely in the summer of 1968 at the eleventh Festival dei Due Mondi of Spoleto,[9] where *The Serpent* by Jean-Claude van Itallie was on the programme:

> Recently, I had the occasion to see in Italy a few performances of the Open Theater, which takes real, well-known elements in order to transform them, putting them in relation with other, equally simple elements and making emerge from their encounter a new guise in a process of continuous proliferation. For me, working in the same direction, this was a captivating experience.
> (Berio 2017 [1969]: 47)

It is precisely the idea of transformation but also the necessity to be able to create a relation between apparently heterogeneous elements (or different levels of meaning) that lies at the foundation of the dramatic construction of *Opera*. In reality, the involvement of the Open Theater already represented in itself a 'layer' of the scenic-musical articulation. Indeed, it was not a coincidence that, for the premiere of *Opera*, one of the fundamental commitments maintained by the theatre group was that of consituting themsleves as a work collective,[10] so much so that in the production of *Opera* in Santa Fe, the Open Theater became essentially part of the authorial sphere of the work.[11] The physicality of the actors, moreover, became

---

9 This date is confirmed by a recommendation letter from May 1969 written by Berio to support a request to subsidize the Open Theater: 'The production of The Serpent (to quote only one) which I saw last year at the Spoleto Festival prompted me to speak to several of the members of the group. As I told them at the time, I would be very much interested in working with the Open Theater.' Kent State University Libraries, Special Collections and Archives; reproduced with kind permission of Talia Pecker Berio.

10 In 1998 Susan Yankowitz wrote: 'The philosophy and method of the Open Theater was greatly influenced by the communal movements of the time. What these movements had embodied was a commitment to a democratic, nonhierarchical structure in which everyone had equal rights and goods were shared. For us this meant that the play did not reflect the vision of only one person (traditionally, the writer or director) but was instead a fusion of many talents. Conventional divisions of labor did not apply – actors contributed text, the director brought in research, the writer conceived improvisations' (Yankowitz 1998: 8).

11 Berio designed the staging of *Opera* at Santa Fe together with Roberta Sklar, co-director of the Open Theater at the time. See Ottomano 2016: 249–51.

68   Vincenzina C. Ottomano

an integral part of the composition's staging: *Opera* was not only interpreted and acted out by the theatrical group, but the actors and their previous practice themselves became 'material' for the composition. Part of the pre-existing text of *Terminal* was included by Berio in its entirety in the libretto of *Opera*, combined with the most diverse sources, from Striggio's libretto to Monteverdi's *Orfeo* to fragments of texts by Umberto Eco, Furio Colombo and Edoardo Sanguineti. Entire scenes of *Terminal* interpreted by the actors of the Open Theater were thus inserted, alternated, and superimposed with the purely musical and/or sung episodes of *Opera* (in particular, scenes featuring the embalming of bodies and those of terminally ill patients in the hospital). A few parts of *Opera* were then freshly written by Berio with the gestural and expressive peculiarities of the Open Theater explicitly in mind. The possibility of working with this type of actor and with this type of text endured beyond the first production's collaboration with the Open Theater. Indeed, for successive performances of *Opera* (in Florence in 1977, in Paris-Nanterre in 1979, and in Turin in 1980) Berio collaborated with other troupes of performers, and despite the substantial revisions that Berio made to the score, the composition similarly posed itself as an answer to the idea of the 'coordination' of different events: musical, scenic, and of meaning, between the singers, the actors, the music and the staging.

A further example of Berio's work with heterogeneous layers and the organization of a 'polyphony' of meaning can be found in 'Air', a piece strategically repeated and progressively varied at the beginning of each act of *Opera* (Air I, Air II, Air III). The stage is dark, a light turns on to reveal an onstage pianist and soprano, and the stage directions specify 'as a lesson' (see Example 3.2).

At the centre of this purposefully conventional frame (the public find themselves in a theatre, watching a musical theatre performance happening right in front of them), the organization of the scenic space, the vocality of the singers, the mimic-gestural actions of the actors, and the (re)-composition of the pre-existent text determine a true de-synchronization between that which is heard and that which is seen, in other words between the audience's expectations and that which is actually attempted during the performative act. This meta-theatrical situation has a double aspect. First, there is the alienatory effect of witnessing a 'concert rehearsal' in the middle of a work signalling (through staged representation, texts borrowed from operatic history, and the venue itself) an operatic situation. Second, the situation of the soprano who sings is not contained within the operatic illusion: she 'incarnates' a performer in the process of 'learning' a piece of opera. This can be understood as an 'autoreflexive' process: that which is seen and heard onstage is not, so to say, a 'finished' result of a piece sung onstage, but the unfolding of an event, that, through various rehearsals, brings the singer to 'construct' and to define the performance of the piece. Upon this is then superimposed the voices of the actors, which introduce the episode taken from *Terminal* regarding the torture of patients at the hospital; the superimposition upon the scenic situation of the soprano occurs gradually, without a solution of continuity (see Example 3.3).

The introduction of a new narrative level not only accentuates the alienating effect of the superimposition of episodes that appear alien to one another, but

Example 3.2 Luciano Berio, *Air I*, from *Opera*, I Act, pp. 1–2. Copyright 1977 by Universal Edition (London) Ltd, London, Copyright assigned to Universal Edition A.G., Wien. By kind permission. *(continued)*

Example 3.2 (continued)

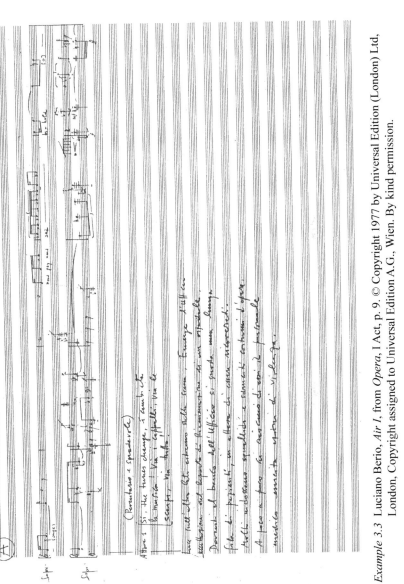

Example 3.3 Luciano Berio, *Air I*, from *Opera*, I Act, p. 9. © Copyright 1977 by Universal Edition (London) Ltd, London, Copyright assigned to Universal Edition A.G., Wien. By kind permission.

72 Vincenzina C. Ottomano

actually adds a new semantic layer. Berio in fact transforms the hospital patients into a sort of traditional opera cast, as we read in the stage directions:

> Spotlight on the other extreme side of the scene. In front of the desk in the office there snakes a long line of patients, waiting to be admitted. Many are wearing filthy and torn opera costumes. Little by little the medical staff carry out acts of violence against each of these patients.
>
> (Berio 1977: 9)

With the effect of a sort of *mise en abyme*, it is almost as if, at the beginning of *Opera*, it is the same culinary experience being portrayed (note the dialogue between the doctor and the patient: 'Did you enjoy that? . . . Why did you enjoy it? . . . Because I needed to enjoy it'). The 'violence' is perpetrated on the public and indeed on the actors themselves, forced to react to the ritual.

The opening of *Opera* provides an eloquent example of the strategies put in place by Berio in his personal definition of musical theatre, one that clearly connects to Abel's theories on meta-theatre and Brecht's epic theatre. As mentioned previously, the idea of the awareness of the characters in the scene, the rejection of a linear plot in favour of a layering of narrative levels and various meanings, just like the idea of a theatre that reflects upon itself, are to be understood not as absolute categories but rather as 'constants', points of reference or reflection that, in different ways, accompanied and traversed the entire experience of Berio's musical theatre.

***

The cases of Berio, Ligeti and Pousseur, here taken as examples of possible 'answers' by composers to the theories of so-called modern drama, certainly cannot be considered paradigmatic of a problem of reception that is complex and inflected in the most disparate ways in the experiences of the new music theatre. At the same time, just this diversity of approach of these three composers demonstrates, if anything, a 'mobility of attitudes' when faced with an urgent question: that of rethinking opera and music theatre 'also', but not exclusively, through the filter of the experience of spoken theatre.

Far from wanting to establish a fully developed 'theory of music theatre', or to appropriate slavishly the theories of playwrights such as Ionesco, Brecht and Grotowski, or even those of philosophers and critics of theatre such as Abel or Bloch, music theatre composers of the 1960s and 1970s opened themselves to different aspects of contemporary theatricality that afforded an infinite array of possibilities. The examples given here show the impossibility, or unwillingness, to give a literal application of dramatical theories to musical theatre: this reflects the different preoccupations of the composers in rethinking theatre above all through the medium of music. They did not furnish an exhaustive response to a surpassingly complex problem, but instead opened up many new questions. Synthesizing this with Berio's own words: 'What is musical theater finally? It is

Theatre as problem   73

the research and development, through music, of an implied dramaturgy. In every situation there is a potential dramaturgy, just as there is, in every perceived form, a potential movement' (Berio 1967: 12).

Acknowledgements

I wish to thank Valentina Bertolani and Bibiana Vergine for helping me in the translation of the text into English, and Robert Adlington for his insightful comments and suggestions.

References

Abel, Lionel (1964), 'Tragedy – or metatheatre?', in Morris Freedman (ed.), *Essays in the Modern Drama*, Boston, MA: D. C. Heath & Co., pp. 367–71.

Beffa, Karol (2016), *György Ligeti*, Paris: Fayard.

Berio, Luciano (1967), 'Problems of musical theater', lecture held in Harvard University (Cambridge) on 11 January 1967; unpublished typescript of 15 pages, original in English; Luciano Berio Collection, Paul Sacher Foundation, Basel. Published in Italian translation as 'Problemi di teatro musicale' in Berio 2013, pp. 42–57.

Berio, Luciano (1977), *Opera*, full score (fair copy, corr. VIII/1982), UE16655, Vienna: Universal Edition.

Berio, Luciano (2013 [1969]), 'Notre Faust', in Angela Ida De Benedictis (ed.), *Scritti sulla musica*, Torino: Einaudi, pp. 398–405; French translation in *Contrechamps*, 1/1 (1983), pp. 51–6.

Berio, Luciano (2013), *Scritti sulla musica*, ed. Angela Ida De Benedictis, Torino: Einaudi.

Berio, Luciano (2017 [1969]), 'Entretien Luciano Berio - Michel Philippot', in Luciano Berio, *Interviste e colloqui*, ed. Vincenzina C. Ottomano, Torino: Einaudi, pp. 43–51.

Bloch, Ernst (1986 [1959]), *The Principle of Hope*, volume 2, Cambridge, MA: MIT Press.

Borio, Gianmario, Giordano Ferrari and Daniela Tortora (eds) (2017), *Teatro di avanguardia e composizione sperimentale per la scena in Italia: 1950–1975*, Venezia: Fondazione Giorgio Cini.

Boulez, Pierre and Zoltán Peskó (1978), 'Musical aspects in today's musical theatre: A conversation between Pierre Boulez and Zoltán Peskó' [1972], *Tempo*, 127, pp. 2–9.

Brüdermann, Ute (2007), *Das Musiktheater von Luciano Berio*, Frankfurt am Main: Peter Lang.

Burde, Wolfgang (1993), *György Ligeti. Eine Monographie*, Zürich: Atlantis-Musikbuch-Verlag.

Butor, Michel (1960), 'La musique, art réaliste: les paroles et la musique', *Esprit*, 280, pp. 138–56; reprinted in Michel Butor (2006), *Œuvres completes*, volume 2, ed. Mireille Calle Gruber, Paris: La Différence, pp. 387–98.

Dack, John (2009), 'The electroacoustic music of Henri Pousseur and the "open" form', in Björn Heile (ed.), *The Modernist Legacy: Essays on New Music*, Farnham, UK: Ashgate, pp. 177–89.

De Benedictis, Angela Ida (2007), 'Opera aperta: teoria e prassi', in Gianmario Borio and Carlo Gentili (eds), *Storia dei concetti musicali. Espressione, forma, opera*, Roma: Carocci, pp. 317–34.

De Benedictis, Angela Ida (2016), 'From *Esposizione* to *Laborintus II*: Transitions and mutations of "a desire for theatre"', in Giordano Ferrari (ed.), *Le théâtre musical de Luciano Berio*, volume 1, Paris: L'Harmattan, pp. 177–246.

Decroupet, Pascal and Inge Kovács (1997), 'Musik und Szene', in Gianmario Borio and Hermann Danuser (eds), *Im Zenit der Moderne, Die Internationalen Ferienkurse für Neue Musik Darmstadt 1946–1966*, volume 2, Freiburg im Breisgau: Rombach, pp. 311–32.

Di Luzio, Claudia (2014), 'Opera on opera, Luciano Berio's *Opera*', in Sabine Lichtenstein (ed.), *'Music's Obedient Daughter': The Opera Libretto from Source to Score*, Amsterdam: Rodopi, pp. 463–82.

Eco, Umberto (1962), *Opera aperta. Forma e indeterminazione nelle poetiche contemporanee*, Milano: Bompiani.

Edwards, Peter (2017), *György Ligeti's 'Le Grand Macabre': Postmodernism, Musico-Dramatic Form and the Grotesque*, London: Routledge.

Esslin, Martin (1960), 'The Theatre of The Absurd', *Tulane Drama Review*, 4/4, pp. 3–15.

Hedges, Inez (2005), *Framing Faust: Twentieth-Century Cultural Struggles*, Carbondale, IL: Southern Illinois University Press, pp. 147–55.

Heile, Björn (2016), 'Toward a Theory of Experimental Music Theatre', in Yael Kaduri (ed.), *The Oxford Handbook of Sound and Image in Western Art*, Oxford: Oxford University Press, pp. 335–55.

Ionesco, Eugène (1960), 'The tragedy of language: How an English primer became my first play', *Tulane Drama Review*, 4/3, pp. 10–13; reprinted in Eugène Ionesco (1964), *Note and Counter Notes*, New York: Grove, pp. 175–80.

Lehmann, Hans-Thies (2016), *Tragedy and Dramatic Theatre*, London: Routledge.

Levy, Benjamin R. (2017), *Metamorphosis in Music: The Compositions of György Ligeti in the 1950s and 60s*, Oxford: Oxford University Press.

Ligeti, György (1983), *Ligeti in Conversation with Péter Várnai, Josef Häusler, Claude Samuel and Himself*, London: Eulenburg Books.

Ligeti, György (2007 [1979]), 'Gedanken zum musikalischen Theater. Über *Artikulation, Aventures* und *Nouvelles Aventures*', in Monika Lichtenfeld (ed.), *György Ligeti. Gesammelte Schriften*, volume 2, Mainz: Schott, pp. 78–85.

Ligeti, György and Adrian Jack (1974), 'Ligeti talks to Adrian Jack', *Music and Musicians*, 22, pp. 27–30.

Ligeti, György and Imre Fabian (1978), 'Nach der ersten Oper weitere Opernpläne. Imre Fabian sprach mit dem Komponisten György Ligeti', *Opernwelt*, 6, pp. 29–30.

Maurin, Frederic (2016), 'L'embarquement pour Santa Fe: la contribution de l'Open Theater à la création d'*Opera*', in Giordano Ferrari (ed.), *Le théâtre musical de Luciano Berio*, volume 1, Paris: L'Harmattan, pp. 285–320.

Ottomano, Vincenzina C. (2016), 'Luciano Berio's *Opera* or a kind of "miroir de moi-même"', in Giordano Ferrari (ed.), *Le théâtre musical de Luciano Berio*, volume 1, Paris: L'Harmattan, pp. 247–84.

Pousseur, Henri (1969), 'Sì, il nostro Faust, indivisibile', translated by P. Gallarati, *Nuova Rivista Musicale Italiana*, 3/3, pp. 281–7.

Pousseur, Henri (1985), 'Les mésaventures de Notre Faust (lettre ouverte à Luciano Berio)', *Contrechamps*, 3/4, pp. 107–22.

Pousseur, Henri (1997 [1967]), '*Votre Faust*. Neue musikalische und theatralische Erfahrungen', in Gianmario Borio and Hermann Danuser (eds), *Im Zenit der Moderne, Die Internationalen Ferienkurse für Neue Musik Darmstadt 1946–1966*, volume 3, Freiburg im Breisgau: Rombach, pp. 267–89.

Pustijanac, Ingrid (2013), *György Ligeti. Il maestro dello spazio immaginario*, Lucca: LIM.

Rebstock, Matthias and David Roesner (eds) (2012), *Composed Theatre Aesthetics, Practices, Processes*, Bristol: Intellect.

Rozic, Eli (2008), *Generating Theater Meaning: A Theory and Methodology of Performance Analysis*, Brighton, UK and Portland, OR: Sussex Academic Press.

Salzman, Eric and Thomas Desi (2008), *The New Music Theater: Seeing the Voice, Hearing the Body*, Oxford and New York: Oxford University Press.

Schwartz, Arman (ed.) (2014), *The Opera Quarterly*, 30/1, special issue 'Opera and the Avant-Garde'.

Searby, Michael D. (2010), *Ligeti's Stylistic Crisis: Transformation in His Musical Style, 1974–1985*, Lanham, MD: Scarecrow Press.

Steinitz, Richard (2003), *György Ligeti: Music of The Imagination*, Boston, MA: Northeastern University Press.

Yankowitz, Susan (1998), '1969 Terminal 1996', *Theater*, 28/3, pp. 7–18.

Part II
Expansions of technology

4 Audio-visual collisions

Moving image technology and the Laterna
Magika aesthetic in new music theatre

Holly Rogers

New music theatre has long been considered a mixed form that hovers between genres. Often, this liminality has been defined in terms of other musical and dramatic practices. Eric Salzman and Thomas Desi, for instance, invoke several existing musical types, explaining that 'contemporary opera, music theater in its various forms, and the modern musical coexist on a continuum and the lines between them are often blurred' (Salzman and Desi 2008: 6). They also propose the value of placing new music theatre within a broader context, suggesting that it is 'closer in many ways to contemporary dance, dance theater, new theater and new performance art than to traditional opera' (ibid.: 4). Along similar lines, David Roesner proposes that

> Composed Theatre is not a genre—it is more a frame or a lens that brings quite disparate phenomena into view and collocates them. At the centre of this frame, the focus is on creation processes that bring the musical notion of composing to the theatrical aspects of performing and staging.
>
> (Roesner 2012: 11)

In the works of Cage, Kagel and others, Roesner argues, the treatment of non-instrumental sounds, human gesture and movement as part of the composition approaches

> the theatrical stage and its means of expression as *musical* material. They treat voice, gesture, movement, light, sound, image, design and other features of theatrical production according to musical principles and compositional techniques and apply musical thinking to performance as a whole.
>
> (ibid.: 9)

Robert Adlington has in turn suggested that new music theatre

> is perhaps ultimately best seen as an 'anti-genre' – which is to say, as characterized by a refusal to conform to traditional or pre-existing genres and categories, rather than by any other consistent traits. Music theatre tends to illuminate the awkward interstices between art forms, the gaps between existing aesthetic categories.
>
> (Adlington 2005: 230)

80 *Holly Rogers*

Latent in these understandings is a move from consideration of new music theatre as a closed genre with a distinct lineage and towards a more lateral and malleable interpretation open to volatile interdisciplinary relationships and contexts. In particular, Roesner's rejection of generic boundaries in favour of a broader understanding of new music theatre as an umbrella heading for a collection of live art practices – encompassing drama, performance, dance and so on – is extremely useful, as it de-emphasises the work as text, focusing attention instead on its multi-textural, performative capacity, not only in terms of how each element fuses or collides with the others, but also on how these new juxtapositions are received within a performance setting.

New music theatre emerged at a time of great disciplinary convergence, connecting it to many other types of experimental culture. In fact, it can be argued that the 'gaps between existing aesthetic categories' stretch well beyond musico-theatrical practices, narrowly defined. The 'awkward interstices' between generic boundaries were further troubled by the inclusion of newly available technologies. The expanding sonic palette of new music theatre often included tape, amplified voices and the spatialisation of sound using loudspeakers, inclusions that enhanced the confrontational relationship of new music theatre with its related historical cousins.[1] But when moving image technology was also included – whether at the request of the composer, or through innovative and forward-thinking stage direction – it contributed to the destabilisation of genre in unique and significant ways: such technology could expand stage space, depth and time, re-energise forms of interaction between performers, activate scenography in new multimedial directions and, perhaps most significantly, refresh and reconfigure traditional relationships between work, performers and audience. As a result, the 'awkward interstices between art forms' were significantly heightened. The porous intertextuality of moving image media opened compositional process to artistic practices that had hitherto remained separate from music theatre traditions, enabling composers to plunder the aesthetic innovations that were driving concurrent experimentation in film, video art and the newly emerging forms of mass media documentation and dissemination.

Building on Salzman's suggestion that music theatre 'reverses the purism of modern art' via its referentiality and intertextuality (Salzman 1988: 245), Adlington surmises that '[o]ne of the ways in which music theatre became symbolic of a move away from the priorities of the avant-garde was its tendency to encourage an intermingling of different musical traditions' (Adlington 2005: 235). And yet, the use of moving image media in specific stagings and performances, while allowing disparate elements to intermingle, could also cause them to repel and undermine each other, forming clashing and confrontational audiovisual textures in which the boundaries between, and even purism of, the individual disciplines remain stark and strident. This oscillation between interdisciplinary collaboration and repulsion

---

1 On the use of tape and sound technology in new music theatre, see the chapter by Andreas Münzmay in the present volume.

suggests a productive relationship between the aesthetics of new music theatre and other domains of collaborative experimentation in Europe and North America during the 1950s and 1960s. The emergence of installation art, for instance, repositioned an attendee's focus from single objects towards the movements and relationships between a number of elements and their contexts (De Oliveira, Oxley and Petry 1994: 1–2). Similar ends could be achieved by the absorption of video into the intermedial textures of performance art and dance, the disruption of traditional cinematic forms through dissonant audiovisual textures, and the use by artists of closed-circuit television feeds to transform the spatial context of a work – including its visitors – into compositional material in real time (Rogers 2013).

When these emergent and process-driven moving-image practices were included in the staging of new music theatre works, the dismantling of traditional generic boundaries and the resultant emphasis on context they encouraged contrasted sharply with previous music-theatrical practice. With this in mind, the productive historicisations of the authors above can be taken one step further: new music theatre can be understood not only in relation to other musical and dramatic traditions, but also in terms of its aesthetic engagement with – and remediation of – concurrent creative moving-image art practices that emphasised process and site-specificity. Shifting the focus thus from object to spatial process promotes a contextual reading of new music theatre based on specific performances. Here, I compare two stagings of Luigi Nono's *Intolleranza* (1961) – as amongst the earliest examples of audiovisual media on the musical stage – to suggest that the use of moving-image technology allowed composers, directors and scenographers not only to expand the physical space of the theatre, but also to promote innovative forms of interactivity and intertextuality that could signify in culturally and politically specific ways. First, though, some context is offered in terms of patterns of use of such technology in both mid-century and more recent music theatre.

Moving image interventions

During the early years of new music theatre, the use of projected images, filmed sequences and live television feeds became a prominent method of intervention into the traditional relationships between music, text and staging, with many composers – including Nono, Giacomo Manzoni, Egisto Macchi and Peter Schat – using moving image technology as an integral narratological tool. Today, filmed and videoed images are common to the operatic stage, where they have formed part of the composition process (as in Michel van der Aa's *Sunken Garden* (2013)), been used to re-imagine existing operas (as in Opera De Lyon's setting of Beethoven's *Fidelio* in space (2013)), or, conversely, as a way to re-sound old film footage, as in Louis Andriessen's re-rendering of Hal Hartley's *La Commedia* (2009). In all these examples, moving-technology is seamlessly integrated into the action, often using large and immersive screens that add depth and a certain filmic believability to the staged action. In *Sunken Garden* for instance, a mystical and elusive hyper-saturated 3D garden indicates a move into an alternative,

82   *Holly Rogers*

transcendent reality that breaks from the stage to bathe the audience not only in sound, but also in image (Rogers 2016).

However, while such hyper-immersive gestures have become relatively normalised, when moving image technology first entered the musical stage during the 1960s, it operated as a radical intervention not only into traditional theatrical gesture, but also into conventional modes of operatic and dramatic consumption. Onstage screens could be used to augment the dramatic space; scenes could have more depth, more intricacy, more realism; they could reach into other geographical locations and enable grand visual gestures, such as crowd scenes, the evocation of speed, close ups and so on. But these immersive qualities could also de-stabilise traditional dramaturgical forms, and that is one of the key differences between the use of new media technologies by mid-century music theatre composers and directors, and the ways in which the moving image is most often configured today. As in *Sunken Garden*, contemporary productions use film technologies to pull the audience into immersive viewing positions akin to those encouraged by mainstream cinematic fiction, where a successful experience is predicated on absorption into the screened world and a loss of bodily awareness, a de-sensitisation that resonates with the Wagnerian *Gesamtkunstwerk* and the desire to bridge the 'mystic gulf' between performers and audience (Wagner cited in Kuritz 1988: 263).

Although there has been ample research into opera's appearance in, and influence on, film (Joe and Theresa 2003; Citron 2010, 2013), investigation into the inclusion of film technology onto the stage has not been so forthcoming. When the role of film in the construction of a new music theatre aesthetic is critically considered, its use is often linked to the rise of neo-realist cinema and other art film traditions as popular forms of storytelling. The dwindling popularity of opera as a form of storytelling and its rejection by many progressive composers as the twentieth century advanced was due to a complex interplay of social and cultural factors, including the expense of staging such work in the post-war financial climate and the mass appeal and aesthetic power of film (Fearn 1997: 57; Salzman and Desi 2008: 8 and 89). For Ralf Remshardt, one of the factors in opera's perceived decline was a shift in narrative gaze initiated by cinema:

> In rapid order, film achieved the status of a normative mode of representation. As the grammar of film integrated into visual discourses, and the homogenous viewer of the discontinuous film image replaced the dispersed viewer of the continuous stage image, film in turn acquired a certain transparency. At the same time, it threw the entire theatrical apparatus into relief and, in a move both hostile and curiously nostalgic, relegated the theatre to a position defined now by its antecedent function and its defective authenticity. We can assume a transitory – almost ineffable – moment when early cinema audiences shifted from *stage seeing* to *camera seeing* and the point of reference no longer remained a previously seen *stage* performance but a previous film performance which had lost trace, if subtly, of its stage antecedent.
>
> (Remshardt 2006: 41, emphasis in original)

In Italy, this shift in gaze and the decline of opera has been related to the popularity of neo-realist cinema (Fearn 1997: 59), a style that sought its inspiration from the post-war working classes and became characterised by storylines of oppression and poverty, a desolation heightened by a self-consciously constructed sense of 'authenticity' garnered from gritty location shoots, the use of non-professional actors, conversational speech and simple editing styles. These traits led André Bazin to describe the genre as 'reconstituted reportage' (Bazin 2011: 33). Sitting somewhat strangely against this naturalism, however, are often grandiose, sweeping orchestral scores (think of Alessandro Cicognini's sumptuous score for Vittorio De Sica's *Bicycle Thieves* (1948), for instance).

Tapping into the complicated cultural resonances of moving image media, composers of new music theatre could incorporate modern technologies as not only a coherent way in which to represent contemporary society, but more significantly, as a tool for direct intervention into its political and cultural fabric. As a result, although many early music theatre works, particularly in Italy, embraced topics similar to those of neo-realist cinema, its audiovisual aesthetics were very different from the smooth textures and structural and immersive cohesion of narrative film. Traditionally, mainstream film, including that in the neo-realist tradition, operates through an audiovisual flow so tightly synchronised as to engender a filmic illusion of unity and realism through discrete editing that effaces its materiality, as can be seen in the paradoxical audiovisual flow of *Bicycle Thieves*. By contrast, the angular textures forged by moving image technologies in early new music theatre productions resonated more clearly with the audiovisual dissonances, audience distanciation and promotion of materiality and artifice evident in much concurrent avant-garde film and video practice. At this time, many experimental filmmakers sought to address what was fast becoming accepted as 'filmic realism' by playing with the ways in which sound and image could contradict each other: music could be rhythmically, texturally or timbrally different from the image, or it could be placed against it in ironic, jarring, unexpected or culturally subversive ways. Earlier in the century, for instance, Sergei Eisenstein and others had theorised that a gap between music and image, forged either via montage techniques or through sounds that contradicted visual information, could activate an audience's interpretative capacity by providing a space for new meanings and forms of engagement to arise (Eisenstein 1949 [1928]). Such dissonance – or what they referred to as audiovisual counterpoint – is difficult to find in mainstream filmmaking, as it can undermine the integrity or coherence of what is being offered. But in experimental film, it not only drew attention to the work as a material piece of art – to its 'opacity' – but also placed film goers in uncomfortable points of reception that embraced the alienating *Verfremdungseffekt* promoted in Brechtian aesthetics. The discomfort produced by audiovisual counterpoint also manifested itself as a theme (and not just a method) within 1960s art. Musicians, such as Nam June Paik and Steina Vasulka, and artists, such as Wolf Vostell and Bruce Nauman, began to use newly available video technology and domestic television screens as sculptural objects to create interactive and site-specific audiovisual works that fractured conventional

84 Holly Rogers

notions of space and problematised what they considered to be the indolent reception of televised content (Rogers 2013).

These forms of dissonance – between music and image; between content and context; between work and audience – can be seen at play in new music theatre productions that use moving image technology. Adlington understands this 'anti-genre' as an anti-realist and ruptured configuration, tracing a move from opera's earliest history as 'the most affectedly artificial of theatrical genres', through its more realistic nineteenth-century configurations of dramatic and psychological upheavals, to a return, in twentieth-century experimentation, to a form characterised by stylised and unnatural gestures (Adlington 2005: 235). If we return to the examples of recent opera works that make use of moving image technology, such as *Sunken Garden*, we can suggest that filmed images have helped the move back into an immersive realism by reducing our awareness of the stage, its construction and limitations in order to draw the audience deeper into the fiction. Contrasted with this, Adlington identifies two forms of anti-realism at play in mid-century music theatre:

> First, narrative cogency may be deliberately exploded – whether by presenting a succession of situations that refuse reduction to a simple narrative sequence, or by combining material that is not clearly related so that the drama appears internally divergent or contradictory. [. . .] [S]econd, taking a cue from Bertolt Brecht, composers have set about the disintegration of the stage illusion that forms such a central part of traditional theatre.
>
> (Ibid.: 229)

If we add to this the powerfully illusory qualities of film and the persuasive, agenda-driven discourses of television and news reportage, these ideas could be pushed to the extreme, particularly when screens were employed visibly and sculpturally to create montages that were not immersive, but instead vibrated with political resonances as sculptural objects.

Laterna Magika

Like Brecht and the experimental filmmakers, many new music theatre composers and directors embraced ruptured forms of storytelling through audiovisual counterpoint and 'the disintegration of the stage illusion', two forms of dissonance easily augmented via moving image technologies. The use of projected images was not new to the stage, however, and can be found in many works of epic or political theatre, particularly those of Erwin Piscator from the mid-twenties on. In *Rasputin, the Romanoffs, the War and the People Who Rose Up Against Them* (1927, co-written by Brecht), for instance, Piscator spread out footage taken from 100,000 metres of feature film, newsreels and documentaries over three screens; these images were then used to contradict or comment on what was happening on the stage (Innes and Shevtsova 2013: 122). The rupture between narrative and visual adjunct supported his desire that theatre become an instrument for social change, able to jolt audiences from their leisurely and inactive gazes.

Audio-visual collisions 85

Although Claudia Georgi has noted that, after an initial flurry of activity in the 1920s, the use of filmed elements on the stage had begun to decline (Georgi 2014), by the mid-century, and contrary to the grain, the synthesis of film and live theatre had become the lynchpin of the newly emerging Laterna Magika, or magic lantern shows, a type of multimedia theatre that combined live and pre-recorded elements to simultaneously unfold multiple narratives and perspectives. The style was developed in Prague's National Theatre by Czech stage director Alfréd Radok and set designer Josef Svoboda, who explained that the screens did not merely accompany the stage action; they were integral to it. A moving image, or travelling screen could direct an audience's gaze to a specific moment, emotion or point of view, explained Svoboda, by 'pick[ing] up different parts of the [scene] as if you were looking through a window at part of your environment' (cited in Burian 2002: 94–5). However, such a gaze could be placed within or against others to initiate what the designer called a 'confrontation of selected realities: actions, objects, people' (ibid.). It could, in other words, be both immersive and antagonistic.

The style can be divided into two types, which developed almost simultaneously: while Laterna Magika combined film with live actors, so-called 'polyekren' (polyvision) performances were more technologically ambitious, using multiple screens and mirrors to fragment the narrative without the help of a live cast. Shortly after the first multi-screen performance at the Brussels Fair of 1958, Svoboda applied his polyphonic visual techniques to the operatic stage, creating the first screen-stage production of a pre-existent dramatic work, a version of Offenbach's *The Tales of Hoffmann* (1881; performance 1962; with the composer and director Václav Kašlík). Unfortunately, the reviewers bemoaned a lack of unification and balance between stage and screen, an issue that perhaps arose from attempting to remould an earlier dramatic structure into polyekren form (Burian 2002: 109).

However, when employed more fluidly, screened images, configured via a Laterna Magika aesthetic, had much to offer new music theatre composers, who were already interested in rejuvenating traditional ideas of dramaturgy, but had found themselves hindered by a traditional proscenium stage. Even though no piece was composed specifically for the Laterna Magika style, Svoboda's technological interventions were most successful when the possibilities of the moving image were taken into account during the compositional process, as Burian explains: 'Scenography is not a background nor even a container, but in itself a dramatic component that becomes integrated with every other expressive component or element of production and shares in the cumulative effect upon the viewer' (Burian 1970: 125–6). The openness to moving image technology was particularly apparent in what Raymond Fearn calls 'the new spirit amongst Italian composers' in the sixties, and although scores do not necessarily contain instruction for visual extension, the knowledge of its possibility was deeply significant to the ways in which work was staged (Fearn 1997: 62). Heavily influenced by both Brecht's thoughts on theatre and the Laterna Magika style, Manzoni and Nono in Italy, and Peter Schat in Holland, were drawn to the possibilities of moving image media. In 1975, for instance, Manzoni described his ideal form of musical theatre as one that emerged through creative convergence:

86 *Holly Rogers*

[O]n the one hand, the inventive, creative levels, of the convergence of various interests, and on the other of present-day techniques of a musical, vocal, scenographic and cinema-technical kind, and therefore an enrichment of artistic research. This means an enrichment of the conscience and of the critical capacity of the listeners-spectators who will increasingly become participants.

(quoted in Fearn 1997: 99)

Significant here are the notions that staged music theatre, when created from a fusion of disciplines, generated a form of artistic *research*; and that the exploratory nature of the form could activate an audience by allowing them not just to consume, but also to participate in the construction of the work's message. Nono voiced a similar sentiment, conceptualising a form of *engagé* theatre – after Jean-Paul Sartre's proposed Theatre of Situations – through which the consciences of an audience would be mobilised as they faced, without fictional cushioning, the horrors of contemporary reality (Suvini-Hand 2006: 22).

As mentioned, the use of moving image technology as something both integral to, and active in the construction of, contemporary life, was significant in forming this type of theatrical engagement. When screened on stage, filmed images could enlarge the psychological ramifications of the story by highlighting and punctuating certain elements of both music and libretto, by evoking memory, or by revealing the inner thoughts of characters. But whereas now, with digital media, the use of moving image audiovisual technologies in post-theatre can operate as a live participant, open to flux and change – responsive, immediate, performative – this was not always the case with early technology, and analogue filmed elements were often immobile and pre-established. Attempting to synchronise pre-recorded footage with live action ran the risk of forming a rigid, rather than a fluid, staging situation able to augment, rather than interact with, the staged actions, as Svoboda warned:

It means that Laterna Magika is to a certain extent deprived of that which is beautiful about theatre: that each performance can have a completely different rhythm, that the quality of a performance can be better or worse, that a production can expand its limits.

(Svoboda 1968: 103)

Such pre-imagined structures can be found in a number of music theatre works staged by Svoboda. For L. J. Werle's *The Journey* (Hamburg, 1969) and Bernd Alois Zimmermann's *Die Soldaten* (Munich, 1969), for instance, Burian notes that

Svoboda's scenography filled the stage with large cubic structures in and on which considerable action occurred accompanied by large-scale multiple projections of a documentary type, keyed in to heighten the impact of the music and libretto. In neither of the last two operas, however, did the projected images directly connect or interact with any on stage character or action as they had in *Intolleranza, The Last Ones* [Maxim Gorky], or *Prometheus* [Carl Orff]

(Burian 1970: 118)

Despite the lack of live and screened interaction, however, Zimmermann, who specified which films were shown and where they were projected, created multiscreen staging that managed to present complex forms of simultaneous action.

In other examples, moving images were a clear part of the actors' world. The mixture of filmed and live action for the staging of Manzoni's 1965 *Atomtod* (*Atomic Death*), for example, powerfully depicted events leading up to, and immediately after, an atomic catastrophe: in Act 1, scene 2, a talking head appears on a giant television screen to attempt to comfort the public initiating a direct interaction between technology and those on stage as well as off (Fearn 1997: 81). However, while the performance flow was heavily mediated by pre-existent visual information, when the images were spread over many screens, they acted like a simultaneous montage that shattered the fixed gaze of a director and distributed point-of-view across numerous spaces and depths.

Intolleranza

The interaction between actors and audience and the distributed form of engagement that this entails was fundamental to Nono's desire to create a politically active and activating form of musical theatre. The composer had experienced Laterna Magika in Prague at the end of 1959 and described Svoboda's work as 'Studies, analyses on history, to overcome it. And to overcome the limitations of Eurocentrism on European theatre culture' (Nono 2018 [1968]: 322). Having long bemoaned the ways in which conventional operatic staging could induce a 'total neutralisation of space' (Nono quoted in Fearn 1997: 68), Nono was seeking a form of total theatre, by which an audience would not simply witness events separated from them by the 'mystic gulf' between stage and auditorium, but rather that audio and visual events would at once swathe and assail their senses from several directions at once. When confronted with 'selected realities' formed not only from a human narrative, but from a bombardment of 'actions, objects, people', the audience is required to assess and construct their own understanding of events. The total work of art, in other words, is paradoxically formed through the promotion of gaps, contrasts and audiovisual counterpoint.

Nono's *Intolleranza 1960* was written quickly, mostly within three months. The self-described 'scenic action' ('azione scenica'), commissioned by the Venice Biennale at the end of 1960, was premiered on 13 April 1961 at the Teatro La Fenice in a production directed by Czech Václav Kašlík. But such quick composition was apt, for the work, which riled against fascism, was directly related to significant social events at the time. In one act divided into two parts, the plot follows a migrant worker, known only as 'The Immigrant', whose attempts to travel from his place of work back home leads him through protests and demonstrations, wrongful arrests, torture and finally to a concentration camp, which he manages to escape only to be washed away in a flood with his female companion. The themes are both local and ahistorical: worker exploitation, unemployment, protest, resistance and natural disaster as the result of human mismanagement. In his Darmstadt lecture delivered the previous year, Nono had problematised John Cage's ahistorical attitude to music, arguing instead that the moment of a work's conception was deeply significant as it could move an audience towards immediate political consciousness (Fearn 1997: 68). Famously, in order to keep the work's immediacy, Nono requested that the date in the title be changed to reflect the year of each performance.

Intolleranza 1960 decentralised and destabilised the established gestures of traditional music theatre through its innovative construction of a compilation libretto and its spatialisation of sound across speakers on either side of the stage (De Benedictis 2012; Santini 2012). Dean Wilcox draws our attention to the negation of linear plot for a scenic action progressing via didactic and episodic montage techniques: 'In this respect *Intolleranza* owes more to the episodically motivated political allegories of the Brecht-Weill collaboration than it does to the narrative process of the operatic tradition', particularly in its preference for 'short scenes, voice-overs, projected slogans and images' (Wilcox 1996: 117). This episodic style lends itself to multimedia and fragmented and simultaneous representation. Aptly, the work became the earliest example of an extended televisual presence on the musical stage. Similarly, in the many histories of experimental film, the coexistence of live and screened bodies is rare and there are only a few instances of what has become known as 'film stage' – Robert Whitman's *Prune Flat* in 1965 and Carolee Schneemann's *Night Crawlers* in 1967 are two notable examples – so this is an important moment in both film and operatic memory (Rogers 2013: 155).

Svoboda was enlisted to reconfigure the work into Laterna Magika form for the premiere. He used polyphonic filmed projections to help achieve some of the ideas outlined by Nono in his first sketches for the work, in particular (as Angela Ida De Benedictis explains) the construction of a 'simultaneity of actions and situations; the rejection of the visual apparatus typical of conventional music theatre; . . . and the need to reduce the text component to a minimum in favour of the action' (De Benedictis 2012: 105). Unfortunately, the premiere production was beset by difficulties (see ibid.). The slides received from Svoboda and Radok in Prague, which were intended to provide the projected material for the Venice stage, were not adequate and some of the footage – particularly that taken from political film – was censored. As a result, the painter Emilio Vedova had to be brought in at the last moment to develop more viable décor and projections. As Svoboda later recalled: 'the 1961 production was politically difficult, very much to the left. The films were not permitted by the head of the city. The stage setup was the same, but Emilio Vedova's paintings were substituted for the political films' (Svoboda 1993: 30). Despite the censorship, the political gesture of staging Nono's politically-charged work in the Teatro La Fenice critiqued the establishment at a time when other productions were moving out of these spaces, initiating a vocal and aggressive protest by an Italian Fascist group on the opening night, a riot described by a reporter for the New York Times as being so disruptive that 'the performance had to be halted while members of the audience were shrieking unprintable names' (reporter quoted in Wilcox 1996: 119; see also Boyd 2012).

While the Venice premiere is the production remembered as a legendary *succès de scandale*, for Svoboda by far the greater achievement was the work's third production by the Boston Opera Company. In a 1993 interview Svoboda described it as 'the biggest, most complicated and best production I have ever done. It has not surpassed since' (Wilcox 1996: 115). He later reminisced in his memoirs *The Secret of Theatrical Space* that the event demonstrated 'how new technologies, new expressive resources emerge' (Svoboda 1993: 104). Directed by Sarah Caldwell and again conducted by Maderna, this production had costume design by Jan Skalický and, significantly, was offered to the American audience in English translation.

Nono had recommended that Svoboda again be employed as scenographer for the production, which ran for two performances, both on 21 February 1965. With the use of technology that he had been unable to get his hands on in Venice and free from the censorship that hampered his previous production, Svoboda was able to extend his Laterna Magika in several significant ways, including the augmented use of pre-existent film footage and live, closed circuit TV able to fold together the spaces of performance and reception. Despite Nono's famously negative reaction to the rehearsals, for which he arrived late due to visa issues and was immediately convinced his intentions were being misrepresented ('When I arrived and saw the work I rejected everything' [Nono quoted in Wilcox 1996: 121]), the performance was a critical success.[2]

Cameras were placed on the stage, in the auditorium, outside the theatre, and, explains Greg Giesekam,

> in two television studios several miles away . . . One studio recorded various documents—photographs, texts, slogans and so on. In the other members of the chorus were filmed—while they themselves followed the conductor's baton on video. In the theatre itself, cameras were trained on both performers and audience: resulting images were mixed live with the other sources and relayed onstage.
>
> (Giesekam 2007: 66)

Still and moving images mixed documentary footage of violent demonstrations and flowing landscapes with pre-recorded footage of the onstage actors and excerpts of the libretto in the form of slogans, which often acted like intertitles. Free from the censorship he had faced in Venice, Svoboda received access to the *New York Times* film archives and proceeded to make use of extreme and distressing footage. As one reviewer outlined,

---

2 It has been impossible to identify the rights holder for surviving photographs of the Boston production. Some photos of this production may be found in Bablet 2004.

90 Holly Rogers

there was a nightmarish montage of 'scenes of injustice'—a Negro lynching, street riots, the desolation of Hiroshima, decaying bodies stacked in graves— flashed on dozens of various-sized screens, some dropped from the flies, others held aloft by the chorus in a jigsaw pattern.

(Anon. 1965: 66)

In addition, Caldwell recalls in her memoir that the production also incorporated 'photographs of incidents of intolerance worldwide', taken from *Time* and *Life* Magazines, used to enhance the composition in a manner that was 'either informational or affectively emotional' (Caldwell 2008: 25).

Soprano Beverley Sills recalled the sense of injustice felt by the (largely American) cast that all the footage depicted questionable activities from within the States, and requested a more diverse representation of atrocity. Wilcox contextualises this reaction well:

[W]hat Ms. Sills fails to take into account is that the political nature of Nono's work demanded that the piece not be presented for an American audience but at an American audience. Nono's work, designed to illuminate the atrocities of the twentieth-century, was aimed at his present audience, an action that allowed the piece to be critical of American ideology as well as foreign and domestic policy.

(Wilcox 1996: 127)

These antagonistic real-world images – far removed from the immersive reconstructed simulacra of neo-realist cinema – were projected predominantly onto a large screen hung on one side of the stage, while on the opposite side, another screen provided what one reviewer described as a 'narrative (as well as pictorial) guide' (Kelly 1965: 21). In addition, differently sized screens placed variously around the space were, explains Caldwell, 'covered in black velour and hung in the air', opening 'mechanically by remote control in different ways, some like the iris of a lens of a camera, while other had shutter openings' (Caldwell 2008: 25). These screens were not always visible, but could appear suddenly to create a strong emphasis or interjection. When spread across the screens, different images could combine and re-contextualise each other to offer an idea told simultaneously from many angles, in a way reminiscent of the multiple unfolded temporalities of a cubist picture. As a result, the screens did not offer mimesis, or mere enhancement, as Caldwell rather oddly suggests; rather the cross-pollination of information was generative and vital to the opera's message, as Svoboda explained:

The play of the actors cannot exist without the film, and vice-versa—they become one thing. One is not the background for the other; instead, you have a simultaneity, a synthesis and fusion of actors and projection. Moreover, the same actors appear on screen and stage, and interact with each other. The film has a dramatic function.

(Svoboda quoted in Burian 1970: 83)

Audio-visual collisions 91

While the screened images at varying instances ran alongside the live action, subverted it and determined its course, there were four moments when, for up to five minutes at a time, *all* the information was being delivered on the screens and via mime (Příhodová 2011: 4–5). However, unlike the immersion of film with its dissolving borders that fade into cinematic blackness, here the materiality of the frames was always evident, as the collage-constructed narrative highlighted spectatorship and the act of viewing. If immediacy is achieved by transparent, 'present' forms of media that emphasise the content of a work over its presentation (the linear narratives and sutured audiovisuality of mainstream film is an excellent example of this), then hypermediacy (at its most basic) describes a work that highlights its 'opacity'. The strong form of alienation garnered by this hypermediacy was heightened by the movement of the screens. After the opening chorus, for instance, written slogans – 'demonstration', 'the refugee is a spectator', 'refugee is arrested' – and disturbing archival stills and documentary footage from demonstrations were projected across several monitors that were moved around the stage, with all of the information given via the moving image (Příhodová 2011: 4). At another moment, the conflict between the single voice and a suppressive power was symbolised by monitors pressing in around the protagonist as he sat in the dark; as one reviewer noted, 'screens pulsating with light moved in to form an ever-contracting prison' (Eaton 1965: 34).

The fractured gaze

The Boston *Intolleranza* has been the subject of several critical readings, including Dean Wilcox's historical reconstruction of the staging, Barbora Příhodová's situation of the performance within the 'pictorial turn', and Andrea Santini's reading of the moving images as 'an ideal visual counterpart to Nono's engulfing musical space, designed to stimulate the listener's critical awareness' (see Wilcox 1996; Příhodová 2011; Santini 2012: 82). If we build on these historical and theoretical ideas through a critical engagement not only with the ways in which the moving image signifies a fractured relationship with other elements of the staging, but also with common modes of audiovisual consumption beyond the auditorium – and in fact the creative world as a whole – a more complex reading based on two contradictory forms of engagement emerges. First, the dissonant use of moving-image technology invites comparison with other art-technological modes of discourse, including the mid-century audiovisual experimentation outlined earlier. Second, if we expand our investigation from the conceptual and practical aspects of staged film and move from the theoretical ideal of experimental theatre, art and music into the domestic sphere of television, an additional form of subversion arises, based on the strategies of audiovisual consumption – variously immersive and distrustful – that informed the everyday lives of the opera goers. By evoking and playing with the paradoxical fallibility and passivity of broadcast television, Svoboda's staging in Boston was historically pertinent. In contrast with the authors mentioned above, I suggest that the key to Svoboda's success in Boston lay in the interplay between the different modes of attention

92   Holly Rogers

and activation required to engage with the experimental arts *and* domestic television simultaneously.

Suggesting that the projected images of the Boston *Intolleranza* garnered an expressivity so significant that 'they often suppressed the action of the performers', Příhodová finds a displacement of power from the live operatic body to the screened image, a slippage she closely aligns with W. J. T. Mitchell's concept of the 'pictorial turn' (Příhodová 2011: 1). The ramifications of Mitchell's reading of a morphing spectatorship in which issues of observation, the gaze and surveillance are complicated and undermined by new modes of representation (what he describes as a 'postlinguistic, postsemiotic rediscovery of the picture as a complex interplay between visuality, apparatus, institutions, discourse, bodies, and figurality'; Mitchell quoted in Příhodová 2011: 1–2) are closely aligned with the ways in which 'images can perform power' (ibid.: 2). But while the pictorial turn that flows through the Boston *Intolleranza* exposes the passivity of mimesis and undoubtedly invests the moving image with great expressive and political power, the complicated interplay between live and screened bodies makes it difficult to assign a complete relocation of the gaze. Taken from television and early documentary footage, the low-fi images clash against the arresting immediacy of the live operatic body, leading not to a replacement of the gaze, but rather a fracturing of a single-point perspective into multiple views, modes of engagement and types of enunciation. Perhaps contrary to Nono's wishes, such distributed attention could free an audience from a fixed point-of-view in a way reminiscent of the sculptural experiments in video installation art at the time. This reveals a dilemma that lies at the heart of 'fractured' theatre and with which Brecht also constantly grappled: is this process of unfastening the audiovisual gaze aimed at freeing the audience, or at a didactic representation of a fractured reality? Does it open a creative space for interpretation, or impose a reading of the splintered and contradictory nature of everyday life?

Just as early audiences of electronic and tape music voiced an unease at experiencing an acousmatic and de-humanised musical presence, we could suggest that here, the juxtaposition between embodied and low-quality two-dimensional forms rendered strange the visual human presence. In his analysis of the performance, Wilcox acknowledges this fractured gaze by highlighting the material incompatibility of screened and live representation:

> The flexibility of the film to change perspective and location with the push of a button cannot be replicated by the materiality of the actor. The film, though unfolding through time, repeats its actions with the precision of a painting or a sculpture.
>
> (Wilcox 1996: 122)

He continues:

> As rehearsed as the actions may be, the actor stumbles, sweats, speeds up, and slows down, responds to the audience, and adjusts his or her performance to individual rhythms for which the film cannot accommodate. All of

Audio-visual collisions 93

this works toward revealing the seams of the construction and dissolving the union between these disparate elements.

(ibid.: 123)

If Nono's experimental timbres required a new form of listening, here the audience was asked to see afresh, not just through the lens of the newly available media and its pictorial turn, but also, and by extension, at how 'real', embodied forms could be transfigured as a result of their relation to their screened companions. Such a move, as Příhodová has accurately identified, from mimesis to a more self-consciously pictorial mode of address further demystifies the Wagnerian gulf between audience and performers. Rather than the fixed point of view of traditional theatre, opera and classical narrative film, experimental montage techniques, spread across the stage and several screens to form an audiovisual simultaneity, left multiple spaces for interpretation. Requiring the audience to take an active role in the construction of meaning, Svoboda's staging dispelled any remnant of traditional theatricality, adding another dimension to Adlington's second form of 'anti-realism' mentioned above. The staging's visibility of construction and embrace of disjuncture ensured that, although the separate elements were plausible, the 'opacity' of their combination rejected immersion and invited instead an objective and active form of reception.

Moreover, the Boston performance highlighted the disjunctive relationship between pre-recorded footage and live, embodied performers through the use of live-feed television projection to further explode the spatial constrictions of the proscenium stage. Svoboda recalls that 'In the Boston theatre I was able to put my hands on equipment and facilities that I previously could only dream about. Part of the dream was industrial television with the possibility and capability of reproducing whatever was being shot' (Svoboda 1993: 41). Images of an offstage chorus could be projected onto the stage at opportune moments in order to draw attention to their sonic, or semantic message; a close-up of a performer in real time could direct the gaze of the audience to a specific visual moment within a crowded *mise-en-scene*. More significantly, it could operate performatively by transmitting elements from beyond the performance space (a radius of three miles was used, as well as footage from the protests that were being staged outside the theatre) directly onto the stage. In a recollection, Svoboda recalls that 'This pictorial collage was given coherence and meaning in the television control booth, which determined the sequences of images filling the giant receiver screen on stage' (Svoboda 1993: 4). Such live and performative gestures were incredibly rare, and were not seen again until Svoboda's scenography for a production of Carl Orff's *Prometheus* (Munich, 1968), in which the protagonist, pinned to a rock, was bathed in a live television projection of his own face to symbolise both his inner turmoil and to suggest, perhaps, a presence larger than that embodied in a single man.

For the Boston *Intolleranza*, Svoboda used a closed-circuit feed several times, including a significant moment in which an image of the overwhelmingly white audience, listening to a protest song, found themselves not only confronted by

94   *Holly Rogers*

their real-time images, but also by a reflection that switched from positive to negative to make them appear black. This unabashed and confrontational gesture itself had a double role, as Wilcox points out: 'By incorporating images of the audience within the stage space, the spectators were both forced to become part of the horrors depicted by the stage action and were directly implicated in the continuation of these horrors', thus enacting visually 'the social and political accusations inherent in Nono's score' (Wilcox 1996: 127–8).

A similarly hostile gesture occurred during the 'chorus of tortured prisoners', in which the protagonist is being held and tortured. Here in Nono's score, the chorus suddenly breaks the fourth wall by turning their attention away from the staged diegesis and towards the audience in what Svoboda called a 'directed happening' (Svoboda quoted in Santini 2012: 82). Firing a string of questions into the auditorium, they asked:

> And what about you?
> Are you deaf?
> Following the herd,
> In its wicked shame?
> Doesn't the wailing
> Of our brothers rouse you?
> Megaphones! Amplify this shout!
> (Cited in Nielinger-Vakil
> 2016: 18)

At this moment, Svoboda used media to amplify clearly an aspect of Nono's quasi-Brechtian dramaturgy: while this direct address to the auditorium threatened the illusory bonds of the theatre, these bonds were re-inscribed in a different way by a brief visual gesture. A closed-circuit feed that showed the angered crowd on one of the large screens suddenly inverted, flashing up a real-time image of the audience shown behind projected prison bars and barbed wire. This moment of broadcasted reflection turned, as Manzoni had hoped, the inactive audience into 'participants'. Of course, to activate an audience is a key technique of new music theatre, but here television technology did so without permission. While the breaking of the fourth wall had become a relatively standard theatrical gesture by the 1960s, the inclusion of an uninvited form of visual surveillance was an intrusive, almost hostile gesture that was at once alienating and immersive as it paradoxically shattered the boundaries of stage and auditorium while at the same time rebuilding it into an entirely different configuration.

In other forms of moving image experimentation of the time where forms of participation and interactivity were being embraced, this kind of process-orientated circularity enabled by the closed-circuit television could give rise to a new form of communal creativity. But if it appeared that Nono and Svoboda were handing over a portion of control to the audience, then this was an illusion. While *Intolleranza*'s moving images and projections flooded the stage space with new depths, there nevertheless remained a 'one-way flow of communication' (Small 1998: 27) common to most theatre, narrative film and television: audience members could be moved by events – even included in them – but could not alter them. Rather, they were used, without consent, as compositional material. The clamour of discrete artforms colliding with each other created a strong sense of *Verfremdungseffekt* that Nono hoped would prove politically rousing and activating, and yet, the work remained removed from visitors at the discursive level.

This televisual moment not only supported and enhanced the libretto and music, as Wilcox has suggested: it also extended them, forming multi-layered commentaries and forms of intertextuality only available via the new moving image technologies. While new music theatre often aspired to a Brechtian form of anti-realism, as Adlington has argued, the Boston *Intolleranza* paradoxically embraced its artifice by rendering fragile the borders between art and life; the real-world, live images made possible by new communication technologies allowed the production to press at the social and cultural structures of contemporary society.

This was a two-way process: first, the audience were drawn across the 'mystic gulf' and into the work itself, albeit at the level of inclusion rather than true inter-activity, and, as we have seen, the voyeuristic nature of this surveillance was also significant. Second, the emphasis on construction – the low-fi image against the fully embodied singers, the multiple screens with their borders clearly in view, the collaged footage from different locations and events, the emphasis on performance as performance – drew attention not just to the story of oppression, but also to the ways in which information about such instances was being relayed and consumed. As a result, the choice of moving images, screens, television technology and documentary footage assumed an extraordinary if coercive power.

The medium is the message

In order to see exactly how these contradictions played out for the Boston audiences, we need to look more closely at the context: at the choice of vehicle for the visual messages. The ramification of a televisual flow, of a distortion of content and its means of dissemination are vital to a coherent understanding of *Intolleranza*'s early performance history. For the 1961 premiere in Venice, the screened images signified at an artistic level, enabling the multiplane narratives to distance audience from work. As we have seen, such an antagonistic style differed significantly from two dominant Italian artistic precursors: the lavish 'realism' that had infused late nineteenth-century operatic customs, with their clearly flowing narratives and overblown staging traditions; and the 'reconstituted reportage' style of neo-realist films, with locational shoots and linear plotlines stitched together by sumptuous orchestral scores. Although, as Remshardt has argued, the contemporary visual gaze was shifting from '*stage seeing* to *camera seeing*' as cinema offered a transparency uncommon on the operatic stage, the Venice *Intolleranza* used the two forms of engagement simultaneously. This duality not only threw into relief the viewing strategies of traditional opera and neo-realist film, encouraging audiences to think about common processes of engagement, it also initiated a critique of Hollywood's influence in their culture at large.

96   *Holly Rogers*

In America in the mid-1960s, several recent televisual occurrences meant that Svoboda's use of screened images may have signified very differently. As we saw above, Nono had a distrustful relationship with America and its political and cultural heritage, prompting Wilcox's suggestion that Nono's political work 'demanded that the piece not be presented for an American audience but at an American audience' (Wilcox 1996: 127). But if we follow this line of argument further, we can suggest that, for an American audience in the mid-1960s, newsreel footage, a structural use of screens and an inability to act despite the immersive lure of a mirrored image had resonances unique to that culture. One event in particular had initiated a troubled relationship with the apparent objectivity of reportage. The Vietnam War, which coincided with great technological leaps in compact cameras, battery power and transmission quality, has famously been referred to as the first 'television war', or the 'living room war' (Arlen, 1969). By 1963, news programmes saw their allocated evening slots increase from 15–30 minutes, and more reporters found their way to Saigon to help fill the time (Mandelbaum 1982: 159). By the time that Nono took his work to America, domestic spaces were starting to fill with quickly captured, locational reportage as it was occurring. This, however, was often an illusion. To ensure good ratings, the camera operators were asked, particularly in the early years, to shoot combat footage, which tended to be of Americans engaging in unspecified, but apparently successful endeavours (ibid.: 160). And yet, to broadcast live via satellite was an expensive business, so television reels were usually sent to the New York broadcasting houses by plane. When breaking news was presented, then, the footage shown was often several days old, and gave the appearance of successful manoeuvres when in fact the images and the spoken word often related to different events.

The brutality of real-world war footage, consumed within personal homes, had a disquieting effect on audiences for several reasons. First, while the infiltration of quickly captured footage was making domestic spaces less insular, at the same time the flow of information into it was becoming normalised, stripped of its potential to shock. And second, trust in the televisual image was being compromised. The high degree of audiovisual fidelity provided by the newsreel footage appeared to give accurate and immediate information in an objective way. But of course, by the time footage reached the home, it had been strongly edited, stylised and censored in the cutting room (Arlen 1969: 240); it could also be several days old and taken from unrelated manoeuvres. Nevertheless, televisual coverage of the war was extensive, beginning in an upbeat manner by celebrating the 'American boys in action', before gradually becoming tempered with anti-war sentiment, scepticism and concern over the increasingly untenable position America was finding itself in. Although a lot of the violence was kept off screen, there were some notable exceptions: in 1965, CBS aired footage of Marines setting light to a village with Zippo lighters, for instance; and in 1968 NBC showed Colonel Nguyen Ngoc Loan shoot a captive in the head (Anderegg 1991; Berg 1986). As events unfolded there developed a perceptible gap between events as they occurred and the way in which they were reported and, in one of the earliest examples of mass distrust in the media, audiences began to question what

Audio-visual collisions 97

they were being told. Communication was fast but information was censored and stylised; and early television audiences had begun to realise that, although reports were readily available, they were not as disinterested as they had once appeared to be (Hallin 1989). The trustworthy nature of televisual delivery had suffered a critical blow.

Svoboda's deconstruction of the performance space fed directly into these concerns about media saturation and control, which were already emerging during the early stages of the Vietnam war coverage. That such distrust of this particular coverage manifested itself quickly was no surprise. The seeds of suspicion had already been planted during the fifties, when the American quiz show scandals exposed the rigging of several popular television game shows and revealed to newly emergent audiences the powerful manipulative power of television (Dunn 2018). It is pertinent that, on the back of such revelations, many of the primary broadcasters reduced the airtime for quiz shows in favour of the increased timeslot for news reportage. For the Boston audience, the use of this highly charged technology could undermine the validity of what was being presented, and its relation to the ways in which the world beyond the stage was being portrayed in the newly emergent media. Svoboda's use of TV footage drew attention to the processes of television viewing and its modes of consumption in several ways: moving image technology enabled the remediation of current news footage and political reportage; violent and shocking events were decontextualised and placed in a montage giving a new reading of occurrences; and the edges of each screen led not to the safety of a domestic setting that could allay shock but to other screens, or to the stage space, in which similarly traumatic scenes were unravelling. Here, screened images provided an intervention onto the stage, but also, and as a result, could themselves be read as a commentary on television viewing and popular culture; on domesticity, reportage, consumption and the way in which to lure audiences away from – or into critical positions about – contemporary American culture.

At the same time, however, the closed-circuit feeds transformed the auditorium space in *real* time, foregrounding the manipulation of information *as it was happening*. Such a transformative critique of established power deconstructed viewing habits in a particularly Brechtian way. With this in mind, Nono's and Svoboda's Boston *Intolleranza* can be read as an attack on intolerance that resonates on several levels: against social injustices of class and race; against modern audiences and their compliant and passive consumption of information; against the nature of television broadcast and its power over truth and opinion; against domesticity and the lack of motivation to act; and against its own operatic and dramatic heritage.

In attempting to embody and substantiate intolerance, then, the Boston *Intolleranza* privileged artistic collision by highlighting its media specificity; the edges of each discipline were left in full view, frayed and angular, enabling the 'confrontation of selected realities' desired by Svoboda. And confrontation is a key word here. Rather than fusion, or cohesion, music, text, narrative and staging seemed to repel each other; and the audience were offered a form of involvement that lacked reciprocity, turning them not into participants, but rather into another visual message designed to reveal the pitfalls of political and artistic inertia.

98 *Holly Rogers*

New realities

Such uses of moving-image technology were very different from the audiovisually sutured, highly cinematic gestures of neo-realist cinema, despite the gritty, historical and political content that both shared. Instead, by embracing the physical, real-time interactive opportunities of moving image media, Svoboda embraced the contextual and radical possibilities of live-streaming that were also being investigated by experimental film and video artists. Significantly, these new technologies were not used as mere decorativism – as part of a staging – but were rather structurally vital, operating as another voice that gives information, affect and information not otherwise apparent in the work. As the designer later explained, 'the objects thereby acquire new relationships and significance, a new and different reality' (Svoboda quoted in Burian 1970: 133). This 'new and different reality' was achieved through the manipulation of both content *and* context: by holding a literal mirror up to the normally physically inactive audience in order to destabilise and objectify their gaze.

Such emphasis on the staging, and, as Carolyn Abbate would say, the 'drastic', ephemeral and experiential nature of music theatre, together with the dissolution of subject from object, posits the genre as an embodied practice, with an unusually close, even reciprocal connection with the world beyond the theatre (Abbate 2004). Today, when the moving image is ubiquitous, present everywhere from the theatre to mobile media, its appearance on the stage is not shocking: we have become well versed in its immersive potential. But the ability of scenography which, as Svoboda has said, 'is not a background nor even a container, but in itself a dramatic component', to take on a life of its own and respond to local cultural resonances is significant. Svoboda's scenography, alongside the ambitious direction of both Kašlík and Caldwell, turned the work into an intertextual tapestry of actual and symbolic references that fed into current and critical concerns about technology, reportage and representation. The resultant performative interplay between content and context enabled the two stagings to harness the power and potential of the newly available live moving image while at the same time exposing their capacity for deceit. Although the audience was not invited to actively participate, this duality de-centred the composerly intentions of Nono, opening the work instead to a form of distributed or network creativity concomitant with the current explorations of experimental filmmakers and video artists.

The shift in emphasis from musical object to intertextual, spatial and performative *mise en scène*, then, is significant for both the staging and reception of *Intolleranza*, and for its historical contextualisation. The destabilising capacity of moving-image technologies positions new music theatre not only within musical and dramatic traditions, but also within the multimedia sensibilities of mid-century avant-garde art, expanded cinema and innovative audiovisual cultures. The hypermediacy that arose from the 'awkward interstices' of these practices was significant as it enabled the prevalent use of dissonant montage techniques; the promotion of screens as sculptural objects for their politicised material presence; and the live-circuit feed that at once encouraged and repelled interactivity. The direct intervention into everyday life and site-specificity that this enabled was historically and culturally contingent, and this encourages a mode of analysis concerned not only with the musico-theatrical work, but also on its performative, transient and 'drastic' potential.

References

Abbate, Carolyn (2004), 'Music—drastic or gnostic', *Critical Inquiry*, 30/3, pp. 505–36.

Adlington, Robert (2005), 'Music theatre since the 1960s', in Mervyn Cooke (ed.), *The Cambridge Companion to Twentieth Century Opera*, Cambridge, UK: Cambridge University Press, pp. 225–43.

Anon (1965), 'Swatches & splashes', *Time*, 5 March, p. 66.

Anderegg, Michael A. (1991), *Inventing Vietnam: The War In Film and Television*, Philadelphia, PA: Temple University Press.

Arlen, Michael (1969), *Living-Room War*, New York: The Viking Press.

Bablet, Denis (2004), *Josef Svoboda*, Lausanne: Editions L'Age d'homme.

Bazin, André (2011), *André Bazin and Italian Neorealism*, ed. Bert Cardullo, New York: Continuum.

Berg, Rick (1986), 'Losing Vietnam: covering the war in an age of technology', *Cultural Critique*, 3, pp. 92–125.

Boyd, Harriet (2012), 'Remaking reality: echoes, noise and modernist realism in Luigi Nono's *Intolleranza 1960*', *Twentieth-Century Music*, 24/2, pp. 177–200.

Burian, Jarka M. (1970), 'Josef Svoboda: theatre artist in an age of science', *Educational Theatre Journal*, 22/2, pp.123–45.

Burian, Jarka M. (2002), *Leading Creators of Twentieth-Century Czech Theatre*, New York: Routledge.

Caldwell, Sarah (2008), *Challenges: A Memoir of My Life in Opera*, Middletown, CT: Wesleyan University Press.

Citron, Marcia, J. (2013), 'Opera and film', in David Neumeyer (ed.), *The Oxford Handbook of Film Music Studies*, Oxford: Oxford University Press, pp. 44–71.

Citron, Marcia J. (2010), *When Opera Meets Film*, Cambridge, UK: Cambridge University Press.

De Benedictis, Angela Ida (2012), 'The dramaturgical and compositional genesis of Luigi Nono's *Intolleranza 1960*', trans. John O'Donnell, *Twentieth-Century Music*, 9/1, pp. 101–41.

De Oliveira, Nicholas, Nicola Oxley and Michael Petry (1994), *Installation Art*, London: Thames & Hudson.

Dunn, Mark (2018), *Quizzing America: Television Game Shows and Popular Culture in the 1950s*, Jefferson, NC: McFarland.

Eaton, Quaintanance (1965), 'Far out Boston', *Opera News*, 1 May, p. 34.

Eisenstein, Sergei (1949 [1928]), 'Statement on sound', in *Film Form: Essays in Film Theory*, trans. and ed. Jay Leyda, New York: Harcourt, Brace, & World, pp. 257–60.

Fearn, Raymond (1997), *Italian Opera Since 1945*, New York: Routledge.

Georgi, Claudia (2014), *Liveness on Stage: Intermedial Challenges in Contemporary British Theatre and Performance* (Berlin and Boston, MA: De Gruyter.

Giesekam, Greg (2007), *Staging the Screen: The Use of Film and Video in Theatre*, London: Palgrave MacMillan.

100 *Holly Rogers*

Hallin, Daniel C. (1989), *The Uncensored War: The Media and Vietnam*, Berkeley, CA: University of California Press.

Innes, Christopher and Maria Shevtsova (2013), *The Cambridge Introduction to Theatre Directing*, Cambridge, UK: Cambridge University Press.

Joe, Jeongwon and Rose Theresa (2002), *Between Opera and Cinema*, New York: Routledge.

Kelly, Kevin (1965), '*Intolleranza* set makes audience into camera . . . that absorbs all the horror', *Boston Globe*, 22 February, p. 21.

Kuritz, Paul (1988), *The Making of Theatre History*, Englewood Cliffs, NJ: Prentice Hall College Division.

Mandelbaum, Michael (1982), 'Vietnam: the television war', *Deadalus*, 111/4, pp. 157–69.

Nielinger-Vakil, Carola (2016), *Luigi Nono: A Composer in Context*, Cambridge, UK: Cambridge University Press.

Nono, Luigi (2018 [1968]), 'Josef Svoboda', in *Nostalgia for the Future: Luigi Nono's Selected Writings and Interviews*, ed. Angela Ida De Benedictis and Veniero Rizzardi, Berkeley, CA: University of California Press, pp. 321-4.

Příhodová, Barbora (2011), 'The power of images in performance: Josef Svoboda's scenography for *Intolleranza 1960* at Boston Opera Company', www.inter-disciplinary. net/wp-content/uploads/2011/10/prihodovappaper.pdf (accessed 23 April, 2017).

Remshardt, Ralf (2006), 'The actor as intermedialist: remediation, appropriation, adaptation', in Freda Chapple and Chiel Kattenbelt (eds), *Intermediality in Theatre and Performance*, New York: Rodopi, pp. 41–54.

Rogers, Holly (2016), '"The public will only believe the truth if it is shot in 3D": Michel van der Aa, "Nine years in an orphanage" (Zenna), *Sunken Garden* Scene 6', *Cambridge Opera Journal*, 28/2, pp. 275–80.

Rogers, Holly (2013), *Sounding the Gallery: Video and the Rise of Art-Music*, Oxford: Oxford University Press.

Roesner, David (2012), 'Introduction: composed theatre in context', in David Roesner and Matthias Rebstock (eds), *Composed Theatre: Aesthetics, Practices, Processes*, Bristol: Intellect, pp. 9–14.

Roesner, David and Matthias Rebstock (eds) (2012), *Composed Theatre: Aesthetics, Practices, Processes*, Bristol: Intellect.

Salzman, Eric and Thomas Desi (2008), *The New Music Theatre: Seeing the Voice: Hearing the Body*, New York: Oxford University Press.

Salzman, Eric (1988), *Twentieth-Century Music: An Introduction*, 3rd edn, Englewood Cliffs, NJ: Prentice-Hall.

Santini, Andrea (2012), 'Multiplicity-fragmentation-simultaneity: sound-space as a conveyor of meaning, and theatrical roots in Luigi Nono's early spatial practice', *Journal of the Royal Musical Association*, 137/1, pp. 71–106.

Small, Christopher (1998), *Musicking: The Meanings of Performing and Listening*, Middletown, CT: Wesleyan University Press.

Suvini-Hand, Vivienne (2006), *Sweet Thunder: Music and Libretti in 1960s Italy*, London: Legenda.

Svoboda, Josef (1968), 'Problémy scény Laterny Magiky', in *Laterna Magika: Proceedings State*, Prague: Film Institute, pp. 98–105.

Svoboda, Josef (1993), *The Secret of Theatrical Space: The Memoirs of Josef Svoboda*, ed. and trans. J. M. Burian, New York: Applause.

Wilcox, Dean (1996), 'Political allegory or multimedia extravaganza? A historical reconstruction of the Opera Company of Boston's Intolleranza', *Theatre Survey*, 37/2, pp. 115–36.

5 Composing new media
Magnetic tape technology in new music theatre, *c.* 1950–1970

Andreas Münzmay

For the time span from 1950 to the mid-1970s, the reference works *Pipers Enzyklopädie des Musiktheaters* and *New Grove Dictionary of Opera* report on more than sixty new music theatre works that assign a fundamental place to new media technologies (Dahlhaus et al. (eds) 1986–97; Sadie (ed.) 1992–98). While opera composers' interest in working with both visual projection technologies and modern communication media (such as telegraph, telephone and radio) goes back to the 1920s and 1930s (think of Satie, Weill, Křenek, Antheil, Milhaud, or Berg), magnetic tape recording and projection technology appears to be an especially prominent feature in operatic scores only after about 1950. Departing from a general survey of the corpus in question – that is, new music theatre works incorporating stored sound and sound projection directly on the level of composition – this chapter aims at proposing a (preliminary and certainly incomplete) categorization by discussing some of the observable paradigms of technological 'extensions' (to borrow an idea of Marshall McLuhan) as found, for example, in works by Mauricio Kagel, Pierre Schaeffer, Bruno Maderna, Renzo Rossellini, Karl-Birger Blomdahl, Luigi Nono, Boris Blacher, and Giacomo Manzoni.

As a starting point to this enquiry it is productive to consider a worklist based on all entries in *Pipers Enzyklopädie des Musiktheaters* and *New Grove Dictionary of Opera* that point in whatever way to works dealing *compositionally* with new media (see Appendix). Here we find works pioneering the use of film in music theatre, such as Satie's *Relâche* (1924), Weill's *Der Zar läßt sich photographieren* (1928), Antheil's *Transatlantik* (1937) – by the way, a most interesting early multimedia opera on the subject of presidential elections and mass media in the United States – and Berg's *Lulu* (1937) with the unfortunately lost film footage bridging the plot gap between the first and second scenes of act two. At the same time, phonographical devices displaying stage music, as in Kurt Weill's previously mentioned comic opera from 1928, in Ernst Toch's *Der Fächer* (1930), Werner Egk's *Peer Gynt* (1938), Carl Orff's 'kleines Welttheater' *Der Mond* (1939) up to American productions such as Robbins'/Bernstein's *Fancy Free* (1944) and Gian Carlo Menotti's opera *The Consul* that premiered in Philadelphia in 1950, hardly, if at all, give an indication of the compositional work with stored sound and sound projection that was to come in the wake of the development of magnetic tape technologies and electronic music. From then

102 *Andreas Münzmay*

on, tape technology offered manifold new possibilities for theatre composition, ranging from acousmatic music/speech, techniques of multiplying and expanding sound (or its sources), through to onstage manipulations of sound devices. One crucial question is what composers 'made' out of these possibilities, or, to put it another way, which concrete dimension of the theatrical media context a composer 'extends' by the use of new media.

'Medialisierung': music theatre historiography and new media

It is not an easy task to get an overview of twentieth-century opera composers' dealings with so-called 'new media'. Works such as Zimmermann's *Die Soldaten* or Nono's *Intolleranza 1960* and *Al gran sole carico d'amore* immediately come to mind as paramount 'multimedia operas'. But how does the field appear as a whole; what does it look like beyond such central works? Extant research literature tends to pay attention to a very restricted number of exceptional music theatre scores – examples include the short, but media-oriented chapters on *Intolleranza* by Joachim Noller, and on *Die Soldaten* by Jörn Peter Hiekel (Noller 1999; Hiekel 2004). And what is more, extant research literature tends *not* to ask systematically how making use of acoustic and/or visual media interacts with opera composition itself. Against this backdrop Werner Heister's chapter 'Medialisierung' ('medialization', or simply 'media') in the handbook *Musiktheater im 20. Jahrhundert* actually appears to be one rare exception as it proposes (among topics such as radio opera, radio play, television opera, rock opera and musical technology) a discussion of the 'theatrical integration of media – music theatre and/as multimedia' (Heister 2002: 420).[1]

In this perspective Heister identifies two pivot points in music media history: first, the beginnings of *musique concrète* in 1948, and second, the comparatively easy availability of sound synthesis from 1951 on. He concludes: 'Both things are significant: now sound reproduction technology reaches also the sphere of "serious", "classical" music' (ibid.: 413; see also Weibel 2016). And that also means: music theatre. Indeed, new technical devices such as Pierre Schaeffer's *pupître d'espace* allowed the 'animation' of monaural – and thus, so to speak, 'static' – tape compositions like Schaeffer's own *Symphonie pour un homme seul* (1948/1950) and the first, non-scenic version of *Orphée: Toute la lyre* (1951) in concert-like presentations by 'moving' projected sound around inside the projection space (for a detailed discussion of Schaeffer's work see Brech 2015). Schaeffer and Henry's production routines were greatly facilitated when from October 1950 onwards they had at hand, for the first time, a magnetic tape machine 'that allowed us to get rid of acetate discs, and without which the idea of a *musique concrète* would have been presumptuous' (Robert 2000: 23). Tape technology actually became more and more accessible and affordable, for example with the first portable tape recorders released by AEG (*AEG Magnetophon AW2* – the 'A' stood for Aufnahme (recording), the 'W' for Wiedergabe (playback))[2] and Ampex (*Ampex 400*)

---

1 Unless otherwise stated, English translations of French, German, and Italian texts are by the author.
2 For more details and photographic images see www.tonbandmuseum.info/magnetophon-aw2.html.

in 1950. Werner Meyer-Eppler had published his influential study on electric sound generation, electronic music and synthetic speech in 1949 (Meyer-Eppler 1949), and from 1951 onwards, the Cologne Studio für elektronische Musik offered sound manipulation and recording facilities based on the combination of subtractive synthesis (noise generators plus filters) and magnetic tape technology.

But as mentioned above, Heister's media-sensitive approach to mid-twentieth-century music theatre historiography is an exception. And what is more, new media, even if notated explicitly in the score, even if lying at the very core of a given music theatre composition, are commonly discussed as an 'additional' or 'external' feature in comparison to supposedly more 'essential' aspects.[3] A second very common explanatory model characterizes any expansion of traditional music theatre language as 'experimental', either in the completely generic sense of 'breaking with traditions',[4] or in the Cagean perspective of an action 'the outcome of which is not foreseen' (Cage 1961).[5] But why should media use always and automatically be tentative, as opposed to carefully planned, precisely calculated? In other words: are such characterizations accurate and satisfactory, or more like a feeble excuse preventing us from taking seriously the compositional use of media *per se*?

Technology/media in theory and on stage

The somewhat ambiguous research situation reveals (at least indirectly) a kind of gap (or tension) between technological media on the one hand, and opera composition on the other. Here arises the more basic question of how media were conceptualized at the time in question. As is well known, media theory (and, not to forget, the term 'media' itself as well) was on the upswing in the early 1960s, especially as a result of Marshall McLuhan's two books *The Gutenberg Galaxy* (1962),[6] and *Understanding Media: The Extensions of Man* (1964) (see Figure 5.1).[7] Searching for an alternative to both the 'appendix' and the 'experiment' formulas, I consider quite attractive McLuhan's idea that

---

3 In principle, this applies also for Heister's survey: 'Aesthetically speaking, in concerts or operas things like film, real sound or magnetic tape are possible or most likely if the collage, or more precisely, the montage, clearly marks them as foreign, as something that is taken in "from outside"' (Heister 2002: 421). Only with Zimmermann's *Die Soldaten* (1965) does Heister see the first major step towards real integration of new media in music theatre, while recognizing Milhaud's *Christophe Colomb* (1930) at least as a 'model'. *Die Soldaten* is also the big exception for Hiekel: 'the opera *Die Soldaten* is unique for its time because there the use of technical media appears not as an extra, but plays a substantial role' (Hiekel 2004: 143).

4 This is, for example, the basic concept of Reininghaus and Schneider 2004; cf. Schneider 2004.

5 Recently Björn Heile has proposed another notion of and set of analytic concepts for 'experimental music theatre' which he defines narrowly as 'a type of performance in which theatrical actions are created by music making', so that a very specific repertoire (in particular Cage and Kagel) comes into consideration (Heile 2016: 335). See also Heile's chapter in this volume.

6 The first edition in German appeared in 1968 under a title that emphasizes in a maybe exaggerated way the thesis of a domination of electronic media: *Die Gutenberg-Galaxis: Das Ende des Buchzeitalters* ('The End of the Book Age').

7 The first edition in German appeared in 1968 as *Die magischen Kanäle. 'Understanding Media'*.

Figure 5.1 Marshall McLuhan, *Understanding Media*, dust jacket (designed by Abner Graboff) of the out-of-print first edition, 1964, with contemporary sound recording and reproduction technology occurring twice (record player; microphone).

media can be defined as 'extensions': with this formula McLuhan stressed that media, so to speak, 'start from' (or 'adhere to') a definable point. According to McLuhan, 'the "content" of any medium is always another medium' (1964: 8), so that even electricity can be considered as a medium that 'contains' any communicative act that uses electricity (telegraph, telephone, radio, TV, tape recording, neon signs, etc.). Applied to sound recording and reproduction this theorem means, for example, that '[t]he phonograph is an extension and amplification of the voice [. . ..,] providing a mechanical extension of the human voice and the new ragtime melodies', and that it was 'the advent of the electric tape recorder that only a few years ago released the phonograph from its temporary involvement in mechanical culture' (ibid.: 275–7). Vice versa, the idea is that, whenever media are involved, this starting point – ultimately, 'man', as McLuhan effectively accentuates in the title of his book – undergoes an extension. As a thought experiment, this idea can easily be applied to art as well, and thus to music theatre, too.

Before the emergence of the concept of 'media' in the early sixties, phenomena we nowadays subsume under '(new) media' were theorized under keywords such as technological progress, mechanization/automation/electronification/computerization, future technologies,[8] communication theory[9], and the like. An exemplary and far-reaching initiative in this sense was surely the conference *Die Künste im technischen Zeitalter*, held in Munich under the responsibility of the Bavarian Academy of Fine Arts in November 1953 (the proceedings appeared as Bayerische Akademie der schönen Künste (ed.) 1956).[10] The welcome address of the Technische Universität Munich's president August Rucker gives an interesting insight into how technology was seen in a dialectical way. Rucker diagnoses a hiatus between the pessimism of the creators of technology – the most important background here is the manifesto of the 'Göttingen Eighteen' (one of whom was academy member Werner Heisenberg) against nuclear rearmament – and an optimistic, collective 'belief in progress' on the side of society as the user of modern technology:

> You are willing to talk of the age of technology. That seems to mean the present age. But the technician will hardly concede that this age, as he understands it, has already begun. To him, the impression of a misuse of technology will prevail. For the moment, I have but one reason to speak of such an age [. . .]. This reason is, that, essentially, our technical achievements are anonymous, non-collective, but cooperative [. . .]. Doesn't this equal the achievements of the highest levels of cultural periods, even their late flowerings? Therefore we could surely speak of a civilization of technology.
>
> (Rucker 1956: 7)

---

8 For a general survey of (political, cultural, social) discourses connected to the 'future' aspect, see Radkau 2017.

9 On the connection of communication philosophy and media theory in the case of Flusser 1963, see Hanke 2006.

10 The first edition attained high print run numbers (at least 17,000); a second edition was published in 1966.

At the same conference, graphic artist and academy president Emil Preetorius agreed with Werner Heisenberg in warning of a profound and irreversible loss of nature as an equal counterpart to man (and arts):

> Hasn't nature, once considered vital and symbolic, opposing mankind as a subject in its own right, as a divine growth in Dilthey's words, hasn't that nature long since descended to become no more than an object, readily available to man? Think of the inexorable, uncannily progressing process of its mechanization: technology may be conceived, in Martin Heidegger's sense, as the power that changes inevitably and increasingly the natural environment, shaping it in our image, in the image of man. It is necessary to recall what Heisenberg has recently said: that for the first time in history man is facing, on this planet, nothing but himself.
>
> (Preetorius 1956: 81)[11]

Nevertheless, technical means *were* used in artistic contexts, including opera (as stated above). In the light of such debates as documented by the *Die Künste im technischen Zeitalter* conference, McLuhan's theorization of media can be understood as the quest for a kind of neutral, more objective view on technological progress, taking, so to speak, a step backward and circumnavigating considerations of opportunities, risks, and 'meanings' of technology, in order to bring to the foreground mediality *as such*. Especially with respect to the arts, and more specifically to the emergence of self-conscious 'media art', the importance of this perspective can hardly be overestimated, because it allows us to analyse the way in which media are applied by artists not only in terms of the 'content' or the 'meaning' of a work, but also poetically, i.e. as an aspect of composition technique that expands the (music theatre) composers' traditional set of means.

In addition to this, it is important to point out that McLuhan's 'extensions of man' paradigm starts from the status of (communication) media in the 'real world', not theatre. This makes it all the more important to take into account that in theatrical contexts media receive a double function: 'man's extensions' not only being *put to use* (as a means of communication), but at the same time also being *set on stage* (a means of communication as 'content' and/or 'medium' of a theatrical representation).

This can be considered precisely the main issue that is analysed onstage, so to speak, in Mauricio Kagel's 'Kammermusikalisches Theaterstück' *Sur scène* (1960). Kagel brings onstage an 'Elektro-akustische Ausrüstung' consisting of three tape machines (for playback of two one-track tapes and one two-track tape) and six loudspeakers (an invisible speaker on both sides of the stage, two speakers on either side of the auditorium; see Figure 5.2). He then literally brings into action this electroacoustic equipment in any thinkable combination and spatial arrangement of (theatrical and musical) performers' bodies/actions/gestures, performers'

---

11 Heidegger also contributed to the 1953 lecture series; see Heidegger 1956.

sounds/voices (coming directly from the performer as usual, but also separated from the actor spatially, or temporally, or both), sound recording (pre-recorded, and recorded live on stage), and sound projection (acousmatic, and amplifying/ pseudo-amplifying stage sound). In a playful way, ('new') technical and ('conventional') non-technical theatre media are theatrically analysed not separately, but on the contrary, on one and the same level. The total absence of a plot, and the neutral, completely black stage decor and clothing of the speaker, mime, singer, and three instrumentalists helps bring to the fore the media theory aspect of the piece even more strongly. (In so doing, it seems no coincidence that the black stage decor and costumes directly follow the example of Béjart, Schaeffer, and Henry's *Symphonie pour un homme seul* from 1955.) Seen from this angle, Kagel, with his very original and far-sighted implementation of, if you will, a 'metatheatre about man and media', is patently ahead of McLuhan. When Kagel, in 1962, stages media, he does so with the purpose of showing man's use of media, man's interaction with media. When McLuhan, in 1964, defines man's interrelation with media, he comes very close to what Kagel had just been doing in *Sur scène* and, a year later, also in *Antithese*, a 'play for one actor with electronic and public sounds', in which the performer operates not only a tape (produced in the Siemens Studio Munich), but also quite a selection of electroacoustic devices of different ages and types.

So in the field of music theatre at least two basic questions regarding new media arise. The first question concerns the 'meanings' conveyed by artistic decisions regarding specific technologies. This question is basically situated on the level of the plot: how do the specific media used in a score contribute to the characterization of man, the subject of the operatic stage work? The second question (and in my opinion the more important one for understanding acts of composing new media) is situated on the level of music-theatrical media situations themselves. If we are ready to adopt McLuhan's notion of mediatic 'extensions', this second question concerns what specific element of a music theatre work the new medium

Elektro-akustische Ausrüstung

2 Tonbandgeräte (einkanalige Wiedergabe), an die Bühnen-Lautsprecher angeschlossen
1 Tonbandgerät (zweikanalige Wiedergabe), an den Saal-Lautsprecher angeschlossen
6 Lautsprecher und Verstärker (Mindestleistung je 60 Watt)
　　　　— zwei davon werden seitlich der Bühne aufgestellt (dürfen vom Zuschauerraum nicht zu sehen sein),
　　　　— die restlichen vier werden an den vier Ecken des Saales angebracht. Vorne und hinten links = 1. Kanal; vorne und hinten rechts = 2. Kanal. (Eventuell genügen auch zwei Lautsprecher an den beiden vorderen Ecken des Saales.)

Figure 5.2 Mauricio Kagel, *Sur scène*, 'Elektro-akustische Ausrüstung', n.p. (detail). © Copyright 1962 by Henry Litolff's Verlag Ltd & Co. KG, Leipzig. Reproduced by kind permission of Peters Edition Limited, London.

108 *Andreas Münzmay*

attaches to, or in other words, where it starts from. As discussed below, such elements (or, if you will, 'starting points') can be the music of a music theatre work or opera, the stage, the characters, but also the spectators and the orchestra. So in sum what I'd like to propose in the following is a conceptualization of new media in terms of 'extensions of theatre'.

As the provisional worklist shows (see Appendix), the magnetic tape issue seems to gather pace in 1953. Naturally, we only can undertake a rather cursory and tentative *tour d'horizon* and address, in loose chronological order, only a fraction of the works in question. Future investigations most certainly could not only examine other works, or examine the works in greater depth, but also identify further types of 'extensions'.[12]

Tape in opera. Extending . . .

a) . . . musical material

Hans Werner Henze's two act 'radio opera' *Das Ende einer Welt* (1953) features a wealth of tape-based sound effects. But at the same time it is revealing that twelve years later the stage version of *Das Ende einer Welt* (premiered in Frankfurt at the end of 1965, the year of Zimmermann's *Soldaten*) took place without any electronics at all. This is due to the fact that in the original radio opera the taped sounds were merely employed in the radio play tradition as background noises and consequently were dispensable in terms of composition. A seemingly analogous, but in fact completely different case is Pierre Schaeffer and Pierre Henry's 'spectacle lyrique' *Orphée 53*, from the same year, 1953 (see Delhaye 2012). This work is also a stage version of an earlier composition broadcast on the radio (5 October 1951), *Orphée 51 ou Toute la lyre* for singers, speakers, and *musique concrète* replayed from mono magnetic tape. Like its radiophonic predecessor, *Orphée 53* comprised taped *musique concrète* and live singers/actors. At the Donaueschingen Festival in autumn 1953 the loudspeakers – placed in the corners of Donaueschingen's Reithalle, 'directed' by Schaeffer from a control desk placed at a central position in the hall, and fed by 'a battery of tape recorders' operated by Schaeffer's 'musicians' – produced a scandal. A critique by Fred Prieberg lay great emphasis on how the technical devices were 'staged', and how they 'acted' together with the human performers (including Schaeffer himself), creating what Prieberg disparages as a 'dilettante world theatre':

> The wide hall, nearly empty, yawned [. . .]. In the middle aisle, to the front, there was a pulpit, obviously for the conductor. But there was no symphonic

---

12 For example, the playful mediatic 'extension of the composer' found at the beginning of Henri Pousseur's *Votre Faust* (1969), where the acousmatic taped voice of 'Henri', a composer, holds a lecture in which he complains about having too many lectures to hold and not having enough time left to compose.

score on it, but a kind of control panel with switches and controls. Cables wound their way to a place to the right of the stage, hidden mysteriously by some decorations. [. . .] Schaeffer flicked through a plan sketch for the distribution of the sound to the loudspeakers, operated some controls, gave directions to his assistants at the tape machines [. . .] The loudspeakers opened their mouths and disgorged cascades of noises, sounds, understandable and incomprehensible snatches of speech into the hall. [. . .] The characters solemnly strode around like statues, reciting philosophy. Everything was overcharged with meaning and lasted much too long – a dilettante world theatre. [. . .] Then the dazzling spotliqhts flared up again. Pierre Schaeffer took hold of his sound direction plan and walked uncertainly on stage towards the battery of tape recorders.

(Prieberg 1960: 76–81)

But there is another detail of Schaeffer and Henry's scenic *Orphée* that must not be overlooked: the integration of a harpsichord. Notwithstanding its possible meanings as a cross-reference to the baroque period and to Monteverdi's or Gluck's *Orfeo*, the integration of this instrument does not primarily increase the conventionality (or 'naturalness') of *Orphée*, but on the contrary functions as a further means for pointing out the fundamental role of sound recording media and magnetic tape manipulations in this composition, for the harpsichord's music, too, counts among the 'concrete' material and is subject to the same type of technical operations (like reversed playback, loops, echoes, filtering) as the other natural and abstract sound material. The composition opens with human breath and a nearly 'natural', although impressively resonating harpsichord arpeggio, which soon reappears in reversed form, in combination with echo effects, and many other 'alienations' (for an analysis and technical description see Fox 2005). Seen from this perspective, in *Orphée 51* the media operate as extensions of the musical material itself, so that the historical panorama begins, as it were, with the most fundamental of possible 'extensions'.

Another example for such a concept, in which the production of new musical sounds is presented as the very content of a music-theatre performance, is Bruno Maderna's 'lirica in forma di spettacolo' *Hyperion*. In the course of the work, an instrumentalist (flautist Severino Gazzelloni at the first performance at the 1964 Venice Biennale) is confronted, amongst other things, with a huge and threatening machine whose appearance and movements on stage are accompanied by Maderna's magnetic tape composition *Dimensioni II* (see Casadei 2014). In this electronic work, realized at the Studio di fonologia musicale RAI in Milan in 1960, shrill laughter and incomprehensible speech is evoked by the synthetic assembly of phonemes pre-selected and pre-ordered by Hans G. Helms, and recorded separately by Cathy Berberian. In *Hyperion*, then, the media technology that makes possible this new and technology-based musical language, is itself given an allegorical 'body' (the metallic, machine-like structure) and an important 'role' (taking control, forcing back the instrumentalist).

110   *Andreas Münzmay*

b) . . . the stage set

Renzo Rossellini's *La guerra*, a one-act 'dramma' premiered in Naples in February 1956, begins programmatically with sound projections from magnetic tape. Immediately after the rising of the curtain, the orchestral accompaniment, marked *ppp* and *lontano*, merges with radio speech and other sounding 'realities' coming from a tape and projected into the auditorium by loudspeakers. In this way, Rossellini integrates a sounding 'reality', that is, 'Radio Libera', a fictitious radio station that announces the end of war and occupation:

> *THE RADIO*: This is Radio Libera. After three years of cruel occupation the hostile army is beaten and retreats. Our troops will enter the city by tonight. The moment of redemption has come: you, who have resisted, suffering most atrocious injustice and most inhuman hardship, you will embrace again your sons, your brothers, all those who have tirelessly fought for you and who . . .

> (Rossellini 1956: 4)

Orchestra and tape merge into an overall sound display that is very reminiscent of mixing strategies familiar from film soundtracks.[13] As can also be discerned from the 1960 recording,[14] Rossellini aims at a seamless integration of recorded speech and orchestral music, resulting in a kind of melodrama produced by tape playback and orchestra. So from the beginning, Rossellini's score helps to establish filmic realism as a general aesthetic concept of this opera.

The plot of the opera, following this 'mediatic melodrama' opening, is a Romeo-and-Juliet story with a lover who has been fighting on the wrong side, namely the side of the besiegers whose defeat has been proclaimed by the initial radio news. Near the end of the opera there are further 'sounding chunks of reality' (sounds of bells and sirens) incorporated into the elegiac orchestral interlude that accompanies the tragic farewell of Erik, the defeated besieger, and Maria, the inhabitant of the liberated town. All in all, Rossellini's starting point for media use is not to be found on the musical (compositional) level proper, but on the level of opera composition in a broader sense, in particular an understanding of the stage as a potentially sounding element of the whole. At the same time, it is revealing that the taped sound is not conceived as something opposed to the orchestra (like usual onstage music or onstage sound), but, on the contrary, systematically occurs in combination with the orchestra. Rossellini is resolute in having both

---

13 Correspondingly, the score sets the scene as follows: 'From outside comes an incessant noise [. . .] interrupted from time to time by raucous shouts, military orders: it is the exodus of a retreating army. Marta, the paralytic, listens to the radio at low volume and looks at the entrance door now and then, like someone who fears being surprised by indiscrete eyes and ears at doing something illegal.'

14 Renzo Rossellini, *La guerra*, Magda Olivero, Nicoletta Panni, Renato Cesari, Giacinto Prandelli, Ottavio Taddel, Walter Albert, Orchestra Sinfonica di Roma della RAI, direttore Massimo Freccia, RAI Roma 8 Oct 1960, CD reissue, Eklipse Records [*c.*1995], 2'20".

work together in order to enhance the spectators' illusion of being 'in' the stage action themselves: through the orchestral 'wrapping' of the loudspeaker projections, the aural stage props blur the border between the stage and auditorium, and help generate an immersive, cinema-like realism. So the 'filmic neo-realism on the opera stage' for which Rossellini is known (see Spohr 1994: 343) owes much to the possibilities of tape-based sound projection, and can in this respect be analysed as grounded in specific mediatic extensions of the stage set.

c) . . . the list of dramatis personae

Karl-Birger Blomdahl's *Aniara* – 'A revue about man in time and space', as the original subtitle reads – is nothing less than a science fiction opera, and as such literally clamours for the deployment of mediatic extensions. Premiered in Stockholm in 1959, the two-act work was quickly produced at other European opera houses as well. Most notably, in the following year, *Aniara* was the first of Rolf Liebermann's numerous 'media opera' productions in Hamburg. (Others included the world premieres of Krenek's *Der goldene Bock*, 1964; Bibalo's *Das Lächeln am Fuße der Leiter*, 1965; Blacher's *Die Notlandung*, discussed below; Schuller's *Die Heimsuchung*, 1966; Goehr's *Arden muß sterben*, 1967; Penderecki's *Die Teufel von Loudon*, 1969; Kelemen's *Der Belagerungszustand*, 1970; Kagel's *Staatstheater*, 1970; Tal's *Ashmedai*, 1971.) The libretto of *Aniara* by Erik Lindegren is based on a 1956 verse epos by Harry Martinson characterized by a wealth of linguistic inventions, including extended passages where the protagonists express themselves in a fictitious language. The exploration of new forms of both linguistic and musical 'language' lies at the centre of interest of this parabolic work. Even more important in our context are the technical circumstances of the odyssey of the spaceship 'Aniara' which carries a group of emigrants from Earth bound for Mars, after Earth has been poisoned by mankind and has been left by both God and the Devil. On the spaceship, man is accompanied by 'MIMA', a sort of technical and mystic Supreme Being that has the capability to record and replay (!) everything that ever happens in space. MIMA is controlled by the 'space sailor' Mimaroben, the main male character of the opera.

Quite obviously the composer – who in 1964 was to found the Elektronmusikstudio in Stockholm (see Groth 2014) – was interested first and foremost in the metaphoric omniscient memory machine MIMA, which he 'translates' musically into magnetic tape music. For the emigrants, MIMA becomes essential at the moment when they realize that they are lost in space and will endlessly continue travelling without ever reaching any planet. At the end of act one, scene two, the two 'engineers in chief' declare:

> We slowly realize that this space in which we travel is totally different from what space formerly meant to us in our imagination on Earth. Now we guess that this space, so crystal clear around Aniara's hull, is spirit, and that we are lost in this ocean of spirit.
>
> (Blomdahl 1959: 75)

112 *Andreas Münzmay*

This passage shows that, philosophically, the piece is also about technology critique, questioning contemporary beliefs in technical feasibility; the question will ultimately be answered – pessimistically – by the behaviour of the machine itself. But to begin with, in scene three, the final scene of the first act, the travellers seek consolation in praying to MIMA. In a kind of mediatic theatre-within-a-theatre situation MIMA shows them images of Earth, their lost home planet. What the reverent crowd of exiles (now transformed into an audience, and in this way unified with the actual theatre audience) hears, is the 'MIMABAND I', a tape with over eight and a half minutes of superb electronic music composed of synthesized sound and (supposedly) synthetic (or at least strongly alienated) speech;[15] what it eventually sees is Earth as it explodes (Example 5.1). Quite obviously, Blomdahl's use of magnetic tape constitutes in a certain sense an extension of both the musical material and the stage set. But another main effect of his compositional use of this medium concerns the field of dramatic roles: in accordance with the extension of the dramatis personae through a God-like machine, or medium, Blomdahl establishes an appropriately mediatic 'supernatural voice' for the mediatic supernatural main character of the opera.

In the course of the second act all passengers, including the Mimaroben and his beloved (female spaceship captain Isagel, a dancing role), will perish. Only the MIMA survives. But it seems as if even the medium will have nothing more to say after the disappearance of mankind: the opera ends with MIMA's electronic tape voice (slowly fading out as if floating off into endless space and time), but this time it is radically reduced to a 'meaningless' pulsating sinusoidal C7 pitch. As something producing meaning and sense, the medium, in Harry Martinson, Erik Lindegren and Karl-Birger Blomdahl's conception, is *not* something self-consistent, but depends essentially on its human operators. In this perspective, *Aniara* can be read as a perfect expression *avant la lettre* of McLuhan's idea that media are 'the extensions of man'.[16]

---

15 The tape can be heard in the 1985 studio production, Karl-Birger Blomdahl, *Aniara*. Operan i konsertversion, Sveriges Radios Symfoniorkester, Stig Westerberg (conductor), 2 LP, Caprice CAP 22016:1–2, 1985, CD reissue Caprice [2002].

16 Similarly, it is unknown whether Arthur C. Clarke and Stanley Kubrick had *Aniara* in mind when they wrote and filmed *2001 – A Space Odyssey* (USA 1968), but there are a lot of parallels, such as the prominence of electronic music for certain interlude-like scenes, or the role of the omniscient computer (called HAL 9000 in Kubrick's film). With regard to the computer–operator (or medium–man) relationship, Kubrick reverts the situation: the operator, space traveller David Bowman, actively deactivates the machine after severe malfunctions. (It appears that the film-makers of 1968 must have known their 1964 McLuhan by heart.) Most remarkably, in this scene tape technology also plays a major role in giving a voice to the machine; as is generally known, the last thing HAL 'says' is the song *Daisy Bell*, continuously getting lower in pitch and slower. As composer Wendy Carlos explains in detail on her web page, this effect was created by processing the tape (with actor Douglas Rain's recorded voice) by a 'Mark II Eltro Information Rate Changer', a tape effect machine intended for speech compression, that allowed for time compression/expansion and pitch alteration independently. See Carlos 2008.

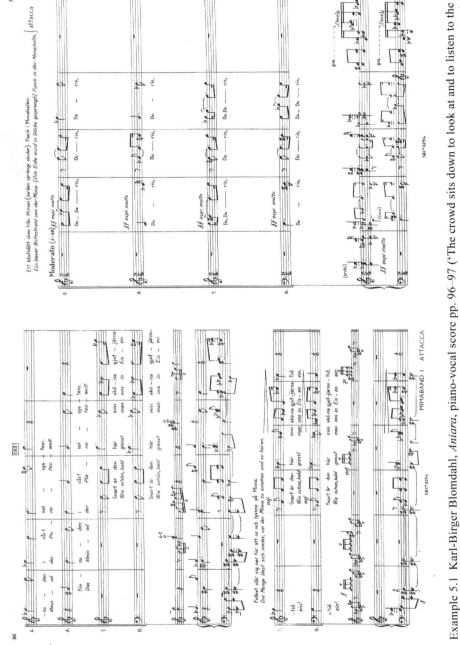

Example 5.1 Karl-Birger Blomdahl, *Aniara*, piano-vocal score pp. 96–97 ('The crowd sits down to look at and to listen to the Mima.' – 'MIMABAND I' [8'37"] – 'Blue flash of lighting from the Mima. Earth is blown up into pieces. Panic in the Mima-hall.'). © SCHOTT MUSIC Ltd, London.

114   *Andreas Münzmay*

As another case of electronic tape music used as the 'voice' of a non-human persona Boris Blacher's operatic 'reportage in two phases' on 'incidents at an emergency landing' (*Zwischenfälle bei einer Notlandung*, Reportage in zwei Phasen, Hamburg 1966) can be cited. Beside the passengers of an aircraft, the dramatis personae also include the characters 'Numbers from One to Infinity' and 'Professor'. Both are part of an artificial intelligence apparatus, an electronic brain controlled by the Professor's human alter ego (the 'Host') able to take over complete control of the fate of the wrecked aeronauts, dialectically promising the only way out of the hopeless situation, and threatening to obliterate the passengers' individual identities. The voice of the A.I. consists of a nine-part magnetic tape produced in the TU Berlin studios by multiplication of the voice of tenor Ernst Haefliger.

d) . . . the auditorium

Nono's *Intolleranza 1960*, not without reason renowned as a 'choir opera', draws massively and in a virtuoso manner on the 'stage extension' strategy encountered *in nuce* already in Rossellini's *La guerra*. But this time, the direction of the extension is reversed, so to speak. Already before the curtain rises, Nono introduces the choir as an acousmatic voice capable of coming from different places in the auditorium: front (1), right side (2), behind the audience (3), left side (4). This choir exposition (combined with visual projections of inscriptions) establishes from the beginning a kind of dialogue that involves not only the stage figures, but also the auditorium which is virtually given a voice, and ultimately something like a 'role' in the piece. So in this case we can not only say that the stage extends over the auditorium, but that at the same time the function of the spectators themselves undergoes a shift towards a more active role, in which the public virtually intervenes and even 'says'/'sings' something in the piece. Quite obviously, this fits perfectly in the political and ethical agenda of *Intolleranza 1960*, appealing to the public's solidarity and personal involvement in the face of a nameless emigrant miner's exposure to injustice, discrimination, and mistreatment. In terms of the media situation it is especially noteworthy that literally the first thing that Nono's score presents is – in combination with Ripellino's passionate appeal to humanity and altruism, 'Vivere è stare svegli / e concedersi agli altri [. . .]'[17] – the use of sound projection technology for the effect of an acousmatic choir in the auditorium.

Also in Roman Haubenstock-Ramati's *Amerika* (Berlin 1966), the tape technology aims at an intensified involvement of the spectators – less politically, more psychologically, less as an outer, more as an inner 'voice'. In this multimedia opera after Franz Kafka's incomplete novel *Der Verschollene* (1913), Haubenstock-Ramati and librettist Max Brod (who had published Kafka's

---

17 'Living means to stay vigilant, and to devote oneself to the others'. See Nono 1962: 2–3 and Ripellino 1990: 21.

fragment posthumously under the title *Amerika* in 1927) confront the spectator with a complex simultaneity of multiple actions and dreams on stage, but also of acoustic layers. The score gives precise indications for the production of four-track tape montages from musical structures that have to be recorded beforehand by the orchestra, the choir, and the soloists, as well as for the mixing and projection of the taped material over speakers placed at the right and left side in the auditorium, to the right and left of the stage, on stage, in the orchestra, and even high up in the middle of the auditorium (i.e. at the hereditary place of the chandelier). In this way, every participant in the opera – orchestra, choir, soloists – is heard both live and acousmatically by playback (or both at the same time), and from whatever position in the theatre. Fragmented, often incomprehensible dialogue, abstract pantomime, absurd simultaneity of actions and settings work together with the holistic sound concept in order to create a mind-expanding theatre that involves each of the spectators as a 'traveller' who at the side of main protagonist Karl Roßmann 'experiences' the confusing new world as a 'dream' and as a series of mental projections of 'the unconscious'.[18] At the premiere in West-Berlin (under the direction of Bruno Maderna) the public was shocked and overwhelmed by this 'new media opera' that, by means of sound display, took hold of the whole performance space and overthrew the traditional role of the audience as mere 'listeners' and 'watchers'; *Amerika* was cancelled after only one more presentation.

e) ... the orchestra

Bernd Alois Zimmermann was not the only one seeking a media-based 'total theatre' in 1965. Only six weeks after the premiere of *Die Soldaten* in Cologne, composer Giacomo Manzoni, librettist Emilio Jona, stage designer Josef Svoboda, and debuting opera conductor Claudio Abbado presented *Atomtod* in Milan. In terms of content, this communist work proposes the vision of a spherical atomic shelter having room only for a select elite (military and church), while workers, soldiers, women, and men outside fall victim to the nuclear destruction of the world. With regard to stage media, this two-act 'teatro integrale' (Jona, cited in Stenzl 1989: 660) called for loudspeakers all around and above the spectators, lighting effects, and a large video screen on stage, i.e. a TV set as a stage prop (but actually a fairly oversized one), symbolizing the mass medium by which

---

18 The preface to the score states: 'Just as we experience in a dream, on the one hand, the real, the well-known and the clear, and on the other, the blurred, the unclear and the ambiguous at the same time (dimensions that [. . .] project one and the same thing in two ways at the same time), the stage must endeavor this TWOFOLDNESS OF THE INSEPARABLE here. On the one hand, the conscious (clear and unambiguous representations of actions, persons, and things), on the other hand, the projections of the same persons, things and actions into the unconscious, by means of blurred, unclear and deformed images and ambiguous, often absurd actions. So on the one hand, [. . .] EXPRESSION of the real, the conscious; on the other [. . .] IMPRESSION of the unconscious, the transcendental' (Haubenstock-Ramati 1970: n.p.).

the 'Speaker' character proclaims the Italian army's emergency instructions for nuclear catastrophes. Musically, within a wide stylistic range (e.g. tonal, jazz, serialist, aleatoric), five magnetic tapes with electronic music play a key role. Consequently, the central function of electronic music and acousmatic sound display is highlighted from the beginning. Manzoni's *Atomtod* can probably be regarded as the first opera (in the more conventional meaning of the word) with an unadorned tape music overture (Example 5.2), preceding by six years Josef Tal's *Ashmedai* (a dodecaphonic allegory about totalitarianism; the King's selfish pact with the devil ends up in apocalyptic destruction), which also features a purely electronic overture.[19] In analogy to the nuclear bomb explosion that takes place between the first and the second act, Manzoni uses electronic sound media as a symbol, or musical placeholder, for the destructive potential of techniques developed by humans in the course of history. In this sense, the voice of the TV speaker, who at the end of Act I cynically requests all the underprivileged people who are not admitted to the shelters built by the upper class to keep calm, comes not 'out of the TV on stage' in a realistic manner, but 'from everywhere in the theatre'. A performance indication in the score specifies that 'from this point on, until the end of act I, the Speaker's voice gets more and more threatening, overwhelming, terrifying, intense and overpowering, but staying calm at the same time, without any agitation' (Manzoni 1964: 73). More and more, the TV speaker's voice loses its concrete context; its enlargement and dislocation can be understood as a long musical *crescendo* that increasingly functions also as a *musical* counterpoint within the orchestral setting.

Just as the opera begins with electronic music, and just as it uses electronic sound projection at crucial points of the action, it also ends with electronic tape music.

Example 5.2 Giacomo Manzoni, *Atomtod*, first page of the score (detail). © Edizioni Suvini Zerboni – Sugarmusic S.p.A., Milano.

---

19 Maderna's *Hyperion* was also introduced at its first performance (Venice 1964) by six minutes of electronic tape music, namely Maderna's *Le rire*; see Casadei 2014: 106.

Composing new media 117

All in all, it can be said that in *Atomtod* tape functions primarily as an extension of the orchestra (or maybe a kind of 'second orchestra'), alternating both musically and semantically with the 'regular' orchestra. In this perspective, the end of the opera is particularly revealing. We see the survivors coming out of their fallout shelters:

> One by one the shelters open; the Owner, the Builder, the General, the Servant, the Priest, Slam, followed by a crowd similar to them, always growing during the choral chant. They all have identical faces: big, sparkling eyes, a stereotypical smile, ambiguous between sweetness and cruelty. They stream past in an orderly manner (while singing).
>
> (Ibid.: 213–34)

This happens with shrill accompaniment by the full orchestra, for the most time producing *fortissimo* sounds on indeterminate pitches. Finally this choir of survivors who seem to have lost their individual identities begins to sing a grotesque song of joy: 'oh sun, I live, finally, brilliant' ('oh sole io vivo finalmente splendente'). A footnote in the score specifies that the voices be detached from the singers' bodies by technical means: 'by no means should the audience perceive the sound produced by the choir as coming directly from the choir, but exclusively by means of electroacoustic amplification and projection' (ibid.: 235). Of the orchestra only the tape ('Nastro E') is left over, forming a disturbing recitative accompaniment to the sinister and bodiless song of joy.

***

In this phase of twentieth-century music theatre history, tape technology plays a considerable role. The few cases discussed in this chapter may already have shown that media use is not *per se* 'experimental', but can first and foremost be regarded as well-determined 'compositional' practice, i.e. not as an 'additional' or 'secondary' feature, but, on the contrary, is situated on the very level of opera dramaturgy and composition itself – even if, naturally, the tape music is not notated *in extenso* in the operatic scores or librettos. It is all the more important not to overlook the indications concerning the use of the tapes and the technical circumstances linked to their playback. And, not least, it must be stressed that the tape music, although often not notated in traditional manner, nonetheless *is* notated by the composers, and is even notated in an especially definite manner – namely, as explicit sound information on the tapes. The McLuhanist idea of media as 'extensions' may help to denote more precisely what media 'do', and to understand the way in which media 'act' in specific cases. As a start, the (allegedly simple) question of how tape music is 'placed' in the complex theatrical space (stage, pit, auditorium . . .), and eventually, what 'role' tape music plays in the dramaturgical conception of a music theatre piece, can serve as a powerful methodological tool for studying composers' uses of new media.

118   *Andreas Münzmay*

Appendix

Chronology of works involving new media as listed in *Pipers Enzyklopädie des Musiktheaters* and *Grove Dictionary of Opera* (numeral after title indicates number of acts):

1920

Francesco Pratella: *L'aviatore Dro*, Opera, 3, Lugo di Romagna 4 Sept 1920
uses Russolo's *intonarumori* for sounds of motor cars and the monoplane

1924

Arnold Schoenberg: *Die glückliche Hand*, Drama mit Musik, 1, Vienna 14 Oct 1924
elaborate scenic effects synchronized with changing coloured lighting

Jean Börlin, Erik Satie, Francis Picabia, René Clair: *Relâche/Cinéma*, Ballet, 2, Paris 27 Nov 1924
ballet intermission: experimental silent film with orchestral accompaniment

1927

Ernst Křenek: *Johnny spielt auf*, Oper, 2, Leipzig 10 Feb 1927
film projections in several scenes

Kurt Weill: *Royal Palace*, Oper, 1, Berlin 2 Mar 1927
film sequence (showing tempting aspects of modern lifestyle)

1928

Weill: *Der Zar läßt sich photographieren*, Opera buffa, 1, Leipzig 18 Feb 1928
telephone and door bells, music from gramophone ('Tango Angèle') as incidental music

1930

Weill: *Aufstieg und Fall der Stadt Mahagonny*, Oper, 3, Leipzig 9 Mar 1930
projections of images and inscriptions

Darius Milhaud: *Christophe Colomb*, Oper, 2, Berlin 5 May 1930
film projections

George Antheil: *Transatlantik (aka The People's Choice)*, Oper, 3, Frankfurt am Main 25 May 1930
film projections; a prepared piano (newspapers distributed on the strings), telephone, telegraph, typewriters

Ernst Toch: *Der Fächer*, Operncapriccio, 3, Königsberg 8 June 1930
sound projection: speaking voices, excerpt from Toch's *Die Prinzession auf der Erbse* (1927), renaissance music

1935 AEG MAGNETOPHON K1, Funkausstellung Berlin 1935

1937

Alban Berg: *Lulu*, Oper, 3, Zürich 2 June 1937
silent film/orchestra intermezzo between II/1 and II/2

1938

Werner Egk: *Peer Gynt*, Oper, 3, Berlin 24 Nov 1938
sound projection (ringing of bells)

Composing new media   119

1939
Carl Orff: *Der Mond*, Ein kleines Welttheater, Munich 5 Feb 1939
offstage choir with megaphones; sound projection (choir in the sky)

1941 AEG MAGNETOPHON K4 (high-frequency pre-magnetization)

1942 STUDIO D'ESSAI DE LA RADIODIFFUSION FRANÇAISE
Frank Martin: *Le vin herbé*, Prolog, 3 Teile, Epilog, Zürich 26 Mar 1942 (concert), Salzburg 15 Aug 1948 (stage)
visual projections
Nico Dostal: *Manina*, Operette, 4, Berlin 28 Nov 1942
music from tape (hymn) behind the stage

1944 AEG MAGNETOPHON K7 (stereophonic)
Jerome Robbins, Leonard Bernstein: *Fancy Free*, Ballet, 1, New York 18 Apr 1944
before the rising of the curtain and orchestral prelude: music from tape (blues 'Big Stuff')

1947
Gian Carlo Menotti: *The Telephone, or L'amour à trois*, Opera buffa, 1, New York 18 Feb 1947
telephone, speaking clock

1950 AEG MAGNETOPHON AW2; AMPEX 300 (portable; record and playback)
Menotti: *The Consul*, Musical Drama, 3, Philadelphia 1 Mar 1950
gramophone disc on stage

1951 GROUPE DE RECHERCHE POUR LA MUSIQUE CONCRÈTE (GRMC) PARIS; STUDIO FÜR ELEKTRONISCHE MUSIK COLOGNE

1952
John Cage: *Water Music. 66 W. 12*, New York 2 May 1952
musical actions, *inter alia* with a radio set

1953 ELEKTRONISCHES STUDIO DER TU BERLIN
Hans Werner Henze: *Das Ende einer Welt*, Rundfunkoper, 2 mit Prolog und Epilog, Nordwestdeutscher Rundfunk 4 Dec 1953
3 tape machines with sound effects (e.g. heartbeat recording)
Pierre Schaeffer, Pierre Henry: *Orphée 53*, Spectacle lyrique, Donaueschingen 10 Oct 1953
for magnetic tape, voice and harpsichord

1955 STUDIO DI FONOLOGIA MUSICALE DI RADIO MILAN
Maurice Béjart, Schaeffer, Henry: *Symphonie pour un homme seul*, Ballet, Paris 26 Jul 1955
musique concrète

120 *Andreas Münzmay*

1956 SIEMENS STUDIO FÜR ELEKTRONISCHE MUSIK MUNICH
Renzo Rossellini: *La guerra*, Dramma, 1, Naples 25 Feb 1956
tape (street sounds, radio news)

c. **1957** RCA MARK II SOUND SYNTHESIZER (Columbia-Princeton Electronic Music Center)

1958 GROUPE DE RECHERCHES MUSICALES (GRM) PARIS; PHILIPPS PAVILLON EXPO BRUSSELS (Xenakis, Varèse: *Poéme électronique*)

1959
Francis Poulenc: *La voix humaine*, Tragédie-lyrique, 1, Paris 6 Feb 1959
telephone
Karl-Birger Blomdahl: *Aniara*, En revy om människan i tid och rum, 2, Stockholm 31 May 1959
3 tape machines (electronic music)

1960
Orff: *Ludus de nato Infante mirificus*, Ein Weihnachtsspiel, Stuttgart 11 Dec 1960
tape (chamber orchestra, choir of angels, voices of sleeping flowers and mother earth)

1961 EXPERIMENTAL MUSIC STUDIO OF NORSK RIKSKRING-KASTING OSLO
Václav Kašlík: *Krakatit*, Televizní opera, 2, ČST Prague 5 Mar 1961 (TV), Ostrava 20 May 1961 (stage)
2 magnetic tapes (concrete sound material, orchestral, jazz, and popular music); film projections (explosions)
Luigi Nono: *Intolleranza 1960*, Azione scenica, 2, Venice 13 Apr 1961
choir projected by loudspeakers surrounding the audience; tape collage/electronic music (II/1: absurdities of contemporary life)

1962
Mauricio Kagel: *Sur scène*, Kammermusikalisches Theaterstück, 1, Bremen 6 May 1962
3 tape machines, 6 loudspeakers
Wolfgang Fortner: *In seinem Garten liebt Don Perlimplín Belisa*, Kammerspiel, 2, Schwetzingen 10 May 1962
tape (5 electronic whistles)

1963 INSTITUT VOR PSYCHOAKOESTIEK EN ELEKTRONISCHE MUZIEK GENT
Alwin Nikolais, James L. Seawright: *Imago – The City Curious*, Ballet, 3, Hartford/CT 24 Feb 1963
electronic music
Kagel: *Antithese*, Spiel für einen Darsteller mit elektronischen und öffentlichen Klängen, Cologne 23 June 1963
scenical actions with tape (Siemens-Studio Munich) and many other historic and recent electroacoustic devices

1964 ELEKTRONMUSIKSTUDION STOCKHOLM
MOOG SYNTHESIZER
Bruno Maderna: *Hyperion*, Lirica in forma di spettacolo, Venice, 6 Sep 1964
tape projections with phonetic material
Křenek: *Der goldene Bock*, Oper, 4, Hamburg 16 June 1964
tape (electronic music); live electronics; complex stage technology

1965

Bernd Alois Zimmermann: *Die Soldaten*, Oper, 4, Cologne 15 Feb 1965
film projections; electroacoustic tape collages; loudspeaker groups on stage and in the auditorium; simultaneous scenes
Giacomo Manzoni: *Atomtod*, Due tempi, Milan 27 Mar 1965
video (speaker in TV screen); tape (electronic music); loudspeakers in the auditorium
Antonio Bibalo: *Das Lächeln am Fuße der Leiter*, Oper, 2, Hamburg 6 Apr 1965
tapes (jazz music); electronic alienation of voices
Rudi van Dantzig, Jan Boerman: *Monument voor een gestorven Jongen*, Ballet, Amsterdam 19 June 1965
tape (adaptation of Boerman's *Alchemie*, 1961)
Larry Sitsky: *The Fall of the House of Usher*, Opera, 1, Hobart, Tasmania, 18 Aug 1965
includes pre-recorded tapes
Sylvano Bussotti: *La Passion selon Sade*, Mystère de chambre, Palermo 5 Sep 1965
lighting effects determined compositionally in the score

1966

R. Murray Schafer: *Loving*, Opera, 1, CBC TV French Network Montreal 3 Feb 1966
score features percussion and electronic sounds
Boris Blacher: *Zwischenfälle bei einer Notlandung*, Reportage, 2, Hamburg 4 Feb 1966
orchestral and electronic composition (4 track tape; Elektronisches Studio der TU Berlin)
Günter Bialas: *Hero und Leander*, Oper in 7 Bildern mit Prolog und Intermezzo, Mannheim 8 Sep 1966
voice echoes via loudspeakers
Roman Haubenstock-Ramati: *Amerika*, Oper, 2, Berlin 8 Oct 1966
tape collages, 4 track tape machine; many loudspeakers on stage and in the auditorium
Gunther Schuller: *Die Heimsuchung*, Oper, 3, Hamburg 12 Oct 1966
use of electronic tape (incl. Bessie Smith's recording of *Nobody knows you when you're down and out*)

1967

Alexander Goehr: *Arden muß sterben*, Oper, 2, Hamburg 5 Mar 1967
piano with microphones and electronic distortion
Béjart, Henry: *Messe pour le temps présent*, Cérémonie en 9 épisodes, Avignon 3 Aug 1967
tape (sound collage) and percussion ensemble
Robert Joffrey, Chrome Syrcus: *Astarte*, Ballet, 1, New York 20 Sep 1967
several film projections (stage, auditorium)

122   *Andreas Münzmay*

1968

Béjart: *Baudelaire*, Spectacle en 8 séquences, Grenoble 9 Feb 1968
tape (collage with Debussy, Wagner, Rolling Stones, Indian music, etc.)

Orff: *Prometheus*, 9 Bilder, Stuttgart 24 Mar 1968
stage music to be pre-recorded and projected from tape

John Cranko, Zimmermann: *Présence*, Ballett, Schwetzingen 16 May 1968
tape (concrete sounds) before each of the 5 episodes

Pavel Šmok: *Listy duverné*, Balet, Prague 27 May 1968
music from tape (Janáček)

Dieter Schönbach: *Wenn die Kälte in die Hütten tritt [. . .]*, Musikalisches Theater, 9, Kiel 23 June 1968
tape with spacially arranged sounds/songs; 6-channel projection system; light sculptures, kinetic light objects

Béjart: *Bhakti*, Ballet en 3 épisodes, Avignon 26 Jul 1968
music from tape (Hindu music, Ravi Shankar)

Glen Tetley: *Embrace Tiger and Return to Mountain*, Ballet, London 21 Nov 1968
music from tape (Subotnick, *Silver Apples of the Moon*, 1967)

Luciano Berio: *Laborintus II*, Brussels 17 Dec 1968
microphones, loudspeaker, 2-track tape

1969

Henri Pousseur: *Votre Faust*, Fantaisie variable genre opéra, Milan 15 Jan 1969
composer's voice ('Henri' in the prologue) from tape, series of tapes shows development of certain instrumental and vocal qualities by means of electroacoustic distortion

Krzysztof Penderecki: *Die Teufel von Loudun*, Oper, 3, Hamburg 20 June 1969
tape with ringing bells

Hans van Manen: *Squares*, Ballet, Paris 24 Sep 1969
music from tape (Satie and others)

Paul Dessau: *Lanzelot*, Oper in 15 Szenen, Berlin 19 Dec 1969
adds stereophonic taped sound to the large orchestra

1970

Milko Kelemen: *Der Belagerungszustand*, Oper, 2, Hamburg 13 Jan 1970
tape/loudspeakers at many places on stage and in the auditorium; typewriter sextet as stage music

Luciano Chailly: *L'Idiota*, Opera lirica, 3, Rome 18 Feb 1970
uses electronic techniques

van Manen: *Situation*, Ballet, Scheveningen 20 Apr 1970
tape (sound effect discs for amateur filmers)

Heinz Holliger: *Der magische Tänzer*, 2 Bilder, Basel 26 Apr 1970
vocal soloists/ensembles to be pre-recorded on tape, 3 loudspeaker groups on stage and in the auditorium

1971 EXPERIMENTALSTUDIO DES SWR FREIBURG

Béjart: *Chant du compagnon errant*, Ballet, Brussels 11 Mar 1971
music from tape (Mahler)

Kagel: *Staatstheater*, Szenische Komposition, Hamburg 25 Apr 1971
9 compositions featuring all kinds of sound sources

Henze: *Der langwierige Weg in die Wohnung der Natascha Ungeheuer*, Show, 17, Rome 17 May 1971
chamber orchestra incl. stereo tape

Alberto Ginastera: *Beatrix Cenci*, Opera, 2, Washington, DC 10 Sep 1971
films and projections

Béjart, Henry: *Nijinsky, Clown de Dieu*, Ballet-soirée, 2, Brussels 8 Oct 1971
music from tape (Henry, Tchaikovsky)

Josef Tal: *Ashmedai*, Opera, 2, Hamburg 9 Nov 1971
blends electronic and orchestral music, five-minute overture contains electronic music only

1972

Flemming Flindt, Thomas Koppel: *Dødens triumf*, Dansedrama, Copenhagen 23 May 1972
tape music (composed collage)

Maja Michailowna Plissezkaja, Rodion Schtschedrin: *Anna Karenina*, Ballet, 3, Moscow 10 June 1972
im III. Akt ein Bellini-Duett vom Tonband

Béjart, Karlheinz Stockhausen: *Stimmung*, Ballet, Brussels 19 Dec 1972
microphones, loudspeakers, tape (*Stimmung für 6 Vokalisten*, 1968)

1973

Maderna: *Satyricon*, Oper, 1, Scheveningen 16 Mar 1973
taped numbers (electronic collages) between the 16 sections

1974

Dessau: *Einstein*, Oper, 3, Berlin 16 Feb 1974
choir from tape

Pascal Bentoiu: *Hamlet*, Opera, 1, Bukarest 19 Nov 1971 (concert), Marseille 26 Apr 1974 (stage)
electronic tape effects (for ghost appearance)

Thea Musgrave: *The Voice of Ariadne*, Chamber opera, 3, Snape, Suffolk, 11 June 1974
Ariadne's voice pre-recorded on tape

Jiří Kylián: *The Odd One*, Ballet, Amsterdam 18 Jul 1974
music from tape (Nordheim, *Solitaire*, 1968)

Robert North, Joan Kelietio, Bob Downes: *Troy Game*, Dance piece, Liverpool 3 Oct 1974
music from tape (Brazilian street music)

Glen Tetley, Henze: *Tristan*, Ballet, Paris 13 Nov 1974
electronic tape sounds in the orchestra

1975

Nono: *Al gran sole carico d'amore*, azione scenica in due tempi, 1st version Milan 4 Apr 1975
extensive use of tape

Manzoni: *Per Massimiliano Robespierre*, Scene musicali, 2, Bologna 17 Apr 1975
tape music in the orchestra and on stage; speaking voices with and without electronic amplification

124   *Andreas Münzmay*

Volker David Kirchner: *Die Trauung*, Oper, 3, Wiesbaden 27 Apr 1975
organ from tape

Béjart: *Notre Faust*, Ballet-comédie, 2, Brussels 12 Dec 1975
tape (Bach, Schaeffer/Henry, Warren, Al Dubin, Argentine tangos)

References

Bayerische Akademie der schönen Künste (ed.) (1956), *Die Künste im technischen Zeitalter*, Munich: Oldenbourg.

Blomdahl, Karl-Birger (1959), *Aniara. Eine Revue vom Menschen in Zeit und Raum / En revy om människen i tid och rum*, piano-vocal score by Alexander Goehr, Mainz: Schott.

Brech, Martha (2015), *Der hörbare Raum: Entdeckung, Erforschung und musikalische Gestaltung mit analoger Technologie*, Bielefeld: Transcript.

Cage, John (1961), 'Composition as process', in *Silence: Lectures and Writings*, Hanover/ NH: Wesleyan University Press, pp. 18–56.

Carlos, Wendy (2008), 'Vintage technologies: the Eltro and the voice of HAL', www.wendycarlos.com/other/Eltro-1967/ (accessed 17 May 2018).

Casadei, Delia (2014), 'Orality, invisibility, and laughter: traces of Milan in Bruno Maderna and Virginio Puecher's *Hyperion* (1964)', *Opera Quarterly*, 30/1, pp. 105–34.

Dahlhaus, Carl and Forschungsinstitut für Musiktheater der Universität Bayreuth (eds) (1986–97), *Pipers Enzyklopädie des Musiktheaters*, 7 vols., Munich: Piper.

Delhaye, Cyrille (2012), ''Orphée 53' de Pierre Schaeffer et Pierre Henry, aux origines du scandale de Donaueschingen', *Revue de musicology*, 98/1, pp. 171–91.

Flusser, Vilém (1963), *Lingua e Realidade*, São Paulo: Herder.

Fox, Barbara (2005), 'Schaeffer stands his ground: Orfée 53 and evocative sound', *EMS05 – Sound in Multimedia Contexts*, EMS Network, www.ems-network.org/IMG/EMS2005-Fox.pdf (accessed 17 May 2018).

Groth, Sanne Krogh (2014), *Politics and Aesthetics in Electronic Music. A Study of EMS – Elektronmusikstudion, Stockholm, 1964–1979*, Heidelberg: Kehrer.

Hanke, Michael (2006), 'Vilém Flussers *Sprache und Wirklichkeit* von 1963 im Kontext seiner Medienphilosophie', *Flusser Studies* 2, www.flusserstudies.net/archive/flusserstudies-02-may-2006 (accessed 17 May 2018).

Haubenstock-Ramati, Roman (1970), *Amerika: eine Oper in zwei Teilen*, score, Vienna: Universal Edition.

Heidegger, Martin (1956), 'Die Frage nach der Technik', in Bayerische Akademie der schönen Künste (ed.), *Die Künste im technischen Zeitalter*, Munich: Oldenbourg, pp. 48–72.

Heile, Björn (2016), 'Toward a theory of experimental music theatre: 'showing-doing,' 'non-matrixed performance,' and 'metaxis'', in Yael Kaduri (ed.), *The Oxford Handbook of Sound and Image in Western Art*, New York: Oxford University Press, pp. 335 55.

Heister, Werner (2002), 'Medialisierung', in Siegfried Mauser (ed.), *Musiktheater im 20. Jahrhundert*, Laaber: Laaber, pp. 413–29.

Hiekel, Jörn-Peter (2004), ''Pluralistisches' Musiktheater als Ausdruck der Katastrophe – Bernd Alois Zimmermanns Oper *Die Soldaten*', in Frieder Reininghaus and Katja Schneider (eds), *Experimentelles Musik- und Tanztheater*, Laaber: Laaber, pp. 140–3.

Manzoni, Giacomo (1964), *Atomtod, due tempi di Emilio Jona*, score, Milan: Edizioni Suvini Zerboni.

Composing new media 125

McLuhan, Marshall (1962), *The Gutenberg Galaxy: The Making of Typographic Man*, London: Routledge & Kegan Paul.

McLuhan, Marshall (1964), *Understanding Media: The Extensions of Man*, New York: McGraw-Hill.

Meyer-Eppler, Werner (1949), *Elektrische Klangerzeugung: Elektronische Musik und synthetische Sprache*, Bonn: Dümmler.

Noller, Joachim (1999), 'Nono zwischen alter und neuer Avantgarde', in Gianmario Borio, Giovanni Morelli and Veniero Rizzardi (eds), *La nuova ricerca sull'opera di Luigi Nono*, Florence: Olschki, pp. 105–8.

Nono, Luigi (1962), *Intolleranza. Handlung in zwei Teilen nach einer Idee von Angelo Maria Ripellino. Deutsche Übertragung von Alfred Andersch*, score, Mainz: Schott.

Preetorius, Emil (1956), 'Die Bildkunst', in Bayerische Akademie der schönen Künste (ed.), *Die Künste im technischen Zeitalter*, Munich: Oldenbourg, p. 81.

Prieberg, Fred K. (1960), *Musica ex machina. Über das Verhältnis von Musik und Technik*, Berlin: Ullstein.

Radkau, Joachim (2017), *Geschichte der Zukunft. Prognosen, Visionen, Irrungen in Deutschland von 1945 bis heute*, Munich: Carl Hanser.

Reininghaus, Frieder and Katja Schneider (eds) (2004), *Experimentelles Musik- und Tanztheater*, Laaber: Laaber-Verlag.

Ripellino, Angelo Maria (1990), *Poesie 1952–1978*, Turin: Einaudi.

Robert, Martial (2000), *Pierre Schaeffer: d'Orphée à MacLuhan. Communication et musique en France entre 1936 et 1986*, Paris: L'Harmattan.

Rossellini, Renzo (1956), *La guerra. Dramma in un atto*, Riduzione per Canto e Pianoforte, Milan: Ricordi.

Rucker, August (1956), 'Begrüssungsworte', in Bayerische Akademie der schönen Künste (ed.) (1956), *Die Künste im technischen Zeitalter*, Munich: Oldenbourg, p. 7.

Sadie, Stanley, ed. (1992–98), *The New Grove Dictionary of Opera*, 4 vols., London: Macmillan.

Schneider, Katja (2004), 'Zur Selbstverständlichkeit wurde, daß nichts mehr selbstverständlich ist', in Frieder Reininghaus and Katja Schneider (eds), *Experimentelles Musik- und Tanztheater*, Laaber: Laaber, pp. 11–15.

Spohr, Mathias (1994), 'Rosselini: La guerra (1956)', in Carl Dahlhaus and Forschungsinstitut für Musiktheater der Universität Bayreuth (eds), *Pipers Enzyklopädie des Musiktheaters*, vol. 5, Munich: Piper, pp. 343–4.

Stenzl, Jürg (1989), 'Manzoni: Atomtod (1965)', in Carl Dahlhaus and Forschungsinstitut für Musiktheater der Universität Bayreuth (eds), *Pipers Enzyklopädie des Musiktheaters*, vol. 3, Munich: Piper, pp. 660–1.

Weibel, Peter (2016), 'Radio Art', in *Musik und Medien: Vom Klang im technischen Zeitalter: Ausgewählte Schriften von Peter Weibel*, Berlin: Hatje Cantz, pp. 171–8; English version as 'Preface', in Sanne Krogh Groth (2014) *Politics and Aesthetics in Electronic Music. A Study of EMS – Elektronmusikstudion, Stockholm, 1964–1979*, Heidelberg: Kehrer, pp. 8–15.

Part III

The critique of established power

6 Guerrilla in the polder
Music-theatrical protests in the Low Countries, 1968–1969

Harm Langenkamp

'It was a firm "no" against the bastards, emerging from the firm "yes" for which we stood.' Thus Harry Mulisch, one of the foremost writers of Dutch post-war literature, remembered his involvement in what had been the *cause célèbre* of the 1969 Holland Festival: *Reconstructie* (Reconstruction), a large-scale music-theatrical work concocted by a collective of two writers (besides Mulisch his Flemish counterpart, Hugo Claus) and five composers (Peter Schat, Louis Andriessen, Reinbert de Leeuw, Misha Mengelberg, and Jan van Vlijmen), all of whom had been bound by their antagonism towards institutionalised power – 'the bastards'.[1] As imaginative as this work was in both its conception and execution, the message it was meant to convey did not leave much to the imagination: facing an eleven-metre statue of Che Guevara substituting for the Stone Guest in a plot that identified Don Juan's sins with the crimes of imperialism, the audience – albeit with a chuckle – was sent away with the exhortation to reflect on their complicity in the exploitation of Latin America by condoning their government's docility to the United States. That a President Nixon-aligned newspaper urged the Dutch government to dismantle this state-subsidised production for stereotyping Americans as 'cigar-smoking exploiters with money-bulging pockets' filled the 'conspirators' with joy.[2]

In *Reconstructie*, a variety of tensions in Dutch (and, by extension, Flemish) society converged, tensions that two years earlier the cultural journal *De Gids* had tried to capture in the word *onbehagen* – a word that embraces meanings such as 'displeasure', 'dissatisfaction' and 'discomfort'. The irony of applying this unpretentious word to such profound topics as the Vietnam War, the welfare gap and the position of women in a 'nuclear technocracy' expressed the scorn of *De Gids*' editors for the perceived pettiness of those who seemed to content themselves with living their lives in their own denominational and ideological *zuilen* ('pillars'), limiting their contacts with the outside world to whatever was necessary to ensure peaceful coexistence (Van Dam, Turpijn and Mellink (eds) 2014).

---

1 Mulisch, cited in Tom Rooduijn, *Haagse Post*, 20 December 1986: 105.
2 The *Washington Star* editorial cited in *De Volkskrant*, 5 July 1969; Schat in a televised interview with Ischa Meijer, *Oog in Oog*, broadcast by the NOS on 25 May 1989.

130   *Harm Langenkamp*

For the authors of *Reconstructie*, this myopic mentality was insufferable. Theirs was a world begging for emancipation, secularisation, democratisation, decolonisation, denuclearisation, de-bureaucratisation, de-alienation – global processes that required each Dutch and Flemish civilian to get from behind the dykes, assume responsibility, empower the imagination and mull over – as *De Gids* did – the meaning of Che Guevara's legacy.[3]

This is what Mulisch, Claus and Schat imagined themselves doing when they – together with another handful of Western European invitees (including from Italy Luigi Nono and from West Germany Hans Magnus Enzensberger and, by proxy, Hans Werner Henze) – answered the call of the Cuban government to participate in the Cultural Congress of Havana.[4] Held from 4–11 January 1968, this meeting convened numerous 'intellectual workers' from Latin America, the United States, Europe, Africa and Asia to discuss the challenges and chances of revolutionary movements who had claimed, or were in the process of claiming, their independence from capitalist-driven hegemony (see Silber (ed.) 1970: 313–21). For the anti-communist Organization of American States, this assembly indicated a reorientation of tactics that, after the failure of rural guerrilla warfare on which Fidel Castro had insisted (in defiance of Moscow) now sought to mobilise urban elites to 'overthrow established governments' through 'ideological penetration and violence' (Organization of American States 1968: 27–8). To the Dutch-speaking invitees, however, the Congress' united expression of solidarity with Vietnam and denunciation of what Castro consistently called 'Yankee imperialism' demonstrated a level of resistance that they feared would never be attained at home. After all, by early 1968, with the Dutch anarchist Provo movement being dissolved, and with Schat and Claus facing prosecution for having challenged bourgeois mores, little was left to sustain faith in a significant alteration of the social power constellation in the Low Countries.[5]

In Cuba, however, their hopes regained new vigour. If the revolution both at home and in the Soviet Union had turned into a petrified reality, Cuba witnessed the birth of a new 'integral man', a man endowed with an independent mind, a creative imagination, a will to act, and a sense of responsibility for keeping the revolution in a river-like state of continuous change (Mulisch 1968: 23–6, 222–6). Indeed, Claus enthused upon his return to Belgium, 'we have all discovered [in Cuba] a completely new society – a far cry from what we can imagine [in Europe or the Communist bloc]'.[6] Impressed by the 'extraordinarily sympathetic Cubans who are engaged in a unique political experiment',

---

3 'There is no science of the future. Nevertheless, now one Guevara has been killed, the rise of many others is to be anticipated, as manifestations of the powerful legend Che has created.' Anton Constandse, *De Gids*, 130/2 (1967): 281.

4 Henze did not attend the congress, but was kept informed by Enzensberger, on whose intercession Henze obtained an official invitation to visit Cuba the next year.

5 Schat was prosecuted for having sheltered the Provo's press centre in his basement, from where cartoons of the Dutch Queen as a prostitute and a policeman as a fascist had been printed. Claus had to defend himself for having represented the Holy Trinity in the nude in his play *Masscheroen*.

6 Claus, cited in Roger H. Schoemans, *Zondagmorgen*, 2 February 1968: 4.

Guerrilla in the polder   131

and undeniably dazzled by the lush cultural, culinary and exotic experiences with which Castro's regime had feted them, Mulisch and Schat immediately established upon their return a solidarity committee to challenge 'the strangling blockade' by which the United States had driven the 'research laboratory of the revolution' into the arms of the Soviet Union.[7] Castro's defence of Moscow's suppression of the Prague insurrection later that year would barely, if at all, affect their infatuation with what appeared to them nothing short of an insular paradise in an otherwise depraved world.[8]

Artistically, the cultural activity in Havana as well as the advanced state of the arts exceeded the expectations of the Western European attendants, as did the freedom that Cuba's 'creative workers' seemed to enjoy regarding the forms in which to express their revolutionary zeal (Mulisch 1968: 43–5). Their multiple reports to the home front effuse about how the Havanese soundscape was graced by electronic music that according to Schat and Nono could compete with international standards.[9] Indeed, the Cuban leadership, following its then recently assassinated cultural ideologue Ernesto Che Guevara, who in 1965 had raised the question of why one would avoid 'true artistic experimentation' and 'strait-jacket artistic expression [in] the frozen forms of socialist realism', prided itself on having married 'the concepts of liberty and artistic expression' to 'the concept of the revolutionary duty of writers and artists' without resorting to the kind of dogmatism that Andrei Zhdanov's revolutionary poetics had imposed two decades earlier (Dorticós 1967: 36–7; Guevara 2003 [1965]: 222–4). In this double resistance towards both 'bourgeois decadence' and 'Soviet staleness', Claus, Mulisch and Schat recognised the guerrilla tactics as theorised and practised by Guevara, a tactics of continuously disorienting the enemy and refusing to submit to his terms of confrontation. Under the sun of Havana, they played with the idea of exporting the guerrilla to their home countries, meaning that they would turn the resources of the capitalist system in which they worked and lived ('the foliage of subsidies', in Schat's words) against itself.[10]

The opportunity to translate theory into practice availed itself even before they had returned home, where an invitation was waiting for them from Maurice Huisman, intendant of both the Royal Theatre of the Mint in Brussels and the Amsterdam-based Dutch Opera Foundation. Huisman requested an evening-filling music-theatrical work, to be staged during the Holland Festival, that would cover – 'in a positive tone' – 'the evolution of, and the revolution in,

---

7 Cited from Mulisch's notes about the Havana Congress and a pamphlet of the Comité van Solidariteit met Cuba [Committee of Solidary with Cuba], 1968, Mulisch Papers, folders 199.11 and 331.3, Museum of Literature, The Hague.

8 Mulisch surmised that Castro, while agreeing with Moscow that Alexander Dubček's reforms were unacceptable concessions to Western ideals, actually considered the Soviet intervention a judicial error. Mulisch, cited in Lidy van Marissing, *De Volkskrant*, 1 October 1968.

9 Claus, cited in Lidy Marissing, *De Volkskrant*, 8 February 1968; Schat, cited in K. L. Poll, *Algemeen Handelsblad*, 25 May 1968; Mulisch 1968: 43.

10 Schat, cited in K. L. Poll, *Algemeen Handelsblad*, 25 May 1968.

132   *Harm Langenkamp*

human relations'.[11] It was Huisman who not only proposed a collaborative effort beyond the usual librettist/composer duo – an initiative of 'stunning progressiveness', according to Mulisch – but also included the name of Guevara in his topical suggestions.[12] Such daring decisions, by which Huisman reclaimed an international position for the Brussels Mint Theatre, had undoubtedly advanced his appointment at the newly established Dutch Opera Foundation, a relaunch of its precursor that in mid-1964, after a crisis-ridden period, had been dissolved. One of Huisman's first decisions on taking up the Dutch role was to pursue the staging of Schat's first music theatre work *Labyrint* (1963–66), which had stalled when Peter Diamand, then-director of the Holland Festival, under whose auspices the work was to premiere, retracted his support on the basis of prohibitive costs.[13] In the months leading up to *Labyrint*'s premiere, the conductor of this production, Bruno Maderna, became the subject of a (failed) campaign launched by Schat and his brothers-in-arms, who insisted on him being appointed as permanent conductor for contemporary music at the Concertgebouw Orchestra alongside Bernard Haitink, who self-admittedly had little affinity with the experimental repertory.[14] In other words, Huisman knew what to expect when he commissioned the Maderna campaigners. In fact, in between *Labyrint* and *Reconstructie*, he sought Maderna's cooperation for another potentially seditious project to be premiered in May 1968 at the Brussels Mint Theatre: the setting of Claus's *Morituri*, a 'grotesque cantata' about a future dominated by computerised warfare, over which the shadow of Vietnam loomed large.[15]

This chapter assesses Huisman's commissions – *Hyperion en het geweld* (Hyperion and the Violence), as Maderna's setting of *Morituri* was titled, and the 'morality play' *Reconstructie* – in relation to their intended political effect: anti-establishment opposition. As barely veiled criticisms on US imperialism in Vietnam and Cuba respectively, these works were not direct attacks on the establishment at home. Yet, by being sponsored through national subsidy programmes, they put the strongly NATO-aligned governments of Belgium and the Netherlands in the delicate position of indirectly sponsoring criticism addressed at their foremost ally from across the Atlantic. The *Hyperion* production was too small to be a serious matter of concern in this regard, but, as will be shown, controversies

---

11 Huisman to Schat, Andriessen, De Leeuw, Van Vlijmen and Mengelberg, 17 January 1968, Schat Papers, box 5016, folder 40, Netherlands Music Institute, The Hague; Huisman to Mulisch, 17 January 1968, Mulisch Papers, folder 86.6.

12 Huisman initially requested from Schat a trilogy about 'people who venture beyond the world', including Che Guevara, an astronaut, and either Rimbaud or Gandhi; see *Reconstructie* team, cited in Wim Boswinkel, *Algemeen Handelsblad*, 21 September 1968; Mulisch 1979: 39.

13 Diamand to Schat, 4 June 1964, Schat Papers, box 5012, folder 336/12.

14 De Leeuw, Andriessen, Mengelberg, Schat and Van Vlijmen, open letter to the Concertgebouw Orchestra Foundation, *Algemeen Handelsblad*, 16 March 1966. Haitink's remark is paraphrased from a press conference, *Algemeen Handelsblad*, 19 September 1964. For a discussion of this campaign, see Adlington 2013: 58–96.

15 Cited from the manuscript's title page. Claus Papers, House of Literature, Antwerp.

surrounding *Reconstructie* drew the attention of the American press and compelled the Minister of Culture to account for her subsidy policy. The discussion of *Reconstructie*, which has obtained an iconic status in Dutch-Flemish cultural history and has been studied in detail (Adlington 2007; Van Putten 2015), focuses on what turns out to be a complex reciprocal relationship between the 'establishment' and its dissenters. The Claus/Maderna production, on the other hand, has been little discussed, perhaps because of its overwhelmingly negative reception. Hitherto untapped archival sources and reviews shed light on the reasons why this collaboration fell through, and why the Brussels *Hyperion* failed to make a splash in the way that *Reconstructie* did in Amsterdam.

Hyperion in Brussels: divergent visions of artistic engagement

A 'grandiose fiasco', a 'still-born protest', a 'disillusion', a 'total failure', 'childish kitsch', a 'comatose experience of ennui', a 'misunderstanding'.[16] The almost unanimous verdict of both the Dutch- and French-language press was harsh on what had been promoted as the high point of the 1968 edition of the 'Nederlandse Dagen' (Dutch Days) festival, an initiative by the Flemish Kunst- en Cultuurverbond (Art and Cultural League) to promote Dutch-language culture in French-dominated Brussels. The target of the verdict was *Hyperion en het geweld*, the fruit of a collaboration between Bruno Maderna and Hugo Claus. Actually, 'collaboration' is not the appropriate word: in 1966, Claus received Huisman's commission to write a libretto that was to appeal 'to all means of expression of contemporary theatre', and more than a year later Maderna was asked to set it on music.[17] At the gala premiere in Brussels on 17 May 1968, however, Claus stubbornly refused to participate in the curtain call. As he explained at an improvised press conference in the theatre's lobby, so much of his text had been omitted and adapted that he fully distanced himself from the work.[18] By way of protest, he published the libretto as he had intended it, under the title he had assigned to the work: *Morituri* – Latin for 'those who are about to die' (Claus 1968).

The collaboration between Maderna and Claus was arguably set up for failure from the very beginning, if only because composer and librettist barely found

---

16 Fernand Papon, *De Nieuwe Gazet*, 29 May 1968; Roger Hofmans, *De Nieuwe Gids/De Spectator*, 25 May 1968; Paul Van Crombruggen, *Het Volk*, 23 May 1968; Figaro, *'t Pallieterke*, 25 May 1968; *Haagsche Courant*, 18 May 1968; M.V., *La Dernière Heure*, 20 May 1968; G.M., *Pourquoi Pas*, 23 May 1968; *L'Écho de la Bourse*, 23–24 May 1968. Clipping file in the Archives of the Royal Mint Theatre, Brussels.

17 Explanation of the opera's genesis in the programme booklet. Archives of the Royal Mint Theatre, Brussels. Initially it had been intended that the Belgian composer Frédéric Devreese would write the music for *Morituri*. Devreese does not recall the exact reasons why the collaboration failed to materialise, but he thinks it was related to Mendel's preference for Maderna; correspondence with the author, 29 May 2018. This explains why an Italian composer came to write an opera for a festival that was supposed to promote Flemish artists – a sensitive point that some critics at the time could not resist highlighting; see Lex van Delden, *Het Parool*, 18 May 1968; Paul Van Crombruggen, *Het Volk*, 23 May 1968.

18 Eugène Eberle, *Algemeen Dagblad*, 26 May 1968.

134   *Harm Langenkamp*

an opportunity to confer about the project due to Maderna's tight schedule of conducting and teaching engagements.[19] The most important reason for their faltering artistic partnership, however, was a fundamental disagreement about the work's overall conception and purpose, which touched on diverging visions on what political commitment in the arts entails. At the time he received the libretto commission, Claus, whose work had always been driven by a belief that 'the immediate reality – inherently political as it is – cannot be obviated by writing about eternal values', was seeking new forms of political engagement that could have a greater social impact (Claus, cited in Auwera 1969: 87). While his more than twenty works in the fields of poetry, novel writing and theatre since his 1947 debut had centred around the 'intimate psychological stirrings' resulting from social pressures, now he sought to shift his focus to what he described as the 'public aspect of humankind'.[20] His so-called *spreekgedichten*, for instance, comprised a type of 'public poem' in which audiences were directly addressed about the social-political controversies of the time, such as NATO's involvement in the Vietnam War and nuclear development programmes, the Belgian government's support for Congolese dictator Mobutu's second *coup d'état*, or the increasing number of instances of censorship to which Claus himself was subjected.

Maderna's understanding of artistic engagement, on the other hand, seemed to have been on a different wavelength from Claus's. Although in the early post-war years, the Cold War-inspired marginalisation of the Communists and Socialists from Italian public life and the appeal of Antonio Gramsci's model of socialism had made him and Nono decide to join the Italian Communist Party (PCI), the brutal suppression of the 1956 Hungarian uprising deprived Maderna (in contrast to Nono) of any confidence in the Party's ability to realise its pre-war promises of social liberation (see Boehmer 2007: 345). Initially, this divergence with Nono did not interfere with their mutual admiration for the synthesis of compositional innovation and socialist engagement as demonstrated by Hermann Scherchen, which came to be sealed in their collaboration (Nono as composer, Maderna as conductor) on *Intolleranza 1960* (Nielinger-Vakil 2015: 10). Yet, the subsequent intensification of Nono's political activism alienated him from Maderna, and culminated in a serious break in 1965 when Nono accused him of 'having been integrated into capitalist society' – this after Maderna had stepped in for Nono, who was denied entry to the United States, to conduct *Intolleranza* at the Boston Opera.[21] As he later explained, Maderna wished Nono to have taken up the social struggle more as a musician rather than as a politician, explaining that effective anti-establishment opposition requires 'more diligence, subtlety and precision'.[22]

---

19 The Maderna Collection held by the Paul Sacher Foundation contains merely three short undated letters by Claus, one of which refers to a work appointment at the Kurhaus in Scheveningen that Maderna apparently had to cancel.

20 Claus, cited in Roland Van Opbroecke, brochure *Derde Programma* of the Belgian Radio and Television Broadcasting Organisation, 3 December 1966.

21 Christina Maderna in the documentary *Terug naar Maderna* by Hans Heg and René van Gijn, broadcast by the NOS on 9 November 1983.

22 Maderna in *Terug naar Maderna*.

Rather than conceiving committed art in terms of Sartrean moral appeals – as Nono did, for instance, in *A floresta é jovem e cheja de via* (1966), *Non consumiamo Marx* (1969), and *Y entonces comprendió* (1970) – Maderna sought to express 'the problem of humans who always try to merge in a community without taking into account that a community cannot exist without a model of individuality'. This was a search for eternal humanistic values from which both Nono and Claus had veered away.[23]

With hindsight, this divergence in Claus and Maderna's artistic aspirations set their collaboration up for failure. At the time, however, there seemed to be sufficient points of congruency for Huisman to assume the potential of a success. When Huisman drew his attention to Claus's libretto, Maderna had been looking out for a 'text of protest' – not 'a strict political protest' but rather 'a cry of revolt [*un cri de révolte chargé d'humanité*]'. In Claus's libretto, he perceived an echo of Friedrich Hölderlin's *Hyperion*, which had intrigued him since the beginning of the 1960s, especially in its 'protest against the degrading and dehumanizing aspects of contemporary life'.[24] Claus, too, was seeking to address contemporary abuses in a way that would extend beyond the political pamphlet and be 'harmonically integrated in the structure of my work'. As he explained, if one does not wish to keep 'muddling in a complacent reactionary art', regardless of how disapproving it is with respect to the object of criticism (such as the Vietnam War), 'the technique of the revolution has to be technically processed into the text as well' (Claus, in Auwera 1969: 90–1). Consequently, Claus, who early on in his career had been fascinated by Antonin Artaud's 'theatre of cruelty', conveyed the anti-war message of his libretto through a staccato and grotesque language that defies identification with anyone from the cast. Situated in a sterile, science fiction-like universe, the action focuses on a 'military unit of the repressive forces', spending their night 'lost in the hostile jungle surrounded by the invisible army of the repressed' (Claus 1968). Enclosed in a plastic dome furnished with a juke box, pinball machine, vending automats, pin-ups and a myriad of screens that show both surveillance images and comic cartoons, the stranded soldiers are assured by their lieutenant of their safety as their computers conduct a 'lawful artillery operation' in retaliation for the enemy's 'treacherous' breach of 'a sacred four-hour truce'. Yet, while being sedated into a one-hour sleep to 'refresh the mind and ease conscience', the enemy ambushes their station and brings them all to their bloody end, leaving a silence that is broken by a female figure's recitation of a Hölderlin fragment about the 'song of union' that can be heard from the 'dissonances of the world'. When the sun rises, the massacred all reappear as mummified versions of themselves, acting in the same 'mechanical manner' as before their death.

From an interview with Claus, it appears that Maderna had asked for the dense dystopian action to be broken with 'somewhat more elegiacal moments

---

23 Maderna, cited in programme booklet of the production of *Hyperion* by The Dutch Opera, 19–20 December 1991.

24 Maderna, cited in M.C., *Beaux Arts*, 18 May 1968.

136 *Harm Langenkamp*

that provide some hope'.[25] Maderna may have found *Morituri*'s theatrical reality too moored in the reality of the day. Although meant as a universal indictment of 'the pointless and immoral actions of liberators and reformers of other peoples' countries', *Morituri*'s references to 'napalm', 'M. 79 bombshells' and 'Telstar satellites' obviously evoke the Vietnam War, whilst references to Popeye, Superman, Donald Duck, Buffalo Bill, King Kong, Lucky Luke, pin-ups, chewing gum, Elizabeth Taylor and frozen turkeys do not fail to identify the repressive faction.[26] Nevertheless, *Morituri*'s hypermodern, claustrophobic and hallucinatory reality resonated with the reality Maderna sought to convey in his open-ended exploration of human experience for which Hölderlin's epistolary novel provided the point of departure (for full discussions of Maderna's *Hyperion* projects see Fearn 1990, Ferrari 2007 and Wetters 2012). In its first manifestation, presented in a staging by Virginio Puecher at the 1964 Venice Biennale, Maderna's *Hyperion* centred on the struggle of the protagonist (interpreted by flutist Severino Gazzelloni) against the forces that frustrate his attempts at meaningful communication, including the orchestra that challenges him into a Goliathian trial of strength, and a 'whorish machine' that strangles him in an uncanny soundscape of electronically manipulated vocal utterances. At the moment he tentatively recaptures himself, he finds himself upstaged by a lone woman (interpreted by Catherine Gayer) who succeeds in what he had been trying all along: giving voice to Hyperion's agonising confession of his alienation from nature and society (see Casadei 2014).

In accepting the commission to set Claus's text, Maderna may have been particularly attracted by the anonymous female character, who outside of the dome comments on the suffering wrought by the violence of war – a dramatic moment which he probably envisioned to cast as a turning point, similar to the appearance of the female figure in *Hyperion*'s 1964 version. If the role of the woman in Claus's libretto was limited to a few minutes, in Maderna's adaptation she came to dominate the second half of the performance.[27] Initially, Claus confirmed his approval of the modifications that Maderna suggested for his libretto, conceding that they had opened his eyes for the 'more universal [rather than confrontational] touch they gave to our work'.[28] Eventually, though, he came to feel that Maderna had made off with his contribution. As he explained at the time, not only had Maderna enforced various alterations, including a change of the title into *Hyperion en het geweld*, but his libretto had also been interpolated with poems by W. H. Auden and Federico García Lorca, without his foreknowledge.[29] Claus's libretto had been

---

25 Claus, cited in Ben Dull, *Het Parool*, 28 February 1968.
26 References to the United States were even more numerous in the libretto's manuscript version. The original name of Padre Jan, the chaplain who justified, in Christ's name, 'the crushing of the vermin that choses to live without Him', was Bill Donovan – perhaps a reference to William J. Donovan, the founding father of the Central Intelligence Agency.
27 Maderna dramatised this conflict by splitting the vocal part in two: a soprano (Liliana Poli) onstage, a mezzo soprano (Jeanne Chanoine) offstage; see *Het Volk*, 20 May 1968.
28 Claus, cited in *France-Soir*, 12–13 May 1968.
29 Anonymous correspondent from Brussels, *Nieuwsblad van het Noorden*, 21 May 1968.

Guerrilla in the polder 137

polytextual as well, including alongside the Hölderlin fragment two excerpts from Karl Frenzel's memoirs of the revolutionaries who perished in the 1848 Berlin uprising, and an unidentified Vietnamese poem from the time of the Korean War. Maderna, however, substituted these texts for Lorca's 'Y después' (And After), a mantra on the passing of time, love and life ('Only desert remains'), and W. H. Auden's 'Ode VI', which begins with the verse: 'Not, Father, further do prolong / Our necessary defeat / Spare us the numbing zero-hour, / The desert-long retreat.' Maderna's choice was obviously inspired by the desert metaphor linking Lorca's and Auden's poems to Hölderlin's *Thalia-Fragment* sung by the female character ('The past lay stretched out behind me like a terrible desert without end . . .'). For Claus, however, such meditations on defeatist resignation – the first with respect to the failure of anarchic resistance during the Spanish Civil War, the second to liberalism's failure in the face of Fascism – must have been unacceptable given the course of activism and blasphemy he had embarked upon. Such differences are arguably emblematic of Maderna and Claus's fundamental disagreement over the purpose of their project: Claus envisioned a work with political repercussion, urging audiences to crusade against what he considered the hypocrisy of NATO liberation missions;[30] Maderna a philosophical contemplation on the modern *condition humaine*, of man's feeble attempts at standing up against what Herbert Marcuse called the 'affluent society' (1991 [1964]: 9).

Another reason for Claus to distance himself from Huisman's commission was his discontent with both the acting, directed by Deryk Mendel, and the staging, designed by Joëlle Roustan and Roger Bernard.[31] Critics were no less disenchanted. For most of the unbroken ninety minutes of the work, the audience looked at a green-greyish lighted stage marked by pillars of irregular length that were 'more reminiscent of Manhattan than a jungle', among which twenty-one so-called 'super soldiers', dressed in plasticised outfits and prodded by the sense-dulling commands of their fascist superiors, endlessly executed marching sequences and aggressively declared their superiority and disdain for the people they were about to liberate (see Figure 6.1).[32] As the opera begins, spectators witnessed a glaring sun projected on a vast circular screen backdrop, followed by a cartoon sequence of the spinach-eating Popeye the Sailorman fighting off a flock of bombers – for some critics the only worthwhile moment of the whole evening.[33] For the nightmare scene, Mendel intensified the multisensorial experience by combining surrealistic projections of monstrous childhood creatures, insects, rats, comic heroes, and robots with specially fabricated stink bombs that simulated the smell of burned flesh.[34] As the ear-deafening violence comes to a halt, the spectator is left with the sight of a few moaning soldiers slipping over

---

30 Claus initially intended to title the libretto *De kruistocht* [The Crusade]. See manuscript in the Claus Papers.
31 Anonymous correspondent from Brussels, *Nieuwsblad van het Noorden*, 21 May 1968.
32 *A.B.C. Antwerpen*, 15 June 1968.
33 Georges Sion, *Beaux Arts*, 25 May 1968; Jacques Stehman, *Le Soir*, 20 May 1968.
34 *Het Vrije Volk*, 20 May 1968.

Figure 6.1 Soldiers taking orders from their captain. Action scene from *Hyperion en het Geweld*, 17 May 1968. Photo: Oscar Vanden Brugge, the Royal Theatre of the Mint, Brussels.

Guerrilla in the polder   139

their own blood – impressive for some spectators, provoking laughs for others.[35] (See Appendix for more details about the staging and music.)

Exceptions aside, the general critical consensus was that the work was too fragmented, the action too static, and the music too incoherent. Some thought Maderna had made things easy for himself by recycling material from previous works, others considered it inappropriate to qualify it as 'music theatre', let alone 'avant-garde theatre', and nearly all predicted its short-lived future.[36] Even the few who were more appreciative of distinct elements of the work had to conclude that as a whole, *Hyperion en het geweld* figured as an 'abnormal hybrid' that would 'disappear with the actuality of the inspiration, like so many operas written during the French Revolution'.[37] Particularly, Maderna's idea to provide Claus's apocalyptic world with 'a counterpoint by a noble song about love and fraternity'[38] failed to convince. The lyrical intermezzo was definitely the most appreciated element of the performance, but almost all critics complained about the lack of its dramatic motivation and its inability to transcend all the preceding violence. In conclusion, as a contribution to Dutch-language opera – the underlying objective of Huisman's commission – *Hyperion en het geweld* had turned into 'a gross fiasco which French-language Brussels still gloats over'.[39]

Some not only declared the work a failure as an opera, but also as a form of protest theatre. Many critics expressed their annoyance with the Nazi-modelled infantry and its vociferous superiors, 'an abuse of a facile device that has become trite in today's theatre'.[40] 'Everything was so totally sterilised', one critic wrote, that it became somewhat 'sexless, neutral – the sphere of a refrigerator.'[41] 'Not for one moment are spectators physically involved in the action', leaving them indifferent.[42] Indeed, 'the efficiency of protest', another critic lectured, depends on its ability to

> crystallise our human complacency and prejudice in characters that can move us as individuals. Haphazard protest without focus is like a television message without listeners: everyone will turn down the volume, and the speaker will turn into an anonymous doll whose incomprehensible mime will affect us as much as the movements of a robot.[43]

As was to be expected, the right-wing press deplored the inclination of 'even our most intelligent and talented artists of today to conform to a mode that considers

---

35 Reinhard Beuth, 'Vietnam, Artaud und die Oper: Zur Uraufführung von Bruno Madernas *Hyperion und die Gewalt*', *Opernwelt* (July 1968): 26–7.
36 Fernand Papon, *De Nieuwe Gazet*, 20 May 1968; L. Schr., *Helmonds Dagblad*, 21 May 1968; Jan Wisse, *Elseviers Weekblad*, 25 May 1968.
37 Willem Pelemans, *Het Laatste Nieuws*, 20 May 1968.
38 Synopsis published in the programme booklet. Archives of the Royal Mint Theatre, Brussels.
39 Fernand Papon, *De Nieuwe Gazet*, 20 May 1968.
40 Gérard Bertouille, *La Phare Dimanche*, 26 May 1968.
41 *De Nieuwe Gids*, 24 May 1968.
42 Fernand Papon, *De Nieuwe Gazet*, 20 May 1968.
43 Roger Hofmans, *De Nieuwe Gids/De Spectator*, 25 May 1968.

140 *Harm Langenkamp*

a work undeserving of attention if it is not animated by the spirit of protest and challenge'.[44] Yet, even the critic of the Belgian Communist daily had to admit that, regardless of how praiseworthy this 'denunciation of American aggression in Vietnam' was, 'the artistic mediocrity of the play defuses any possible effect of the ideological message on the public, and will unfortunately serve as a pretext for the bourgeois press to contest the one by devastating – alas justified – the other'.[45]

The directorship of the Mint Theatre consoled Huisman: 'It is better to have ten misfired creations than to remain passive and present nothing but stock repertory.'[46] Likewise, the critic of *Le Patriote Illustré* conceded that the work may have been 'a partial failure', but 'a necessary failure' nonetheless:

> As long as one wraps oneself exclusively in the forms of the past, will one not, in the long term, suffocate theatre? If art does not join the crowd, will the crowd not seek the spiritual escape it seeks elsewhere?[47]

For Claus and his *Reconstructie* colleagues who accompanied him at the impromptu press conference after *Hyperion*'s premiere, these questions had to be answered in the affirmative. Critically disposed towards the forms of culture to which both the bourgeoisie and the hippies resorted for their spiritual escape (apoliticised 'timeless' art in the one case, marihuana-inspired beat music in the other), their ambition was to come up with a convincing alternative to what they saw as the calcified institutions of the performing arts.

Che in Amsterdam: the tactics of subsidised subversion

'We are unanimously excited about a commission as you describe it', Schat responded to Huisman on behalf of himself and his colleagues.[48] After negotiations that resulted in an increase of the team's honorarium of 15,000 guilders by 50 per cent and the inclusion of Claus as a partner for Mulisch, the team started its operation.[49] Initial disapproval by Mengelberg and Van Vlijmen for dedicating the collective work to Che Guevara was quickly overcome by the prospect of having another chance to provoke the cultural establishment. At the time of accepting Huisman's invitation, four of the five composers were in the final stages of preparation for their response to the failure of the Maderna campaign: a concert with premieres of works by Schat, Andriessen, and Mengelberg for ad hoc ensembles, designed to demonstrate an alternative performance model for the idiosyncratic

---

44 Jacques Stehman, *Le Soir*, 20 May 1968.
45 P. B., *Le Drapeau Rouge*, 24 May 1968.
46 Editorial, *Pourquoi Pas*, 6 June 1968.
47 J. M., *Le Patriote Illustré*, 26 May 1968.
48 Schat to Huisman, 5 February 1968, Archive of the Dutch Opera Foundation, Netherlands Theatre Institute, Amsterdam University Library, box 64, folder 100.
49 Nando Schellen, DOF executive director, to Claus, 4 April 1968, Mulisch Papers, folder 86.6. Initially, 5,000 guilders had been earmarked for the libretto. With the addition of Claus, this sum was raised to 7,000 guilders, to be divided between the two writers.

fruits of experimental composition. The concert was to be presented on 30 May 1968 at the Carré Theatre, a venue commonly presenting operettas, cabaret, musicals and variety shows, and as such, the opposite of the 'elitist' Concertgebouw. When the group applied for funding from the Prins Bernhard Cultuurfonds (a cultural fund established by the spouse of the reigning head of state, Queen Juliana), the project had not carried an overtly political tone. Yet, two weeks before the concert, the escalation of the Parisian student protests into a society-wide revolt led to the decision to turn the event into a demonstration against 'our late-capitalist social system' and a 'declaration of solidarity with the world revolution'.[50] As to the salient detail that the concert had been enabled by the sponsorship of the very establishment that it sought to undermine, the initiators mounted a robust defence: 'After all, we also drink Coca Cola', and so are 'willy-nilly accessory [to the acts of the establishment]', Schat argued. 'So yes, we use the techniques and the money of this society to say what we think must be said.'[51]

Schat expounded on this Trojan horse strategy in his opening essay to the programme booklet that the curious attendants of what now was called a 'political-demonstrative experimental concert' (Politiek-Demonstratief Experimenteel Concert) were handed (at the price of 1,50 guilders) as they entered the Carré Theatre. Sceptical about music's capacity to transform society, or even to reflect 'late capitalism and its inherent economic and fascistic violence', the choice to politicise the concert arose from a felt need to 'avoid falling into the hands of the established order' and being used as its tool to prove its progressiveness in tolerating resistance. Admitting that 'we breathe from the (subsidy) oxygen of this system', the concert was meant to prevent this system from abusing its generosity by not changing anything (Schat 1968: 5–6). The way in which Peter Weiss's documentary play *Viet Nam Diskurs* – a remorseless attack of 'the American free enterprise system' that had just premiered in Frankfurt and for which Schat had provided the incidental music – had been smothered by the tolerance of the authorities exemplified for Schat the mechanism of what Marcuse called 'repressive tolerance'.[52] Indeed, as the young composer Konrad Boehmer, to whom the ideological justifications of the concert may be ascribed, declared, 'the euphony-loving system' would only grant composers freedom of resistance insofar as they 'would not notice that the essential is forbidden to them', namely, structural reform of the musical infrastructure towards their needs (Boehmer 1968: 29).

On the night of the concert, the 'system' was more tolerant than anything else. Anxious about Parisian scenes at Carré, crowded as it became with Vietnam

---

50 Schat, cited in *Trouw*, 16 May 1968; Andriessen cited in *Algemeen Dagblad*, 29 May 1968.

51 Schat, cited in *Trouw*, 16 May 1968. Subsidies for the concert not only flowed in from the Prins Bernhard Cultuurfonds. Andriessen's contribution, *Contra tempus*, was commissioned by the Ministry of Culture, Mengelberg's *Hello Windyboys* by the VPRO broadcast network, and Schat's *On Escalation* – dedicated to Guevara and framed as an enactment of a guerrilla revolt whereby a percussion ensemble increasingly undermines the authority of the conductor – by the Amsterdam municipality.

52 Schat, cited in K. L. Poll, *Algemeen Handelsblad*, 25 May 1968.

142   Harm Langenkamp

demonstrators, Guevara idolisers, communists, anarchists, Paris-inspired students, and weed-smoking hippies amidst 'ordinary' concertgoers, the police force standing by in the vicinity of the building refrained from intervention, even though the disarray inside inflated to a point that even concerned the concert's initiators.[53] Likewise, in reference to Boehmer's scepticism, 'the system' indeed did not change, at least as far as its support for commissions it had already contracted was concerned.[54]

When it got hold of the first synopsis for the new music theatre work, which was also to take place at the Carré Theatre, it was clear to the directorship of the Holland Festival that they were in for more of the same: Huisman's commission was to evolve into 'an anti-American evening'.[55] The memory of two years earlier, when Schat's lavishly subsidised *Labyrint* disclosed itself as a downright challenge of the Dutch establishment, was fresh on everyone's mind; the question was raised whether the Holland Festival could bear the responsibility of another such incident, both politically and artistically. Eduard Reeser, patriarch of Dutch musicology, and Wim Polak, Amsterdam alderman of cultural affairs, opined that, while the festival should certainly be open to experimentation and politics, this particular experiment threatened to devolve into a work marked by a '*Muette de Portici* stamp' that 'leaves little illusion about any aesthetical pleasure'. Polak's Rotterdam counterpart, Jan Reehorst, agreed and foresaw that the project would claim all attention, either negatively or positively, at the expense of other events on the programme. Unexpectedly, it was none other than the board's governmental representative, Jan Hulsker, director-general of the Ministry of Culture, who came to the defence of the Dutch Opera Foundation, which had overcome its initial reservations by trusting the *Reconstructie* team's artistic reputation and prioritising its right to free expression. By ensuring that the Opera alone was responsible for the commission and that the *Reconstructie* team had promised to mount no other known figures on the stage next to Guevara, Hulsker managed to tilt the Holland Festival's balance of approval in favour of the project.

Indeed, no other real-life characters would be drawn into the commission. Neither would the 'principles of guerrilla warfare' affect the performer/audience relationship as seemed to have been contemplated at an early stage.[56] The references to real-life geopolitics, however, were no less conspicuous, and went beyond 'the positive tone' that Huisman had asked for in his commission letter.

---

53 For extensive reports, see *Het Parool, Algemeen Handelsblad* and *De Tijd*, 31 May 1968. For a full discussion of this event, see Adlington 2009.

54 An exception in this regard concerns two of the four broadcast networks that abandoned their intention to record the Carré concert as they felt misled by its sudden politicisation; see *Het Parool*, 29 May 1968.

55 Hendrik Jan Reinink, director of the Holland Festival, cited from the minutes of the Holland Festival Board of Directors, 15 July 1968, Holland Festival Archive, Netherlands Theatre Institute, Amsterdam University Library, box 16. All other quotes in this paragraph are taken from this document.

56 At one point Schat jotted down in his *Reconstructie* notebook the phrases 'setup up main camp', 'occupying environment', 'ambush', 'self-explosion', 'spectators become participants', and 'spectators become potential enemies'. Schat Papers, box 336, folder 17(1).

In what was conceived as a morality play, that, in marked contrast to Henze and Enzensberger's Cuba-inspired works *El Cimarrón* (1969–70) and *La Cubana* (1973), was to focus 'not on the tears of the oppressed but on the fist of the oppressor', the 'apparatus of repression' effective in Latin America was to be 'reconstructed' on three levels.[57] On the first level, the motives behind Che's murder are exposed through a cartoonesque ensemble representing the directors of the 'Total American Company', flanked by their 'frigid and sterile' spouses and CIA abettors, who visit Latin America to plot the elimination of 'a villain' bent on obstructing their 'civilising work'. Along the way, the company's director general, driven as much by altruism as a desire to unravel the secret of his heritage, finds his lost parents: Tarzan, the personification of 'the law of the jungle', and a humongous fission fungus, a symbol of the dissent capitalism engenders in Latin America (Andriessen *et al.*, 1969: 34). On the second level, Latin America's exploitation is allegorically enacted in a miniature opera in Mozartean style – Cuba and Bolivia being the 'brides' raped by Don Juan on a Latin American-shaped bed, and Bolivia's father ('Commendatore' Guevara) being killed in the ensuing confrontation by the Don's gun. Needless to say, the Don pays for his sins: in what cannot be mistaken for anything other than a call for revolution, his pregnant victims turn against him, aided by an 11-metre high Styrofoam statue of Che's image (see Figure 6.2) that during the length of the performance was erected by seven stage hands (i.e., the third level of

Figure 6.2 Cast in front of the Guevara statue. Action scene from *Reconstructie*, 28 June 1969. Photo: Joost Evers, National Archives of the Netherlands / Anefo, CC0.

---

57 Synopsis by the *Reconstructie* team, early June 1968, DOF Archive, box 64, folder 100.

144   *Harm Langenkamp*

reconstruction), and which, like the vengeful Commendatore, finally condemns the perpetrator to death by freezing.

Had it not been for the *Reconstructie* team's ambition to 'reconstruct the opera genre from its very core', the project could easily have faltered.[58] Based on the premises that a 'revolutionary topic' required a 'revolutionary method', and that the project's success depended on the will of each member to yield his ego to 'a dispossession of the production processes', the team devised an intricate method through which the composition procedures were decided upon collectively, and the contribution of each member passed hands as much as was needed in order to flatten stylistic differences. The result was nevertheless a highly heterogeneous score, in which strict serialism was pitted against jazz improvisation, operatic arias alternated with cabaret songs, revue ballet contrasted with static choirs – in short, to speak in the terms of the day, 'highbrow' met 'lowbrow' and vice versa (see Adlington 2007: 185–8). 'This method of the guerrilla – of a small group of individuals bound by solidarity and unanimity – works so well', Andriessen told the press at the time, 'that it feels as if an eighth man is involved'.[59]

To the collective's sponsors, it must have seemed they were paying for an eighth man too. Even though an extra subsidy had been awarded by the Buma Culture Foundation in order to 'guarantee the success of the experiment' – this despite a perception that the experiment had 'got out of hand' – the team's creativity drove the Dutch Opera Foundation to despair.[60] More than once the team was informed that the budget had been far exceeded.[61] Yet conceptual fine-tunings, with concomitant financial consequences, continued to be made until shortly before the premiere, such as the demand for 'twenty girls in bathing suits and scarves in various national colours'.[62] That the financial troubles did not come to mean the end of the project was due to a certain B. P. Wagemans, a senior official at the Ministry of Culture in charge of the Music and Dance Division, on whom Fernand Schellen, the Opera's executive manager, could rely each time 'the boys' were asking for money (Schellen, cited in Van Putten 2015: 474–5).

The most important factor contributing to *Reconstructie*'s viability, however, seems to have been the outrage that its governmental sponsorship provoked from the right-wing press. In what evolved into a staccato of attacks, *De Telegraaf*, the mouthpiece of Dutch conservatism, relentlessly raised the question of why the government should continue supporting the Holland Festival, which more than once had wasted public money on ephemeral experimental operas such as Schat's *Labyrint*, and now funded *Reconstructie*, a 'smear campaign against America and a glorification of the Cuban revolution'. When asked for a reaction,

---

58 Cited from Schat's *Reconstructie* notebook. Schat Papers, box 336, folder 17(1).
59 Andriessen cited in *Algemeen Handelsblad*, 21 September 1968. That this unanimity had its limits as well, is pointed out by Adlington 2007: 191–2.
60 Theo Limperg to Jaap den Daas, 28 February 1969; Fernand Schellen, memorandum, 10 March 1969, DOF Archive, box 64, folder 97.
61 Schellen to *Reconstructie* team, 19 February 1969; Schellen, situation report, 2 April 1969, DOF Archive, box 64, folder 97.
62 Schellen to Schat, 8 May 1969, Schat Papers, box 5016, folder 40.

the Holland Festival's executive director, Jaap den Daas, invoked his duty to guarantee artistic quality only, adding that the United States was unrecognisable as *Reconstructie*'s object of criticism: 'It could just as well have been Asia – imperialism is not confined to America.' Not only was this attempt at rebuttal unconvincing, it was also – unintentionally – nullified by Schat, who in another press reaction stated that, although the opera indeed should be taken as a generic condemnation of imperialism, it was 'abundantly clear' that *Reconstructie* would demonstrate this by the example of the Americas. The Ministry of Culture, for its part, refrained from commentary since, in accordance with the Dutch constitution, its subsidies came with no strings attached.[63]

The *Reconstructie* team was elated by *De Telegraaf*'s branding their project as 'a political scandal', as they knew it would assure them of political support. 'If one thing was certain, it was that you could not flinch at the wrath of the *De Telegraaf*', De Leeuw remembered.[64] Indeed, when *De Telegraaf*'s outcry prompted parliamentary member Hubert Kronenburg to ask the Minister of Culture, Marga Klompé, to share *Reconstructie*'s libretto with the House of Representatives, Klompé responded negatively, invoking the authors' copyright. Neither did she allow herself to be pressed into questioning the opera's subsidies, clarifying that the expenses of *Reconstructie* were borne by the Dutch Opera Foundation, not the publicly funded Holland Festival.[65] Significantly, a preliminary version of her reply concluded with the statement that 'I cannot grant subsidies to artistic companies on the condition that their performances should be agreeable to the government'.[66] Why this sentence apparently did not make it to the parliamentary floor is not known. She nevertheless made the point when Kronenburg followed up her reply with a question about whether she judged the matter of the Politiek-Demonstratief Experimenteel Concert to attest to the good faith of *Reconstructie*'s authors: 'It is not up to me to forbid those involved to express their engagement in political or any other domain.'[67]

Klompé's defence of *Reconstructie* articulated a firm belief in the need of artistic freedom in the social welfare state. Recognising the presence of 'displeasure' (*onbehagen*) among citizens about governmental interference in their lives, she saw her role as one of facilitating 'new, even revolutionary artistic ideas' for the sake of 'preventing us from becoming little robots in this crazy world of ours'. Also, she deemed it a sign of social health if artists could 'knock on the door of society and say that things are going in the wrong direction.'[68]

---

63 Henk van der Meyden, *De Telegraaf*, 1, 8 and 11 February 1969. Schat delivered his statement in a news broadcast by the AVRO at 9 February 1969.

64 De Leeuw cited from an episode in the historical documentary series *Andere Tijden*, broadcast by the VPRO on 31 May 2005.

65 *Handelingen van de Tweede Kamer* [Parliamentary Proceedings], 43rd assembly, 6 March 1969, 2138.

66 J.F.M.J. Jansen, Arts Division, to the Minister, draft version of the answers to the questions of parliamentary member H.Ch.J.M. Kronenburg, 3 March 1969, Archive of the Ministry of Culture, Recreation and Social Work, National Archives, inventory 2.27.19, folder 4397.

67 *Handelingen van de Tweede Kamer*, 6 March 1969, 2139.

68 Klompé, cited in K. L. Poll, *Algemeen Handelsblad*, 23 November 1968.

146 *Harm Langenkamp*

Thus nothing prevented the *Reconstructie* team from venting its criticism against its patron. The delicate issue, however, was that *Reconstructie*'s target was not so much the Dutch government as its NATO ally, the United States. That the centrist-right cabinet of Piet de Jong neglected to intervene in the staging of blatant anti-American stereotypes at a government-sponsored platform could become a source of diplomatic trouble. Yet, the risk (if it was construed as such) seems to have been accepted, and perhaps intentionally so. In the face of society-wide resistance that engendered a parliamentary motion and internal division within his coalition, De Jong considered himself to have earned credit with the U.S. for never having retracted his support of American military interventions in North Vietnam (Van der Maar 2007: 132–8). Consequently, calculating that Washington would understand that 'government subsidy does not constitute government approval',[69] De Jong's cabinet may have seen in the non-interference with Reconstructie a strategy to counter the negative image that its unswerving loyalty had created of itself as an obedient follower – in *Reconstructie* personified by the figure of Erasmus, who as Don Juan's sidekick does not give in to his qualms about his master's conquests, just as his historic counterpart had failed to support Lutheran dissent.[70]

For the *Reconstructie* team, nothing may have seemed any longer to stand in the way of a success. The producers, however, kept sleepless nights. A month before the start of the rehearsals, the singing choir retracted its participation after having failed 'to find anything positive in the lyrics'.[71] Earlier, one of the main actors had retreated for the opposite reason: he deemed the work to be unworthy of its topic, contrasting his own political engagement with the 'salon socialism' of *Reconstructie*'s authors.[72] Short-term engagements and the complexity of the parts also prompted actors and soloists to ask for exorbitant fees, which put another strain on the hapless budget. The rehearsals themselves were ruled by chaos, which to an important extent was to blame on the inexperience of the team members in opera directing and conducting, as well as their inability to keep up the united *guerrilla* spirit. Until the moment of the premiere, disagreements on all matters, small and large, 'brought musicians to despair, the choir to terrorism, and the boys' choir to tears' (Léon Schoenmakers, cited in Van Putten 2015: 493–4).

All the concerns and controversies about *Reconstructie* may have predicted a failure. As it turned out, nothing was less true. Perhaps as the unintended outcome

---

69 Joseph Luns, minister of Foreign Affairs, cited in airgram no. A-328, 1 July 1969, Records of the Department of State, Central Foreign Policy Files, National Archives and Records Administration, College Park, entry A1 1613, box 325.

70 In 1967, Claus, Mulisch, Schat, Van Vlijmen and Maderna had been asked by the Ministry of Culture to contribute to Rotterdam's quincentennial celebrations of Erasmus through an 'actualised music-theatrical adaptation' of *In Praise of Folly*. Although all seemed to have been receptive at first, a few months later they returned the commission for 'a lack of affinity with the topic'. *Het Vrije Volk*, 21 May 1968.

71 Rie Vranken, spouse of Toon Vranken, artistic director of the Collegium Musicum Amstelodamense, to Léon Schoenmakers, dramaturg, 14 May 1969, DOF Archive, box 64, folder 97.

72 Lo van Hensbergen to Den Daas, 18 March 1969, DOF Archive, box 64, folder 100.

Guerrilla in the polder   147

of *De Telegraaf*'s high-profile publicity campaign, all six performances were sold out and plans to take the production to the Brussels Mint Theatre and the Festival d'Avignon were made (but did not materialise). The premiere, attended by Minister Klompé and an unofficial delegation from Cuba, was received in a manner that left the creators dumbfounded.[73] When asked about her first impression, Klompé referred to the press for a verdict, although she could not hide her doubts as to whether the goals of the artists had been realised to their fullest extent. She was sure, however, that *Reconstructie* did not intend to overthrow democracy, and considered the criticism prior to the premiere to have been premature.[74] To a certain extent, some critics indeed admitted that the result had surprised them – even *De Telegraaf* (albeit from the pen of another correspondent than the one who conducted the smear campaign) could appreciate the 'Romantically revolutionary' qualities underneath its foil of anti-Americanism.[75] The international press, too, generally reported back in admiration and envy about the 'courage' of the Holland Festival to present 'the youngest and most radical of art forms', including a 'possible way for new music theatre'.[76] Nevertheless, as in the reception of the Brussels *Hyperion*, complaints about superficiality, crassness and haphazardness abound in the press reviews.[77] Communist critics, too, returned home disillusioned, finding in *Reconstructie* mere 'corny parody' rather than a tool for revolution.[78] The critic of *The New York Times* took the criticism a level further, pressing on what is arguably *Reconstructie*'s weakest spot: the silence about the *Dutch* (and *Flemish*) share in global exploitation.[79]

Conclusion

Although *Reconstructie* was received with more acclaim than *Hyperion en het geweld*, critics did not fail to point out that both specimens of protest theatre were 'no *Muette de Portici*' – Daniel Auber's opera that, as legend has it, sparked the Belgian Revolution of 1830–1.[80] As for *Hyperion*, this became painfully clear at

---

73 Mulisch and De Leeuw cited from *Andere Tijden*, broadcast by the VPRO on 31 May 2005. According to Schellen, there had been plans to get Castro himself to Amsterdam (Van Putten 2015: 495). The premiere was attended by Lisandro Otera, Vice-President of Cuba's National Council of Culture, who seized the opportunity to inquire with Klompé about the possibility of tightening cultural relations. Klompé, memorandum, 3 July 1969, Archive of the Ministry of Foreign Affairs, National Archives, inventory 2.05.313, folder 9136.

74 Klompé paraphrased from an interview with Henriëtte Klautz, The Netherlands Institute for Sound and Vision, item 167315.

75 H. J. M. Müller, *De Telegraaf*, 30 June 1969.

76 *Le Monde*, 1 July 1969; *Süddeutsche Zeitung*, 2 July 1969; *Der Spiegel*, 7 July 1969: 114.

77 See, for instance, Mia Aleven-Vranken and Gabriël Smit, *De Volkskrant*, 30 June 1969: 5; Everett Helm, *Frankfurter Allgemeine Zeitung*, 5 July 1969.

78 Wim Gafefl, *De Waarheid*, 30 June 1969.

79 Clive Barnes, *New York Times*, 8 July 1969. At an early brainstorming session, *Reconstructie*'s objective had been formulated as 'the demonstration of the Benelux's share in the world's oppression, specifically in Latin America'. The final version, however, does not fulfil this intention. Claus Papers, folder 308.

80 Joost Kirez, 'Reconstructie', *De Internationale* 12/5 (1969): 3; anonymous correspondent from Brussels, *De Volkskrant*, 22 May 1968.

148   *Harm Langenkamp*

an anti-censorship read-in, which was convened a few days after *Hyperion*'s premiere, on the occasion of Claus's trial for offending public decency. As it turned out, the revolutionary spirit at this meeting never rose above a few random cries for 'subsidised cultural revolution', amidst abstract lectures from 'representatives of the establishment' who only sympathised with the protesters insofar as reforms could be effectuated within existing judiciary provisions. The discussion left one reporter to quip that the only destiny *Hyperion* would come to share with *La Muette* is its disappearance into oblivion.[81] *Reconstructie* managed to attract more attention, but as some members of the Holland Festival directorship predicted, fifty years after its premiere it merely lives on as an emblem of the 'roaring sixties' rather than as a lasting contribution to the opera repertory.[82] Likewise, the *Reconstructie* team's high-flown ambition to 'arrive at a verifiable example of collective composition for future generations' proved to be short-lived.[83] Plans for a follow-up project were made, but foundered as the interests of the guerrilleros went in different directions.[84]

The general lack of appreciation for the Brussels *Hyperion* cannot merely be explained by an overriding 'climate of mediocrity and narrow-mindedness', as Claus did at the Brussels read-in. On the contrary, as my reception analysis demonstrates, the charge of mediocrity boomeranged on Claus himself. Most reviewers ascribed the perceived mediocre quality of the Brussels *Hyperion* to a fundamental disagreement between its authors over the poetics of artistic engagement: the direct, confrontational way of Claus versus the subtle, musing way of Maderna. Significantly, most of the reviewers of both *Hyperion* and *Reconstructie* did not object to the notion of politically committed art; their criticism concerned the way in which it was effectuated. Several of them did not conceal their weariness at seeing 'trite' theatrical techniques reminiscent of, for instance, The Living Theatre or the Grotowski Laboratory.[85] Another criterion by which several reviewers measured the efficiency of radical music theatre was its affective power: some indicated that the grotesque staging and ever-switching music deprived them of the possibility to identify with the action/actors. If – in Klompé's words – art should prevent citizens from turning into 'little robots', visitors to *Hyperion* and *Reconstructie* were precisely presented with deliberately dehumanised acting. Considering the various reprises it has enjoyed since its 1976 premiere, it seems that Henze and Edward Bond's *We Come to the River* has better succeeded in the objectives that Claus set for himself. Although equally imbued with the grotesque, the text, actions and polystylistic music in this work serve a single affective and effective strategy that aims to sensitise the audience for the atrocities taking place in the world through unvarnished enactments of violence.

81 Anonymous correspondent from Brussels, *De Volkskrant*, 22 May 1968. For another report that confirms the lethargic sphere at the read-in, see Lieselot Van Son, 'Nederlandse Dagen in Brussel', *Ons Erfdeel* 12/1 (1968–69): 187.
82 See minutes of the Holland Festival Board, 1 December 1969.
83 Cited from Schat's *Reconstructie* notebook. Schat Papers, box 336, folder 17(1).
84 Martin Schouten, *Haagse Post*, 3 November 1973: 65–6.
85 P.B., *Le Drapeau Rouge*, 24 May 1968; Georges Sion, *Beaux Arts*, 25 May 1968.

Finally, the case of *Reconstructie* in particular demonstrated the extent to which the dissenters' conceptualisation of the 'establishment' as a monolithic machine working against the interests of its subjects obscures the dynamics of conflicting interests within and across the various sectors that constitute the established order. Under the leadership of Marga Klompé, the Dutch Ministry of Culture, Recreation and Social Work conducted a cultural policy that not only proved to be amenable to experimentation and anti-establishment criticism, but also facilitated it through its subsidy and commission programmes. To critics including the *Reconstructie* team, this policy may have come across as a strategy of containing dissent and evading true reforms, turning – in Guevara's words – 'a weapon of protest' into a societal 'safety valve' (Guevara 2003 [1965]: 224). Considering the unrelenting financial and moral support granted to *Reconstructie*, despite ever-new demands and dubious prospects for its completion, this perception may be questioned. Even if the government's support for progressive causes was intended to counterbalance the discredit caused by its unwavering support of U.S. operations in North Vietnam, the dissenters seemed blind to their own complicity in sustaining this strategy by accepting state support. Once Marcusean speculations are set aside, an image of the 1960s polder emerges in which establishment and its dissenters were bound in an interdependent and mutually beneficial relationship, and in which avant-garde resistance, if anything, was tolerated – and facilitated.

Appendix: Tentative reconstruction of *Hyperion en het Geweld*

In the absence of a master score or a recording of the Brussels performance, the exact compilation of *Hyperion en het geweld* is difficult to trace. The following reconstruction is based on Mario Baroni and Tiziano Popoli's intensive source studies (1985), the materials located in the Maderna Collections of the Paul Sacher Foundation and the University of Bologna's Music and Theatre Department, and the numerous reviews contained in the clipping files of the Munt Theatre.

Action	Music (live and/or electronic)
With squeaking noise, the iron stage screen opens, showing twenty-one soldiers wrapped in plasticised uniforms.	*Messaggio* (flute cadenza from *Dimensioni III/2*), subsequently combined with the second part of the tape *Le rire* that was originally used in the 1964 Venice version of *Hyperion*.
A Popeye animation, fighting off a shoal of bombers, is meant to distract the soldiers who are nervously awaiting the commencement of hostilities.	Accompanied by the first part of *Le rire*.
As a Chaplain tries to sooth the men, the Captain enters, informing his troop that a breach of truce by the enemy has put operation 'Prairie Dog' into action.	No music.

(continued)

(continued)

Action	Music (live and/or electronic)
The battle is controlled by an intimidating Machine. As the stage fills with smoke and noise, two Guards (Castor and Pollux) report on the battle.	Signalling sounds of a computer, probably followed by *Entropia II* for orchestra (episode from *Dimensioni III/3*).
The war effort is followed by 'recreation', provided by slot machines and a jukebox.	Registration of a 'religious waltz' and a 'Captain's waltz'.
The Captain raves about the enemy's miserable life, and announces that three days' leave will be given for every 'rat' killed.	After the Captain's message, *Psalm* for choir and orchestra on texts by W. H. Auden and Federico García Lorca, and combined with fragments from *Stele per Diotima*, is performed.
The soldiers are scared by enemy lights that they glimpse through portholes, but their superiors assure them of the infallibility of the Machine that protects them. As the Chaplain preaches of their duty to spread the Lord's teaching of love to the enemy, the soldiers doze off in an artificial sleep.	No music.
Although supposedly protected by the Machine, the 'rats' begin to be heard over loudspeakers, at first gently, later with threats and jests. Castor and Pollux, who stand guard, are afraid and powerless.	A combination of various sounds and music for flute, choir, orchestra and tape, including *Entropia I*. Maderna's archive includes a manuscript of this 'Scene of the Guards' (*Scena delle sentinelle*).
Again a battle ensues, this time with images of childhood monsters and heroes, represented by puppet-monsters dressed as Dracula, the Werewolf, Robot Robbie, Doctor Demon and Superman.	*Contrasti*, combined with the tape-work *Dimensioni II/Invenzione su una voce* and a 'Choral of Puppets', in which all creatures recite: 'We are the dreams, the nightmares, the desires enclosed in the dark gardens of men.'
The Captain wakes up his men, informing them that 'the mice attack'. A battle follows in which the soldiers fall one by one under the blows of the enemy. The battle only leaves three survivors: Castor searching for Pollux, the Chaplain reading from the Bible, and the Captain praising the self-sacrifice of his men.	During the whole confrontation, the loudspeakers emit sounds of computer and battle (tapes titled *Battaglia I and II*). Other indications refer to an orchestral tape called *Battaglia Hyperion*.
As in the 1964 Venice version of *Hyperion*, a Woman appears singing verses from Hölderlin's *Hyperion-Fragment*.	*Aria I* for soprano, flute and orchestra (three nights sung by Liliana Poli, three nights by Beverly Bergen).
The ending is unclear, but elements seem to have been the reappearance of the puppet-monsters, the soldiers' resurrection as Mummies, and the Woman's general lamentation on the destruction of nature and humanity.	Untitled music, drawn from *Stele per Diotima* • *Zombieschorus* for choir and tape • *Aria II*.

Acknowledgements

I am grateful to the archivists of the Paul Sacher Foundation (Basel), the Netherlands Music Institute (The Hague), the Netherlands Theatre Institute (Amsterdam), the Museum of Literature (The Hague), the House of Literature (Antwerp) and the Royal Theatre of the Mint (Brussels) for facilitating my research for this article. Special thanks are extended to Robert Adlington, to whose helpful suggestions and extensive work on Dutch post-war musical life I am much indebted.

References

Adlington, Robert (2007), '"A sort of *guerrilla*": Che at the opera', *Cambridge Opera Journal*, 19/2, pp. 167–93.

Adlington, Robert (2009), 'Forms of opposition at the "politiek-demonstratief experimenteel" concert', in Robert Adlington (ed.), *Sound Commitments: Avant-garde Music and the Sixties*, Oxford: Oxford University Press, pp. 56–77.

Adlington, Robert (2013), *Composing Dissent: Avant-garde Music in 1960s Amsterdam*. Oxford: Oxford University Press.

Andriessen, Louis, Hugo Claus, Reinbert de Leeuw, Misha Mengelberg, Harry Mulisch, Peter Schat and Jan van Vlijmen (1969), *Blauwdruk van de opera Reconstructie: een moraliteit*, Amsterdam: De Bezige Bij.

Auwera, Fernand (1969), *Schrijven of schieten?*, Antwerp: Standaard Uitgeverij.

Baroni, Mario and Tiziano Popoli (1985), '*Hyperion en het geweld*', in Mario Baroni and Rossana Dalmonte (eds), *Bruno Maderna: Documenti*, Milan: Edizione Suvini Zerboni, pp. 266–75.

Boehmer, Konrad (1968), 'Repressieve kunstpolitiek', in *Muzikale en politieke commentaren en analyses bij een programma van een politiek-demonstratief experimenteel concert*, Amsterdam: Polak & van Gennep, p. 29.

Boehmer, Konrad (2007), 'Retour à Maderna', in Geneviève Mathon, Laurent Feneyrou and Giordano Ferrari (eds), *À Bruno Maderna*, volume 1, Paris: Basalte, pp. 341–53.

Casadei, Delia (2014), 'Orality, invisibility, and laughter: traces of Milan in Bruno Maderna and Virginio Puecher's *Hyperion* (1964)', *Opera Quarterly*, 30/1, pp. 105–34.

Claus, Hugo (1968), *Morituri*, Amsterdam: De Bezige Bij.

Dam, Peter van, Jouke Turpijn and Bram Mellink (eds) (2014), *Onbehagen in de polder: Nederland in conflict sinds 1795*, Amsterdam: Amsterdam University Press.

Dorticós Torrado, Osvaldo (1967), speech given at the closing session of the Preparatory Seminar for the Cultural Congress of Havana, 2 November, pamphlet, Havana: Cultural Congress of Havana.

Fearn, Raymond (1990), *Bruno Maderna*, Chur: Harwood Academic Publishers.

Ferrari, Giordano (2007), '*Hyperion*, les chemins du poète', in Geneviève Mathon, Laurent Feneyrou and Giordano Ferrari (eds), *À Bruno Maderna*, volume 1, Paris: Basalte, pp. 89–121.

Guevara, Ernesto (2003 [1965]), 'Socialism and man in Cuba', in David Deutschmann (ed.), *Che Guevara Reader: Writings on Politics and Revolution*, Melbourne: Ocean Press.

Maar, Rimko van der (2007), *Welterusten mijnheer de president*, Amsterdam: Boom.

Marcuse, Herbert (1991 [1964]), *One-Dimensional Man: Studies in the Ideology of Advanced Industrial Society*, London: Routledge.

152 *Harm Langenkamp*

Mulisch, Harry (1968), *Het woord bij de daad: Getuigenis van de revolutie op Cuba*, Amsterdam: De Bezige Bij.

Mulisch, Harry (1979), 'Een geldig recept? Korte reconstructie van *Reconstructie*', in *Paniek der onschuld*, Amsterdam: De Bezige Bij.

Nielinger-Vakil, Carola (2015), *Luigi Nono: A Composer in Context*, Cambridge, UK: Cambridge University Press.

Organization of American States (1968), *Against the Subversive Action of International Communism: Cultural Congress of Havana*, Washington, DC: Pan American Union.

Putten, Bas van (2015), *Alles moest anders: Biografie van Peter Schat*, volume 1, Amsterdam: De Arbeiderspers.

Schat, Peter (1968), Introduction to *Muzikale en politieke commentaren en analyses bij een programma van een politiek-demonstratief experimenteel concert*, Amsterdam: Polak and van Gennep, pp. 5–6.

Silber, Irwin (ed.) (1970), *Voices of National Liberation: The Revolutionary Ideology of the 'Third World' as Expressed by Intellectuals and Artists at the Cultural Congress of Havana, January 1968*, New York: Central Book Company.

Wetters, Brent (2012), 'Idea and actualization: Bruno Maderna's adaption of Friedrich Hölderlin's *Hyperion*', *19th-Century Music*, 36/2, pp. 172–90.

7 René Leibowitz's *Todos caerán*

Grand opéra as (critique of) new music theatre

Esteban Buch

The new music theatre that emerged in Europe in the fifties and sixties was not always greeted with enthusiasm.[1] New music theatre pieces were often accused of being failures, and of being examples of a failed genre; indeed, hostile criticism was arguably instrumental in new music theatre coming to be perceived as a genre in the first place. Negative reactions were frequent whenever these works were exposed to broader audiences than contemporary music circles, starting with those opera critics and fans prone to think that music drama had ended with, say, Giacomo Puccini in 1924. But they could also be found amongst other groups, including contemporary composers. In a sense, the divide between opera and music theatre was also an inner dispute of the contemporary music world. Many composers who dismissed opera as reactionary and *bourgeois* avoided calling their avant-gardist pieces *operas*, as if to enhance their own aesthetic identity. In turn, other composers who called their works *operas* differentiated them from what they described as *anti-operas*. Some even talked of *anti-anti-operas*. And these critics of new music theatre were no less vociferous than the proponents; on the contrary, their modernist credentials gave them the authority – or so they thought – to claim, louder than others, that the king had no clothes.

René Leibowitz (1913–1972) is a case in point. Born in Warsaw and established in Paris in the 1920s, he was recognized in France after the war as the modernist musician *par excellence*, especially as teacher of composers interested in twelve-tone technique. The author of important books on the Viennese School, he was also influential as a music critic for *Les Temps modernes*, Jean-Paul Sartre's and Simone de Beauvoir's journal, and for *Critique*, led by his friend Georges Bataille (see Kapp 1987; Mosch 1992; Meine 2000; Schürmann 2010). An active conductor of the classic and operatic repertoire, his performances of Beethoven and Offenbach were appreciated at the time, and are still worth hearing today. He also published in 1957 a *Histoire de l'opéra*, meant to accompany the 'very special

---

1 The author thanks Antoinette Molinié, Humbert Camerlo, and Heidy Zimmermann (at the Paul Sacher Stiftung) for their support and help, and Cora Leibowitz, Tamara Leibowitz, and Monique Lévi-Strauss for their authorization to reproduce excerpts of René Leibowitz's scores and to quote his correspondance with Claude Lévi-Strauss. A previous version of this essay was presented at the international conference *Hommage à René Leibowitz*, Centre de Documentation sur la Musique Contemporaine (CMDC), Paris, 3 October 2013.

154   *Esteban Buch*

favour' enjoyed by the genre at the time (Leibowitz 1957). And, most important for our topic, he was a prolific composer with a long-established interest in music for the stage, whose catalogue includes *La nuit close* op. 17 (1949), '*drame musical*' on a libretto by writer and critic Georges Limbour (1900–1970); *La circulaire de minuit* op. 30 (1953), '*opéra en trois actes*', also after Limbour; *Les Espagnols à Venise* op. 60 (1963), '*opéra bouffe*', his last with Limbour ; *Labyrinthe* op. 85 (1969), '*drame musical*' on a text of his own after Baudelaire; and *Todos caerán* op. 91 (1971), '*opéra en deux actes et cinq tableaux*', on a libretto of his own – his most ambitious stage work, never performed in its entirety to this day.[2]

In fact, of Leibowitz's five operas, only one was ever performed, namely *Les Espagnols à Venise*, in 1970 at Grenoble's Maison de la Culture, directed by Humbert Camerlo and conducted by himself. By no means a man of the opera establishment, even if he did conduct major works of the repertoire, he was known for modernist achievements such as the first French performances of Schoenberg's *Erwartung* (1966) and *Die glückliche Hand* (1968), both with Camerlo. Just before his untimely death in 1972, he shared his thoughts on contemporary music theatre in his last book, *Les fantômes de l'opéra*, dedicated to the history of opera from Monteverdi to Schoenberg, published fifteen years after his first book on the topic (Leibowitz 1972). Even if his views on recent productions appear only fleetingly in the prologue and the epilogue, they are important because they frame Leibowitz's discourse on opera as a genre, which he set out now to defend and promote in times of unpopularity and ideological defiance.

In this book, he claims that the great opera composers of the past were 'true revolutionaries', since their works were the result of 'an opposition and a revolt against the society that generated them'. One of his favorite examples is *Tosca*, an *opéra contestataire*, a 'dissenting opera' whose subject matter – he adds, borrowing Sartre's vocabulary, as he already did in 1957 – is proof of Puccini's '*engagement*' (Leibowitz 1972: 263). Along these lines, he opposes in the prologue the authentic 'revolutionary will' of the composers of operatic masterpieces to the *dilettantisme* and *amateurisme* of contemporary composers and artists:

> The common trait to all we usually talk of as 'avant-garde' (be they *happenings*, 'improvisations', or 'artistic laboratories' travelling around the world), is that, more often than not, it relies on clichés and hackneyed formulas.
>
> One might think that if it did not exist, someone should invent it. The problem is that *all this has already been invented*, and if our dilettantes were not such, they would know that since the beginning of our century there have been several 'movements' – German expressionism, Italian futurism, Surrealism – of which our current 'avant-gardists' only produce pale imitations.
>
> (Leibowitz 1972: 15, emphasis in original)

---

2 Scenes 4 and 5 and the Interlude of the Premier Tableau of Act I were performed in a concert version by the Schola Heidelberg and the Ensemble Aisthesis, conducted by Walter Nussbaum, at the Klangforum Heidelberg, on 28 October 2017.

René Leibowitz's Todos caerán   155

In the epilogue, Leibowitz dedicates a whole section to 'the complex of the avant-garde', debunking '*les fantoches de la contestation*', the 'puppets of dissent' that, he says, have been particularly active since May 1968. He goes on :

> Most of the avant-garde ignores even the existence of lyric art, or has of it a limited idea that can't but inspire contempt and distrust. This makes it prone to surrender to *fantoches*.
>
> Some did try, though, here and there. Without going into details – the topic is not worth it – let's say they do it in a spirit that, for want of a better word, I call 'nihilist'. They want to produce operas that are not operas, or that represent some 'emancipation', as a kind of opera that was 'never done before'.
>
> Again, the futility of it all does not merit closer examination. Their real and deep motivations are *à la mode* imperatives that are meaningless, and actually not new at all. In order to scandalize, not only the singers, choirs and extras get dressed – or undressed – but also the members of the orchestra and the conductor (they all participate in the 'action'); with the help of eroticism and simple pornography [. . .], opera is supposed to have been 'revolutionized'.
>
> (Leibowitz 1972: 367–8)

It is a pity that Leibowitz declined to 'go into details'. One might wonder, for example, what he had in mind when he talked about 'pornography'. Even if there was no explicit eroticism in it, a candidate is Sylvano Bussotti's *La Passion selon Sade*, whose first performance in 1966 at *Le Domaine musical* had been the target of violent criticism. The critic of *Le Monde* dismissed it as 'a college student's hoax', a 'kind of farce' without 'any reason to exist', nor true novelty: 'It's rather like a resurgence of the epidemic of Dadaism' (Siohan 1966). While this last might suggest dislike not only for Bussotti's work but also for historical Dadaism, the critic regarded the new piece as an involuntary and impoverished remake of historical avant-gardes, just as Leibowitz later did. Yet, he also expressed disappointment regarding his hopes of living 'the experience of a new music theatre' – by which he implied that he *was* looking forward to a new music theatre in the first place (ibid.). Now, claims of support for true novelty, as compared to the actual novelty being judged, are typical reactions of conservative critics. But this shows that Leibowitz's skeptical position, far from being idiosyncratic, was part of a larger debate.

At an international level, Leibowitz was close not only to some professional critics, but also to composers such as Alberto Ginastera (1916–1983), who saw his atonal operas, set in historicist contexts with a kind of Verdian dramaturgy, as counter-examples to contemporary 'anti-operas' (see Buch 2003). As Eric Drott has documented, while a new *théâtre musical* developed in France by the early 1970s with people such as Georges Aperghis, Michel Puig, and Claude Prey, there were 'a number of individuals questioning the "false audacity" and "false subversiveness" of contemporary composers' (see Drott 2011: 208–9). Even if there is no reason to think that Leibowitz was targeting Puig in *Les fantômes de l'opéra*, the fact that this last was a former pupil of his, whose 'chamber opera' *Stigmates* against the Algerian war he had conducted in 1962, shows his proximity to what he was now rejecting (Vichniac 1962).

Leibowitz's dismissal of what he calls avant-garde had a personal dimension, which inspired in him passionate *coups de sang*, rather than systematic analysis of the field. His quarrel with new music theatre after May 1968 had roots in the early fifties, when his former pupil Pierre Boulez succeeded in presenting him, in his article 'Schoenberg is dead' and other texts, as a paradigmatic example of academicism and conservatism. In later years, his attachment to Schoenbergian dodecaphony and his plea for twelve-tone 'athematicism' could appear as *passé*, compared to integral serialism, indeterminacy, instrumental theatre, and other tendencies of contemporary music. Of course, the triumph of Boulez's aesthetics over Leibowitz's was no law of history but the result of a symbolic fight, whose result, nevertheless, consigned the latter for decades to a reactive position, a fate that resonates in the harshness of his vocabulary (see Kapp 1988; Buch 2018).

Leibowitz's aggressive disdain of avant-garde experiences might appear today as paternalistic and full of prejudice. From a historical perspective, though, it also reminds us that composers and artists of an older generation shared with younger composers the will to renew the field of music theatre, while diverging radically as to the means to achieve it. Leibowitz, for one, was convinced that atonal operas were an appropriate response to the crisis of the genre, and in a provocative Verdian *torniam'al antico* spirit he composed works that addressed contemporary issues while being consciously clothed in vintage dramaturgy. This was the case of *Les Espagnols à Venise*, the story of the revolt of the people of Venice against an alleged conspiracy of sixteenth-century Spaniards, disguised as modern German tourists.[3]

This *opéra bouffe* achieved only modest success. An unconvinced critic of *Le Monde* noted that 'the tradition of this musical genre is no longer really blossoming', and wrote that even regardless of its genre 'his *opéra bouffe* is a sad farce whose scenic and musical intentions are hard to understand' (Dandrel 1970). But such reactions notwithstanding, Leibowitz was confident that, thanks to his knowledge of the history of opera and the avant-gardes, and his command of twelve-tone technique, he was better armed than others to revive the great composers' 'revolutionary' spirit. As he says in *Les fantômes de l'opéra*, this claim was related to his skepticism towards May 68, a youthful movement that in private conversations he tended to dismiss as immature, illusory, and not really revolutionary.[4] This was not only a matter of age – Leibowitz was 55 years old in 1968 – but also one of political sensibility. His views on May 68 were not unlike those of some people with leftist views and/or who were close to the Communist Party. In 1968, writer Philippe Sollers denounced the movement's 'counter-revolutionary

---

3 René Leibowitz, *Les Espagnols à Venise. Opéra bouffe en un acte de Georges Limbour*, vocal score. Facsimile of the manuscript, Bibliothèque nationale de France, Paris.

4 Antoinette Molinié, personal communications, 18 October 2013 and 25 July 2017; Humbert Camerlo, personal communication, 5 August 2017.

leftist spontaneism', a view that in his case was soon to change radically, in favor of Maoism (cited in Hourmant 1996: 115); many years after, an intellectual like Claude Lévi-Strauss still expressed retrospectively his 'repugnance' for the *événements* (Éribon 1998/2001: 115–17). Leibowitz, not a revolutionary himself, was familiar with the French left's discourse and pathos, as a long-time collaborator of Sartre, a signatory in 1960 of the *Manifeste des 121* and other statements against the Algerian War, and a man who, in 1967, composed *Four songs Che Guevara in memoriam* op. 80, shortly after the iconic guerrilla's death in Bolivia. Against what he perceived as the failure of the new generation to produce convincing stage works dealing with crucial issues such as revolution and eroticism, and maybe against what he perceived as the failure of political and sexual revolution as such, he was ready to show that he – a man in his late fifties, of forward-looking tastes and outlook – could stage a *better* tale of love and revolution.

Thus, between July 1970 and May 1972 Leibowitz composed an opera that, aside from its atonal language, corresponds to his own definition of the *grand opéra français*: '"Wide-reaching", historical (rather than mythological) topics, characters in prey to violent passions, many sumptuous settings, crowd scenes with large choirs, many orchestral effects to enrich and give colors to the drama, dance interludes (and sometimes important ballet scenes)' (Leibowitz 1972: 214). Except for the lack of dance, this is a fitting description of *Todos caerán*, a work in two acts and five tableaux that features five main characters, twenty-two secondary roles, two choirs, a brass ensemble onstage, and an imposing orchestra with triple winds and a big percussion set. It pictures a bunch of leftist revolutionaries trying to debunk and kill a cruel right-wing dictator, while getting trapped in tortuous and sublime love affairs, in the exotic setting of an imaginary, contemporary Latin-American island. Close to the title, the manuscript score has the words 'pour Antoinette', the woman who, identified as 'A.', is also the dedicatee of the prologue of *Les fantômes de l'opéra*, as if Leibowitz was giving her name to the connection between his critique of new music theatre and his contribution to the renewal of opera.[5]

* * *

Why, of all possible subjects, did Leibowitz write an opera on a Latin-American revolution? At the time, Latin America was often a matter of debate in France – especially Cuba and Chile – and for many it was common sense that a revolution *of some kind* was a positive political and/or cultural horizon (Bantigny 2016). But in 1971 the 'Padilla affair' – the name of a writer persecuted by Castro's regime – estranged many of Leibowitz's friends, such as Sartre and Michel Leiris, from the Cuban revolution, thus casting the very figure of the revolutionary under a darker, controversial light.[6] And, except for his songs for Che Guevara, Leibowitz had never directly addressed political subjects in his music before, nor did he have a

---

5 René Leibowitz, *Todos caerán. Opéra en deux actes et cinq tableaux*, op. 91, orchestral score and vocal score. Facsimiles of the manuscripts, Bibliothèque nationale de France, Paris.
6 'La lettre des intellectuels à M. Fidel Castro', *Le Monde*, 22 May 1972.

158   *Esteban Buch*

strong political interest in revolution, nor a lasting personal connection with Latin America, which he had briefly toured in 1957 as a conductor (see Schürmann 2010: 413–15).[7]

Yet, a new element in the composer's private life might explain his decision to deal intensively with the topic in 1971 and 1972. The composition of *Todos caerán* can be partially reconstructed thanks to the letters he wrote to Monique and Claude Lévi-Strauss, this last being not only a famous specialist of Latin-American cultures but also a passionate Wagnerite and opera lover, who in his books compared music and mythology.[8] The musician and the anthropologist met in the late 1940s, and became closer friends during the sixties (Faivre d'Arcier 2013; Meine 2000: 64–9). Their relationship became a collaboration in 1970, when Lévi-Strauss made a scenography for Leibowitz's and Camerlo's production of Ravel's *L'heure espagnole*, given in Grenoble as a complement to the first performance of *Les Espagnols à Venise*. The costumes and scenography for this last piece were made by Victoria von Hagen, an archeologist close to Lévi-Strauss who also specialized in Latin America (see von Hagen 1972), and with whom Leibowitz had a lasting, intimate relationship.

On 17 May 1970, Leibowitz's long-time friend and collaborator Georges Limbour drowned on a Spanish beach, leaving him without a librettist. In August, the composer wrote to Lévi-Strauss:

> I still don't know for sure what I'll be busy with this summer. I'd like to write a new opera (a 'grand' one, in 3 acts), but – since Limbour's death – I don't know how to do it. I wrote musical sketches for several scenes, but I don't feel ready to write a libretto. I'll take with me Shakespeare's Chronicles and other Elizabethan historical plays, hoping to find there at least a 'plot'.[9]

The two men must have discussed Leibowitz's new project, for shortly after that Lévi-Strauss lent him an unidentified theatre piece as a basis for a libretto. But the composer had already made his mind for a different kind of subject :

> Thank you for thinking about a libretto for me. I don't want to take your copy away from you, but perhaps I could read it at your place, without bothering you. Also, if you had an hour, and if you don't mind, I'd like to show you some notes I took for my 'historical' (or 'political') subject. That might give you some idea of a play for me to read.[10]

---

7 In 1957 Leibowitz gave concerts in Mexico and Venezuela. A second tour to Chile and Argentina was planned for 1958 but was probably cancelled, according to sources in Buenos Aires. Silvia Glocer to author, 19 April 2008.

8 Unfortunately, Lévi-Strauss' answers to Leibowitz's letters are apparently lost (except for the last one, quoted below). On Lévi-Strauss and music, see Nattiez 2008 and Meine 2000: 65.

9 René Leibowitz to Claude Lévi-Strauss, 3 August 1970, manuscript letter, collection NAF 28150 (195), Bibliothèque nationale de France.

10 René Leibowitz to Claude Lévi-Strauss, 26 September 1970, manuscript letter, collection NAF 28150 (195), BnF.

René Leibowitz's Todos caerán   159

Besides suggesting that Leibowitz could start writing music for an opera before having the libretto and even before knowing the subject matter, this letter shows that the choice of a 'grand' opera on a 'historical' or 'political' subject came before finding the subject in question. By March 1971 his thoughts had evolved a little further:

> I've worked quite a lot on my new opera (two and a half scenes from Act 1), and I start to have some ideas for the plot. But I need your advice again, and also Monique's. Can I show it to you in the coming days, without abusing of your time and patience?[11]

A couple of months later, the 'ideas for the plot' had become precise enough to make headway with the structure of the second act:

> I thank you again for your interest in my work, I really appreciate your advice and your ideas. I'll try to organize the dramatic action of the second act, and I'll show it to you, hopefully without trying your patience.[12]

The letters to Lévi-Strauss suggest that Leibowitz found his subject between October 1970 and March 1971, a subject that was actually less 'historical' than 'political', in the sense that it was based on contemporary events. But how did he find it? By the end of 1970, at a dinner at his friend Salomon Resnik's – an Argentine-born psychoanalyst connected with Latin-American circles – the composer met Antoinette Molinié, an anthropologist just returned from her PhD fieldwork in Peru, focused on the impact of agrarian reform on Indian populations (Fioravanti-Molinié 1971). The young woman was fully consubstantiated with the cause of Latin-American revolution: 'The massive introduction of money in the community', she wrote in a paper on the Huanchay valley, 'tends to develop wage labour', thus 'destructuring' traditional society (Fioravanti-Molinié 1975: 106). Close at the time to the Communist Party, she was soon to abandon her Marxist orientation and embrace a culturalist approach more akin to Lévi-Strauss, whom she eventually met through her new friend.[13] Thirty years younger than Leibowitz, she was to be his *dernier amour*.

During her first fieldwork in Peru, Molinié visited the revolutionary leader Hugo Blanco, then resident in a prison island near the Callao port, and one of the key figures of the *guevarista* movement in South America, in opposition to general Velasco Alvarado's military government which had been in power since 1968.[14] Blanco, a Trotskyist union leader, had been in jail since 1963, and had

---

11 René Leibowitz to Claude Lévi-Strauss, 27 March 1971, manuscript letter, collection NAF 28150 (195), BnF.
12 René Leibowitz to Claude Lévi-Strauss, 7 May 1971, manuscript letter, collection NAF 28150 (195), BnF.
13 Antoinette Molinié's books on Peru include Molinié 1982 and Molinié and Galinier 2006.
14 Antoinette Molinié, personal communications, 18 October 2013 and 25 July 2017. See Niedergang 1970.

160   *Esteban Buch*

escaped the death penalty partly thanks to the mobilization of Sartre, Beauvoir, Leiris and other intellectuals,[15] before being given an amnesty by Velasco in December 1970, shortly after the anthropologist's visit. Another intriguing episode of her trip was her encounter with an American travel companion who – she learnt afterwards – was suspected of being a CIA agent. There are few doubts that what Antoinette told her friend René about the Peruvian revolutionary scene was a powerful inspiration for his opera project: 'The story of *Todos caerán* ran in all our conversations', she says.[16] Leibowitz used a text by her for the opera's last aria, where a character named Esmeralda sings, just before throwing herself into the sea:

> I kissed the flowers, hurting my hands. How beautiful they were, and how much they trouble me. You ask me to tell you more about my silence, as you often do, without any hope of understanding it. [. . .] You know so many things, that I feel isolated as the red of your flowers. [. . .] Are you the one who talked about death? But everything is so beautiful, and I care for it as if it were some imaginary treasure in an island.[17]

In July 1972, Antoinette returned to Peru, leaving René to write passionate letters while dreaming of living together in Chicago, as he had proposed before her departure. Almost at the same time, the composer wrote to his friend Paul Dessau: 'My opera is ready. I'm quite satisfied. Still no title.'[18] And two weeks later, to Lévi-Strauss: 'I finally finished my opera, and now I'll have to wait 3 or 4 years before having it (perhaps) performed.'[19] Lévi-Straus answered a few days later: 'Congratulations for the completion of the opera, I hope we'll soon be able to hear it (maybe first played by you at the piano?). I warmly thank you for sending me – and for having written – this text that touches me.'[20] To Dessau again, on 4 August, he spoke of 'my unnamed opera (but the title is forthcoming)'.[21] The title must have been decided in the very days that followed, while preparing fair copies of the orchestral score and the vocal score, where it appears on the cover sheet; the typewritten libretto has the title and the mention 'Pour Antoinette' written in ink, as if added afterwards.[22]

On 22 August, the composer wrote to his friend Camerlo: 'I have some circulatory disorders and I have to do lots of medical tests, X-rays, etc. (Nothing really

---

15 'Le leader paysan péruvien Hugo Blanco menacé d'exécution', *Le Monde*, 26 November 1966.

16 Molinié, personal communication, 25 July 2017.

17 René Leibowitz, Libretto for *Todos Caerán*, n/p, and Antoinette Molinié, manuscript, Archive Antoinette Molinié.

18 René Leibowitz to Paul Dessau, 29 June 1972, cited in Schürmann 2010: 540.

19 René Leibowitz to Claude Lévi-Strauss, 12 July 1972, manuscript letter, collection NAF 28150 (195), BnF.

20 Claude Lévi-Strauss to René Leibowitz, 17 July 1972, manuscript letter, Sammlung Leibowitz, Paul Sacher Stiftung, Basel.

21 René Leibowitz to Paul Dessau, 4 August 1972, cited in Schürmann 2010: 540.

22 Archive Antoinette Molinié.

serious, *almeno lo spero*).'[23] On the evening of 28 August, in Paris, he suffered a fatal heart attack. Soon after, Antoinette Molinié received in Peru a telegram from Claude Lévi-Strauss, announcing to her the death of René Leibowitz.

* * *

Todos caerán, Spanish for *Everyone must fall*, is the title of a picture by Goya with no direct relationship to the revolution, nor to Latin America (Figure 7.1). It is one of his *Caprichos*, number 19 of the famous print series published in 1799, which Molinié remembers admiring in a book, together with the composer.[24] The etching shows an old woman and two girls impaling with a stick a human-headed bird, while in the sky other anthropomorphic male birds fly around a sitting female character with human head and breasts, and the body of a bird. The title is written down below. The artist supposedly commented, in a manuscript held at the Museo del Prado in Madrid: 'Y que no escarmienten los que van a caer con el ejemplo de los que han caído! pero no hay más remedio todos caerán' ['And those who are about to fall won't take warning from those who have fallen! But there is no remedy: all will fall'].[25] In Goya, the words *Todos caerán* seem to allude to men's moral weaknesses and to their vulnerability to corruption by prostitutes, as well as to women's cruel revolt against their oppressive power. The *Caprichos*' most famous title, 'The sleep of reason produces monsters', coupled to Goya's reputation as a non-conformist artist, must have resonated with Leibowitz's interest in developing a critical, 'revolutionary' art (see Nehamas 2001). In fact the picture itself appears less related to his opera than these Spanish words, read as a prophecy of the fall of the actors of his Latin American tale. While the libretto is in French, the characters all have Spanish names (except for Isabella, whose spelling is Italian, perhaps as a mistake for Isabel).

'The action is set today in an imaginary island', says the score. The work stages a right-wing dictator, Salvador (bass), backed by the Army and the Church, and a group of revolutionaries led by Carlos (tenor). It is hard not to think of Cuba under Batista on the eve of Castro's revolution, even if one can dream of some other Latin-American country led by a cartoon-like character such as General Alcázar in Hergé's *Tintin*. In that respect, this fiction does differ from 1971 Peru, governed by General Velasco Alvarado, a dictator with leftist leanings who, whatever his wrongdoings, does not qualify for the sinister cliché incarnated by, say, General Somoza in Nicaragua, General Trujillo in Guatemala or General Stroessner in Paraguay (see Stephens 1983). In Leibowitz's opera, a statue of Bolívar, the nineteenth-century hero of South-American independence, is set in front of the Presidential Palace.

---

23 René Leibowitz to Humbert Camerlo, 22 August 1972, cited in Camerlo, unpublished essay.
24 Molinié, personal communication, 25 July 2017.
25 Translation from Heckes 1978.

Figure 7.1 Francisco de Goya, *Todos caerán* (*Los caprichos* no. 19).

The first act begins in the street, at night, with the entrance of Rodrigo (baritone), a revolutionary just escaped from Salvador's prison, and deeply troubled after confessing under torture the names of his comrades, including that of his lover Isabella. His sense of guilt, his ambition, and his existential anguish define a tortuous psychology, shared by other masculine characters of the opera. Salvador is a cruel and megalomaniac tyrant, haunted by the loneliness of power and the betrayal of his lover; Carlos is a sacrificial hero, probably modeled on Che Guevara, yet he is plagued by all-too-human desires. The intertwining of political action and personal passion, reminiscent of Sartre's theatre plays, rules the drama throughout the work.

The female characters, far from leading the revolt, as in Goya's picture, are defined by their relationship to men: Isabella, 'lover of Rodrigo, collaborator of Carlos', and Esmeralda, 'lover of Salvador, in love with Carlos', says the libretto. The two sopranos represent opposite types, the sublime Isabella and the treacherous Esmeralda, who despite their musical importance are secondary in the political plot. Isabella resists Carlos' passionate advances by claiming that loyalty to the Revolution excludes romantic feelings. Esmeralda betrays Salvador not out of political conviction but because of her desperate love for Carlos, and eventually kills Isabella out of jealousy. Even if Isabella's idealism and virtuoso singing make of her a heroine, from a feminist perspective Leibowitz's libretto looks as conservative as most traditional operas. It is true that here the 'undoing of women' is but a consequence of the general rule that *everyone must fall* (see Clément 1999).

This melodramatic plot has a comic counterpoint in Pico, Paco, and Pongo, a trio of conspirators who try to destabilize the country for the sake of an obscure foreign power, without backing either Salvador's regime or the Revolution. An obvious allusion to Ping, Pong, and Pang from Puccini's *Turandot*, and perhaps a more obscure one to Paul, Boum, and Puck from Offenbach's *La Duchesse de Gérolstein*, they are cartoon-like CIA agents, seen in the eye of the anti-imperialist left: ridiculous and mean, yet dangerous and smart enough to survive when everybody else has fallen, leaving the island with an ominous promise to return. All these sub-intrigues are embedded in grandiose crowd tableaux, a public trial of prisoners greeted by the priests, the setting fire to the University by Salvador, a funeral procession for the dictator, and the final explosion of the Presidential Palace. During an interlude, a choir of prisoners who wait for their death brings an echo of *Fidelio*. The revolution seems to fail at the end of the first act, when Salvador arrests Carlos and his friends. Yet in the second act the dictator is shot by Rodrigo in a moment of confusion, while Carlos lies dying in a dungeon jail. Rodrigo's and Esmeralda's deaths follow. Mortality rates are high in *Todos caerán*, even by the lethal standards of the operatic tradition.

Indeed, the first death is that of an old man from the people, coldly shot by an officer for mumbling a protest against the dictator. The true subject of the plot is less the Revolution than the inexorable fall of everybody, dictators and revolutionaries, men and women alike. From that point of view, Leibowitz's is a desperate, even nihilistic view of the world's state and future. Yet, despite this nihilism, 'the people' progressively reveals itself to be the true hero of the story: ready to back the dictator's cruellest actions in the first act, it storms the Presidential Palace in the second, as in a remake of the October Revolution, only to be stopped by the bloody explosion set off by the three *agents provocateurs*. After this grandiose climax, during which the crowds led by a 'young priest' and a 'young man' occupy the stage over pure orchestral music, the end is open-ended, for survivors sing simultaneously of *espoir* (hope) and *désespoir* (despair).

Overall, the story seems to echo Leibowitz's description of *Tosca*, an opera that 'shows us in the crudest possible way the conflict between, on one side, the "official" will of oppression, and, on the other, the desire for freedom (implying a challenge to established power)' (Leibowitz 1972: 263). What he says about *Don Carlos* also applies here: 'situations and characters so diverse, that the imbroglio would be inextricable, without the music's grandiose synthesis' (Leibowitz 1972: 179). Now, the music of *Todos caerán* does operate a (perhaps grandiose) synthesis of the heterogeneous elements of the libretto, but of course Leibowitz's language is very different from Puccini's or Verdi's. As Leibowitz knew very well, atonal operas seldom found their way to opera houses. The work starts with a dodecaphonic series that heralds the musical style of *Todos caerán* (see Example 7.1).

Throughout the score, the intervallic structure privileges minor seconds and major thirds. Their function was described in 1980 by Jan Maguire, a disciple of the composer:

> He maintains integral variation throughout the opera with only two musical elements, his thesis and antithesis: the second and the third. These two intervals, with their inversions, used vertically and horizontally, expressed in an infinite number of forms, rhythms, registers, dynamics, instruments and voices, form the entire work – the fifth, their sum, acting as synthesis between them.
>
> (Maguire 1980: 7)

Even if this description is quite unspecific, Maguire's stress on 'integral variation' does echo a fundamental feature of the score, namely its athematicism.

Since the late 1940s, athematic composition was Leibowitz's envisioned *telos* for twelve-tone music, soon to be opposed to Boulez's integral serialism;

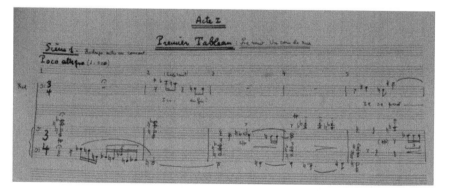

Example 7.1 Leibowitz, *Todos caerán*, vocal score: Act I, Tableau 1, Scene 1, bars 1–2.

in this late work, it leads him to avoid motivic characterization as a basis for dramatic action (Leibowitz 1949; see Buch 2006). Even if serial operations are not easy to reconstruct in the absence of sketches or other traces of the creative process,[26] it is also pretty clear that series are not used to identify the characters nor to suggest relationships between them, as happens typically in Berg's *Lulu*. Indeed, contrary to received wisdom about Leibowitz's Viennese school 'academicism', the frequent use of incomplete series and/or repeated notes deviates from standard, 'classic' twelve-tone technique. Coherence, instead, is largely based on atonal style itself and the dominant Expressionist orchestral idiom – sometimes infiltrated by chamber-like sonorities, as in Isabella's first aria with bass clarinet and cello solo *obbligati* – and the alternation of lyric, *Sprechgesang* and *parlato* vocal techniques (as in Rodrigo's outburst; see Example 7.2).

As a result, characters are most distinguishable in how they relate to the operatic repertoire. Esmeralda is a kind of Donizetti's Lucia, Isabella is an heir of Puccini's Tosca, Carlos a grandson of Beethoven's Florestan, Salvador a tenebrous bass much in the fashion of Verdi's Philippe II (see Example 7.3), and so on. This web of classical references is only partially unified by *bel canto*, for the classical melodic impulse is inflected by Viennese-school features such as huge intervallic leaps (ninths, tenths, and more) and the general avoidance of closure. The only exception is the thematic function of major thirds in the characterization of Pico, Paco, and Pongo, as a reminiscence of *Turandot*'s lighter, operetta-like register (see Example 7.4).

As to the crowd scenes, their dramatic importance and atonal style might evoke Schoenberg's *Moses und Aron*. Political issues are often mirrored in differentiated writing for the choirs, like the anticlerical stance of the stiff *Requiem* section, and the emancipatory sign of Expressionist outbursts. In the second Tableau of Act I, though, when Salvador is at the height of his power, the prisoners who denounce the tyrant and the people who praise him are musically indistinguishable, as if to underline the fundamental political ambiguity of the masses (see Example 7.5).

* * *

René Leibowitz once noted that 'more than anything else, operas are made out of operas' (Leibowitz 1970). According to Jan Maguire, in *Todos caerán*

> references to traditional opera are intended as parody, but they are also intended in a broader sense to imply all opera itself, not only its passions but also its structure, its existence, and to stand it up against the absurdity of the contemporary political situation, and the pathos of humanity.
>
> (Maguire 1980: 10)

---

26 Neither sketches nor other documentary materials related to the opera are included in the René Leibowitz Collection at the Paul Sacher Stiftung, Basel (Heidy Zimmerman to author, email, 17 August 2017). The original manuscripts of the vocal and orchestral scores, whose photocopies (kept at the BnF) were the basis of this study, have not been located.

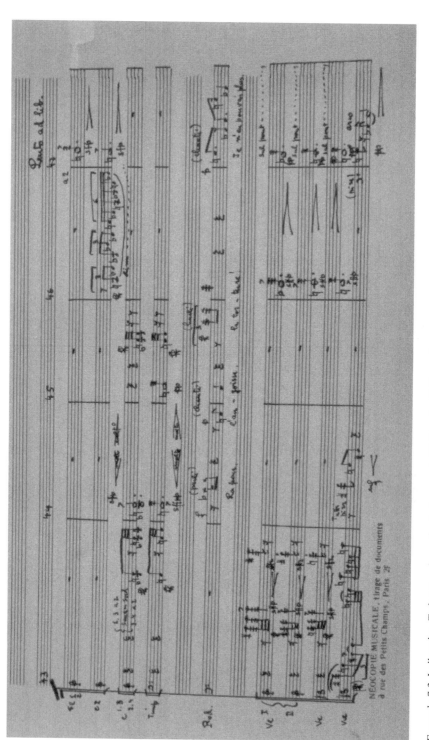

Example 7.2 Leibowitz, *Todos caerán*, orchestral score: Act I, Premier Tableau, Scene 1, bars 44–6.

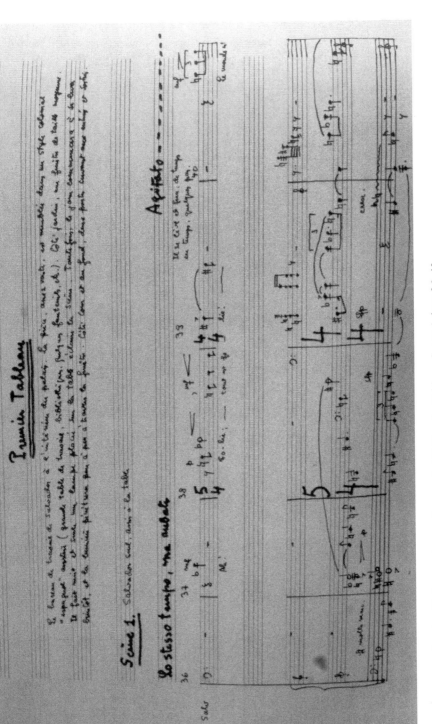

Example 7.3 Leibowitz, *Todos caerán*, vocal score: Act II, Premier Tableau, Scene 1, bars 36–40.

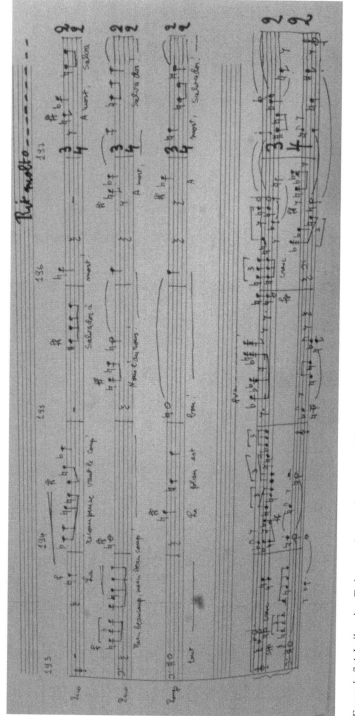

Example 7.4 Leibowitz, *Todos caerán*, vocal score: Act I, Premier Tableau, Scene 2, bars 193–8.

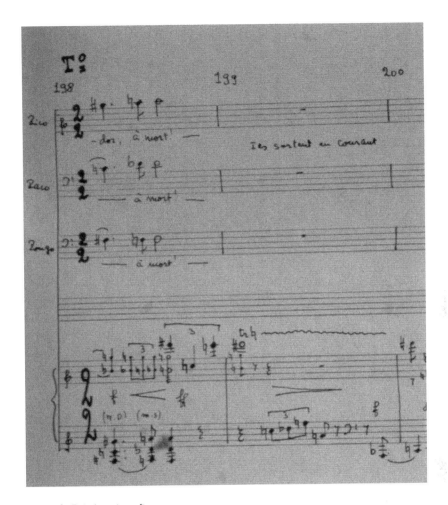

Example 7.4 (continued)

Parody, here, should not be taken as designating humour, but rather cross-relationships between genres. *Todos caerán* is a dodecaphonic *grand opéra*, and also a parody of *grand opéra*, in part precisely because it is dodecaphonic. If the suspension of collective action to leave room to *bel canto* solos gives *grand opéra* its characteristic dramatic thrust, *Todos caerán* seeks to achieve the same thing by way of dodecaphonic *bel canto*, as when Isabella's vocal line hints chromatically at C major, on the words '*le combat*' ('the fight'; see Example 7.6).

Now, the three CIA characters, who might also evoke the Marx brothers, introduce a comic dimension that differs from the tragic spirit of, say, Auber's *La*

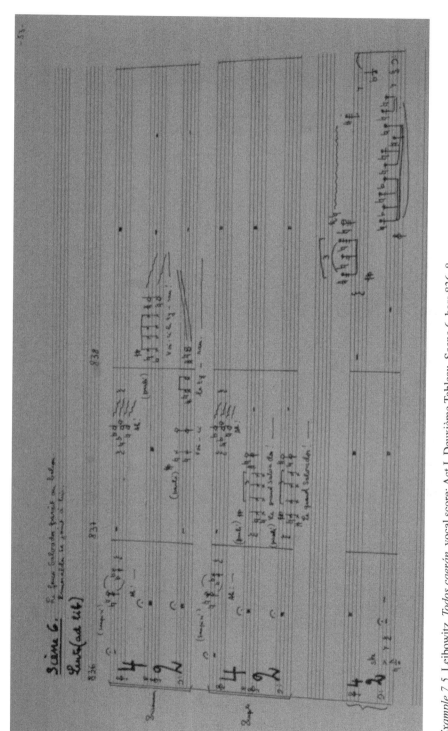

Example 7.5 Leibowitz, *Todos caerán*, vocal score: Act I, Deuxième Tableau, Scene 6, bars 836–8.

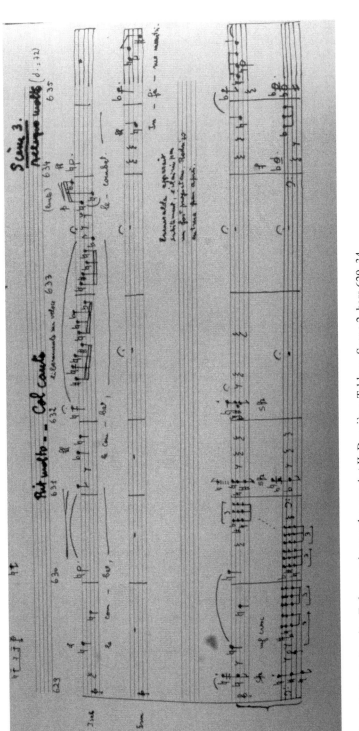

Example 7.6 Leibowitz, *Todos caerán*, vocal score: Act II, Deuxième Tableau, Scene 2, bars 629–34.

172 *Esteban Buch*

muette de Portici (1828), the paradigmatic example of *grand opéra* which also tells the story of a revolution. It cannot be discounted that Leibowitz had in mind pieces such as Offenbach's *La Périchole* (1868), an *opéra bouffe* that features a strange Viceroy from Peru and his unsubordinated mistress. Even if *Todos caerán* is very far from Offenbach, the sinister Salvador is literally a *dictateur d'opérette*, an expression that in today's French language does not allude to opera, but rather to actual authoritarian leaders, fond of theatrical apparatuses and phony gesticulations. Maybe Leibowitz wanted to write a satire of the Revolution, as a way to express his skeptical views on Revolution itself. And, contrary again to *grand opéra*, whose subjects were past events that required interpretation in order to relate to the present of the audience, he meant to address current political issues, revolution in Latin America being at the time a hot topic of public debate.

At the same time, as a man overtly hostile to *art engagé* and socialist realism, he did not try to intervene directly in the political arena, as in a kind of *agitprop*. This was coherent with another aspect of the *grand opéra* tradition. 'With its sympathetic, heroic rebels', writes Peter Mondelli, 'French grand opera thus presented something seemingly implausible: an officially sanctioned portrayal of historical events running contrary to the beliefs and desires of the ruling classes' (Mondelli 2013: 41; see also Fulcher 1987). But while the nineteenth-century ruling classes had efficient ways to neutralize these works' subversive potential, the ruling classes of Leibowitz's world, i.e. the French intellectual elites, were more prone to sympathize with rebels than with officials, and this he shared with friends such as Claude and Monique Lévi-Strauss, Michel Leiris, and also Antoinette Molinié. By the way, it is ironic that Lévi-Strauss accompanied the creative process of a music work so influenced by Sartre, precisely at the time when a public controversy between both intellectuals led the composer to take sides with the first and against the latter.[27] As a matter of fact, *Todos caerán* totally ignores the anthropological specificities of Latin American cultures, starting with the Indians so dear to Lévi-Strauss and Molinié.

Leibowitz's untimely death prevented *Todos caerán* from being considered for production by an opera house. But even before that, prospects for a performance were not very good, as the composer acknowledged in his last letter to Lévi-Strauss. By the time he started writing *Todos caerán*, he couldn't ignore that the exorbitant technical demands of his new score would make a premiere all the more unlikely. Things are not very different today, forty-seven years after his death, with Leibowitz trapped in an endless purgatory. Yet the virtual oblivion of this operatic monster can be seen as part of its historical substance. According to Humbert Camerlo – by the time of his friend's death the best candidate to direct the new opera – the composer was prone to disregard feasibility issues out of pure artistic idealism.[28] Maybe this very idealism led Leibowitz to stage his vision of the revolution knowing already quite well that it would be almost as impossible

---

27 Leibowitz to Lévi-Strauss, 22 April 1972.
28 Camerlo, personal communication, 5 August 2017.

René Leibowitz's Todos caerán   173

to perform as revolution itself. Far from being a mainstream, conservative project, adapted to the taste of bourgeois opera and opera-goers, *Todos caerán* was an ambitious, challenging project, for the standards of the genre and its political imaginary. This conjecture makes of *Todos caerán* a kind of conceptual work, and puts it in a paradoxical company with the avant-garde the composer was so eager to dismiss while working on his own piece. Pushing this reasoning to its limits, it can be argued that, as an unperformed and unknown *grand opéra révolutionnaire*, René Leibowitz's last opera *is* a work of new music theatre.

References

Bantigny, Ludivine (2016), 'Flux et reflux de l'idée révolutionnaire', in Christophe Charle and Laurent Jeanpierre (eds), *La vie intellectuelle en France. II. De 1914 à nos jours*, Paris: Editions du Seuil, pp. 639–61.
Buch, Esteban (2003), *The Bomarzo Affair. Ópera, perversión y dictadura*, Buenos Aires: Adriana Hidalgo Editora.
Buch, Esteban (2006), 'Notes sur l'engagement de la musique, et en particulier sur *Un Survivant de Varsovie*', in Martin Kaltenecker and François Nicolas (eds), *Penser l'œuvre musicale au XXe siècle : avec, sans ou contre l'histoire?*, Paris: CDMC, pp. 95–110.
Buch, Esteban (2018), 'René Leibowitz, Pierre Boulez et Pierre Schaeffer dans le huis clos de la liberté', in Laurent Feneyrou and Alain Poirier (eds), *De la Libération au Domaine musical: Dix ans de musique en France (1944–1954)*, Paris: Editions Vrin, pp. 244–56.
Clément, Catherine (1999), *Opera : The Undoing of Women*, Minneapolis, MN: University of Minnesota Press.
Dandrel, Louis (1970), 'Création d'un opéra bouffe de René Leibowitz', *Le Monde*, 9 February.
Drott, Eric (2011), *Music and the Elusive Revolution. Cultural Politics and Political Culture in France, 1968–1981*, Berkeley, CA: University of California Press.
Éribon, Didier (1998/2001), *De Près et de loin*, Paris: Odile Jacob.
Faivre d'Arcier, Catherine (2013), 'Claude Lévi-Strauss et René Leibowitz. L'anthropologue à l'opéra et le compositeur en poésie', *Revue de la BNF*, 45, pp. 54–66.
Fioravanti-Molinié, Antoinette (1971), 'La réforme agraire péruvienne: premier bilan', *Politique Aujourd'hui*, 7–8, pp. 103–19.
Fioravanti-Molinié, Antoinette (1975), 'Rapports de parenté et de production à San Juan (Haute Vallée du Chancay, Pérou)', *Bulletin de l'Institut Français d'Etudes Andines*, 4/1–2, pp. 97–106.
Fulcher, Jane (1987), *The Nation's Image: French Grand Opera as Politics and Politicized Art*, New York: Cambridge University Press.
Hagen, Victoria von (1972), 'Distance biologique et endogamie', *L'Homme*, 12/4, pp. 85–96.
Heckes, Frank I (1978), 'Goya's Caprichos', *National Gallery of Victoria Art Journal*, 19, www.ngv.vic.gov.au/essay/goyas-caprichos/ (accessed 19 August 2017).
Hourmant, François (1996), '*Tel quel* et ses volte-face politiques (1968–1978)', *Vingtième Siècle, revue d'histoire*, 51, pp. 112–28.
Kapp, Reinhard (1987), 'Materialien zu einem Verzeichnis der Schriften von René Leibowitz', *Musiktheorie*, 2/3, pp. 275–83.

174 *Esteban Buch*

Kapp, Reinhard (1988), 'Shades of the double's original: René Leibowitz's dispute with Boulez', *Tempo*, 165, pp. 2–16.

Leibowitz, René (1949), *Introduction à la musique de douze sons*, Paris: L'Arche, pp. 267–70.

Leibowitz, René (1957), *Histoire de l'opéra*, Paris: Buchet-Chastel.

Leibowitz, René (1970), 'L'heure espagnole – Les Espagnols à Venise', *Rouge et noir. Journal d'information de la Maison de la Culture de Grenoble*, 14, http://webmuseo.com/ws/mc2/app/file/download/RN014-0170.pdf (accessed 19 August 2017).

Leibowitz, René (1972), *Les fantômes de l'opéra*, Paris: Gallimard.

Maguire, Jan (1980), 'Rene Leibowitz (II): the music', *Tempo*, 132, pp. 2–10.

Meine, Sabine (2000), *Ein Zwölftöner in Paris: Studien zu Biographie und Wirkung von René Leibowitz (1913–1972)*, Augsburg: Wissner.

Molinié, Antoinette and Jacques Galinier (2006), *Les néo-Indiens. Une religion du IIIè millénaire*, Paris: Odile Jacob.

Molinié, Antoinette (1982), *La Vallée Sacrée des Andes*, Paris: Société d'Ethnographie.

Mondelli, Peter (2013), 'The Sociability of History in French Grand Opera: A Historical Materialist Perspective', *19th-Century Music*, 37/1, pp. 37–55.

Mosch, Ulrich (1992), '*L'artiste et sa conscience*. René Leibowitz und Jean-Paul Sartre', *Mitteilungen der Paul Sacher Stiftung*, 5, pp. 46–50.

Nattiez, Jean-Jacques (2008), *Lévi-Strauss musicien. Essai sur la tentation homologique*, Arles: Actes Sud.

Nehamas, Alexander (2001), 'The sleep of reason produces monsters', *Representations*, 74/1, pp. 37–54.

Niedergang, Marcel (1970), 'Le syndicaliste Hugo Blanco conteste que le régime péruvien soit "révolutionnaire"', *Le Monde*, 29 January.

Schürmann, Yvonne (2010), 'René Leibowitz: Ein Pionier für die Musik des 20. Jahrhunderts', PhD thesis, Vienna: University of Vienna.

Siohan, Robert (1966), '"La Passion selon Sade" de Bussotti', *Le Monde*, 10 December.

Stephens, Evelyne Huber (1983), 'The Peruvian military government, labor mobilization, and the political strength of the Left', *Latin American Research Review*, 18/2, pp. 57–93.

Vichniac, Isabelle (1962) 'Création à Lausanne d'un opéra de chambre d'une nouvelle formule: "Stigmates"', *Le Monde*, 31 August.

Part IV
New venues and environments

8 A survey of new music theatre in Rome, 1961–1973

'Anni favolosi'?

Alessandro Mastropietro

New music theatre composition in Rome

Following the premiere in 1961 of *Collage*, an 'azione musicale in un tempo' with music by Aldo Clementi and visual elements by Achille Perilli, Rome became a very lively hub for the creation – and, to a certain extent, the dissemination – of a new music theatre. The body of music theatre works composed in Rome up to 1973 (ranging from 'instrumental theatre' or 'gestural music' to 'fully-staged', in so far as the distinction is meaningful) amounts to no fewer than fifty entries.[1] This manifold cluster of works, each with its own approach to the combination of media, spans the entire spectrum of problematics common to all new music theatre of the period: a questioning and/or recombination of disciplinary genres and competences, together with their implications regarding different media; a reconsideration of theatrical space; the disintegration or disappearance of a dramatic-narrative system; a non-linear relationship with the verbal component; the testing of new vocal qualities; and so forth.

However, in Rome this burgeoning activity cannot be explained independently of the appearance of a new generation of composers converging upon the Italian capital for various reasons: besides being the point of intersection for political and diplomatic as well as artistic and international relations (which carried advantages when it came to keeping up-to-date with the artistic horizon internationally),[2] Rome was home to kinds of cultural renewal, new lifestyle and communication-based industries (cinema, radio, television, newspapers and magazines), and the growth of educational and cultural institutions. All this made for increasing job opportunities for musicians, artists and intellectuals. Many young composers were

---

1 A chronological table of this body of work can be consulted in Mastropietro 2019 (at the time of writing, this book is in production): divided into two columns ('fully-staged' versus 'instrumental theatre' or 'gestural music'), it includes works by composers not strictly belonging to the neo-avant-garde, but who were nonetheless receptive to new music-dramaturgical strategies and based in Rome (such as Henze and Bucchi).

2 The foreign State Academies and Institutes in Rome played an especially important role, among which the most active during the 1950s and 1960s – as far as new music was concerned – were the American Academy, the Goethe Institute and the German Academy in Villa Massimo (which reopened in 1957 after its requisition in 1945).

178   *Alessandro Mastropietro*

able to begin their teaching jobs shortly after graduation, often in new conservatories that were opening throughout the peninsula and could be easily reached from Rome. The worlds of cinema and broadcasting also offered an alternative – or a supplement – to the educational job, especially after the reopening of the Cinecittà studios in 1947 and the launch of Italian television broadcasts in 1954 (with offices in Rome from 1960). Ennio Morricone, today a guru of film music, began his activity in this context very early, but he also composed the music for a ballet (*Requiem per un destino*, 1967) that retains some traits of a new-music-theatre dramaturgy (Mastropietro 2019).[3] Egisto Macchi worked basically as a composer for movies (short ones, rather than long ones). Paolo Renosto began his career within the Italian national broadcasting service (RAI). Many others – including Domenico Guaccero and Vittorio Gelmetti – also had opportunities in these fields where, as in state education, the government role (through institutions like RAI and other specific initiatives) was more fundamental than the market in sustaining the cultural side of the industry. Aside from the job domain, Rome was thereby becoming an even more appealing city as far as culture and lifestyle are concerned. Musical, artistic and cultural magazines opened or moved their editorial office there, thus giving to composers and critics an opportunity to make an intervention, sometimes an interdisciplinary confrontation, on their pages. One Roman neighbourhood even acquired the reputation of an interdisciplinary district in the years leading up to 1968: the zone south of Piazza del Popolo and around Via del Corso hosted both the Conservatorio di Musica di Santa Cecilia and the Accademia di Belle Arti, a lot of small (sometimes progressive) art galleries and painting studios, book and music shops, and editorial offices; people from all of these gathered at the end of the day at elegant cafés or popular taverns of the quarter, engaging in endless aesthetic debates as part of a very convivial as well as pleasant lifestyle (Salaris 1999: 167–255; Mafai 2002).

Educational opportunities were also of primary importance for the new musical generation: in addition to the natives, many young musicians moved to Rome, some already in the course of their studies. In terms of composition, Goffredo Petrassi, who taught at both the Conservatorio and the Accademia of Santa Cecilia, was seen as a key point of reference during the post-war period: young composers including Clementi, Guaccero, Bertoncini, Morricone, Heineman, Panni and Zosi studied under him, while Evangelisti and Pennisi worked under Petrassi's students. Petrassi's teaching was regarded as progressive and open-minded (Guaccero 2005 [1964]): it provided models (moreover, by no means limited to his own music) only as historic examples in solving compositional problems, amongst which music dramaturgy was an issue for Petrassi himself.[4]

---

3 The plot and the music for this ballet are a non-linear reorganisation of those from the movie *Un uomo a metà* (directed by Vittorio De Seta, 1966).
4 Petrassi's last stage work, the one-act *Morte dell'aria*, falls very early in his career (1950): it demonstrates how the coordinates of the traditional dramaturgy were still a strong reference point for the 'older' generation, who tried to renew it through inventing quite allegorical plots (often with ethical implications), so challenging the interpersonal and psychological preoccupations of nineteenth-century opera, instead of rethinking the vocals and/or relationship of the different media.

A survey of new music theatre in Rome   179

Petrassi's methods broadened his students' education to a wider cultural training, for instance, through visiting painter's studios near the Conservatorio, with a view to stimulating the search for a different, original way of thinking in music: an experience that had a substantial part in the birth of *Collage*.

Collage was a seminal occurrence in many respects: like most of the fully-staged new music theatre works conceived in Rome, its planning and production involved a representative of other neo-avant-garde disciplines, here the painter and man of theatre Achille Perilli.[5] Moreover, as a result of the authors' aversion towards any melodramatic vocalisation, the vocal medium is confined to a montage of jazz singing (fragments from recordings of Bessie Smith) which serves as a soundtrack to just one of the work's twelve scenes, consisting of a short surrealist-like black and white film (see Lux and Tortora (eds) 2005). The dramaturgy arises from the superimposition of contrasting scenic-visual and instrumental components. Clementi's music consists of sound surfaces partly adopted from his two instrumental *Ideogrammi* (1959); the earlier works are re-read in retrograde, their figures integrated according to procedures similar to Perilli's pictorial ones (veiling, proliferation, contrast of timbral colour and so on; see Mastropietro 2011: 217–19). Clementi's score is, therefore, even more of a collage than the scenic-visual contribution of Perilli, which stages objects and forms (including varied lighting, self-propelled pneumatic sculptures, backdrops and transparent screens, the above-mentioned film, and mannequins moved on rails), all the while maintaining the minimal and abstract narrative of an alchemical as well as a psychological process. Such a combination of quite autonomous expressions is intended – according to Perilli – to offer an 'increase and expansion of the imaginary potential of a story' entrusted to the audience, so that the radically self-referential, loosely structured spatio-temporal presentation, not dissimilar to a Cagean 'event', is not substantively received, but rather (so to speak) kept in mind, together with its links – apparent from the title – to its modernist premises.

Disciplinary co-authors thus aimed both to foster a substantial rethinking of dramaturgy, and to give each work a new, individual cipher, which depended on the features of the specific media and the relationship between them. From this arose a concern central to works of complex and heterogeneous design: whether to instil an organic – namely contrapuntal – relationship between the media and elements at play; or, on the contrary, to neglect any effort to integrate them, as a conscious aesthetic choice following the example of Dada and Cage (particularly suitable to the gestural-instrumental theatre and to mixed-media happenings).

Especially in the earlier part of the period under consideration here, the paradigm most frequently adopted by Roman creators of new music theatre was that of counterpoint between the media-layers. This model is clear in a sketch draft contained in one of the very first letters sent from Clementi to Perilli, during the gestation of *Collage*, which indicates the presence or absence of three referential

---

5 Perilli (Roma, b. 1927) founded multidisciplinary periodicals, covering fields of artistic experimentation that in Italy had long remained unknown (e.g. the theatre of the Bauhaus, Schwitters and surrealist Paris) or forgotten (the theatre of dynamic forms of futurism).

180   Alessandro Mastropietro

categories (chaos, man, nothing: 'le tre voci'), thereby mapping the average density of the different layers (Lux and Tortora 2005: 155). Similar sketches were drawn up by Domenico Guaccero early in the elaboration of his vast project *Scene del potere*, developed with the painter and stage designer Franco Nonnis. They fall into three main types. The first adheres to a minimal formula (already detected in the *Collage* sketch) that shows the presence or absence of different components. Figure 8.1 provides an example: at the top of the page is a sequential chart showing the distribution of the components (music, sung word, [spoken] word, action, scenic elements) through the five main scenes (A–E) – and their internal sub-scenes – of the piece, in the shape of a quasi-digital absence/presence; the lower part of the page then shows a serial redisposition of the five scenes (twenty-four different permutations).[6] The second type of sketch offers a synopsis of a specific component. Figure 8.2 shows a sequential summary of the behaviour of an individual voice of the media-counterpoint, in this case the lighting component (light on/off, colours, increase/decrease, flash-effects and so on), through all the three parts – and their scenes – of the final version of the work, with special attention to the articulation of stage space in distinct zones. The third type of sketch offers detailed schemes for each scene. Figure 8.3 gives a synchronic snapshot of media behaviours (and materials too) in the first scene of the work's first version: each box, devoted to one specific media component, is doubled in mirror fashion, reflecting the fact that the project was – at this early stage – imagined as a 'double opera' with parallel actions. Guaccero's aim here seems to be to break continuity, by shaping each scene differently in its relationship of media and each component's flow through the scenes, and at the same time to control the media machine through permutational and contrapuntal tools. More than any other figure of the period, Guaccero sought to develop a theoretical and aesthetic basis for contrapuntal dramaturgical structures of this kind: he saw them as a legacy of a general analytical tendency (the 'extraction of individual parameters') expressed by the aesthetics of the first avant-garde (Guaccero 2005 [1963]: 146).

The most explicit sketch from the Roman compositional context is perhaps the columned one drafted by Guaccero in order to serve as a structural media-chart for his *Rot* (1970–72), a choreographic action conceived and developed together with the dancer Amedeo Amodio (reproduced in Mastropietro 2016a: 67). Here, each column presents the course of an individual 'dramaturgical formant' (sound-musical, gestural-choreographic, figural-chromatic, etc.), intertwined with the others in a plot shaping a 'media-polyphony'. The relational characteristics of this kind of polyphony are: overall density (presence or absence); relative fore- or background – or equal status – for each component; a more or less defined

---

6   The upper part of the sketch is transcribed in Caputo 2017: 276; this sketch is apparently connected with the first version of the work, around 1963. The whole group of sketches, which includes also those reproduced in Figures 8.2 and 8.3, is now preserved at the Institute of Music of the Fondazione Giorgio Cini, Venice (Guaccero Archive, *Scene del potere* folder), and is discussed in Mastropietro 2003: 136–40. Figures 8.1–8.3 reproduced by courtesy of the Institute of Music of the Fondazione Giorgio Cini and Guaccero's heirs.

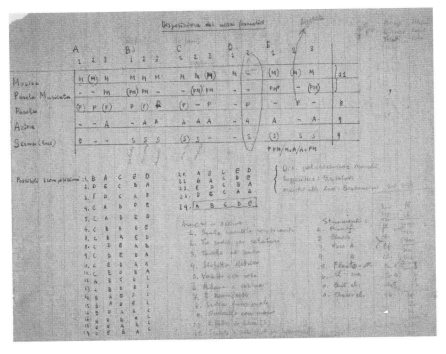

Figure 8.1 Domenico Guaccero, *Scene del potere* (first version), preparatory sketch. Reproduced by courtesy of the Institute of Music of the Fondazione Giorgio Cini and Guaccero's heirs.

synchronisation of events; and a more or less open content (or overt avoidance of a referential frame). Similar foundations for a free media-polyphony can be detected elsewhere thanks to comparable prearranged diagrams of a flowing counterpoint of components: they are once again deployed, as columned or multi-layered scenarios, for other works by Guaccero,[7] as well as by Egisto Macchi[8] and Franco Evangelisti.[9] Even in Sylvano Bussotti's works, the idea of

---

7 Sketches for *Kombinat Joey* (described later in this chapter); now preserved at the Institute of Music, Fondazione Giorgio Cini, Venice.
8 Fragments of a scenario survive for *Anno Domini*, while scenarios (named 'pre-score') are the only complete sources for the unfinished *Parabola* and the project *Processo a Giovanna*, all three being collaborations – dating from 1961–64 – between Egisto Macchi and Antonino Titone. See Mastropietro 2016b for reproductions.
9 Prearranged as well as final diagrams are available for *Die Schachtel*, 'azione mimoscenica' by Franco Evangelisti and painter-scenographer Franco Nonnis (1962–63): its scenes (referred to as 'structures') do not reflect a syntagmatic (or sequential) strategy, rather an argument on the status of society in three paradigmatic phases: initial state; alienated individual and/or collective reactions; eventual choice. The voice element is even more objectified than in Clementi's *Collage*, since singing is banned in all its forms, and the word often appears as a mere signal, displayed or played, or as an alienated element in relation to urban noises on tape. See Ferrari 2000: 177–218 and 259–79.

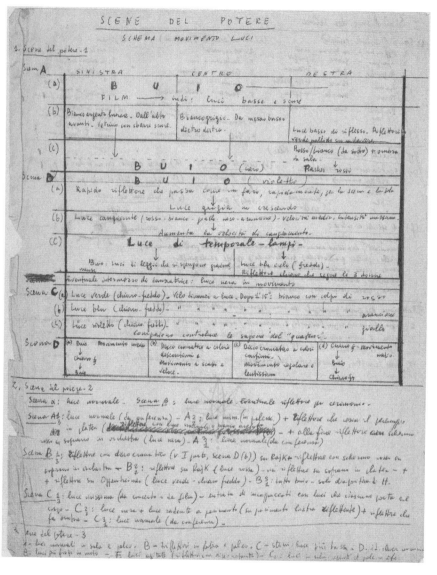

Figure 8.2 Domenico Guaccero, *Scene del potere* (final version), preparatory sketch. Reproduced by courtesy of the Institute of Music of the Fondazione Giorgio Cini and Guaccero's heirs.

a counterpoint of dramaturgical components may be detected, albeit that it is overwhelmed 'from within' by the author's action and self-projection over each component. In a synoptic scenario prepared (but not completed) for *Raramente* – a 'mistero coreografico' of 1971, consisting of five pre-existent works plus

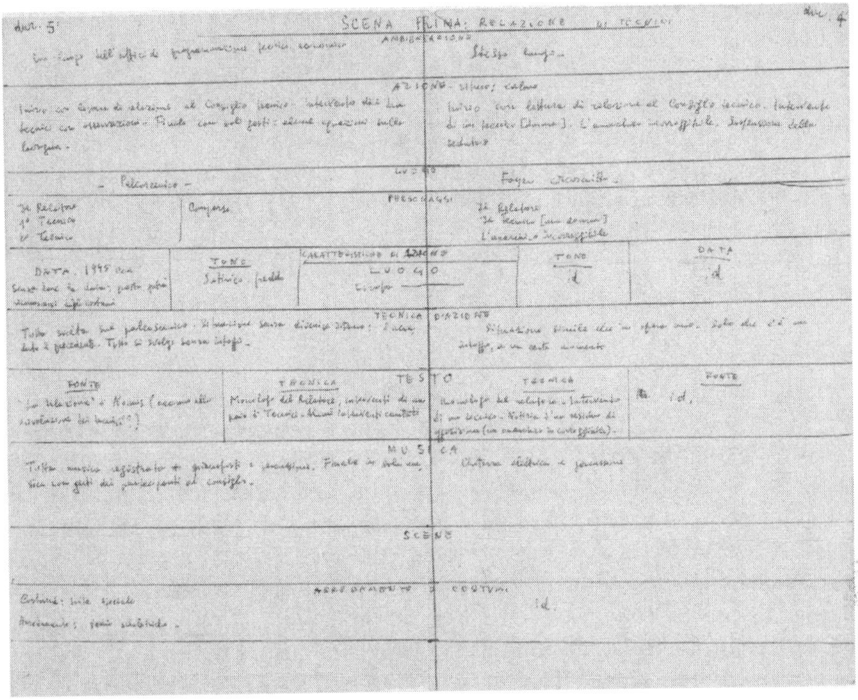

Figure 8.3 Domenico Guaccero, *Scene del potere* (first version), preparatory sketch. Reproduced by courtesy of the Institute of Music of the Fondazione Giorgio Cini and Guaccero's heirs.

one read text, all in a choreographic reading by Aurel Milloss – Bussotti specified the coordination of sung texts and music, choreography, lights and stage movements/actions, a plan probably intended to serve the parallel function of a pre-ordered media plot and a production book, as he could not in this case have total personal control over them all (for a reproduction see Mosch 2017). In a more analytical personality, such as Francesco Pennisi, the parallel composition of music, text and projected images by a single creator (as in *Sylvia Simplex*, 1971–72) produces an elastic counterpoint of media, built around the dramatic topic of a surrealist lecture.[10]

As regards the approach favouring a conscious *non*-integration of the media involved, the first works composed in Rome were by the Americans living

---

10 The lecture, a recurrent anti-dramatic *topos* in the musical avant-garde, is here given by a bizarre ornithologist whose interest in birds lies mainly in hunting and feasting on them. Pennisi's imaginative paintings for the slides illustrate a mechanical and unattainable nature; this, however, does not change the analytical structure of the dramaturgy. See Mastropietro 2014: 22–37.

there – notably, from 1966, Fredric Rzewski and Alvin Curran of the Musica Elettronica Viva (MEV) group – as well as Vittorio Gelmetti. Rzewski's works belong to the mixed-means typology: they develop an environment where, thanks to an ingenious use of basic technology (sensors, microphones and resistors), sound and light signals influence each other through visible gestures existing outside any diegetic code (e.g. *Impersonation*, 1966; *Selfportrait* – mixed-media version, 1967; *Portrait*, 1967; see also below). Here the starting model is seemingly Cage's experimentation, together with that of Cunningham, Tudor and others, on mixing and interference between heterogeneous signals (*Variations V* and *VI*). Rzewski probably had a first-hand knowledge of the previous steps in this field (including those made by the ONCE group), having participated in the first of Charlotte Moorman's Avant Garde festivals in New York; nonetheless, his above-mentioned works are substantially connected to the Roman context and the experiments of MEV, as nothing similar can be found in his output before or after. In Curran's *La lista del giorno* (1967) and Gelmetti's *La descrittione del gran paese* (1966–68), a partially or totally unpredictable result is obtained from a montage – sequential and superimpositional – of an open selection of fragments. Apart from the abrasive Dadaism of Giuliano Zosi's Kagel-like pieces, where absurdity becomes a means for a psychoanalytic unchaining, a more consistent quasi-Cagean lineage is traceable – as far as Roman figures are concerned – in *Klangfarbenspiel* (1972), a 'progetto scenico' by the painter Piero Dorazio, the theatrical experimenter Mario Ricci and the composer Marcello Panni. This work lies between a so-called 'happening' and a stage performance: between the sound panels by Panni, Ricci's playful actions with objects and colourful shapes, and Dorazio's paintings, there is only a neutral time connection, allowing the streams of information from different material (music, actions, colours) to occupy more or less the same total duration. A mild analogy between materials exists – both actions and music are based on modular repetition, just as Dorazio's abstract-geometric painting develops through iterations of simple forms that the stage performers try to trace – without producing strong time or referential structures.

In parallel, other figures were trying to overcome the contrapuntal formula, through a functional and organic model. In the Roman context, Mario Bertoncini was a forerunner, already arriving in *Spazio-Tempo* (1970) at a methodical, multifaceted network between sound, gestural and visual elements. (This work is described in greater detail below.) Sciarrino offers a different organic solution: in *Amore e Psiche* (1971–2), the whole score is built as – and leads to an experience of – a gigantic saturation, obtained through exhaustive procedures of mirror-reflection of sound figures (vocal as well as instrumental), from the smallest to the largest time-dimension; the smallest figures obtain such a volatility and a permeability that their dense kaleidoscope forms a floating timbral hallucination, the mirroring of episodes and vocal phrases creating a similarly hallucinatory time sense. In this way the dramaturgy reacquires a narrative component, solely because it is strongly tied to compositional processes (Psyche's vocal and gestural signs are more or less reflected over all the

A survey of new music theatre in Rome   185

other personae), while the other theatrical elements have to adapt to the features already contained in the sound dramaturgy.[11]

A different path to making an organic entity out of heterogeneous components is the so-called 'scrittura scenica' (scenic writing), a practice developed in Italy by some theatre companies (and so named by the critics) during the second half of the sixties. In scenic writing, the only text is the concrete performance, the acted text (or text of actions): it comprises every kind of scenic and audio-visual outcome, which are thoroughly moulded from materials developed during the rehearsal process. In the original theatrical context, the goal was to avoid the tyranny of the verbal text, which – if present – was subjected to the same deep performative elaboration and general montage as the other components.[12] Evangelisti's *Die Schachtel* already tends towards this sort of solution, by leaving to the production team and musical supervisors the realisation of some of the materials (e.g. the magnetic tapes), and decisions over the relevant indeterminate elements of the multimedia score. The musically richest 'scenic writings' are those that involve Guaccero, namely *Kombinat Joey* (1970) and *Novità assoluta* (1972). *Kombinat Joey*, a theatrical piece involving both vocal and concrete sound, resulted in a collective work, signed equally by all the participants to the production, although its schematic script was prepared by Perilli. Guaccero had responsibility (together with Walter Branchi) for the sound component, which he elaborated during months of working directly with the stage performers, using charts that allocated classes of materials to particular scenes, but without formalising a score (Kombinat Joey 1972, Mastropietro 2019). *Novità assoluta*, a chamber theatre piece for a new festival, had a similar genesis, evolving through intensive work in Rome together with the director (Ezio Alovisi) and the performers; but this time Guaccero wrote down a score filling the original, generic scenario with verbal sounds, gestural instructions, and musical fragments (see Example 8.1).[13] Regardless of the kind of notation used (from free-measured to indeterminate and graphic), every description of outcomes in every presentational media is timed in the score through an indicative duration in seconds, that seems to originate in a negotiation between pre-compositional structures and their embodiment during rehearsal work (Mastropietro 2009).

This group of works, by re-thinking relations between the theatrical components, tended also, in one way or another, to raise two pivotal institutional issues: first, the role of the audience, not only as a presence in the concrete space of

---

11 This is the reason why Sciarrino and Pes disowned the first and sole staging (Piccola Scala, Milan, 1973) due to the divergence of stage elements (the dance movements in particular) from the naked, ritualistic theatre they imagined. Later, they preferred to entrust this work to the 'sound-listening dramaturgy' of the radio drama.

12 For scenic writing practice in the spoken theatre, see the chapter by Stefania Bruno in the present volume.

13 D. Guaccero, *Novità assoluta*, autograph score, p. 8, preserved at the Institute of Music of the Fondazione Giorgio Cini, Venice, Guaccero Archive, *Scene del potere* folder (courtesy Institute of Music of the Fondazione Giorgio Cini and Guaccero's heirs).

Example 8.1 Domenico Guaccero, *Novità assoluta*, autograph score, p. 8. Reproduced by courtesy of the Institute of Music of the Fondazione Giorgio Cini and Guaccero's heirs.

performance, but also as an addressee (social, cultural, institutional) of a proposal that was limited neither to a single event, nor to works exclusively by Rome-based authors; and second, the connection with producing institutions, and more generally the issue of new music theatre projects for which the frame of traditional venues and performers' ensembles appeared unsuited (in their receptivity to new ideas, new performance texts and new kinds of creativity), albeit not always unusable. This awareness of a need for new relationships with audiences, performers and organisations generally emerged shortly after authors' first theatrical projects, with their associated difficulties or failures. Nonetheless, the power of established institutions, especially the operatic ones, sometimes attracted experimentalists to attempt to relocate their own projects into an existing institutional frame, if not to a revolutionary subversion of such a frame. The following sections will survey these two 'institutional' issues as they emerged in Rome in the period 1961–75, and the answers that arose in different situations. The discussion will necessarily address the dissemination of international new music theatre works, alongside the production of works conceived and composed locally.

Off–off/Underground

The Compagnia del teatro musicale di Roma (CTMR; 1965–68) represents the first serious Roman attempt to develop, out of established networks, a proposal for the creation and circulation of a new music theatre (Mastropietro 2017a). Its founders Guaccero, Macchi and Bussotti had already shared two performances, mainly of 'gestural' works, at the first festival of Nuova Consonanza in 1963, and one year later at a university theatre in Rome, in both cases rotating their roles as performer, composer and ideologue-introducer. By the end of 1965, after the official debut of the company in Florence (with the label 'Teatro musicale da camera di Roma'), Bussotti, who earlier that year had obtained a *succès-de-scandale* with *La Passion selon Sade* in Palermo (see Tortora 2013), quitted the partnership. The company was thereafter run by Guaccero and Macchi (Kagel declined the invitation for a fixed collaboration), whose own works ended up comprising very nearly the entirety of its repertoire.[14] Its larger plans thus remained a utopia, both in terms of the inception of a big festival of musical theatre – whose programme was realised only as a published collection of scenarios from the foreseen works[15] – and in consolidating a stable team. Guaccero and Macchi imagined the company as a cooperative endeavour between composers, performers and a crew who would share its artistic aims, as well as any profits. But insufficient engagements, as well as interpersonal tensions aroused by the problematic staging in Palermo of Guaccero's *Scene del potere* – a work of very complex spatial conception, described further below – destroyed the company as such.[16]

---

14 It's significant that the leading figures were composers, not directors: on the director-driven versus the composer-driven new music theatre, see Salzman and Desi 2008: 99.

15 *Marcatrè*, 30–33 (July 1967), pp. 36–121.

16 A precious audio-video document of this staging is available from Rai-Teche; see Mastropietro 2017a: 155–7.

188 *Alessandro Mastropietro*

Nonetheless, the CTMR marks an important step in developing a wide range of formulas in the field of small-scale music theatre, augmented with sound and film projection and enriched by unconventional theatrical concepts. Starting from a multidisciplinary organisation in which all of the members, performers and technicians included, are requested to put at the disposal of the team their own specialised competence, the CTMR ultimately came to follow an ultra-disciplinary model. Its penultimate staging was of Guaccero's *Rappresentazione et Esercizio*, mounted inside a church.[17] Here the company acted as a community celebrating a rite, initially in a representation of the birth and death of *logos-Christos*, then an initiatory process from darkness towards light. This process, being an 'exercitium' (an action on oneself) more than a representation, focuses on performers: the audience, whom Guaccero and Macchi wanted to shock in 1965, now should help rather than attend to the performance, as the score explicitly declares in its preface (reprinted in Guaccero 2005: 475) and as the whole action (voicing, sounds, text, acting) of *Esercizio* implies. Consequently, the performance almost drifts away from the realm of theatre, following a direction that Grotowski was pursuing in the same years (see Lombardi Vallauri 2015). Performance competences were now totally shared by each of the twelve performers (conductor-composer and director included): no more a matter of 'everyone does something', rather 'everyone does everything (or almost everything)'. The model was by this time the theatrical commune epitomised by The Living Theatre, a group that appeared bound by a strong – and strongly palingenetic – concept, by which the individual could attain an ideal fullness and unity of being.

This club-like audience was far removed from the myth of popularity that sustained the Italian operatic theatre, a myth that still intrigued these composers. Nevertheless, the fervent world of small, dank 'cantine romane' (never more than 100 seats, often less than 50) became both the headquarters for new theatrical conceptions, and a trendy node for a new cultural sociability, one that extended beyond the cultural elite (Carandini (ed.) 2012; Margiotta 2013: 168–94; Mastropietro 2019).[18] Other small-scale performances were also hosted by these venues. The most famous 'cantina', Beat 72, promoted a series of 'Monday concerts', where premieres and famous works (such as *Theatre Piece* by Cage, who was a guru for all the Roman experimentalists, in art and theatre as well as music) were given during the seventies. Among the premieres, Beat 72 hosted the début of Alvin Curran in his first solo performance, *Songs and Views from the Magnetic Garden* (1975): this work comprises a kind of minimal theatre,[19] where

17 Such a space is mandatory, and the actions take place sometimes in the central nave, sometimes at other *loci deputati* (designated places); Mastropietro 2017a: 152–4.
18 Beat 72 was attended, among others, by Alberto Moravia, Ingeborg Bachmann, and almost all the writers from the avant-gardist Gruppo 63.
19 After Curran's gestural works composed in 1967–68 for the MEV group, this turning point is related to Young and Zazeela's Theatre of Eternal Music (see Kostelanetz 1968: 183–218). Curran did not know La Monte Young in New York, where he studied, but encountered him later in Rome, where Young had concerts with Marian Zazeela in 1969 and 1972.

A survey of new music theatre in Rome   189

the performer brings himself into the *mise-en-scene*, manipulating various sound objects and materials – his own voice included – for an hour and a half, sitting before a ready-made background that is part of the performance environment.

Similar mixed-media performances were to be found in Roman art galleries already during the 1960s. From the autumn of 1968, the Galleria l'Attico began systematically to host such performances, as a way both to challenge the aesthetics of art as a permanent object, and to promote the newest American music or dance (Massimo Barbero and Pola (eds) 2010). This was preceded by the Galleria La Tartaruga, which in May 1968 programmed a month of different daily performances,[20] including events making use of sound elements by Bussotti (*La più rararara*), Enrico Castellani and Loreto Soro. In September, Bertoncini premiered his *Epitaffio alla memoria di un concerto* at the Galleria dell'Oca, during which he offered bystanders an etching, printed from the metallic amplified sound-surface on which one of the performers had scraped contours and texts from a score during the performance.

Something of a model for such performances had been established the previous year, when a multidisciplinary day-long programme of performances (*Grammatica Teatro No-Stop ore 12*) took place in and outside the bookshop of Feltrinelli, the main publisher of the Italian literary neo-avant-garde, Gruppo 63. This venue had already hosted a series of performances (music, readings, dance) and exhibitions supervised by the writer Nanni Balestrini and the composer Vittorio Gelmetti; the musical events, *I concerti del Marcatrè*, had borrowed the name of Rome's most significant avant-garde journal. The 1967 event involved leading figures from the art, music, theatre and cinema worlds, and was organised to celebrate a multidisciplinary issue of Perilli's periodical *Grammatica*, devoted to experimental theatre. Surviving video documentation gives the impression of an avant-garde celebration, expressed in an anarchic sequence of various actions. Among the individual and collective performances, the more significant as regards music theatre were those by Fluxus artist Giuseppe Chiari (*Whisky*), Bussotti (*Solo*, performed by a group of trusted singer-actors with projected films by photographer Gianfranco Mantegna and moviemaker Alfredo Leonardi), and Rzewski (a mixed-media version of *Selfportrait*). All day long, readings, experimental film projections, basic theatrical actions and other performances alternated continuously (sometimes overlapping, but without a predetermined intention), extending even to food-art as a gesture of sensory enlargement (Mastropietro 2019).[21]

This day of performance at the Feltrinelli bookshop shares with the events at L'Attico an important characteristic: a tight and unconventional connection with the audience. The bookshop was packed, with attendees standing or sitting on the floor in the low-ceilinged space; as part of the performance, some were later

---

20 A full review of the whole series was published as 'Il teatro delle mostre' – literally 'Exhibition theatre' (Bonito Oliva 1968).

21 The video-documentation, actually an experimental montage-film, is due to Alberto Grifi (who reworked it in 2009 with the title *Anni '60 No Stop*).

190 *Alessandro Mastropietro*

provocatively thrown out in the street, in the midst of dangerous traffic. From December 1968 to June 1976, L'Attico relocated to a garage under a residential building, mounting environmental expositions there, together with performance art events – notably, two festivals in 1969 and 1972. Photos and videos from the performances show the audience positioned close to the performers (who included dancers from the New York Judson group, such as Simone Forti, Steve Paxton and Debora Hay), either sitting – or lying – on the ground, or standing against the garage's bare walls.[22] Even in L'Attico's original location – an attic of a building located in the centre of the city – the audience–performer relationship had been similar, and was emboldened by the obstructive smallness of the rooms. For two MEV performances, the famous artist Michelangelo Pistoletto realised an environment that synthesised the uncomfortable disposition of the viewers at Pascali's previous exhibitions with his own characteristic obstruction of the space (here by means of shreds of ripped dresses and scrap paper) that on this occasion impeded the performers as well as the viewers (see Figure 8.4).[23]

While many of the actions at L'Attico were substantially concert-like, without any theatrical implication, these festivals also offered a systematic criticism of the institutions of the established art world by erasing the borders between the disciplines. Together with the unconventionality of venues and audience/performer behaviours, this idea seems to have developed partly side-by-side with corresponding international phenomena, drawing on specifically Roman and Italian premises that are nevertheless coherent – aesthetically and historically – with that international horizon (above all, the American one, with its authoritative and well-known antecedents), and partly in direct dialogue with New York precedents. The Roman context was able to put to use those hints either as a stimulus, or a model to be developed in autonomy, or even corroboration of an already taken path: L'Attico's magazine printed the first and only Italian review of the 1966 show *9 Evenings: Theatre and Engineering* involving Cage, Tudor and other experimental luminaries, although it appeared only in January 1969 (Balzarro 1969), when the aesthetic commitment of the gallery to performance art was already clear. Adding the circumstance that the core of their audience was made up of devotees of the experimental galleries, rather than members of Rome's musical avant-garde, one can deduce that the Roman context was particularly predisposed toward a wide, poly-centred, radically multidisciplinary

---

22 The whole 1969 festival (the programme for which is available at https://fabiosargentini.it/) is documented in a mid-length film (*Festival di danza, volo, musica, dinamite*, directed by Francesco degli Espinosa, dur. 57'). Similar presentational formats can be seen on live video-documents (made by Luciano Giaccari) of both the second Festival (1972) and the music and dance sections from the interdisciplinary exposition *Contemporanea* (1973–74), located in an underground parking lot.

23 Photos from performances at L'Attico are available, together with the brochure, at https://fabiosargentini.it/, while shots of Pistoletto's environment for MEV performance may be found in *Cartabianca*, 4 (15 January 1969), pp. 32–4.

A survey of new music theatre in Rome 191

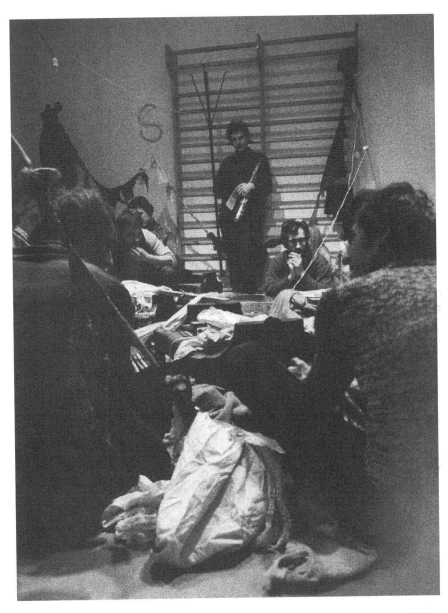

Figure 8.4 Musica Elettronica Viva, *Zuppa*, 25–26 October 1968, L'Attico, Piazza di Spagna; courtesy Fabio Sargentini, L'Attico Archive; photo Marco Cresci.

experimentation, albeit one characterised by a discontinuity of groups and spaces, rather than a direct, mutual knowledge and a consistent communion of experiences between its operators.

(Quite-)Off contexts: festivals and the Accademia Filarmonica Romana

After the fateful year of 1968, the Roman milieu around new music theatre appeared to pursue two seemingly opposite tendencies: an increasing radicalism in the spatial, social and aesthetical conception; and a growing interest amongst established institutions towards the new phenomena. This provided the basis for the success of the organisation Teatromusica, founded by Marcello Panni in 1970 as a chamber ensemble within the Nuova Consonanza festival, which thrived until 1979. Teatromusica had a longer and less troubled life than Guaccero and Macchi's company, and presented ordinary concerts as well as more ambitious theatrical events. Its signature productions, however, were a series of music theatre (or sometimes, more properly, mixed-media) projects, that involved renowned experimenters in art, scenic design, film, and theatre (both directors and actors), and that found space in the programmes of many concert series, festivals (often well-established) and opera houses. Teatromusica was even able to organise two festivals in Rome (the first in 1973) that encompassed its own theatrical productions; and yet, theatre evenings comprised only two or three out of many others in the festival programme, and moreover were restaged from Teatromusica's previous productions for bigger institutions.[24] The creative activity of Teatromusica is equally significant, bearing in mind especially the interest of its creative collaborations, albeit conducted from an aesthetically freer and theoretically less rigorous (but also more pragmatically professional) perspective than that of CTMR.

Contemporary music festivals in Rome and elsewhere offered another natural opportunity for performance, besides the above-mentioned theatrical and cultural 'off–off' venues of interdisciplinary exchange. A festival is an institutional and intellectual frame as much as a physical one,[25] not necessarily enjoying a well-established material and productive situation: and yet Nuova Consonanza, a Roman association of avant-garde composers (Evangelisti, Guaccero, Macchi, Clementi, Pennisi and others; see Tortora 1990), started programming gestural works already in its first festival,[26] and in 1965 produced the second part of *Scene del potere*. This last work offered an especially complex dramaturgical, spatial and performative concept (Mastropietro 2003; Caputo 2017). Each of the three parts unfolds a different conception of space and performer–audience relationships,

---

24 For example, from the 1972 Venice Biennale, in the case of *Sylvia Simplex* and a half-staging of Schnebel's *Glossolalie 61*; or Maggio Musicale in Florence, in the case of *La Partenza dell'Argonauta*, a work originating in an intense 'scenic writing' collaboration between Panni and Memé Perlini, a landmark director for the so-called Roman 'teatro-immagine' (Mastropietro 2019).

25 Nonetheless, almost all the concerts in Nuova Consonanza festivals from 1967 onward were placed at the Galleria Nazionale d'Arte Moderna, and a collaboration for social activities was agreed between Nuova Consonanza and other private galleries around 1970.

26 The programme of this 1963 concert, mentioned earlier, which Guaccero and Bussotti took part in, included Schnebel's *Réactions (Abfälle I.1)* for a performer and audience, and (notably) the Italian première of Cage's *Theatre Piece* (Mastropietro 2019).

A survey of new music theatre in Rome   193

suggesting a path from the usual distinction between the world of the drama and that of the audience (in the first part), through a breaking of this scheme (in the second part, involving actions on stage and amongst the audience), to a complete spatial merging inside the hall (with performers and acting audience simultaneously taking up both stage and seating areas); two further scenes take place in the foyer, during the first intermission and then after it (whilst the second part is taking place in the auditorium, so without the audience in attendance!). This spatial trajectory is intended to correspond to a transition from outer (social-economic) to inner (individual) power.

Also closely connected to the Roman scene was the Festival 'Settimana Nuova Musica' in Palermo (see Tessitore (ed.) 2003; Tessitore 2013: 157–91; Mastropietro 2019), the intellectual and managerial leadership of which was close to, and partially overlapped with, that of Nuova Consonanza. In Palermo, new music theatre was programmed only in the last two Festivals (1965 and 1968), with substantial attention given to composers active in Rome (i.e. Macchi, Bussotti, Gelmetti, Guaccero, Heineman).[27] These editions were significant for pursuing an overtly multidisciplinary programme, including an evening of theatre with texts by Gruppo 63 writers in 1965,[28] and – in both years – experimental film projections and the newest art exhibitions curated by Mario Diacono, Macchi's collaborator for his Artaudian theatre piece *A(lter)A(ction)* (described below). New music theatre, hence, was presented here within a horizon of experimental art experience, which it reflected in its own interdisciplinary disposition, and by which it was legitimated. If Nuova Consonanza didn't propose an interdisciplinary agenda so explicitly, this was because Rome itself already offered it in a very dense way every day, while in Palermo – notwithstanding a tradition of attention towards modern art – such experiences were rarer.

Nuova Consonanza always suffered from restriction of means, as it was barely supported by the Italian government. After 1965, its music theatre programming was limited only to gestural works, like those of Bertoncini, or the performance of the ensemble MW2 from Kraków (which included a work by Bogusław Schaeffer), at least until 1974 when Perilli's new theatrical collective Gruppo Altro was hosted in its second production, *Altro-Experimenta*. This group, active between 1972 and 1981, developed a mode of elaborating performances named 'intercode', which was based on an exchange between disciplines so strict that the outcome could be viewed as transdisciplinary. For instance, *Altro-Experimenta* included the gestural piece *Synergy* by Walter Branchi, which treats theatrical elements (two mimes' gestures, and a continuously controlled play of light and shadow) in the same way as the work's sound material (from a solo trombone) – namely, as absolute, non-semantic material (Gruppo Altro 1981: 65–8).

---

27 During the animated sixth Settimana (1968), a monographic performance was devoted to some of Kagel's theatre works (*Phonophonie, Variaktionen über Tremens, Montage à titre de spectacle*).

28 Already in 1963, short texts by Gruppo 63 writers were staged, some of them by the American director Ken Dewey, with his (at that time) Rome-based Action Cooperative Theater (ACT).

194 *Alessandro Mastropietro*

Similar constraints of resource could also be felt by better established festivals: the Venice Biennale's production of Bertoncini's *Spazio-Tempo* (1970) resorted to musicians from the orchestra of La Fenice, who were far from accustomed to the codes (sonic, semiographic, relational) of the composer's *informel* conception; the result, as it emerges from the surviving audio-visual document, was a certain clichéd quality of the instrumental component against the complex inter-media machine.[29] Moreover, the space was not big enough to permit a complete setting of the sonic installations conceived by the composer. Nonetheless, this project endures as one of the most organic cross-media experiments, as well as one of the most radical and consistent in conceiving a new kind of creation that synthesises elements of an exhibition as well as a performance. The work is notable for the strictly non-diegetic nature of the codes and materials used by all performers (instrumentalists in four groups, mime-dancers, sound- and lights-directors), which are partly projected over the sound objects and installations (a labyrinth of suspended cymbals and bells, electronically amplified wooden platforms to be stepped on by the performers, resonant surfaces hung from the wall, and so on) in the space, forging mutual relationships of dependence or autonomy that also implicate the relations between performers and spectators. Other striking characteristics are the presentation of the instrumental score as a variable sequence of slide projections, not determined in duration, and a presentational frame hovering somewhere between a performance and an exhibition. The audience is alternately forced to the perimeter of the hall (while the mime/dance performers are active at its centre and the instrumentalists at the corners), or let free to explore (either alone or together with the performers) the sound installations arranged around the space. Sometimes disoriented and embarrassed, sometimes enthusiastic, those present at the 1970 performance appear from the video to have enjoyed a remarkable experience (see Mastropietro 2019).

Two years later, the Biennale was able to give a fully satisfying staging of Bussotti's vast *Lorenzaccio*, a deconstruction of an operatic dramaturgy fragmented across multiple planes (sometimes epic or dreamlike) and performative expressions (sung or spoken word, mime, dance, film), and encapsulating Bussotti's latest tendency towards a free summary of every element made available by music-theatre history (from the happening to the romantic opera or ballet; from Artaud to an imaginary ancient funeral pantomime; see Mastropietro 2019).[30] This work was more favourable to the participation of an operatic theatre such as La Fenice, whose spatial concept *Lorenzaccio* explicitly sets out to deconstruct. Nevertheless, this event remained the sole Italian production (and the sole one directed by the author himself) of this *monstre*-opera, as *Lorenzaccio* never reached the Roman opera house.

---

29 The video-document (unfortunately lacking audio in some cuts) is preserved at the Biennale ASAC (Archivio Storico per le Arti Contemporanee, Venice).

30 The video and audio documents, separately preserved, will be more extensively discussed in a forthcoming article on *Lorenzaccio*.

A survey of new music theatre in Rome   195

Back in Rome, the well-established Accademia Filarmonica Romana (or AFR, which continues to exist as an enduring concert season; see Quattrocchi 1991) was almost the only 'generalist' musical institution to be curious toward the new music theatre in Rome during the sixties. Its interest in the avant-garde had begun as early as January 1959 with a historic concert given by Cage, Berio and Cathy Berberian, including the première of Cage's *Aria* plus *Fontana Mix*. Earlier still, in 1958 (thus three years before the première of *Collage* together with the Italian première of Brecht-Weill's *The Seven Deadly Sins*) the AFR had staged a one-act opera by the dodecaphonic composer Vittorio Fellegara, *Una gita in campagna*. Later, AFR staged a major work by Egisto Macchi, *A(lter)A(ction)* (1966), with a set designed by the artist Jannis Kounellis: in this work, a character resembling Antonin Artaud is split into four personae that sing, act and howl about the vexations of society upon the unfit poet-victim; miscellaneous found objects dominate both the stage setting and the sound palette (with fragments of pop-riffs and recordings on vinyl), embodying the deranged situation (Tortora 1998; Mastropietro 2017a; Cosci 2017). During the same season (1966–67), AFR promoted two avant-garde music festivals, whose programmes were compiled by Musica Elettronica Viva (MEV), at the time not yet a group focused mainly on improvisation but instead a radical compositional collective devoted – like the ONCE group – to a real-time, sometimes mixed-media use of electronics.[31] In Rzewski's *Portrait* (a revision of the earlier *Selfportrait*), gestures by some of the performers upon Clyde Steiner's four-channel 'photocell mixer' controlled both a sound projection and a chromatic light beam upon an opaque screen; behind it, another performer acted as a silhouette and generated with her larynx heavily amplified cries that, together with a kind of electro-acoustic jungle of noises, were projected from all around the space: hence, the same gestures were responsible for the lighting and shadowing as for the sounding of the space.

At the time, AFR was directed by figures such as Goffredo Petrassi, Valentino Bucchi and Roman Vlad, who looked with interest to the younger generation of composers, as well as to a small-scale music theatre. This should have led to a festival of new music theatre in 1968, where the première of the first, now forgotten stage work by Castiglioni, *Tre misteri*, took place; unfortunately, it ran into protests from both right-wing and left-wing activists (including even musicians involved in the production), which dissuaded the institution's managers from proceeding with further editions of the festival. Berio's works also appeared in the Filarmonica's schedules. Nevertheless, both the mime performance of Ann Halprin in *Visage* (1963) and the Roman premiere of *Passaggio* (1971) were half-staged productions: being a concert society, albeit owning a theatre, AFR had neither the means nor the in-house workforce sufficient to mount demanding stage productions. Therefore, the 'scenic version' of Bussotti's *Sette fogli*

---

31 On MEV (Musica Elettronica Viva), founded mainly by American composers living by then in Rome, see Beal 2009 and Pizzaleo 2014. The American ONCE group, based in the academic city Ann Arbor, gathered – even before its official birth in 1961 – around visual artist Milton Cohen's mixed-media projects; see Dietrich 2009 and Mumma 2015: 3–38.

196 *Alessandro Mastropietro*

(performed the same evening as Berio's *Passaggio*) was actually a staged concert with dance interventions, albeit an important event in attesting to Bussotti's evolution towards yet more sumptuous and calligraphic stage productions. In conclusion, AFR was the institution closest to the cause of a new music theatre, and some of its productions were landmarks (either for the novelty of the concept, the impact on the critics and the audience, or the productive test of an experimental project), even if it was unable to exceed either a certain level of economical and organisational constraint, or a merely sporadic presence of experimental works within the generalist annual programmes.

The Opera di Roma: love and hate

The most official institution regarding music theatre in Rome, the Teatro dell'Opera di Roma, gave admittance to the Italian neo-avant-garde only in March 1968, with an evening comprising a new staging of Berio's *Allez-hop*. The otherness – both aesthetic and practical – of such music-dramaturgies was obviously a strong deterrent to serious consideration by an artistic management whose paragons of modernity at the time were Berg's operas and a couple of Henze's recent works.[32] At the end of the sixties, however, thanks also to a consolidated centre-left political orientation in the city which was supportive of the newest works, the by-then recognised neo-avant-garde found themselves in a better position to be taken seriously by an operatic theatre, whilst the Opera could in turn also hope to gain legitimation by so doing. This however would neither mitigate the hostility towards the themes and forms of new music theatre's dramaturgies from the conservative (or better, reactionary) element of the Opera's audience, nor overcome the lack of inclination to quickly renew the theatre's habits of production. The results during the following years, both in production and in reception, were controversial, to say the least, but in some way also emblematic of a reciprocal, albeit asymmetrical or misunderstood, appeal: often love-and-hate-like from composers, sometimes bureaucratically dutiful from the established institution.

The programme of the first attempted encounter in 1968 was in certain respects typical for the Opera, with its mixed ballet-opera evening arranged in three parts.[33] *Work in progress*, an assemblage of three pre-existing tape-music works (by Clementi, Maderna and Castiglioni) with stage actions inspired by Calder's artwork and 'acted' by pictorial or plastic forms as well as stage performers, was indeed a kind of abstract ballet.[34] This production, similar (although more abstract) to the

---

32 Namely, *Boulevard Solitude* (staged 1954) and *Der junge Lord* (staged 1965). *Moses und Aron* was staged only thanks to a hosting of Hamburg State Opera (1966), and *Parade* had its Roman première (in Bejart's choreography) in 1964. Annual chronologies of the performances at Teatro dell'Opera are given in Tognelli (ed.) 1979: 201–66.

33 The opening title in the evening was Malipiero's *Torneo notturno*, a landmark work in its questioning of the operatic tradition.

34 Sketches and stage sketches and photos preserved at the Archivio Storico del Teatro dell'Opera di Roma are reproduced in Malusardi and Reggiani 2010.

media-concept of Clementi-Perilli's *Collage*, was restaged by the same theatre in 1977 in a slightly more favourable season for the presence of the avant-garde; but even in 1968 the reception was not wholly negative: the audio recording registers some applause during the performance and, at the end, more of an animated perplexity than a revolt of boos. The tumultuous element of the evening in March 1968 was due mainly to the pre-organised provocation by the reactionary part of the audience against *Allez-hop* and its staging by Missiroli.[35] Some elements of the staging, involving dancer-hippies who descended into the stalls to paint flowers and hearts on the faces of the stunned audience members, reflecting the director's reading of the plot in terms of the anti-war sentiments of that year, had been performed a few weeks earlier – without any scandal – in leftist Bologna.[36] During the Rome production, however, a negative campaign against the performance was waged by conservative newspapers: the critics stigmatised both the work and its staging, expressing polemical disapproval of the Opera's board of directors for their use of public money. This led the Opera's management, who feared protests during the performance, to prohibit the most provocative elements of the production: the face-painting was replaced by the distribution of paper flowers, for instance. Nonetheless, as many other elements (the set, the costumes, the miming, even – in an allusive way – the final song added for this 1968 version by Calvino and Berio) were explicitly leftist or pacifist, the ambush from the extreme-right could not be wholly neutralised. Berio and Missiroli even faced physical aggression, as an extreme-right procession converged just in front of the Teatro dell'Opera the morning before the première: both figures protested verbally against the demonstrators' fascist slogans, only to be set upon, without any protection from the attending police.

When Guaccero's *Rot* reached the Teatro dell'Opera stage in 1973, after a postponement of two years, its production suffered similar difficulties at the hands of the audience, as well as others from the Opera's technical teams. The abstract painter Agostino Bonalumi had conceived an irregular cladding in foam rubber for the floor in the first scene (in black), in order to obtain from the dancers the unbalanced movements and the softened sounds prescribed by the choreographer and the composer (see Mastropietro 2016a): this cladding was not realised. Additionally, of the three musical groups in the score (three voices, three live-electronics performers, six percussionists, all positioned in the pit), only the voices were able to perform live; because of technical difficulties, the other two were heard only on tape, thus depriving the score of part of its timbral dazzle.

---

35 Live recording (21 March 1968) on magnetic tape, both of *Work in progress* and *Allez-hop* performances, are preserved at the Archivio Storico del Teatro dell'Opera di Roma, together with the press review.

36 Audio-video recordings of Bologna's staging (in February 1968) of *Allez-hop* and its Roman revival have been made by the Italian national broadcasting service (Rai), and cut into two different programmes (respectively *L'Approdo: Opere teatrali d'avanguardia*, 1968, and *TVS Valori espressivi della musica contemporanea*, 1969; documents preserved in Teche Rai, n. C7828 and C9706).

198   *Alessandro Mastropietro*

As Amodio unwound a gigantic red flag from a crevice in the backdrop up to the proscenium, intended as the culmination of the choreography and to coincide with the climax of a sonic crescendo, the conformist and prejudiced audience responded with uproar. As with many of the newspaper critics, the audience was unable to seize in this concluding gesture anything but a political sign, totally losing sight of potential alternative and more alchemical meanings.

In sum, the Teatro dell'Opera for several years confined new music theatre largely to the choreographic dominion, as Bussotti's *Bergkistall* (1973, staged 1974) confirms. Composers from the avant-garde to a certain extent took advantage of this circumstance: especially when directly involved in the commission, they minimised, or simply avoided, the troublesome – for an experimental dramaturgy – element of the sung word. At the same time the operatic institution could deceive itself about a less direct reception of revolutionary meanings by the conservative audience. *Il coccodrillo* (1969) by Valentino Bucchi, a large work in four acts, and the last one by a composer from an older generation, was in Rome transformed into an experimental opera substantially thanks to the pop-art, Duchamp-like scenic and film elements contributed by Gianfranco Baruchello: the verbal and musical dramaturgy shows a certain heterogeneity of materials, with an expansion of signs and features towards those of new music theatre, without any profound challenge to traditional linguistic bases (Mastropietro 2019).

By way of conclusion

Rome was a centre of great fermentation in the field of new music theatre from 1961 until at least the mid-1970s. Beyond the density of conceived, composed and performed works, each with its own new dramaturgic arrangement, this creative wave reflected the larger innovations of new music theatre internationally, notably: a close interaction (from planning to performing) with personalities from other disciplinary fields; a reconfiguration of authorship and sometimes also of the concept of the 'work', further emboldened by the phenomenon of the single impermanent realisation ('opus' as an action, more than a fixed text/object); a consequent reconfiguration of the works' textual entities, which were often heterogeneous and meta-textual; a profound rethinking of the music-theatre performer, and of the space of performance; a substantial difficulty in tracing the borders or boundaries of a precise (new) genre, leading one to speak of a hyper-genre. Considering the venues involved, the last issue appears particularly complex, as the space of experiencing was also often the site for various cross-media or expanded art-actions, as well as for intellectual exchange and a freer sociability. Consequently, any convergence of experimentations that included a musical element combined with other kinds of live performance action seemed to classify within the fluid, experiential category of the 'new music theatre'.

If something similar happened in other cultural capitals (including New York and other European cities), where there existed a comparable supply of flexible, uninhibiting performance spaces (potentially embodied even in an official venue, albeit one subverted from its standard use), the Roman scene nonetheless exhibits some particularities.

First, to the extent that new music theatre was conceived as an anti-operatic (or anti-balletic) gesture, this opposition did not always extend to relationships with established organisations, operatic or not. As production houses and hubs for existing audiences, established organisations could sometimes be entrusted with an internal renewal by experimenters who at the same time criticised them. These experimenters felt confident that such a radical renewal – not a complete collapse – could be achieved by virtue of a re-motivation of the constitutive elements of the music-theatrical enterprise, so leading to the demise of opera except as a museum genre. Guaccero's attempts with operatic and other high-status organisations are emblematic,[37] as is the Accademia Filarmonica Romana's involvement in promoting new music theatre.

Second, one perceives in the Rome scene a high level of diversity and fragmentation, especially after 1968. Up to that year the constellation of single operators, thanks to the personal relationships between them, may be considered almost a unified, if internally articulated, experimental fringe; after 1968, this constellation explodes, partly because of the appearance of a powerful establishment institution (the Teatro dell'Opera), even if its function as a reference point did not extend much beyond journalistic rumours. Naturally, a big city with a year-round cultural life could not operate like a small one that concentrates its forces into a radical seasonal festival (as in the case of Avignon).[38] In another metropolis such as New York, the experimental scene, whilst similarly internally articulated, also seems more cohesive, since the most significant 1970s figures and groups (such as The Kitchen, or Meredith Monk's House Foundation) appear as fruits of the common soil of the 1960s downtown (Salzman and Desi 2008: 226–35; Chevalier 2013). The more scattered scenery of Rome's music-theatre experimentation remained a distinction as well as a limit.

Third, there was an absence in Rome of certain types of venue, both as promotors and hosts. If this is obvious in the case of the lack of Protestant churches with social and cultural missions (such as New York's Judson Church),[39] the lack of educational and/or research institutions, above all of high schools or universities, is more notable. This precluded the growth in Rome of an alternative circuit for

---

37 During the 1970s Guaccero designed other new music theatre projects inside very official institutions (including Italian broadcasters, and Roman and other municipalities; Mastropietro 2017a: 160–2), succeeding four years before his death in realising for the Teatro dell'Opera (but outside its main stage) a two-part programme combining his and Monteverdi's music (*Fatti d'amore e di guerra*, texts from Tasso, stage direction and co-conception by Ezio Alovisi, 1980).

38 On Avignon see Jean-François Trubert's chapter in this volume.

39 Judson Church was at the same time venue for Charlotte Moorman's avant-garde festivals (in 1964, its hall hosted the famous US première of Stockhausen's *Originale*) and the domicile of the interdisciplinary collective Judson Dance Theater, whose performers would later participate to L'Attico's Roman festivals. Even in Rome, the American Church hosted in its crypt some borderline events during 1966: an art exhibition, with electro-acoustic sound by Alvin Curran; and a concert by MEV composers, which was filmed in an experimental short – *Organum multiplum* – by the movie-maker Alfredo Leonardi.

200 *Alessandro Mastropietro*

experimental performances, a protected (culturally, economically, institutionally) laboratory for creative research, and a link with leading bodies in technological research, which were anyway located far from the Italian capital.

Fourth and finally, music theatre activity in Rome showed an inclination, especially when a performance took place in overtly unconventional venues and borderline situations, towards the ephemeral dimension of the festive celebration, with all the problems that ensue in retracing the realised text and its context.

A further issue concerns the relation of the actual achievements to the intended projects; in the case of the most complex dramaturgies, the outcome was frequently disappointing for the authors (even if in some way effective for the audience) for various reasons, including inadequacies of implementation within conservative institutional contexts. This poses a question concerning the famous Italian expression about the sixties, the so called 'favolosi anni Sessanta': are we to understand *favolosi* in the sense of the fabulous, exciting years, brimming with interactions, deep innovations and stimulating challenges, marked by a move towards general renewal (in politics, culture, lifestyle); or rather in the sense of a utopian, imaginary condition (as in *favoloso*, like a fairy tale), one in which reality is blended with expectation and fantasy?

References

Balzarro, Marco (1969), 'Lettera da Philadelphia', *Cartabianca*, 4, 15 January, pp. 2–11.

Beal, Amy C. (2009), '"Music is a universal human right": Musica Elettronica Viva', in Robert Adlington (ed.), *Sound Commitments: Avant-garde Music and the Sixties*, Oxford: Oxford University Press, pp. 99–120.

Bonito Oliva, Achille (1968), 'Il Teatro delle Mostre', *Sipario*, 23/267, pp. 5–10.

Caputo, Simone (2017), '"Musica, parlato, azione, scena, film: teatro lirico con film": *Scene del potere* di Domenico Guaccero', in Gianmario Borio, Giordano Ferrari and Daniela Tortora (eds), *Teatro di avanguardia e composizione sperimentale per la scena in Italia: 1950–1975*, Venezia: Fondazione Giorgio Cini, pp. 259–301. Retrieved from http://omp.cini.it/index.php/FGCOP/catalog/view/3/3/11-1 (accessed 1 May 2018).

Carandini, Silvia (ed.), (2012) *Memorie dalle cantine. Teatro di ricerca a Roma negli anni '60 e '70, Biblioteca Teatrale*, 101–03, Roma: Bulzoni.

Chevalier, Pauline (2013), 'Topographie d'une avant-garde: *downtown* New York 1961 – 1976', in Jean-Paul Aubert, Serge Milan and Jean-François Trubert (eds), *Avant-Gardes: Frontières, Mouvements. Volume I. Délimitations, Historiographie*, Sampzon: éditions Delatour France, pp. 317–39.

Cosci, Marco (2017), 'La scena media(tizza)ta: teatro, cinema e televisione in *A(lter) A(ction)*', in Gianmario Borio, Giordano Ferrari and Daniela Tortora (eds), *Teatro di avanguardia e composizione sperimentale per la scena in Italia: 1950–1975*, Venezia: Fondazione Giorgio Cini, pp. 235–57. Retrieved from http://omp.cini.it/index.php/FGCOP/catalog/view/3/3/11-1 (accessed 1 May 2018).

Dietrich, Ralf (2009), 'ONCE and the Sixties', in Robert Adlington (ed.), *Sound Commitments: Avant-garde Music and the Sixties*, Oxford: Oxford University Press, pp. 169–86.

Ferrari, Giordano (2000), *Les débuts du théâtre musical d'avant-garde en Italie*, Paris: L'Harmattan.

A survey of new music theatre in Rome 201

Gruppo Altro (ed.) (1981), *Altro. Dieci anni di lavoro intercodice*, Roma: Edizioni Kappa.

Guaccero, Domenico (2005) *'Un iter segnato'. Scritti e interviste*, ed. Alessandro Mastropietro, Milan: Ricordi-LIM Libreria Musicale Italiana.

Guaccero, Domenico (2005 [1963]) 'Un'esperienza di "teatro" musicale', in Alessandro Mastropietro (ed.), *'Un iter segnato'. Scritti e interviste*, Milan: Ricordi-LIM Libreria Musicale Italiana, pp. 143–60.

Guaccero, Domenico (2005 [1964]) 'Petrassi: l'empirismo illuminato della didattica contemporanea', in Alessandro Mastropietro (ed.), *'Un iter segnato'. Scritti e interviste*, ed. Alessandro Mastropietro, Milan: Ricordi-LIM Libreria Musicale Italiana, pp. 342–55.

Kombinat Joey (ed.) (1972) *Kombinat Joey, Grammatica*, 4.

Kostelanetz, Richard (1968), *The Theatre of Mixed Means*, New York: The Dial Press.

Lombardi Vallauri, Stefano (2015), 'L'*anti-opera* come veicolo: il teatro musicale come pratica autotrasformativa per il performer', in Alessio Ramerino (ed.), *Teatro e Musica*, Roma: Bulzoni, pp. 131–46.

Lux, Simonetta and Daniela Tortora (eds) (2005), *Collage 1961, un'azione dell'arte di Achille Perilli e Aldo Clementi*, Roma: Gangemi Editore.

Mafai, Miriam (2002), 'Roma, dal 18 aprile alla dolce vita', in Maurizio Fagiolo dell'Arco and Claudio Terenzi (eds), *Roma 1948–1959. Arte, cronaca e cultura dal neorealismo alla dolce vita*, exhibition catalogue (Rome, Palazzo delle Esposizioni, 30 January to 27 May 2002), Genève-Milano: Skira, pp. 5–21.

Malusardi, Alessandra and Francesco Reggiani (eds) (2010), *Alexander Calder, Work in Progress. Memoria di una messinscena*, Roma: Teatro dell'Opera di Roma – Archivio Storico.

Margiotta, Salvatore (2013), *Il Nuovo Teatro in Italia 1968–1975*, Corazzano: Titivillus.

Massimo Barbero, Luca and Francesca Pola (eds), (2010) *Macroroots of the Contemporary. Fabio Sargentini's L'Attico 1966–1978*, Milano: Mondadori Electa.

Mastropietro, Alessandro (2003), 'L'interno/esterno della voce: su "Scene del potere" di Domenico Guaccero', in Daniela Tortora (ed.), *Voce come soffio, Voce come gesto. Omaggio a Michiko Hirayama*, Roma: Aracne, pp. 123–72.

Mastropietro, Alessandro (2009), 'Ancora una "scena del potere": *Novità assoluta* (1972)', in Daniela Tortora (ed.), *Domenico Guaccero. Teoria e prassi dell'avanguardia*, Roma: Aracne, pp. 297–316.

Mastropietro, Alessandro (2011), 'Music theatre as space-time reversal: Aldo Clementi from 1961 to 1979', *Contemporary Music Review*, 30/3–4, pp. 212–34.

Mastropietro, Alessandro (2014), 'Il teatro musicale di Pennisi, da *Sylvia Simplex a Descrizione dell'Isola Ferdinandea*', in Alessandro Mastropietro (ed.), *Il dubbio che vibra. Francesco Pennisi e il teatro musicale*, Lucca: LIM Libreria Musicale Italiana, pp. 19–62.

Mastropietro, Alessandro (2016a), 'Un teatro musicale danzato "polifonico" e polisenso: *Rot* (1970–72) di Domenico Guaccero', *Gli Spazi della Musica*, 5/1 (2016), pp. 32–77. Retrieved from www.ojs.unito.it/index.php/spazidellamusica/article/view/1801 (accessed 1 May 2018).

Mastropietro, Alessandro (2016b), '"Lo voglio alla Nino": Titone, Macchi e "l'idea di un nuovo teatro musicale" all'inizio degli anni '60', *InTrasformazione*, 5/2, pp. 209–39. Retrieved from www.intrasformazione.com/index.php/intrasformazione/article/view/237/pdf (accessed 1 May 2018).

Mastropietro, Alessandro (2017a), 'Intorno alla "Compagnia del Teatro Musicale di Roma": un nuovo modello operativo, tra sperimentazione e utopia', in Gianmario Borio, Giordano Ferrari and Daniela Tortora (eds), *Teatro di avanguardia e composizione sperimentale per la scena in Italia: 1950–1975*, Venezia, Fondazione Giorgio Cini, pp. 105–62. Retrieved from http://omp.cini.it/index.php/FGCOP/catalog/view/3/3/11-1 (accessed 1 May 2018).

Mastropietro, Alessandro (2019) *Nuovo teatro musicale fra Roma e Palermo, 1961–1973*, new revised edition, Lucca: LIM Libreria Musicale Italiana.

Mosch, Ulrich (2017), 'When the composer's artistic aims clash with the choreographer's autonomy. Sylvano Bussotti, Aurel Milloss, and the "choreographic mystery" *Raramente* (1970–71)', in Patrizia Veroli and Gianfranco Vinay (eds), *Music-Dance: Sound and Motion in Contemporary Discourse*, Abingdon, UK: Routledge, pp. 157–74.

Mumma, Gordon (2015), *Cybersonic Arts: Adventures in American New Music*, Urbana, IL: University of Illinois Press.

Pizzaleo, Luigi (2014), *MEV Musica Elettronica Viva*, Lucca: LIM Libreria Musicale Italiana.

Quattrocchi, Arrigo (1991), *Storia dell'Accademia Filarmonica Romana*, Rome: Presidenza del Consiglio dei Ministri – Dipartimento per l'Informazione e l'Editoria.

Salaris, Claudia (1999), *La Roma delle avanguardie. Dal futurismo all'underground*, Roma: Editori Riuniti.

Salzman, Eric and Thomas Desi (2008), *The New Music Theatre: Seeing the Voice, Hearing the Voice*, Oxford: Oxford University Press.

Tessitore, Fiorella (ed.) (2003), *Visione che si ebbe nel cielo di Palermo*, Roma: Cidim/Amic – Nuova Eri.

Tessitore, Fiorella (ed.) (2013), *Palermo anni Sessanta. Le Settimane Internazionali Nuova Musica*, Palermo: Fondazione Teatro Massimo.

Tognelli, Jole (ed.) (1979), *Cinquant'anni del Teatro dell'Opera. Roma 1928 1978*, Roma: Bestetti.

Tortora, Daniela (1990), *Nuova Consonanza. Trent'anni di musica contemporanea in Italia (1959–1988)*, Lucca: LIM Libreria Musicale Italiana.

Tortora, Daniela (1998), '*A(lter) A(ction)*: un tentativo di teatro musicale d'avanguardia', *Il Saggiatore Musicale*, 2, pp. 327–44.

Tortora, Daniela (2013), 'Da * *selon Sade* a *La Passion selon X*: intorno alla *Passion selon Sade* di Sylvano Bussotti', *Studi Musicali*, 4/1, pp. 203–35.

9 Avant-garde music theatre at the Festival d'Avignon between 1967 and 1969

Jean-François Trubert

When Jean Vilar founded the Festival d'Avignon in 1947, he had been charmed by places and spaces: the Cour d'Honneur (Court of Honour) in the Palais des Papes (Pope's Palace); the Cloître des Célestins (Celestine Cloister); the Verger d'Urbain (the Orchard of Urban V). The most striking feature of this unique festival, which lives on today, is its eminently topographical feel, during which the historic city of Avignon is itself transformed. The emergence in France of a new experimental or avant-garde music theatre in 1969 found roots in this soil, a phenomenon located from the outset at the intersection of several events, all located in Avignon and linked through a particular topographical feature, the stage. It built upon aspects of the new theatre – what Michel Corvin in 1963 described as the 'avant-garde theatre' of Samuel Beckett, Jean Genet and Arthur Adamov (Corvin 1987 [1963]: 3) – whose dramatic writing called into question the linearity that prevailed until the mid-1950s:

> The new œuvre is not an analytical demonstration of our condition, it does not 'talk' about our anxieties or uncertainties, it 'shows' them. Its language is action [. . .] insofar as it is based on objects, on gestures that are no longer indicative of a character or a soul, as in classical or symbolist theatre, but are significant in and of themselves.
>
> (Corvin 1987 [1963]: 5)

It also built upon the innovative experiments of the new music theatre whose foundations had been laid in Italy, Germany and the United States (Ferrari 2000). Just as language became action in the new theatre, so singing was supplanted by other kinds of embodiment in new music theatre – as Vilar's colleague Paul Puaux noted:

> Lying between two extreme poles is the *concert éclaté* (broken concert) or wordless or physical opera, similar to dramatic ballet or pantomime, and opera, in which all means of expression are permitted and there is no right or prescribed way of doing things. It seems however that singing, in the sense of *bel canto*, has lost its dominant role to voice, musical speech, dramatic music and its alliance with the other expressive sonic or visual sources.[1]

---

1 Paul Puaux archives, Maison Jean Vilar, Avignon, call number 4-ACOL-1 684-2 1976. All original translations are by the author.

204   *Jean-François Trubert*

The factors that came to the fore in Avignon between 1967 and 1969 were many and varied. While the festival established itself as a meeting place and platform for experimentation where heritage and innovation could exist side-by-side, it is customary to give credit to the Office de Radiodiffusion-Télévision Française (O.R.T.F.), to Radio France, and to one of its producers, Guy Erismann, for introducing the genre of music theatre to France (Loyer and de Baecque 2007). Erismann was especially instrumental in defining music theatre at the time of its emergence – which was late compared to the experiments of composers elsewhere. In Avignon, now-emblematic French composers, including Georges Aperghis, Gérard Massias, Claude Prey, Michel Puig, Francis Miroglio, and Girolamo Arrigo, were to conduct their first experiments with the stage as a medium. However, the documents held in the Maison Jean Vilar in Avignon show a late 1960s reality characterized by growing experimentation in which everything converged in the transdisciplinarity specific to new music theatre. Without minimizing the real contribution of services provided by O.R.T.F., nor the undeniable share of credit due to Guy Erismann, to whom we will return below, this article aims to set this emergence in a context centred on Jean Vilar, especially on those events in Avignon that acted as catalysts, such as the performance of Maurice Béjart's company Ballets du XXe siècle, and the events of 1968 as they manifested themselves during the festival. The presence of the Living Theatre company during the 1968 festival was an especially notorious moment; the events fostered a desire to create a new and concerted cultural action enabling music theatre to emerge in full in 1969.

Jean Vilar and music

The Festival d'Avignon – whose history is also closely intertwined with the history of stage genres, focused as it was to begin with purely upon spoken theatre – formed around a group of individuals engaged in an ongoing reflection on programming: Jean Vilar, its director; his close collaborator Paul Puaux; and from 1967 Christel D'Ornjhelm, who was put in charge of musical programming. Vilar hosted Avignon's first 'week of the dramatic arts' in 1947. In 1951 he was appointed head of Paris's Théâtre du Palais de Chaillot, later the Théâtre National Populaire (TNP). It was during this period that he mounted famous productions of *Le Cid* and especially *Mother Courage* by Bertolt Brecht. From 1959 onward, an element of TNP programming was set aside for contemporary authors; Vilar also began to work increasingly overseas, whilst continuing to direct the Festival d'Avignon. From 1963, he started to direct opera, underscoring his interest in music,[2] including Verdi's *Jérusalem* at the Teatro La Fenice in Venice, Verdi's *Macbeth*, and Mozart's *Le nozze di Figaro* at La Scala in Milan. In 1969, he also produced *Don Carlo* by Verdi in the Verona Arena. These first operatic productions drew considerable attention. In 1965, his reputation as an artist favourable to contemporary forms attracted a group from Belgian radio hoping to produce Henri

---

2 Guy Erismann recalled that Jean Vilar studied music in his childhood, including the violin. See Erismann 1995: 265.

Pousseur's *Votre Faust* – a project which unfortunately would go unrealized. In a letter dated 21 June 1965, Georges Carael, head of the Belgian Broadcasting Office's music division, addressed Vilar directly:

> As I told you over the phone last Saturday, I have asked you to produce Butor-Pousseur's *Votre Faust* and to take on the role of the Theatre Director.
>
> The following is a summary of our conversation:
>
> A group of five radio stations (O.R.T.F., Italian Radio, la Radiodiffusion Télévision Belge – Belgische Radio en Televisie, Swiss Broadcasting Corporation) have joined forces to produce the first performance of *Votre Faust*. This initial performance is planned for September 1966, at the time of the awarding of the Prix Italia (though *hors concours*). There are also plans for a second performance in Italy. Four performances are featured in Théâtre de Genève's subscription season. At least two performances will be given in Paris in November, in collaboration with the O.R.T.F. of course, as well as another performance in Belgium on 14 or 15 December 1966. I should add that the National Theatre of Belgium (not the Opera) has shown keen interest in this production for its own shows.
>
> The musical production is already underway. At the moment, we are recording the magnetic tape used to back part of the action; this underlines the seriousness of the aforementioned offer. [. . .]
>
> You also told me that, for this period, you had a large amount of publishing work [probably a reference to Vilar's *Chronique romanesque*, finally published in 1971]. I should think that the *Votre Faust* solution will leave you enough leisure time to tend to your upcoming major productions in August–December 1966.[3]

In a letter dated 16 October 1965, Carael wrote again to Vilar:

> I have just returned from a quick trip to Paris where I obtained assurance from the O.R.T.F. of a series of at least four performances in the latter half of October. Everything is looking up, you see, because Jacques Huisman of the National Theatre of Belgium is also quite eager to see our project through. [. . .] All of the organizations interested in *Votre Faust* are enthusiastic about the idea of your collaboration.[4]

This initiative, led by Carael, was put on hold when he left for Canada, and in his absence, the Director of Programs terminated the production, breaking the news to Vilar in November:

---

3 Letter from Georges Carael to Jean Vilar, June 21 1965, Brussels. Maison Jean Vilar Archives, Jean Vilar Collection, file 4-JV-223-3.

4 Letter from Georges Carael to Jean Vilar, October 16 1965, Brussels. Maison Jean Vilar Archives, Avignon, Jean Vilar Collection, file 4-JV-223-3.

206   *Jean-François Trubert*

I regret to inform you that several insurmountable calendar and funding-related difficulties prevent us from carrying out the *Votre Faust* project in 1966. I'm writing to let you know that we must cancel the option requested by Mr. G. Carael.[5]

The timing of this correspondence is interesting, as during the same period Vilar was in contact with Maurice Béjart's ballet company, les Ballets du XXe siècle, in residence at the Théâtre de la Monnaie in Brussels. Béjart, who since 1955 had enjoyed a fruitful collaboration with Pierre Henry (in 1967 they would create the *Messe pour le temps présent* for Avignon), was also working at the time with the actress Maria Casarès on a show combining theatre, cinema, music, and dance, *A la Recherche de Don Juan*, created in 1961 and subsequently performed in Avignon in 1968 (Béjart 1995: 168). Another multimedia piece written by Béjart, *The Green Queen*, was also performed by Casarès. Casarès then invited Vilar to see this piece. The premiere left a deep impression on Vilar, who confided his thoughts in a 1963 letter to the choreographer:

How can one be anything but astonished in the presence of such a precise and pure arrangement of on-stage elements? [. . .] I felt like I was in the presence of new signs, a new alphabet. While one is a bit puzzled, at least at the beginning of the play, by your way of demonstrating a, b, or etc., differently from the rest of us (authors or directors), one is also thrown off balance by the intermixing of various disciplines (the art of speech, mime, dance, music, of musique concrète – I mean, electronic [. . .]).
In short, you've shaken us up.[6]

(Béjart 1995: 169–170)

Béjart borrowed from Jean Vilar's letter the term 'polygamy' to define this new meeting of the different disciplines, which he dubbed an 'inter-racial mix between dance and theatre' (1995: 169–170).

Vilar was exposed to these experiments at precisely the time that his interest shifted toward opera. It followed that Vilar would opt to overhaul the programming for the 1966 Festival d'Avignon: that year marked a turning point in the history of the festival, its twentieth anniversary, because it headed in a new direction, opening up to disciplines other than the spoken theatre. Dance would be programmed for the first time in the cour d'honneur (Court of Honour) inside the Palais des Papes; Vilar naturally invited Béjart and the Ballets du XXe siècle:

It is my hope and desire that you will make a creation – of your choosing, of course – for the 20th Festival d'Avignon [. . .] Twenty years is a landmark

---

5 Letter from C. Mertens to Jean Vilar, November 17 1965, Brussels. Maison Jean Vilar Archives, Jean Vilar Collection, Avignon, Jean Vilar Collection, file 4-JV-223-3.
6 Letter from Jean Vilar to Maurice Béjart, 26 October 1963.

Music theatre at the Festival d'Avignon 207

anniversary, and we would like to celebrate it not as a sign of age but as a renewal. The Palais is in my opinion a perfect venue and 'acoustic courtyard' for your work.[7]

(Loyer and de Baecque 2007: 211)

Béjart's programme reflected the tendency toward multidisciplinary experiences. A new piece, *L'Art de la barre*, imagined situations and movements developing out of dance study exercises; but there was also a shift toward indeterminate form, as in *Variations pour une porte et un soupir* to music by Pierre Henry, whose subtitle reads 'exercise in collective improvisation'. Also featured would be Wagner's *Bacchanale, Pas de deux* set to the music of Anton Webern, *Sonate à trois* set to the music of Bartók, *Peter and the Wolf* by Serge Prokofiev, and Ravel's *Boléro*, as well as more institutional choreographic compositions.

In 1967, French culture minister André Malraux wanted to launch a major project with the goal of rehabilitating the operatic arts at Paris's Opéra Garnier. Malraux entrusted the project's management to Vilar, who surrounded himself with two great figures of modernity: for dance, his new companion Maurice Béjart; and for music, Pierre Boulez, who was later to remark on how 'Vilar's operatic stagings in Italy had certainly given him a real ambition for operatic theatre' (Boulez 1995: 175). Vilar thus found himself at the crossroads of disciplines and cultural institutions. This position would exert a strong influence on his own aesthetic orientations in programming the festival.

1967 and the addition of music to the Festival

As Vilar wrote in his 1967 festival editorial, it was then a question of 'creating', of both proposing novel programming and bringing something new to the festival's spirit, because, as he stated, 'When dealing with cultural affairs, how does one separate activity from doctrine?'[8] The 1967 festival featured a programme commensurate with his ambition: six new theatrical creations and more than forty-eight performances, including fifteen concerts featuring a different instrumental ensemble. The transition that began in 1966 was now in full swing. In 1967, the Festival d'Avignon became multidisciplinary – with performances in music, dance, theatre, and cinema – and placed an emphasis on diversity. In addition, new spaces were established for public debate and for research (symposia), as well as an area devoted to music: the Verger d'Urbain V (the orchard of Urban V). The programming was sponsored by the O.R.T.F., which managed the production and contracts of musical artists. Notable, for example, was the presence of the Percussions de Strasbourg, in 1967 still called the 'Groupe instrumental à Percussion de Strasbourg', in a programme of music by Milan Stibilij, Miroslav Kabeláč and Michel Puig; Puig's *Provisoires Agglomérats* offered a

---

7 Letter from Jean Vilar to Maurice Béjart, 8 September 1965.
8 Jean Vilar, excerpt from the 1967 Festival d'Avignon program, editorial, Maison Jean Vilar Archives, Avignon.

208   *Jean-François Trubert*

graphic sonic depiction of the aftermath of an atomic explosion, made more gruelling by the groans and howls of two actors (Claude Petitpierre and Karen Fenn).[9]

That same year, the theatre director Jorge Lavelli participated for the first time in the production of Goethe's *Triumph der Empfindsamkeit*, based on a French translation by Jacques Decourdemanche and with incidental music composed by Diego Masson, the founder of the ensemble Musique Vivante (which would participate later on in the festival and become a great promoter of new music in France). But the highlight of the 1967 festival was without question the world premiere of the ballet *Messe pour le temps présent* by Maurice Béjart, set to the music of Pierre Henry. At the time of the performance, Béjart stated in a television interview that he saw Avignon as a 'unique place' and that he did not think that he could have 'done as good a job [with this piece] elsewhere'. The piece was described by Béjart as a 'total spectacle' because 'actors participate in the show, there is bodily expression, dance, a wide variety of music, and percussion. But it is still a very focused spectacle, just like a liturgical service.' He went on to explain that the show is very 'composite', giving an image of the 'present time', ranging from the 'the purest' classical to the 'most contemporary dances, like the *jerk* [original in English]'.[10] Two years prior to the festival's wholehearted incorporation of musical theatre in 1969, Béjart's *Messe pour le temps présent* set in motion a genuinely forward-looking aesthetic programme. It did so by mixing and hybridizing artistic disciplines; by intermingling periods and styles within the same work; by blending the learned with the popular; and by combining extreme contemporaneity – Pierre Henry's *musique concrète* and electronic music – and tradition, with interludes for percussion alone.

On the strength of these successes, Vilar was encouraged to ponder a completely different event for the following year's Festival d'Avignon by inviting the Living Theatre, with the purpose of amplifying and solidifying its policy of openness. The year 1968 proved to mark a change of course for its programming, concerning not only disciplines, but also their social and political content.

1968: the breaking point

As we have just seen, from 1967, Vilar was on the lookout for new theatrical forms weaving together artistic disciplines and genres. Without referring yet to music theatre, Vilar took inspiration from creators close to him, such as Béjart, to imagine new possibilities for stage performances in the festival's secular venues. The programming of the festival's twenty-second edition was therefore undertaken in this spirit of exploration and innovation, in a manner designed to transform the new theatre's stage. One need only glance through the final programme: three plays by the Living Theatre, which gave its performances a dimension of total spectacle; a production by Jorge Lavelli; Oscar Panizza's *The Council of Love*;

---

9 Details from the 21st Festival d'Avignon playbill, 1967, Maison Jean Vilar Archives, Avignon.

10 Maurice Béjart, interview with the TV news, O.R.T.F., broadcast 4 August 1967, National Audiovisual Institute Archives (INA), Paris.

Music theatre at the Festival d'Avignon   209

and a piece by Béjart, *A la Recherche de . . .* which mixed dance and theatre and involved Maria Casarès.

These developments caused concern for Vilar's usual collaborators, starting with his stage director counterparts such as Antoine Bourseiller. Hailing from the TNP, Bourseiller was stage director for the Centre Dramatique National du Sud-Est, which mounted two productions for the 1968 festival. The first, *American Hurrah*, based on a script by Jean-Claude van Itallie, was a piece featuring stage music announced as 'Live Psychedelic Music'. Van Itallie, a Brussels-born author living in New York, was actively involved in the Open Theatre, an offshoot of the Living Theatre which later collaborated with Luciano Berio on his *Opera* (1970). The second piece, *Crénom*, based on a script by Charles Baudelaire, was produced in collaboration with Eugène Ionesco and Slawomir Mrozek. Upon learning that the Living Theatre was slated to perform, Bourseiller immediately called Paul Puaux, Vilar's collaborator, as Puaux later reported in a letter to Vilar:

> I received a phone call from Bourseiller.
> In short:
> 'I'll be able to let you know the events for the cloister by month's end. But the presence of Living [*sic*] has me a bit worried. They are, after all, the finest theatre movement around at the moment. And we are all striving to work the way they do – including Planchon, whose production should reflect the same spirit. In a sense, their presence should impel us to strive further. But from a commercial standpoint, they're our competition!' End of quote [. . .][11]

For the 1968 edition, Vilar also sought to forge a bond between festival audiences and artists. Talks and symposia were held regularly on themes relating to culture and its dissemination. Both urban and popular events in Avignon drew crowds to a variety of venues, including the Verger d'Urbain V and the Cloître des Célestins, to see personalities including Julian Beck, Maurice Béjart, Antoine Bourseiller, Jorge Lavelli, and Georges Wilson.

In parallel, the musical programme of the 1968 festival saw the inclusion of contemporary repertoire. Sponsored by the French Ministry of Cultural Affairs' music division and the O.R.T.F., the festival's music stage, in the Verger d'Urbain V, featured almost exclusively contemporary pieces, reflecting the theme *Music of our time*. As the festival programme stated, 'Most of the musical works presented this year at the Avignon Festival belong to contemporary artistic practice [. . .] A number of young composers and performers from France and abroad are showcasing a varied pallette of modern sound arts.'[12] These included works on the programme of the O.R.T.F.'s Simonovitch Orchestra, the presence of Boulez's Domaine Musical concert society (building upon Vilar's and Boulez's collaboration in the Malraux mission at the Garnier), and the hosting of 'current jazz' nights.

---

11 Letter from Paul Puaux to Jean Vilar, 21 December 1967, Maison Jean Vilar Archives, Avignon, Jean Vilar Collection, file 4-JV-180-1.

12 Excerpts from the 1968 festival programme. Maison Jean Vilar Archives, Avignon.

210   *Jean-François Trubert*

Under Vilar's direction, the Festival d'Avignon at this time sought to draw performers on the cutting edge of artistic creation – one might also say the most audacious artists. The pieces performed by Julian Beck's and Judith Malina's Living Theatre were without a doubt the high point of the 1968 festival (see Figure 9.1). The American troupe's acting style was based on improvisation and intensity of bodily expression, sometimes reaching extremes through the violence of the situations represented and the use of vocal utterances. Ideologically influenced by Antonin Artaud, the company had been banned from America in 1963, and so began an international tour away from their home stage on New York's 14th Street, which had been shut down by the American government. The Living Theatre's performances at Avignon were held at the Cloître des Célestins in the south of the city, some distance from the Cour d'Honneur. The programme included three plays: Sophocles' *Antigone*, in an adaptation by Bertolt Brecht; *Mysteries and Smaller Pieces*, a series of exercises and scenic situations symbolizing the work of the Living Theatre; and lastly *Paradise Now*, a collectively improvised play involving audience participation. A special improvisation night bringing together the Living Theatre with the dancers of Maurice Béjart's Ballets du XXe siècle was planned for the festival at midnight on 10 August. This served to highlight two approaches being taken at the time by two companies dedicated to unusual forms of spectacle: on the one hand a mixed-discipline choreography; and on the other, a total theatre that went beyond scripts in favour of a physical action-language completely unfettered by academicism.

The programme would, however, be turned on its head by the civil unrest of May 1968, a student strike movement originating in Nanterre that rapidly developed into riots in the heart of the capital. During these events, the position of French president Charles de Gaulle shook the convictions of Jean Vilar – in particular, with his policy of violent repression of demonstrators. During this period, Vilar resigned from the position that had been granted to him at the Opéra Garnier, without even giving Béjart or Boulez notice (Téphany 1995). Because of the many movements that had shut down parts of the country, Georges Wilson, Jorge Lavelli, and André Bourseiller could not make it to Avignon, forcing Vilar to modify his programming (Adler and Veinstein 1987: 110). A left-leaning individual, confident in the soundness of his ideals, Vilar organized ongoing public forums at the Verger where 'everyone will be free to speak, and discuss the artistic revolution' (Adler and Veinstein 1987: 110).

The festival officially began on 17 July, but tensions were already running high a week earlier. The actors of the Living Theatre had been in France for several months, arriving in Avignon by May.[13] They were rumoured to have participated in the occupation of the Odéon Theatre in Paris. On 11 July, an actor from the Living Theatre was arrested for breaching public morality. At the same time, Paul Puaux received a visit from the French intelligence services who informed

---

13 Chronicle of the 1968 edition's events by the festival team, Maison Jean Vilar Archives, Avignon, Jean Vilar Collection, file 4-JV-181. This is the principal source for the following account of the festival's upheavals in 1968.

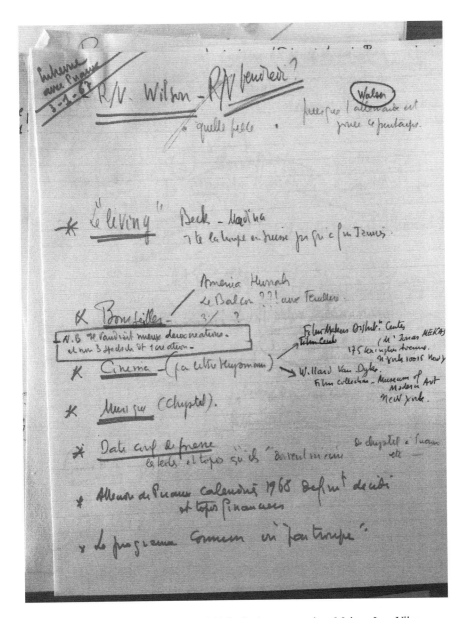

Figure 9.1 Preparatory notes for the 1968 festival programming. Maison Jean Vilar archives, 4-JV-180-1, 1967.

him of several 'dissenting' groups travelling down from Paris with plans to occupy Avignon. Among these dissenters, there were students from the Sorbonne and especially the École des Beaux-Arts, including Jean-Jacques Lebel, who had organized the occupation of the Odéon Theatre. On 12 July, the law enforcement

212   Jean-François Trubert

agencies and Paul Puaux agreed to cooperate, although Puaux's concern that the event 'must not be a festival of the CRS [i.e. Compagnies Républicaines de Sécurité, the police division responsible for public order and crowd control]'[14] led to an agreement with the local police commander, who promised not to intervene without prior consultation. Accordingly, the festival opened without incident. On 18 July, however, news spread that the prefect of the neighbouring département had banned a theatre piece in Villeneuve-les-Avignons, *La paillasse aux seins nus* (The Bare-Breasted Tramp) by Gérard Gélas, in a production by the Chêne Noir theatre troupe – a playwright, play, and troupe unknown to the festival management. The company took their protest to Vilar and his team, and leaflets were distributed. Julian Beck of the Living Theatre offered to let the Chêne Noir perform its play at the Cloître des Célestins ahead of *Antigone*, but the festival management opposed the idea, suggesting that a letter of protest be read instead. Beck categorically refused this solution. At 6:30 p.m., a demonstration was organized at the Place de l'Horloge, the town's central square, in front of the town hall; Jean-Jacques Lebel dominated the meeting. Around 7 p.m., the crowd became hostile, and the CRS organized a charge to disperse demonstrators. At 9:15 p.m., Beck declared that the evening's performance would not take place so long as demonstrators were being held by the police. Vilar, Puaux, and Beck negotiated until midnight at the Cloître des Carmelites, which was gradually being emptied of the protagonists and festivalgoers who came for the event; the planned performance of *Antigone* did not take place.

On 19 July, a compromise seemed to have been reached between Vilar and the actors of the Chêne Noir troupe; it was agreed that following the evening's performance of Bejart's *Messe pour le temps présent*, the Chêne Noir's actors would stand on stage and read their protest publicly. The following day, public participatory meetings were held in the Verger, and that night the Living Theatre performed *Antigone*. The Chêne Noir's actors were invited, out of solidarity, to stand symbolically at the back of the stage throughout the play with adhesive tape placed over their mouths. At midnight, extremist anti-left hooligans broke into the old high school where the Living Theatre company was spending the night; a member of their entourage with long hair was seized and his hair shorn off in the street. Young festival attendees and people from protest groups occupying the Place de l'Horloge and some of the theatre stages took up the Living Theatre's cause, seeking explanations from the festival organizers. On 24 July, *Paradise Now* premiered in a particularly challenging environment for Vilar, who tried to pacify the crowd as it attempted to rush the stage. Relations became tense between Julian Beck and the mayor of Avignon: on July 25, Living Theatre actors put on a second performance of *Paradise Now* under heated conditions, from 10 p.m. to midnight. Then, they continued the show away from the festival's premises until 3 a.m., moving into the city to perform 'street theatre'. The following day, the

---

14 Report of the chronology of events of 1968, Maison Jean Vilar Archives, Avignon, Jean Vilar Collection, file 4-JV-181.

Music theatre at the Festival d'Avignon   213

Avignon city hall board of directors banned any street performance of *Paradise Now* following numerous complaints by local residents – but the Living Theatre were still permitted to perform on stage.

In this overall context, the ban on the Living Theatre was sorely resented by the company. It recalled not only painful memories of censorship at home, but echoed the ban on Chêne Noir a few days previously. On 28 July, Julian Beck publicly announced to the press and a crowd of people that he was leaving the festival. With his troupe, he handed out leaflets in the streets of Avignon:

> We are leaving the festival because the time has finally come for us to refuse to serve those who want the knowledge and power of art to belong only to those able to pay for it, those who wish to keep people in the dark, who work to keep power in the hands of the elite, who wish to control the lives of artists and those of other men. The struggle lives on for us too.[15]
>
> (cited in Loyer and de Baecque 2007: 238)

From 30 to 31 July, a few minor incidents affected the performances, and the festival's final days in August were dampened by inclement weather. Vilar remained profoundly impacted by the criticisms levelled against him during these events. Enduring chants of 'Vilar, Béjart, Salazar', Vilar remained a target of harshly worded tracts and slogans ('supermarket of culture'), standing accused of summoning and hiding behind the military police. This was evidently not the case, as the archives show that Vilar and Puaux had consistently done their utmost to deal with the police and the prefect to avoid massive intervention, ensuring that the public was respected and that the festival security service intervened before the police. Be that as it may, the events of 1968 rather confirmed Vilar's declared hope that 'La ville entière doit devenir le lieu du festival' ('The whole city must become the place of the festival') (Loyer and de Baecque 2007: 241). They encouraged Vilar to even greater innovation and reflection in terms of programming. He took stock of those performances that met with success, including Béjart's *Messe pour le temps présent* and *À la Recherche de . . .*. Public participation, novel forms, new writings: it was within this context that the idea for a new music theatre gradually emerged.

1969: the avant-garde festival

The 1968 festival's aftermath played out over an extended period.[16] Julian Beck's lawyer called to express doubts about future programming. The festival was running a deficit, and it was time to find new ways of operating. The festival team met. Vilar was in the habit of taking notes over the course of the festival; he roamed the streets of Avignon, observing plays, writing down ideas, determining what worked and what did not. Elements of these handwritten notes today

---

15 Leaflet posted in the streets of Avignon during the 1968 festival.
16 Jean Vilar experienced his first cardiac episode in September 1968.

214   *Jean-François Trubert*

attract the researcher's attention, especially those forward-looking ideas, that is to say, ideas calling for new forms, a 'new theatre' as stated in a document dated December 1968.[17]

Directors and the national companies were more circumspect towards the festival because of the previous year's incidents, using strong language to describe the peculiar climate on the heels of the 1968 edition: as Loyer and de Baecque remark, 'the desperate quest for a prestigious creation for the Cour d'Honneur in the years after 1968 is met with many refusals. Supply becomes scarce, and demand heterogeneous' (Loyer and de Baecque 2007: 277). Public opinion was divided into two large groups: on the one hand the proponents of a text-based theatre influenced by the festival's first years and the great moments of the TPN; on the other hand, a younger audience yearning for experimentation. To these multiple, even 'irreconcilable', expectations, there was the added difficulty of having to fill several spaces and sites in Avignon: the Cour d'Honneur, the Cloître des Carmes, the Cloître des Célestins, and the Jardin du Verger. It was therefore necessary to welcome new genres to the 1969 festival, taking into account current experimentation, new writing, and transgressive forms of performance. The idea progressively emerged to bring multidisciplinary performances to the stage, a logical evolution of a programming policy that had been pursued since 1965 and whose founding principles were forged by contact with the parallel activities of Vilar as stage director.

Another factor, rarely emphasized in the historiographies devoted to the festival, was Vilar's involvement with UNESCO's cultural programmes. At the time, Vilar was in close contact with Yves Brunsvick, the Secretary General of the French National Commission for UNESCO; Raymond Lyon, the Secretary General of the National Music Committee (the French Section of UNESCO's International Music Council); and especially Jack Bornhoff, the General Manager of the International Music Council. In 1965, Vilar organized a festival symposium with the French National Commission on the theme 'education and culture'; and during the 1968 festival, a second symposium was held, involving UNESCO representatives and having as its theme 'cultural development policy in cities'. Vilar and Brunsvick had both attended a UNESCO symposium in 1967 in Monaco.[18] Vilar's personal library contains a copy of the 1968 proceedings for a major UNESCO symposium on music theatre, which he almost certainly received from one of his personal contacts, either the publisher, Jack Bornhoff, or Yves Brunsvick.[19] The volume, *Music Theatre in a Changing Society*, provided both historical and practical insights into experimental lyrical practices in a broad sense, ranging from a repertoire review to interventions by directors. The major works regarded as being emblematic of this new genre of experimental theatre were: Nono's *Intolleranza*; Berio's *Passaggio*; Manzoni's *Atomtod*; Zimmermann's

---

17 Maison Jean Vilar Archives, Avignon, Jean Vilar Collection, file 4-JV-182-3.
18 Maison Jean Vilar Archives, Avignon, Jean Vilar Collection, file 4-JV182-2.
19 Maison Jean Vilar Archives, Avignon, Jean Vilar Collection.

Die Soldaten; Peter Schat's *Labyrint*; Stockhausen's *Originale*; Butor/Pousseur's *Votre Faust*; Mauricio Kagel's *Sur Scene*; Ann Halprin's *Parade and Changes*; Maderna's *Hyperion*; and Ligeti's *Aventures*. Also included were the collaboration of Brecht and Weill, the experiments of John Cage, and finally *L'Histoire du soldat*, all of which served as forerunners to forms combining several disciplines on stage. The book gave insight into 'experimental music theatre', in which the musicians themselves participated in on-stage action, claiming in addition that 'almost all make use of electronic components in their musical or sound structure' (Bornhoff 1968: 37).

One may therefore consider that Vilar and his team adhered very precisely to the era of the 'present time', to paraphrase Béjart, in order to seek new forms of stage expression. Vilar also involved television and other media for the 1969 festival. The O.R.T.F.'s television programmes and broadcasts of festival events made their debut, capturing the atmosphere of the streets, concerts, and rehearsals. Subsequent O.R.T.F. coverage of the festival used a more appropriate medium: radio, and more specifically the France Culture station. Guy Erismann, a music theatre enthusiast and director of musical programmes, organized this initiative, and for good reason: during festival preparation he became Vilar's principal contact for fostering the implementation of a new focus on music theatre at the festival. Most commentators have considered Guy Erismann to be the main instigator of music theatre's emergence at Avignon (e.g. Loyer and de Baecque 2007: 284).[20] His role as a producer, as well as the financial role played by the channel, are indisputable. The O.R.T.F. also operated as a financial partner in previous editions and, in his 1968 press conference to present the festival, Vilar emphasized the value of this partnership and of his festival associates (although in 1968 Erismann's name was not yet explicitly cited[21]):

> I would like to say that this music-promoting endeavour [programmed at the Verger d'Urbain V] in Avignon would hardly be possible had we not obtained the effective collaboration of the O.R.T.F.'s music division, that of Michel Philippot and of his collaborators.[22]

Several handwritten notes found in the Maison Jean Vilar archive show that a genuine cooperation existed from then on, and that Vilar, even before meeting

---

20 Interview with Gaston and Brigitte Sylvestre, November 2016. These informants were both members of the Ensemble Musique Vivante (directed by Diego Masson) and involved in numerous new music theatre premieres.

21 Although the name of Guy Erismann does appear in a preparatory note for the 23rd Festival, 1968, file 4-JV 181-1, where the question of O.R.T.F. arose: 'Erismann is Philippot's deputy. He has particular responsibility for the commentated musical programmes. He has written a book about songs; he is ambitious and he seems well attached to Avignon.'

22 Jean Vilar, handwritten preparatory notes for the press conference of the 22nd Festival d'Avignon, Maison Jean Vilar Archives, Avignon, file 4-JV180-3. Note also that Michel Philippot's primary collaborator was none other than Guy Erismann, his assistant. It is worth noting that Jean Vilar often spoke not of the festival, but of 'Avignon', emphasizing his desire to extend the festival to the city itself.

216   *Jean-François Trubert*

Erismann, had developed the founding principles for a new, total theatre that integrated several disciplines (see Figure 9.2). As these notes show, Vilar was shifting his preoccupation away from spoken theatre and towards the 'quest for a "lyrical theatre"' or even a 'music and song theatre'. He asked himself, 'to which musicians, singers, and directors should I reach out?' And finally, at the bottom of the page, after the choirmaster and conservatory professors, Vilar wondered if he shouldn't rather turn directly to Guy Erismann, who is named here. Other notes show that several plans were envisaged, including entrusting the artistic direction for the musical aspects to a third party:

> I'll take care of the music.
>
> 1   Ask [Diego] Masson what he would do if he were responsible for the general direction of music in Avignon. For this year.
>
> Next year . . . Béjart?
> Another year . . . Puig?[23]

In October 1968, contact was finally made with the O.R.T.F. and Guy Erismann. The minutes from the meeting held in Paris show that Vilar's team were the first to pitch a new lyrical work for the festival:

> Contacts with Erismann:
>
> Overview – Erismann was very satisfied with Avignon and wanted to develop the event. Following a discussion with Chrystel [D'Ornjhelm], the idea of creating a musical show at the Festival seemed to interest the O.R.T.F. I [Puaux] reached out to Février [from the ministerial office] who thought that the idea of such a creation could give rise to a Festival-Opera-Cultural Affairs-O.R.T.F. collaboration, and that a working meeting on this topic is possible. Funding will remain the biggest problem. All parties seem to agree that Avignon's festivalgoers are the best argument for trying operatic experiments.[24]

We see here that events were becoming more precise, but above all that the idea of putting on 'operatic experiments' was the result of a concerted cultural will at the highest level of France's decision-making bodies.

A further meeting, still in October 1968, then specifically addressed musical programming (see Figure 9.3). The organization of the notes on this page is significant, presenting the festival's iconic venues on the left, and toward the right, ideas for troupes or shows to occupy these venues during the festival. Thus, from

---

23 Preparatory notes for the 23rd festival, Maison Jean Vilar Archives, 4-JV-181-1. Michel Puig (b. 1930) is a French composer who studied with René Leibowitz, and contributed to numerous music-theatre stage productions in France.

24 Preparatory notes for the 23rd Festival, dated October 1968. Maison Jean Vilar Archives, Avignon, file 4-JV-182-1.

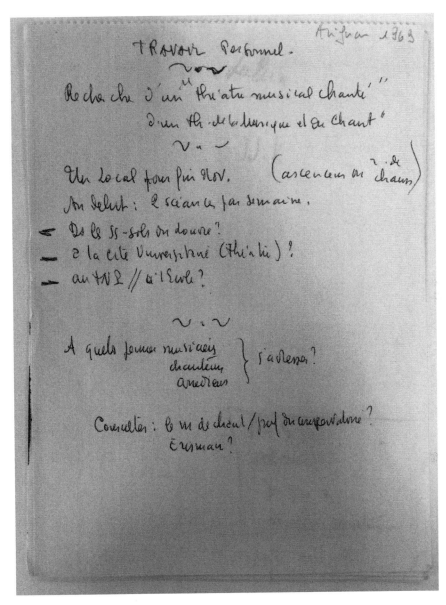

Figure 9.2 Preparatory notes for the 1969 festival programming, October 1968. Maison Jean Vilar archives, 4-JV-182-1.

late 1968 onward, it was foreseen that the Cloître des Célestins would be entirely dedicated to music, with a question near the bottom about 'musical theatre', comprising either a pair of troupes or a single troupe. At this time the festival program was not yet finalized, even though the names of Ariane Mnouchkine and Peter

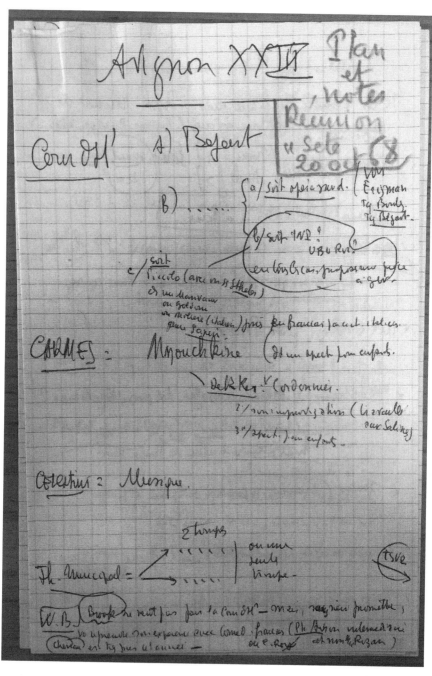

Figure 9.3 Preparatory notes for the 1969 festival programming, October 1968. Maison Jean Vilar archives 4-JV-182-1.

Brook were already under consideration. Erismann's name appeared once again next to those of Béjart and Boulez as a source of advice about the main programme in the Cour of the Palais des Papes; and on the same note, 'music theatre' appears at the bottom of the page, showing the importance the organizing committee attributed to it as a 'genre'.

It seems clear from these documents and the existing documentation about the creations that would be the preserve, starting in the 1970s, of the Théâtre d'Angers, the Atem d'Aperghis, and the Atelier Lyrique du Rhin, that one of the central issues concerned the revival of operatic art, the adaptation of the stage format to new theatre, to new dramaturgies, and to contemporary music. Vilar was fully aware of the experiments taking place in the contemporary music scene. We have already seen that he came very close to actively participating in one of them: *Votre Faust*, with its on-stage orchestra, dialogues, sung passages, quotations, and collages, as well as audience participation that directly shaped the plot via a voting system, fell directly in line with the search for new theatrical forms, as well as for a new kind of collaboration between a contemporary director, librettist, and composer. It is symptomatic that, in notes made by Vilar during the 1968 festival, we find a proposal to introduce an orchestra on the acting stage, one of the most characteristic features of music theatre since Stravinsky's *L'histoire du soldat* (Figure 9.4).

It followed that emerging plans for the 1969 festival would adhere to this aesthetic line, providing a venue and a programme dedicated to music theatre for the first time in France. The first edition's playbill and press conference listed music theatre works to be performed in the Cloître des Célestins in the following order:

- *On veut la lumière, allons-y*, music by Claude Prey, adapted script depicting the Dreyfus affair, directed by Pierre Barrat.
- *Syllabaire pour Phèdre*, by Maurice Ohana, poem by Raphaël Cluzel, directed by Roger Kahan.
- *Tjurunga*, set to music by Gérard Massias, texts by Antonin Artaud.
- *Wacjwa* (later to become *Orden*) by Girolamo Arrigo, script by Pierre Bourgeade and directed by Jorge Lavelli.

At the same time, a new group called the Ensemble Instrumental de Musique Contemporaine de Paris proposed a special evening entitled 'Une expérience de Théâtre musical', directed by Konstantin Simonovitch and presenting *Conditionnement* by Jeannine Charbonnier, based on a text by Michel Butor, and *Pas de Cinq*, the music theatre piece by Mauricio Kagel. The festival programme also featured an original musical theatre creation performed by the Atelier de Composition du Groupe de Recherches Musicales, directed by François Bayle: *Musiques Éclatées*. The work was collaborative, open, indeterminate, and involved the audience, whose members were provided playbills that served as sheet music (see Figures 9.5a and 9.5b). The piece presented itself as a huge event in which the boundaries between stage and audience were 'shattered' and where the transgressive dimension was very clearly emphasized. In an exquisitely post-Dada spirit, the programme begins as follows:

220 *Jean-François Trubert*

Please note: two possible errors:

1　Mistaking *Musiques Eclatées* for a concert
2　Mistaking *Musiques Eclatées* for a non-concert[25]

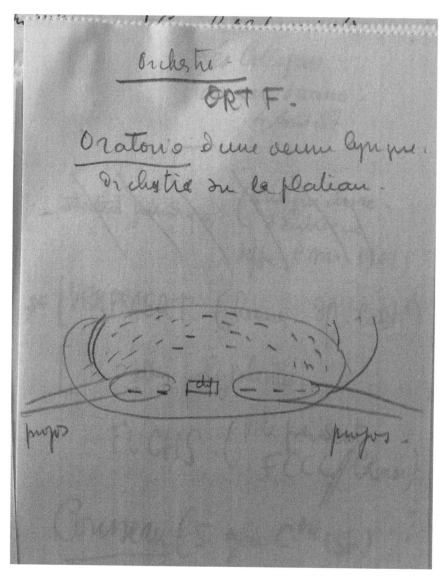

Figure 9.4 Note by Jean Vilar during the 1968 Festival. Maison Jean Vilar archives, Avignon, 4-JV-182.

25　Excerpt from the playbill, dated 7 August 1969.

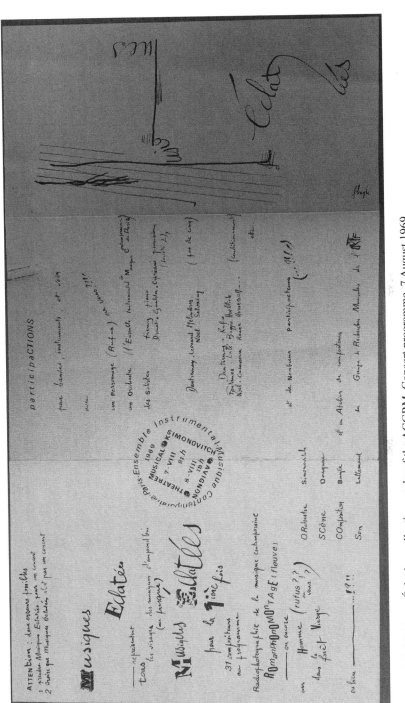

Figure 9.5 Musiques Éclatées, collective works of the ACGRM. Concert programme, 7 August 1969.

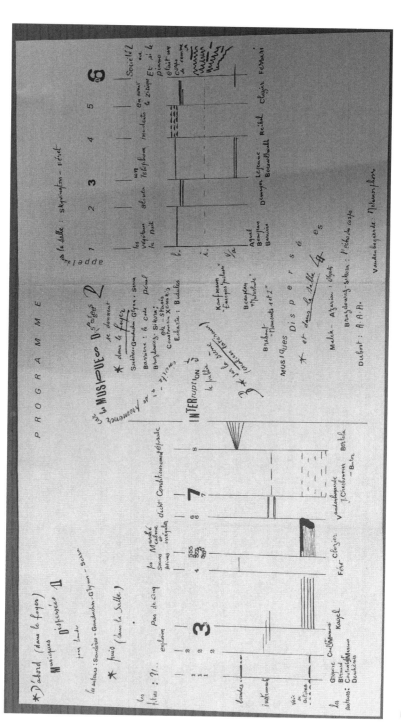

Figure 9.5 (continued)

Music theatre at the Festival d'Avignon 223

However, the highlight of the festival was undoubtedly the music theatre work *Orden* by Girolamo Arrigo, directed by Jorge Lavelli. Pierre Bourgeade's text addressed the question of repression and totalitarianism in Spain. The stage directions fully integrated the new artistic and aesthetic exigencies. The actors and musicians were mixed on stage, with everybody taking part in the action. The scene began with a particularly striking moment: a battalion loading their rifle breeches while gradually beating a deadly rhythm, announcing the repression to come.[26] Girolamo Arrigo's score included not only instrumental sounds but also an electro-acoustic tape fitted out for the different scenes. According to contemporary critics, the performers gave a very impressive representation of a total work of art, in which actors, musicians and singers were held in perpetual tension, opening up a multi-sensory universe, a veritable 'polyphony of signs', to quote Roland Barthes (1993: 1362). The mix of Brechtian techniques and the wrenching Artaudian expressive intensity grabbed spectators' attention, making *Orden* a music theatre hit, and a promotional piece for the genre.

The O.R.T.F. was thus able to continue its policy of commissioning and producing young composers, leading to the discovery of talents such as Georges Aperghis, who were able to develop thanks both to the festival and to the will of the O.R.T.F., of Radio France, and of the Ministry of Culture to foster creative endeavours. In a historically confused period, in which the public authorities were gradually withdrawing from the collective sphere in many areas, it is striking to see the contrast with the 1970s, when, as Georges Aperghis puts it:

All you had to do was go into the office with an idea for a performance, pitch it to Guy Erismann for an hour, and wait for him to say 'sounds good' and sign off on grant funding, with complete carte blanche for the production.[27]

***

Thus, between 1966 and 1969, the Avignon festival established itself as a multidisciplinary artistic festival without any comparison in France. The events that marked the programme during this period gave it an unmistakable notoriety, renowned for releasing new and independent creations, free of the usual institutional straightjackets. In this context, the new music theatre, the fruit of a combination of new theatre and poetry, contemporary and experimental music, and the renewal of approaches to the stage, found a privileged mode of expression, and benefited from cultural policies that proved highly supportive. Jean Vilar played a pioneering role here, anticipating the development of this genre in France, and demonstrating his ability to give French programming an international dimension – at a time when the new music theatre had been established in Germany and Italy for several years. The Festival d'Avignon enabled the discovery of new composers such as Michel Puig, Claude Prey, and Gérard Assayag,

---

26 Interview with Gaston and Brigitte Sylvestre, November 2016.
27 Interview with Georges Aperghis, October 2016.

224 *Jean-François Trubert*

and talented directors such as Jorge Lavelli. It later brought together great tutelary figures such as Georges Aperghis and Antoine Vitez, who collaborated on an emblematic piece for the festival (Paul Claudel's *Le Soulier de Satin* in 1987), the stage director Pierre Barrat (who worked on Aperghis' *Histoire de Loup* in 1976), and last but not least Mauricio Kagel, who officially invested the Festival in 1976 with *Mare Nostrum*. Kagel's encounter with Aperghis at Avignon was to prove especially productive; the two worked together during the 1980s at the Centre Acanthes in Aix-en-Provence, sharing performers such as the percussion trio Le Cercle (for the plays *Dressur* and *Les Guetteurs de son*), the harpist Brigitte Sylvestre, and the comedian Martine Viard (in Kagel's *La Trahison orale* (1983)). The Avignon Festival, as a place of exchange and transmission, of creation, of questioning the stage both through the modernity of creative thought and the city's unique architecture, thus brought the inception of a new approach to musical and theatrical composition, and a new spirit faithful to its director, Jean Vilar.

References

Adler, Laure and Alain Veinstein (1987), *Avignon, 40 ans de festival*, Paris: Hachette.
Barthes, Roland (1993), *Œuvres complètes*, edited by Éric Marty, volume 1, Paris: Seuil.
Béjart, Maurice (1995), 'Bien plus que le théâtre', in Jacques Téphany (ed.), *Jean Vilar*, Paris: Edition de l'Herne, pp. 168–73.
Bornhoff, Jack (ed.) (1968), *Music Theatre in a Changing Society: The Influence of the Technical Media*, Paris: Unesco.
Boulez, Pierre (1995), 'Questions d'exigence', in Jacques Téphany (ed.), *Jean Vilar*, Paris: Edition de l'Herne, pp. 174–8.
Corvin, Michel (1987 [1963]), *Le Théâtre nouveau en France*, Paris: PUF.
Erismann, Guy (1995), 'Jean Vilar, homme de musique', in Jacques Téphany (ed.), *Jean Vilar*, Paris: Edition de l'Herne, pp. 264–87.
Ferrari, Giordano (2000), *Les débuts du théâtre musical d'avant-garde en Italie: Berio, Evangelisti, Maderna*, Paris: L'Harmattan.
Loyer, Emmanuelle and Antoine de Baecque (2016 [2007]), *Histoire du festival d'Avignon*, Paris: Gallimard.
Téphany, Jacques (ed.) (1995), *Jean Vilar*, Paris: Edition de l'Herne.
Trubert, Jean-François (2013), 'Théâtre musical et théâtre instrumental', in Nicolas Donin and Laurent Feneyrou (eds), *Théories de la composition musicale au XXe siècle*, volume 2, Lyon: Symétrie, pp. 1269–96.
Vilar, Jean (1990), *Avignon*, Paris: Autrement.

Part V
Reconceiving the performer

10 Reconceptualising the performer in new music theatre

Collaborations with actors, mimes and musicians

David Beard

Performance has been continually reconceived throughout music history, but increased notational complexity and the introduction of aleatory techniques in the 1950s redefined the performer in radical ways, whilst inadvertently highlighting the inherent theatricality of all musical performance. It is widely argued that these developments, combined with a desire to re-engage with the body, helped inspire the emergence of instrumental and new music theatre works from around 1955 (see Griffiths 1995; Clements 2001; Adlington 2005; Salzman and Desi 2008). Such works explore the relationship between sound, movement, mind and body, anticipating neuroscientific and psychological studies that demonstrate the body's fundamental role in shaping cognitive processes (Laws 2014).[1] In the language of embodiment theory, new music theatre highlights the body's role in *creating* meaningful (or meaningless) musical acts and, arguably, reconceptualises music itself as performance.

There are numerous ways in which performers were reconceived in new music theatre. My focus is on the widespread practice of reaching out explicitly to other art forms, engaging directly with actors, mime artists, dancers, visual artists and non-professional musicians, in ways that culminated in the dancing musicians in Stockhausen's *Licht* cycle (1978–2003), and the mime artists and puppets in Birtwistle's *The Mask of Orpheus* (1973–1983), which, although operatic in scale, are directly informed by the smaller-scale experimentation of instrumental and new music theatre (Cross 2009; Beard 2012: 79–158). There are two important reasons for focusing on this 'reaching out' to other art forms. First, it highlights the collaborative nature of new music theatre, in which, to cite Vlad Petre Glăveanu, creative agency is 'distributed between multiple actors, creations, places and times' (Glăveanu 2014: 2), or, following Georgina Born, 'between persons, between subjects and objects, and across space' (Born 2005: 24). This reflects an emerging conviction among psychologists, social scientists and others that 'significant creations are almost always the result of complex collaborations' (Sawyer and

---

1 Laws uses the term 'embodied cognition' (2014: 131). For more on this concept, see Cox 2016, especially pp. 36–57.

228 *David Beard*

DeZutter 2009: 81; see also Clarke and Doffman (eds) 2018),[2] and the more general argument that all creativity 'is social' (Born 2005: 15).[3] Second, this approach offers a way of defining new music theatre, which is notoriously varied and hard to pin down. Certainly, collaboration is not unique to new music theatre, but artists working in this field tend to express an interest in avant-garde theatre techniques, the notion of embodiment, and a desire to combine expertise from different aesthetic and artistic disciplines.

Although I will discuss these interactions in relation to general trends across Europe, my emphasis is on Britain where developments began around 1963 and peaked in 1977. As demonstrated by Michael Hall's *Music Theatre in Britain: 1960–1975* (2015), this was a diverse and thriving period. Yet there is considerable scope for further research into this period, especially in terms of the ways in which British perspectives differed from or critiqued those in continental Europe and America. Hall's work is therefore developed and extended in this chapter, but with a focus on two forms: first, combinations of music with mime and dance; and second, collaborations between musicians and actors. I approach these forms from three perspectives: 1) the level of prescription in a work, or, to use John Cage's term, the extent to which embodied actions are 'disciplined' by an idea, a textural instruction, or some form of musical notation that enables the work, however conceptual in nature, to be reproduced; 2) the kind of performers required; and 3) the pragmatic question, for researchers, of how to access a performance, especially when no audio or visual recording exists.

The third perspective raises the topic of performance analysis.[4] The principal problem in this context is that historical performances, for which live ethnographic research is not an option, are only available through layers of mediation (interviews with the artists involved, press reviews, photographs, audio or video recordings, and so on), which record performances from their own, biased perspectives – in the sense that *all* perspectives are inevitably selective and therefore biased in some way. It therefore follows that performance analysis needs to be mindful of the kind of evidence it is using, which may require different methodological approaches. It also requires us to think carefully about 'what' is being performed, which is to say, how scores and other textual instructions function:

---

2 According to Sawyer and DeZutter, distributed creativity refers to 'situations where collaborating groups of individuals collectively generate a shared creative product' (2009: 82); see also Ravet 2016. Even in terms of brain activity, it has been observed that 'creativity is a whole-brain function, drawing on many diverse areas of the brain in a complex systematic fashion' (Sawyer 2006: 95).

3 Similarly, regarding the social nature of 'performance creativity' R. Keith Sawyer observes: 'creativity is fundamentally social and collaborative [. . .]. By explaining performance, we can ultimately better explain all creativity' (Sawyer 2006: 257); see also Sawyer 2003. On the concept of 'situated creativity', in which art is considered to be contingent on social context, see Wolff 1993 and 1983, Becker 1982, and Bourdieu 1993 and 1996.

4 I use the term 'performance analysis' in the sense defined by Nicholas Cook, whereby performance is seen 'as an object of analysis', and performers 'appear in the role of informants, consultants, or co-researchers', although he gives great attention to the analysis of recorded performances (Cook 2013: 49).

are they, for example, prescriptive, or suggestions for performance techniques, or imperfect attempts to record a performance after the event? If the latter, the score mediates a performance that evolved previously, for example in workshops where performers were co-creators.[5]

These considerations inform the discussion that follows by directing attention to the specific nature of physical performance assisted by two related theoretical concepts, namely 'disciplined action' and 'embodied technique'. Following Cage, the term 'disciplined action' (used in the instructions to *0'00"* (1962), to distinguish from an everyday action), has been proposed by Björn Heile to refer to, among other things, the 'choreographically precise placing, planning, and specification of actions' and their 'meticulous' performance by 'trusted interpreters' (Heile 2016: 341). Of course, this description describes what all self-respecting performers do: plan and execute actions with precision. However, it also prompts further questions: What kind of disciplined action? How was it determined? What instruction was provided, and how did that shape the performer's interpretation? What degree of freedom was permitted? For example, contrary to what one might assume, given his association with chance and indeterminacy, Cage's music theatre pieces are highly structured; most are performed in relation to a stopwatch or clock. Even Cage's use of indeterminacy in performance is 'primarily a concept tied to notation' (Fetterman 2010: 227), in the sense that the score is 'a prompt for action rather than a description of sound', often requiring the performer to interpret the score and prepare their performance in some detail (Thomas 2013: 96; see also Thomas 2009). For my purposes, 'disciplined action' is a *process* of performance interpretation that may or may not be influenced by a score but that is developed in workshops and rehearsals, from which trusted interpreters – and, as will be seen, even scores – emerge (for evidence of this with regard to Kagel, see Vaes 2014).

Some of the disciplined actions discussed in this chapter are non-representational or do not relate to conventional notions of plot or character. This reflects the influence of Happenings and other experimental theatre, such as Richard Schechner's The Performance Group, in which performers do not 'act' in the strict sense but rather 'do things' as themselves or draw attention to actions that have no narrative framework. Michael Kirby describes this as 'not-acting', which he labels 'non-matrixed performance' (Kirby 1972). When contextual features such as costume are involved, meaning is more likely to be inferred and Kirby refers to this as 'non-matrixed representation'. Whilst several examples in this chapter fit with one or other of these categories, Kirby's terminology is actually misleading because a lack of plot does not remove the matrices of performance. Rather, it reduces and

---

5 Underpinning this are ontological and phenomenological questions. What is performance, and how is it brought into conscious experience? Is it the experience of the performer, or the perceiver, or some combination of these? Even if present at a live performance, numerous factors determine (or compromise) the way a perceiver frames their interpretation, including where they sit, what they choose to focus their attention on, and what preconceptions and other knowledge they bring to the experience.

230 *David Beard*

focuses them, highlighting other kinds of matrices, such as time, space, coordination and structure, all guided by some kind of instruction, context or concept. In this sense, new music theatre spotlights and reconfigures the fundamentals of performance – the operations and disciplined actions with which I am concerned.

Another way of thinking about disciplined action is through the more cognitive concept of 'embodied technique'. In his book *What A Body Can Do*, Benjamin Spatz refers to 'embodied practice' and 'embodied technique'. For Spatz, embodied practice is the field of physical action, in the broadest sense. Embodied techniques are the 'transmittable (and hence researchable)' ways of using the body (Joseph Roach, 'Foreword' to Spatz 2015: ix). In whichever domain (whether dance, acting, martial arts, yoga or everyday life), technique is the 'knowledge that structures practice'. In other words, embodied practice is 'fundamentally epistemic – structured by knowledge' (Spatz 2015: 1–2). Spatz accordingly describes his methodological approach as an 'epistemology of practice' (ibid.: 1), and he sees his project as part of what has been dubbed the 'practice turn' in theory and philosophy (see Schatzki *et al.* 2001). Spatz's motivation is his belief (following Spinoza) that we 'do not yet know what a body can do', and that what matters is the 'continuous creation and transmission of knowledge' through what he calls research 'in', rather than 'on', performance, the purpose being to generate new technique (Spatz 2015: 4).[6]

There are notable differences between Spatz's intentions and my own, not least his concern to find new ways of thinking about the body in order to foster and support '"research culture" in diverse areas of physical culture, performing arts, and everyday life' (ibid.). However, his ideas prompt two perspectives on new music theatre: 1) that it can be interpreted as a search for new knowledge and technique with which to structure the body and what it can do; and 2) it highlights the problem, for the researcher, of how and where to locate those techniques, and how they are transmitted.

Mime

> [M]ime lives in the depths of silence, where gesture does not replace words.
>
> (Lecoq 2006: 68)

I turn now to consider ways in which mime has contributed to the reconceptualisation of performance in instrumental and new music theatre, and the kinds of disciplined action and embodied technique that occur in this context. The ideas discussed below centre on the question of whether, and if so how, mime and music relate to one another. The focus is primarily on the performer's perspective but composer intention and audience perception are also taken into account.

---

6 Spatz proposes the term 'research in acting' in place of 'method': 'While research *on* acting produces scholarly and intellectual knowledge about acting, research *in* acting produces new acting technique. The latter must be acknowledged if we hope to understand how acting changes, or to compare acting practices, across time and space' (2015: 118).

Reconceptualising the performer 231

Table 10.1 Six kinds of relationship between mime(-dance) and music

- Mimed musical performance.
- Sound and mime closely integrated in the score.
- Actions used to intervene and prompt instrumentalists to perform differently.
- Mime gestures not notated but generated in response to the music.
- Mime actions that are loosely related to the music, including situations in which music and mime respond to a narrative or text but do so independently.
- Mime actions that are totally independent of the music, including situations in which actions and sounds simply coexist, interaction arising from coincidence, overlap or juxtaposition.

I have identified six broad approaches to this question, although these distinctions could be broken down further, and they might operate simultaneously or in succession (see Table 10.1).

At one end of the spectrum outlined in Table 10.1 is mimed musical performance. Examples of this approach exist in instrumental theatre works, including moments when a mute actor mimics the performing gestures of the musicians in Mauricio Kagel's *Sur scène* (1959–60), a section of Kagel's *Sonant 1960/. . .*, in which the performers appear to play their instruments but emit no sound, and Dieter Schnebel's *Visible Music 1* (1960–2) and *2* (1962), in which musicians are required to mime musical performance and conducting. In *Sonant*, the mime, or 'virtual interpretation', requires the players to read musical notation (this occurs in 'Pièce jouée, pièce touchée'). Heile observes that in making musicians pretend to perform actual music, they do not need to step outside their roles as musicians. This, he feels, is effective because musicians often make poor, self-conscious actors, and therefore the rupture between music performance and acting is avoided (Heile 2006: 36). And yet the reconceptualisation of performers in new music theatre often requires them to re-examine, modify or think *beyond* their roles as musicians. This highlights an important focus of this chapter: namely, the ways in which musicians, actors and mimes are encouraged to expand the sense of their performing selves, precisely by stepping outside their 'normal' roles and established training.

An interesting example of this is provided by the 'Trommel-Mann' in Kagel's *Staatstheater* (1967–70), as featured on the cover of this book. Here an instrumentalist becomes a mime, but in a way that is different in kind from, for example, the dancing clarinettist in Stockhausen's *Harlekin* (1975). As directed in the score, the drum-man wanders uncertainly about the stage 'like a blind man', his arms hanging by his sides, his body turning slowly to the left. He continues this motion 'in spite of' the actions of the drummers, who perform a kind of dance around him as they strike their moving targets, a series of drums strapped to his head, legs, arms, hands and body (Kagel 1973). The 'Trommel-Mann' is both performer and instrument, a semi-conscious agent with whom the surrounding percussionists enter into a visual-sonic dialogue.

232 *David Beard*

Mimed gesture is also central to Harrison Birtwistle's *For O, For O, the Hobby-Horse is Forgot* (1976), for six percussionists (see Figure 10.1). Here conventional playing techniques are extended into an elaborate series of mimed gestures using the players' sticks, suggesting a game or ceremony of some kind (Birtwistle 1976).[7] Surplus gestural information (sticks crossed, held aloft, silent mimed notes, and so on) draw attention to the strictly choreographed rhythms of the players' bodies, their musical actions and the sounds we expect to hear from them (in the work's powerful opening, we see stick movements but hear no sounds).[8] This work also

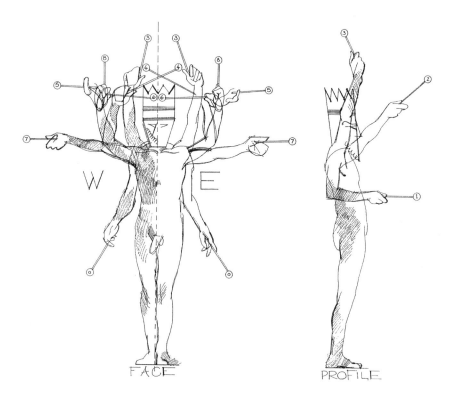

Figure 10.1 Stick Positions from the 'Performance Notes' for Harrison Birtwistle's *For O, For O, The Hobby-Horse is Forgot* (1976). © Copyright 1976 by Universal Edition (London) Ltd., London. Used with the permission of Universal Edition (Vienna).

7 The idea for this piece may have emerged in Birtwistle's mind during composition of *The Mask of Orpheus*: one of the earliest conceptual sketches for the opera, from 1973, includes the abandoned idea that it should employ 'some sort of mimed percussion on stage', which would involve 'v. beautiful stylized gestures . . . (the[y] must not be percussion players but actors)'. Paul Sacher Stiftung, Birtwistle Collection, microfilm 0530-0592.
8 For an example performance, see www.youtube.com/watch?v=SqavaxEhEME (accessed 10 May 2018).

reconceptualises the players by placing them in a theatrical framework – most obviously, by arranging them in a circle, facing inwards. The players to stage left and stage right, named King and Queen in the score, signal when certain actions should begin and end. The performers are required to be 'more than' musicians, and to execute their stick actions with precision and commitment. Erika Fox's *Round for Fourteen Strings* (1974) also places musical ideas in a theatrical context and reconceptualises the performers by requiring them to move (see Figure 10.2). Here the conventional hierarchy between the violins as melody-bearing instruments, and the other instruments as accompanists, is reversed musically but also visually. The violins are arranged in a circle, facing inwards towards the violas and cellos, seated in the centre. At certain moments the first viola moves to and from a solo position outside the circle, and at the end of each of the piece's seven sections, the violinists move in a clockwise direction to their next position, while continuing to play.[9]

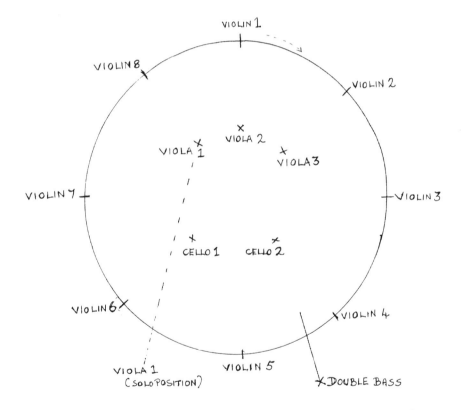

Figure 10.2 Performer positions in Erika Fox's *Round for Fourteen Strings* (1974). © Copyright Erika Fox. Used with the composer's permission.

9 From the 'Notes on Performance' in the unpublished score of Erika Fox's *Round for Fourteen Strings*, completed on 6 June 1974. I am grateful to Brenda Townsend for allowing me to consult her late husband Michael Hall's copy of this work.

234   *David Beard*

At the other end of the spectrum laid out in Table 10.1 are works in which mime was not intended to relate to music in any shape or form. A radical example of the asynchronous coexistence of action and sound is provided by Cornelius Cardew's *Schooltime Compositions* (1968) and 'Paragraph 5' of *The Great Learning* (1968–70). The latter comprises a seven-part 'dumb show' in which physical movements are precisely described but performed alongside separate schemes for speech, chant, instrumental sound and optional solo songs, each devised and executed independently of one another, so that any correspondences are purely fortuitous. Less extreme, although also asynchronous by design, is Alexander Goehr's *Triptych*, from 1968–72. According to John Cox, who directed *Naboth's Vineyard* (the first of this series of works, composed and premiered in 1968): 'The composer insisted at the outset that the mime should not be choreographed, or even be musical in feeling. Consequently the mime was created in silence, our only guide the stop-watch. In performance the music accompanies the mime' (Goehr 1973: n.p.). In other words, the mime action was devised independently. In an interview before the piece was completed, Goehr also spoke about using 'clowning gestures' in the mime to create dramatic incongruity with the text, noting that he was 'not so attracted to the Berio-Kagel type of musical theatre' but instead wanted to create a new form of semi-cabaret theatre, but with 'real music' (Goehr and Sadie 1968: 625–6).

Cox's note on 'Staging' suggests that instructions in the score concerning the use of masks, when the mimes should be still, and brief descriptions of narrative events (for example: 'Naboth appeals to the Elders, who become the Sons of Belial. He realizes it is a frame-up; he is trapped'; Goehr 1976: 40), were added after the first performance. Regarding his *Sonata About Jerusalem*, Goehr went further, stating: 'It is not the function of the mimes to reduplicate the telling of a story already told in the text' (Goehr 1973). In his review of the premiere of *Sonata*, Peter J. Pirie noted: 'it is a tribute to the effectiveness of the stage spectacle that it is often hard to concentrate on the music, which becomes an almost unconscious part of the total effect' (Pirie 1971: 687). This observation implies that even though the sound and visual languages were conceived separately, the result, in terms of audience perception, was a form of synthesis in which the music was secondary to, but contingent upon, the mime action. Reaching a definitive conclusion on how this relationship actually worked in the original productions is impossible because evidence of the stylised movement and masks is limited to a handful of photographs of *Naboth's Vineyard*, and there are no video recordings.[10] However, some insight into Goehr's Brechtian separation – or independent combination – of mime and music is provided by Michael Nyman, who describes a scene in *Naboth's Vineyard* in which we hear Jezebel reading as she writes a letter, 'the Elders simultaneously reading what she has written, in a

---

10   Fifteen photographs taken by the composer's mother, Laelia Goehr, are held in the Musikarchiv of the Akademie der Künste, Berlin; see https://archiv.adk.de/objekt/2432011 (accessed 24 August 2017). One of these images is reproduced in Hall 2015: 118.

Reconceptualising the performer 235

less emotional idiom, while the mimes carry out the action suggested by Jezebel' (Nyman 1968). This suggests a loose, conceptual relation between music, plot and embodied action, but no direct relationship or planned synchronicity.

By contrast, it is hard to imagine a more integrated approach than the one adopted in Stockhausen's *Inori* (1973–4) for one or two 'dancer-mimes' and orchestra, created by Elizabeth Clarke and Alain Louafi. The hour-long piece requires performers trained in dance and mime (see Stockhausen 1983), although they are mostly confined to sitting, kneeling and standing on a platform high above the orchestra. Exhaustive, detailed instructions are provided in a volume that accompanies the score, along with an explanatory seminar on the work's techniques, titled 'Lecture on HU', which can be performed before *Inori* (see Stockhausen 1979). This guidance enables the performers to translate a notated musical melody into physical movements based on prayer gestures from around the world (the melody may also be played by an instrument). In other words, this is a clear example of physical action based on embodied technique, as theorised by Spatz: the performers' actions are structured by knowledge of global prayer gestures, collated by the American anthropologist Nancy Wyle (see Figure 10.3; the 'Lecture on HU' also includes 224 photographs to illustrate the use of these gestures). Each prayer gesture is assigned a specific pitch (associated with a harmonic spectrum), dynamic level, tempo and instrumentation, the intention

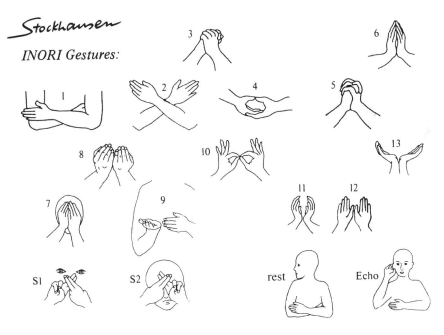

Figure 10.3 Prayer Gestures for Stockhausen's *Inori* (1973–4), compiled by Nancy Wyle and reproduced in the published score. © Copyright 1979 Stockhausen-Verlag. Used by permission of the Stockhausen-Stiftung für Musik.

being to fully integrate physical and musical gesture – although some perceive the sounds as direct responses to the mime (Maconie 1974: 32). Clearly, the piece requires dedicated performers with a serious commitment to learning a new language, in which, for example, a sustained *pianissimo* middle G translates to a gesture closest to the human heart, and a crescendo mark equates to motion away from the heart. The idea that performers should translate a notated melody into an 'action-melody', however, is a conceit that integrates sound and movement at a purely abstract level. In one sense, this is an attractive method, which avoids conventional responses, such as moving more quickly when the music speeds up. On the other hand, there is less room for performer interpretation, the mime gestures being strictly determined by Stockhausen's esoteric scheme.

There is no direct equivalent to this piece in British new music theatre that I am aware of, although Richard Orton's *Mug Grunt* (1972) and Michael Finnissy's *Bouffe* (1975) both require disciplined action, of the kind prescribed in the score. Arguably, however, there is a closer relationship between sound and physical action in these works than in *Inori* because they are located in a single source – the mime-musician – and there is more room for performer interpretation. Orton's work calls for three actors, although its complex gestural counterpoint requires, in Orton's words, 'the command of the musician' (Orton n.d.). Indeed, the premiere

Figure 10.4 Roger Marsh, Archer (Tom) Endrich, and Bernard Rands performing Richard Orton's *Mug Grunt* (1972), at the Shaw Theatre, London in 1974, with the York University music theatre group 'Clap'. © Copyright Peter Harrap/Report-IFL Archive/reportdigital.co.uk; used with their permission.

Reconceptualising the performer 237

was performed by three musicians, including the composer Bernard Rands (see Figure 10.4).[11] Dressed in working men's clothes and seated on chairs, as if taking a tea break, all three were members of the 'Clap' new music theatre group at York University. The piece is a strictly choreographed mime with twenty-four positions for the head and right arm, holding a mug. There are also grunting sounds (high, middle and low), and, towards the end, muffled speech. Orton devised a clear notational method for prescribing the action, in which the emphasis is on the placement of events in time, and the rhythm formed from grunts, with some sections to be performed as fast as possible (for an example, see Hall 2015: 261–2). As an 'action plan' (I deploy the term in the sense intended by Brüstle 2009) the score is certainly disciplined, but there is still room for interpretation. Tempo is left to the performers to decide, and their gestures could be comic or sinister, or both.

By contrast, Finnissy's *Bouffe* falls back on the written word to prescribe its disciplined actions, which amount to a kind of 'absolute mime' (Lecoq 2006: 72). Inspired by Artaud and by Beckett's *Act Without Words 1* and *2*, it is scored for a single performer, whose only prop is a sheet that conceals the body. Part of Finnissy's original rationale had been to bring the often-separated conventions of words, pictures and music notation into juxtaposition, which Kagel, he notes, 'had already accomplished in *Staatstheater* and elsewhere'.[12] However, Kagel's interest in more representational and expressive devices (Heile 2016: 347) is condensed and intensified by Finnissy, creating a strong psychological effect. The score's instructions portray an individual in considerable distress, with rapidly changing movements and emotions suggesting fear, confusion, pain, shock, and occasionally pleasure. The mime is also required to emit various sounds, approximately notated in the score, including growls, sniffles, giggling, a nasal squawk, sucking, short intakes of breath, howling, 'infantile grizzling', and even, at one point, an intricately notated vocal outburst (see Example 10.1) (Finnissy 1975). This may suggest Finnissy had conceived the piece for a trained singer, but he has indicated that the musical notation is not something that can be sung accurately. Therefore, he suggests, an actor with some musical ability would be suitable to perform the role.[13]

I have proposed *Inori, Mug Grunt* and *Bouffe* as examples in which mime and sound are closely integrated, but the performance styles are very different. In *Inori*, the performers' absorption in a sophisticated mime language arguably deepens the music's spiritual meaning. In *Mug Grunt*, the prosaic language of workers drinking is transformed into an intricate, hieratic display. And in *Bouffe*, invented musical mime highlights the breakdown of language in society, with an effect that is raw and direct.

---

11 The two other performers were Roger Marsh and Archer (Tom) Endrich, both of whom composed music theatre works in the 1970s.
12 From an email to the author, 11 April 2018.
13 From a personal conversation with the author, University of Huddersfield, 18 November 2016.

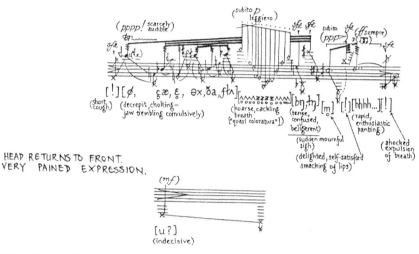

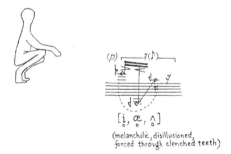

Example 10.1 Page four of Michael Finnissy's *Bouffe (for a person alone on stage)* including a precisely notated vocal outburst for the actor-mime (1975). © Copyright Michael Finnissy. Used with the composer's permission.

Workshops with artists, mimes and musicians

An important factor in the development of mime in new music theatre was the role of workshops, which acted as incubators for the discovery of new embodied techniques. These workshops arose across Europe in the context of a 'significant increase', from the 1970s, 'in the amount of devised performance which emphasized movement, gesture and mime as the main expressive tools of theatre,' in reaction against the dominance of the playwright and the spoken word (Murray 2003: 3). This didactic tendency was especially prominent in Britain due, among other factors, to an increased awareness of the need for actors to broaden their experience beyond Stanislavskian and 'method' approaches, influenced by the experimental work of Peter Brook, the rise of theatre studies in universities, and state funding policies that increasingly sought evidence of educational training and widening participation, all of which fuelled an explosion of workshops in the 1980s and 1990s (see Murray and Keefe 2016), run by organisations such as the Mime Action Group (founded in London in 1983), International Workshop Festival (London 1988),[14] National Theatre Studio (London Southbank 1985), and Centre for Performance Research (Cardiff 1988, previously the Cardiff Laboratory Theatre 1974).

Among the earliest music theatre workshops in Britain were those held at the Dartington Summer School in 1970 and 1971, the first led by Birtwistle and Peter

Figure 10.5 Hans Keller, Peter Maxwell Davies, Harrison Birtwistle and Milein Cosman at the Dartington Summer School of Music, 1970. Photograph by Charles Davis. © Copyright Dartington Summer School of Music Archive; used with their permission.

---

14 For archival documentation on this group's activities up to 2001, see http://blogs.bl.uk/english-and-drama/2014/09/the-international-workshop-festival-collection-1988–2001.html (accessed 24 August 2017).

240   *David Beard*

Maxwell Davies, the second by Birtwistle alone.[15] Figure 10.5 shows the two composers at the School in 1970 with the broadcaster and musicologist Hans Keller and his wife, the artist Milein Cosman.[16] During these workshops, young composers were asked to compose pieces after performing exercises with the mime artist Mark Furneaux, who I will return to later.[17] Birtwistle advised that the students should think of an idea or gesture 'that could be realized both musically and visually', and that the relationship between sound and movement was stronger when based on 'contrast rather than similarity' (Hall 2015: 218, 76).[18] He then 'drew two parallel lines on the blackboard, told them this was the idea, and instructed them to get on with it' (Hall 2015: 218).

Annual workshops were also held with art students at Falmouth College, in Cornwall. A documentary film, broadcast by the BBC in 1971, shows Birtwistle, composer Bruce Cole and clarinettist Alan Hacker at this 'Sound and Dance Course', working with art students in ways that are reminiscent of Cornelius Cardew's Scratch Orchestra, for trained and untrained musicians.[19] During the documentary, Birtwistle explains that the idea is for the art students to work in a medium (sound) with which they are unfamiliar, taking them out of their comfort zone. The intention is to invent music, 'to start as if music never existed', something that would not be possible to achieve in the Royal Academy of Music, Birtwistle argued in the documentary, where the students 'would all know musical notation and they would be tied up with it, and the whole history of music [. . .] would be behind them'. The exercises culminate in a composition devised by the students, who play various percussion and wind instruments in conjunction with a mime or dancer. Birtwistle conducts, using a basic form of graphic notation in which events are plotted in time.

15 According to a report of the 1970 Dartington Festival, 'Daily morning classes, mainly restricted to professional musicians, are also held. This year [. . .] the composition class given by Harrison Birtwistle and Peter Maxwell Davies was a very interesting one in which students were guided on how to combine mime and music. This was a three-week course, at the end of which some of the new works were performed at the Friday-afternoon students concert' (Tecker 1970: 50).

16 I am very grateful to Jeremy Wilson, archivist for the Dartington Summer Arts Foundation, for providing me with this image, as well as programme details from 1970 and 1971.

17 Instruction was also provided by Photes Constantinedes, although more briefly (Hall 2015: 76).

18 Davies's *Vesalii Icones* was used as a model during the workshop and performed at the School on 10 August, with the Pierrot Players and dancer William Louther. Louther's contribution to this seminal piece has been elided in a similar manner to that of Roy Hart's in *Eight Songs for a Mad King*: these artists were co-creators to a degree that is seldom acknowledged (although see Francesca Placanica's chapter in the present volume for a discussion of Hart's role in *Eight Songs*). In addition to photographs of Louther's original performance, many of which have been posted on the Internet, drawings of Louther's dance were made by Eilean Pearcey during rehearsals and performances; these are stored in a dedicated collection in Archives and Special Collections, Surrey University.

19 'A Couple of Things About Harry' was broadcast on 4 April 1971 as part of the BBC Two series *Art on Two*. A handwritten poster for the course, shown in the programme, refers to the involvement of 'a female dancer', although I have been unable to establish who this was. According to Bruce Cole, four members of the Pierrot Players were in attendance, including Hacker (Hall 2015: 240), but this is not verified by the documentary.

Reconceptualising the performer 241

Another BBC documentary programme, broadcast in 1977, reveals Peter Maxwell Davies and Michael Finnissy directing a music theatre workshop at a festival organised by Hans Werner Henze, the Cantiere Internazionale d'Arte Montepulciano, which Henze had founded the previous year under the auspices of the Italian Communist Party.[20] Henze described the 'Cantiere' as 'a workshop where young artists could invent and experiment with new forms of communication' (Henze 1982: 262–3). Consistent with the festival's emphasis upon the involvement of non-professionals, the workshop included a happening with schoolchildren and local residents, conceived by theatre director Memè Perlini, which combined Davies's *Antechrist* (1967), *Missa Super L'Homme Armé* (1971), *Renaissance Scottish Dances* (1973), and *Psalm 124* (1974) with Cage-like experimentalism and Cardew-like social commitment. Titled *Tradimenti*, the happening 'took place in the Edmondo d'Amicis school, on all three floors, in corridors, classrooms, even in the lavatories, and was a kind of exhibition of the horrors of provincial life, with its bigotry, frustrations, its hopelessness, its weird and absurd petit-bourgeois habits' (Henze 1982: 265). Here, new music theatre performance is reconceived as something social and inclusive, something to be shared with non-professionals. By contrast, at the workshop in Falmouth, the exercises were motivated more by Birtwistle's personal interest in analysing the relationship between sound and movement. Nevertheless, such cross-disciplinary experiment, and the use of mime in particular, was suited to both sets of interests – the desire for social inclusion, and the concern for grappling with theatrical essentials.

Mark Furneaux

I referred earlier to the mime artist Mark Furneaux and his involvement in workshops held in Dartington. Furneaux was a founder member of the Raree Show, a travelling group of clowns performing 'old English street entertainment', in which he went by the name Cheskoo the Clown (Lust 2003: 119). He also gave solo performances, for example at the Little Theatre Club in London. Especially relevant, however, was his background. Furneaux had trained in Prague with Ladislav Fialka and in Paris with Jacques Lecoq, at the Jacques Lecoq International School of Theatre, which opened in 1956. Prior to this, Lecoq had established the Piccolo drama school in the Piccolo Teatro, Milan, where, with actors who he had instructed in mime, he choreographed Berio's *Mimusique No. 2* (1952–5) and *Allez-hop* (1952–9), the latter based on a libretto by Italo Calvino (Lecoq 2006: 109). Lecoq's training involved an emphasis on masks, beginning with neutral masks and gradually reducing their size down to the clown's red nose. Three of the principal skills that he encouraged in his students were *le jeu* (playfulness), *complicité* (togetherness) and *disponsibilité* (openness). His classes on working with music included music by Bartók, Bach, Satie, Stravinsky, Berio and

---

20 'Festa in Montepulciano' was broadcast on 13 March 1977 as part of the BBC Two series *The Lively Arts*.

242   David Beard

Miles Davis. The so-called 'Bartók Lesson' begins by imagining the placement of sounds around the mime, in space, then attempting to touch the sounds, and investigating whether they are pushing or pulling the mime. Gradually, music and mime enter into a 'state of mutual belonging', after which the mime chooses a point of view, 'to be for, against or with [. . .] to create a relationship of play, for the aim is always to play with the music' (Lecoq 2016: 53).

Some indication of this training, in particular the notion of pushing and pulling sounds, and of play with the music, can be seen in a video recording of a 1972 production of Birtwistle's *Down by the Greenwood Side* (1969).[21] The mimographer for the production was Mark Furneaux; the video therefore provides an insight into Lecoq's methods, although the main theatrical model for the piece is the Mummer's Play, a folk tradition dating back to the Middle Ages. In one scene, Wayne Pritchett performs the role of Jack Finney (the Green Man) reviving St George after he has been slain in battle. Considerable freedom is granted to the mime at this point, as the instruction in the score is simply: 'Enter Finney, as Green Man. He performs an elaborate, ritualistic cure' (Birtwistle 1971: 52). Furneaux's knowledge of Birtwistle's work, which stretched back to his creation of the role of St George in the original production in 1969, rendered him a trusted interpreter, and the actions are disciplined and precisely executed, with comic touches (for example, as he attempts to raise St George, the Green Man momentarily loses his balance before steadying himself). The music assists in this process through its sparse, gestural language, including wave-like motions in the flute and bass clarinet, a snapping pulse on the slap stick (mirrored by sharp body movements), and a rising scale at the end, accompanied by the instruction 'St. George very slowly begins to rise' (Birtwistle 1971: 53). In other words, Birtwistle's music provides a suggestive framework in which a 'state of mutual belonging' between music and mime can be realised. Moreover, Furneaux's response reflects Lecoq's encouragement to his students to be a creator rather than interpreter, a '(co-)author-maker of material, whether it is physical, spoken, musical or imagistic' (Murray 2003: 223).

Mark Furneaux also performed Goehr's music theatre works (he is listed in the cast for a performance of the *Triptych* at the 1971 Edinburgh International Festival, with Goehr's company the Music Theatre Ensemble), and he collaborated with Peter Maxwell Davies, notably on *Blind Man's Buff*, premiered in 1972 at the Roundhouse with the BBC Symphony Orchestra, conducted by Pierre Boulez. There is no video recording of this production, however, and the performance instructions in the score are restricted to a handful of general directions, such as when to perform dances or to remove masks. Davies's musical sketches for *Blind Man's Buff* suggest that he gave little thought to the actions

---

21 This was produced by London Weekend Television and broadcast across ITV regional channels as part of Humphrey Burton's *Aquarius* series on Sunday 16 December 1972, billed as 'A Programme with a Difference'. Birtwistle is listed in the credits as being responsible for stage production. Prior to this, an extract from a piano rehearsal for the original production was televised on BBC2's *Music Now* programme in May 1969, as reported by Raynor 1969: 5.

Reconceptualising the performer   243

of the mime, instead preferring to translate aspects of the plot into quite complex pitch-set procedures (a ten-note set is subjected to numerous transformations, although the first three notes recur whenever the King asks the mime 'Who are you?', prompting the mime to peel off a succession of masks asking 'Am I this?, or this, or this or that?').[22] However, in a later collaboration with Furneaux, titled *Le Jongleur de Notre Dame* (1978), for mime, baritone, chamber ensemble and children's band, Davies elevates the mime to the role of the central character, a street jester accepted into a monastery.[23] Photographs of the production stored at the British Library show Furneaux entering through the auditorium, dressed as a medieval jester, balancing a large ball above his head; other images show him juggling on stage and interacting with onstage musicians. The set design reflects the medieval monastic setting. Written instructions in the score direct three instrumentalist monks (flute, clarinet and percussion players), the Statue of the Virgin (violin), and a mime (the Jester monk), to interact in specific ways. In section No. 4, Scene 2, for instance, the clarinettist (onstage and in costume) is asked to improvise around five melodic figures and to use these to create a dialogue with the mime, to be worked out between the performers (Davies 1978: 20). The score directs:

> The clarinettist (Bro. David) uses the following five figures quite indepen- dently of the 'cello and piano in an order, form and tempi worked out in collaboration with the Mime, Bro. Mark, to fit in with, comment upon & elaborate the pantomime, so that a dialogue between Bro. David & Bro. Mark emerges, with much slapstick comedy in their interactions. The clari- nettist is free to improvise upon the given figures to fit the needs of different situations – one indicator of the kind of improvisation is written out below each given clarinet figure.
>
> (Davies 1978: 20)

Archival evidence indicates that Furneaux may have had a vital role in helping to shape the nature and detail of the music–mime drama. A letter from Furneaux to Davies outlines routines he could use in his depiction of the Jester and a list of props, but also his need to organise the musicians' actions.[24] The letter was written after Furneaux received a version of the libretto, but it seems likely that Furneaux's experience directly informed both the plot outline cited at the start of the score,[25] and verbal directions inserted throughout the score, written in Davies's hand.

Clearly, Davies intended there to be close interactions between mime and musicians in this piece, including moments when the mime prompts musicians

---

22 British Library Add MS 71267: 1972.

23 For plot details, see www.maxopus.com/work_detail.aspx?key=121 (accessed 28 May 2017).

24 British Library Add MS 71272: 1977. The letter is dated 12 December 1977; Davies's first draft of the score (including stage directions) is dated 28 December 1977.

25 These two sides of text are unattributed but are likely to have been written by Davies.

244 *David Beard*

to perform in certain ways. However, the instructions in the score leave a fair amount of scope for performers to work out the details themselves, effectively encouraging an unpredictable and improvisational rehearsal process of a kind that Sawyer and DeZutter refer to as 'collaborative emergence', in which the moment-to-moment responses of performers are interactive, each contingent on the other (2009: 82).[26] In other words, the mime artist has a crucial co-creative role in defining the relationship between sound and mime in this work, with 'initiatives and ideas' coming from all of the players (Clarke *et al.* 2013: 647).[27] Of course, this is a reminder that in art music more generally a performance is created by 'the interaction of players, conductor, and composer, organized but not completely determined by the score' (Frith 2012: 64; see also Born 2005), and that degrees of 'creativity in performance' are expected in Western art music (Clarke 2012). And yet Furneaux's role in this and other works has been elided,[28] in a similar way to the elision of session players in famous rock and pop recordings (see Frith 2012: 64–6).

The idea of more complex interactions between mimes and musicians was pursued by a number of others directly influenced by Furneaux's workshops in Dartington, including Bruce Cole and Nicola LeFanu, in whose work mimes become fully integrated into the drama. LeFanu's *Anti-world*, from 1972, is a tour-de-force in this respect. The score notates complex, carefully choreographed relationships between a mime, who transforms gradually into a dancer, and a soprano, baritone and three instrumentalists.[29] All performers move around, listen and react to one another, in such a way that the music would not make sense without the mime. The mime's attempts to seek a rapport with the musicians are initially rejected, and she responds uncomfortably to their music. Eventually, however, her fortunes change: the instrumentalists imitate her rhythms and provide the kind of music she wants, although the soprano remains aloof. The mime then rips up the soprano's music and threatens her with a heavy object, which turns out to be a feather. It is a fascinating piece, whose mixture of playful and serious actions is concerned with breaking down the invisible barriers between performers as a metaphor for restrictions to personal freedoms and divisions in society more generally.

---

26 Sawyer and DeZutter refer to 'the moment to moment contingency of collaborative emergence', in which a 'wide range of actions is possible at each moment; the actors do not know what is going to follow an action, and they do not know how their actions will be interpreted and elaborated' (2009: 83).

27 On the role of instrumental performers as co-creators in workshops, helping to establish new performance techniques and influencing the evolution of a piece, see Clarke *et al.* 2013, especially pp. 640–1.

28 For example, there is no reference to Furneaux in Friedrichs 1997.

29 The score is unpublished; the present author consulted a photocopy given to Michael Hall by the composer herself. The piece was devised for the Focus Opera Group, based at Morley College, London, and it was first performed at the Cockpit Theatre, Marylebone, London, in 1972. For a score example, see Hall 2015: 179.

Experiments at London's National Theatre and the Roundhouse

Theatre had been reaching out to music, finding ways to incorporate musical devices and techniques, from as early as the 1920s, notably in the work of Appia, Artaud and Meyerhold (see Roesner 2014). The musicalisation of British theatre in the 1960s and '70s is not well documented, however, despite the fact that this was a crucial time in its development. The year 1963 saw the foundation of a National Theatre in London. Its first newly commissioned play was Peter Shaffer's *The Royal Hunt of the Sun* (1964), with music by Marc Wilkinson. Shaffer's production very clearly reflects the climate of experimentation in the 1960s, which included Peter Brook's work with Jean-Louis Barrault and actors from the Royal Shakespeare Company, and Brook's Noh-influenced production of *The Tempest* at the Roundhouse in London in 1968. Evidence held at the National Theatre Archive reveals that Wilkinson pioneered a more active role for music and musicians in the theatre. He is not well known today, but Wilkinson studied with Varèse and Messiaen, then at Columbia and Princeton, and at Darmstadt in 1956 and 1957.[30] As a fascinating series of contact sheets reveal, Wilkinson, who became Director of Music at the National, took a hands-on approach, energetically choreographing actors in the chorus, inventing instruments, and devising ways in which musicians would take a more active role, using a host of invented or specially adapted percussion instruments (see Figure 10.6).[31] A full score of *The Royal Hunt* exists in the National Theatre archive, and a film adaptation made in 1969 uses some of the music from the original production. The play concerns the sixteenth-century Spanish massacre of the Incas, and its combination of mime, dance, ritualistic percussion and stylised vocal parts for trained singers and actors generates a distinctly hieratic, at times Orientalist, yet thoroughly immersive experience. The film version of the climactic scene is especially revealing.[32] The Inca King, Atahualpa, has been killed, at his own agreement, since he believes he will be resurrected. The climactic scene is set in a ceremonial chamber; at one end sits the King, wearing a large golden mask, at the other stands Pizarro, the Spanish expedition leader. Robed Inca courtiers flank the room on either side. Pizarro approaches the King (his slow steps echoing in the hushed space), and when he touches the King's arm the mask falls off, clattering to the stone floor, followed by the King's dead, semi-naked body. This triggers a violent outburst from the courtiers, whose grimaces call to mind Jerzy Grotowski's notion of masks 'created solely by the facial muscles' (Grotowski 2015 [1968]: 64–5), joined by percussive sounds and a high, soprano solo. In other words, the scene evokes (almost to the letter) Peter Brook's description of Artaud's imaginary productions as reflecting 'a certain preference

---

30 Wilkinson had a solo clarinet piece performed at Darmstadt in 1957, which was originally to have been performed by Birtwistle (Delaere 2015: 278).

31 I am grateful to Jennie Borzykh and Pawel Jaskulski at the National Theatre Archive in London for providing digital scans of these images.

32 See www.youtube.com/watch?v=6YKSC81Qtlc from 1:30:15 to 1:31:53 (accessed 30 May 2017).

for darkness and mystery, for chanting, for unearthly cries, for single words rather than sentences, for vast shapes, masks, for kings and emperors and popes, for saints and sinners and flagellants, for black tights and writhing naked skin' (Brook 2008 [1968]: 68).

The musicalisation of British theatre is further illustrated by an intriguing, previously undocumented production titled 'The Wheel', staged at the Roundhouse during the Camden Festival in May 1972. This was advertised as 'a freewheeling tower of words, notes, sounds, shapes, movements, lights, colours', and described as 'an attempt to bring actors more into the musical area'.[33] The action

Figure 10.6 Marc Wilkinson at the National Theatre, London, preparing the use of invented percussion instruments and rehearsing with actors and musicians for Peter Shaffer's production of *The Royal Hunt of the Sun*. Photographs taken at the Old Vic Theatre, London, *c*. 1963, by Angus McBean, stored at the National Theatre Archive, London. © Copyright Houghton Library, Harvard University; used with their permission.

33 From a flyer for the production contained in a file marked 'The Wheel, 1972', THM/271/2/1/30 from the Arts Council of Great Britain Records, 1928–1997, Theatre and Performance Archive, Victoria and Albert Museum Archive, London.

Figure 10.6 (continued)

(continued)

Figure 10.6 (continued)

(lasting 70 minutes) placed the instrumentalists (flute, clarinet, trumpet, percussion, violin and cello) in the centre of the hall next to the audience, who stood but were encouraged to move around the venue. Four actors performed on a platform to the side. Seven sections, named after colours, were determined by the spin of a wheel, which introduced an aleatoric dimension intended to 'develop [the] actors' ability to improvise and relate to one another'.[34] This British Arts Council funded project brought together influential figures, including the

34 Ibid.

Reconceptualising the performer   249

director Geoffrey Reeves, who had worked with Peter Brook and shortly after became director of the Cologne State Theatre, and composer David Bedford, a former pupil of Nono who by this time had received several high profile BBC commissions. The project was conceived by the Yugoslav-born actor, opera singer and poet Bettina Jonic, who was married to Samuel Beckett's publisher, John Calder, and had acted and collaborated with Beckett. Her passion for experimental theatre traditions is writ large in the programme note, which comprises quotations from Gropius, Grotowski, Brecht, Beckett and Meyerhold, and correspondence reveals her urging the director of the Roundhouse to subscribe to *Der Spielplan* and *Theater Heute* which, Jonic argued, 'give an absolute picture of what is going on in Germany and in contemporary theatre in most parts of the world'.[35] According to Keith Horner, reviewing the production for *The Times*:

> *The Wheel* is Mr Bedford's first theatre work, a multi-media aggregation of four actors, revolving lights and small band of instrumentalists [. . . the musicians were] a frequently entertaining, improvising group working on three spaced stages [. . .] Like many of Mr Bedford's compositions, *The Wheel* uses atmospheric, freely and economically notated sonorities, illustrating the text or action.
>
> (Horner 1972: 9)

Regarding the action, Horner refers to an 'improvized nautical allegory', a 'charade of love', and a 'contorted religious scene within a black-magic framework', which he appears to suggest would have been more effective in the hands of Maxwell Davies (Horner 1972: 9). He notes, however, that contrary to Jonic's claims the actors 'largely remained mutually exclusive from the musicians', and he concludes, surprisingly, that the production broke 'little new ground'. To verify Horner's verdict requires more concrete information on the performance, but details remains elusive: there are no extant photographs,[36] few reviews, no recordings, and no score is listed in Bedford's catalogue, or even in his entry in the *New Grove Dictionary*.

Wilkinson clearly contributed in important ways to raising the profile of music at the National, and in 1975 Harrison Birtwistle became the new Director of Music. This appointment resulted not only in incidental music for productions of Shakespeare, Marlowe and others, but also a series of collaborative ventures in which Birtwistle sought new synergies between music, speech, sound and movement. I have discussed these works in detail elsewhere (Beard 2012 and 2010),

---

35 Letter from Bettina Jonic to George Hoskins, dated 29 September 1971. Arts Council of Great Britain Records, Victoria and Albert Museum Archive.

36 The Arts Council records indicate that the photographer Ronald Gunn took pictures of the production. However, Gunn passed away in 2013, and I have been unable to locate his pictures.

250   *David Beard*

but it is worth briefly restating here how they illustrate both the musicalisation of British theatre and the reconceptualisation of the performer.

Birtwistle's *Bow Down*, which premiered in 1977, grew from workshops with actors based on a libretto by the poet-dramatist Tony Harrison, in which different versions of the Ballad of the Cruel Sister were compiled and elaborated. Five actors and four musicians face the audience on an empty stage, seated in a semi-circle that defines the area in which the action takes place.[37] Although acting is reserved for the actors, and oboe and transverse bamboo flute are played only by musicians, the piece also explores the region in between, where there is no distinction between actor and musician. All performers play an instrument of some kind, and all performers chant, speak and move, although the musicians' movements are restricted to position changes in the semi-circle. The idea of the performing body is central both to the ballad of the Cruel Sister and to *Bow Down*. In the ballad, the Cruel Sister drowns the Fair Sister, who is later transformed into a harp, who then exposes the Cruel Sister through song. Mime is key to the expression of these narrative themes. The harp, for example, is represented through a mime sequence, which culminates in the form shown in Figure 10.7.

Shortly before *Bow Down* was performed, Birtwistle and Tony Harrison began another, major collaboration on a performance of *The Oresteia* using Harrison's translation. A series of workshops was organised, described as the 'Agamemnon Experiments', which Harrison recorded on audiocassettes.[38] The purpose of the workshops was to reinvent the idea of an Ancient Greek chorus. Sixteen actors were involved with two musicians. Birtwistle explained to the actors that they were there to help him 'liberate the text'. Tensions arose, however, because the actors felt they first needed to learn the rhythm of the text, otherwise its meaning and their personal interpretations would be lost. In other words, the actors were reluctant to relinquish hard-won embodied technique (their classical training), and there were some heated debates.

---

37 I am grateful to Jennie Borzykh at the National Theatre Archive for providing digital scans of images from the original workshops and dress rehearsal, for research purposes. The concept of mimed action in an egalitarian, circular space, was actually anticipated by Elisabeth Lutyens in her music theatre work *The Linnet From the Leaf* (1972), in which two instrumental groups are arranged either side of a raised circular platform divided into five zones, with five seating positions for each of the solo singers. Each character must pass through the centre circle before performing their next scene, and the work begins with a mute pantomime performed by all the singers. The work was not performed until 1979, however, and then only for a BBC audio recording, conducted by Lionel Friend on 11 November. Sketches, draft and published scores are stored in the British Library, Add MS 64466–64469: 1972.

38 Audio recordings of over ten hours of workshops, which took place from 10 to 14 January 1977, are stored at the Archive of Performances of Greek and Roman Drama (APGRD), Faculty of Classics, University of Oxford. I am grateful to Amanda Wrigley for drawing my attention to the existence of these tapes. For a discussion of the contents, see Beard 2012: 290–95.

Reconceptualising the performer 251

Figure 10.7 Actors Fred Warder and Morag Hood mime the transformation of the Fair Sister into a harp, in Harrison Birtwistle's *Bow Down* (1977), from the original performance in London's National Theatre. Photograph by John Haynes. © Copyright Lebrecht Music & Arts; used with their permission.

Trusted interpreters

Neither *Bow Down* nor the 'Agamemnon Experiments' began with a score. In both cases, the score was assembled later, and in neither case by Birtwistle.[39] For *Bow Down*, the score leaves considerable scope for interpretation, particularly with regard to the use of masks and other mimed actions. A performance during the 2012 Spitalfields Music Summer Festival in London by The Opera Group, directed by Frederic Wake-Walker, made no use of masks, and virtually no symbolic or stylised use of mime, with mixed results. It seems that much depends on a performer's belief and commitment when they approach this, or any other piece, and that performers coming to these works now would benefit greatly from

---

39 The National Theatre Archive has an incomplete full score of the music for the *Oresteia*, some of which is in Birtwistle's hand, but much of which was written out and compiled by Benedict Mason (see Beard 2010). The score for *Bow Down* was prepared later by Jonty Harrison and published by Universal Edition in 1983. For more on the music, see Beard 2012: 296–305.

252 *David Beard*

understanding the context in which a work was conceived, the aspirations behind it, and an awareness of the original rehearsal processes.

This chapter has demonstrated that through the use of mime and collaborations with actors, new music theatre reconceptualised performance by encouraging performers to think outside established performance practice traditions, bringing them into dialogue with artists from other performing backgrounds, and in some cases creating synergies between these forms. We have seen that notation can be important in determining disciplined actions, but that it is often more useful to think of this concept as a *process* developed in workshops and rehearsals, from which trusted interpreters emerge. As Cornelius Cardew remarked in one of his scores, albeit with a degree of irony: 'Instructions to be followed only by qualified person' (Cardew 1968).

References

Adlington, Robert (2005), 'Music theatre since the 1960s', in Mervyn Cooke (ed.), *The Cambridge Companion to Twentieth-Century Opera*, Cambridge, UK: Cambridge University Press, pp. 225–43.

Beard, David (2010), '"Batter the Doom Drum": The music for Peter Hall's *Oresteia* and other productions of Greek tragedy by Harrison Birtwistle and Judith Weir', in Peter Brown and Suzana Ograjenšek (eds), *Ancient Drama in Music for the Modern Stage*, Oxford: Oxford University Press, pp. 369–98.

Beard, David (2012), *Harrison Birtwistle's Operas and Music Theatre*, Cambridge, UK: Cambridge University Press.

Becker, Howard (1982), *Art Worlds*, Berkeley, CA: University of California Press.

Birtwistle, Harrison (1971), *Down by the Greenwood Side*, London: Universal Edition.

Birtwistle, Harrison (1976), *For O, For O, the Hobby-Horse is Forgot*, London: Universal Edition.

Born, Georgina (2005), 'On musical mediation: ontology, technology, and creativity', *Twentieth-Century Music*, 2/1, pp. 7–36.

Bourdieu, Pierre (1993), *The Field of Cultural Production: Essays on Art and Literature*, Cambridge, UK: Polity Press.

Bourdieu, Pierre (1996), *The Rules of Art*, Cambridge, UK: Polity Press.

Brook, Peter (2008 [1968]), *The Empty Space*, London: Penguin Books.

Brüstle, Christa (2009), 'Timekeepers – sound artists – drum machines', *Twentieth-Century Music*, 6/1, pp. 6–81.

Cardew, Cornelius (1968), *Schooltime Compositions: An 'Opera Book'*, n.p.: Gallery Upstairs Press.

Clarke, Eric and Mark Doffman (eds) (2018), *Distributed Creativity: Collaboration and Improvisation in Contemporary Music*, Oxford: Oxford University Press.

Clarke, Eric (2012), 'Creativity in performance', in David Hargreaves, Dorothy Miell and Raymond MacDonald (eds), *Musical Imaginations: Multidisciplinary Perspectives on Creativity, Performance and Perception*, Oxford: Oxford University Press, pp. 17–30.

Clarke, Eric, Mark Doffman and Liza Lim (2013), 'Distributed creativity and ecological dynamics: a case study of Liza Lim's "Tongue of the Invisible"', *Music & Letters*, 94/4, pp. 628–63.

Clements, Andrew (2001), 'Music Theatre', in Stanley Sadie and John Tyrrell (eds), *New Grove Dictionary of Music and Musicians*, volume 17, London: Macmillan, pp. 534–5.

Reconceptualising the performer 253

Cook, Nicholas (2013), *Beyond the Score: Music as Performance*, Oxford: Oxford University Press.

Cox, Arnie (2016), *Music and Embodied Cognition: Listening, Moving, Feeling, and Thinking*, Bloomington and Indianapolis, IN: Indiana University Press.

Cross, Jonathan (2009), *Harrison Birtwistle's* The Mask of Orpheus, Farnham, UK: Ashgate.

Davies, Peter Maxwell (1978), *Le Jongleur de Notre Dame*, London: Chester Music.

Delaere, Mark (2015), '*Gigue Machine* and other gigs: Birtwistle in Europe and beyond', in David Beard, Kenneth Gloag and Nicholas Jones (eds), *Harrison Birtwistle Studies*, Cambridge: Cambridge University Press, pp. 264–92.

Fetterman, William (2010), *John Cage's Theatre Pieces: Notations and Performances*, London: Routledge.

Finnissy, Michael (1975), *Bouffe*, London: Universal Edition.

Friedrichs, Frank (1997), '"You or I must be he!" Peter Maxwell Davies' Opera *Blind Man's Buff*', in Peter Petersen and Hans-Gerd Winter (eds), *Büchner-Opern: Georg Büchner in der Musik des 20. Jahrhunderts*, Frankfurt: Peter Lang, pp. 71–103.

Frith, Simon (2012), 'Creativity as a social fact', in David Hargreaves, Dorothy Miell, and Raymond MacDonald (eds), *Musical Imaginations: Multidisciplinary Perspectives on Creativity, Performance and Perception*, Oxford: Oxford University Press, pp. 62–72.

Glăveanu, Vlad Petre (2014), *Distributed Creativity: Thinking Outside the Box of the Creative Individual*, Heidelberg: Springer Verlag.

Goehr, Alexander and Stanley Sadie (1968), 'Naboth's Vineyard: Alexander Goehr talks to Stanley Sadie', *The Musical Times*, 109/1505, pp. 625–6.

Goehr, Alexander (1973), *Naboth's Vineyard*, London: Schott & Co.

Goehr, Alexander (1976), *Sonata About Jerusalem*, London: Schott & Co.

Griffiths, Paul (1995), *Modern Music and After: Directions Since 1945*, Oxford: Oxford University Press.

Grotowski, Jerzy (2015 [1968]), *Towards A Poor Theatre*, London: Bloomsbury.

Hall, Michael (2015), *Music Theatre in Britain: 1960–1975*, Woodbridge: Boydell & Brewer.

Heile, Björn (2016), 'Toward a theory of experimental music theatre: "showing-doing," "non-matrixed Performance," and "metaxis"', in Yael Kaduri (ed.), *The Oxford Handbook of Sound and Image in Western Art*, New York: Oxford University Press, pp. 335–55.

Heile, Björn (2006), *The Music of Mauricio Kagel*, Aldershot, UK: Ashgate.

Henze, Hans Werner (1982), 'The Montepulciano Cantieri, 1976–80', in *Music and Politics: Collected Writings, 1953–81*, London: Faber & Faber, pp. 260–73.

Horner, Keith (1972), 'The Wheel. Roundhouse', *The Times*, 13 May, 9.

Kagel, Mauricio (1973), *Staatstheater: Szenische Kompositionen, 1967–70*, London: Universal Edition.

Kirby, Michael (1972), 'On acting and not-acting', *The Drama Review*, 16/1, pp. 3–15.

Laws, Catherine (2014), 'Embodiment and gesture in performance: practice-led perspectives', in Darla Crispin and Bob Gilmore (eds), *Artistic Experimentation in Music: An Anthology*, Leuven: Leuven University Press, pp. 131–42.

Lecoq, Jacques (2006), *Theatre of Movement and Gesture*, trans. and ed. David Bradby, London; Routledge.

Lecoq, Jacques (2016), *The Moving Body: Teaching Creative Theatre*, in collaboration with Jean-Gabriel Carasso and Jean-Claude Lallias, translated by David Bradby, London: Bloomsbury.

254   David Beard

Lust, Annette (2003), *From the Greek Mimes to Marcel Marceau and Beyond. Mimes, Actors, Pierrots, and Clowns: A Chronicle of the Many Visages of Mime in the Theatre*, Plymouth: Scarecrow Press.

Maconie, Robin (1974), 'Stockhausen's 'Inori', *Tempo*, 111 (December), pp. 32–3.

Murray, Simon and John Keefe (2016), 'Preparation and training', in *Physical Theatres: A Critical Introduction*, second edition, London and New York: Routledge, pp. 146–202.

Murray, Simon (2003), *Jacques Lecoq*, London: Routledge.

Nyman, Michael (2013 [1968]), 'Alexander Goehr's *Naboth's Vineyard*', in Pwyll ap Siôn (ed.), *Michael Nyman: Collected Writings*, Farnham, UK: Ashgate, p. 36.

Orton, Richard (n.d.), *Mug Grunt*, Willoughby on the Wolds: Unique Music.

Pirie, Peter J. (1971), 'Festivals. Brighton', *The Musical Times*, 112/1541, p. 687.

Ravet, Hyacinthe (2016), 'Negotiated authority, shared creativity: cooperation models among conductors and performers', *Musica Scientiae*, 20/3, pp. 287–303.

Raynor, Henry (1969), [n.t.; review] *The Times*, 2 June, p. 5.

Roesner, David (2014), *Musicality in Theatre: Music as Model, Method and Metaphor in Theatre-Making*, Farnham, UK: Ashgate.

Salzman, Eric and Thomas Desi (2008), *The New Music Theater: Seeing the Voice, Hearing the Body*, Oxford: Oxford University Press.

Sawyer, R. Keith and Stacy DeZutter (2009), 'Distributed creativity: how collective creations emerge from collaboration', *Psychology of Aesthetics, Creativity, and the Arts*, 3/2, pp. 81–92.

Sawyer, R. Keith (2006), *Explaining Creativity: The Science of Human Innovation*, Oxford: Oxford University Press.

Sawyer, R. Keith (2003), *Group Creativity: Music, Theater, Collaboration*, Mahwah, NJ: Erlbaum.

Schatzki, Theodore R., Karin Knorr Cetina and Eike von Savigny (eds) (2001), *The Practice Turn in Contemporary Theory*, London: Routledge.

Spatz, Benjamin (2015), *What A Body Can Do*, London: Routledge.

Stockhausen, Karlheinz (1979), *'Vortrag über HU' für ein Sängerin oder Sänger und Beterstimme aus* Inori *für 1 oder 2 Tänzer-Mimen (Musikalische Analyse von* Inori *mit 224 Fotos der Betgesten). Werk Nr. 38½*, Kürten: Stockhausen-Verlag.

Stockhausen, Karlheinz (1983), *Inori: Anbetungen für einen oder zwei Solisten und Orchester*, Kürten: Stockhausen-Verlag.

Tecker, Hans (1970), 'Summer in South Devon: on the joys of Dartington', *Music and Musicians*, October, p. 50.

Thomas, Philip (2009), 'A prescription for action', in James Saunders (ed.), *The Ashgate Research Companion to Experimental Music*, Farnham, UK: Ashgate.

Thomas, Philip (2013), 'Understanding indeterminate music through performance: Cage's *Solo for Piano*', *Twentieth-Century Music*, 10/1, pp. 91–113.

Vaes, Luk (2014), 'On Kagel's experimental sound producers: an illustrated interview with a historical performer', in Nick Crispin and Bob Gilmore (eds), *Artistic Experimentation in Music: An Anthology*, Leuven: Leuven University Press, pp. 214–24.

Wolff, Janet (1983), *Aesthetics and the Sociology of Art*, London: Allen & Unwin.

Wolff, Janet (1993), *The Social Production of Art*, 2nd edn, London: Macmillan.

11 Embodied commitments
Solo performance and the making of new music theatre

Francesca Placanica

Avant-garde music and its ethos have been subjected to close and contentious scrutiny in recent scholarship. The musical avant-garde of the period 1955–75 frequently presented its innovations as a socially and politically radical gesture, sometimes overtly antiauthoritarian in nature. However, for many commentators, the pursuit of refined conceptual procedures by a generation of composers led to the rise of a social and intellectual élite, and implied the disavowal of musical practices and languages associated with mass cultural consumerism (Born 1995; Taruskin 2005). As a result, the demands made by avant-garde composition survived through the support of state institutions such as culture ministries, broadcasters and educational organisations, and thereby through its partial absorption into the status quo. The initial programmatic *élan* that led its criticism of and responses to established mindsets and social structures seems to have faded into a negation of its earliest incarnations. The revolutionary intellectual backdrop of avant-garde music was instead re-elaborated by popular genres into protest songs and psychedelic rock.

In documenting various politicised and collaborative endeavours by the 1960s avant-garde, Robert Adlington has attempted to challenge this narrative, predominant in Anglo-American musicology, which frames avant-garde music as the expression of an autarchic élite of composers who emphatically rejected the practices of worldly engagement (Adlington 2009). Although many composers eventually retired from the militant scene to pursue their own aesthetic ideals, their music remained immersed in an era of cultural upheaval and, especially in the 1960s and 1970s, could still be perceived as representations of political criticism.

In this chapter I argue that, in order to grasp more fully the political significance of the artistic production of new music theatre at this time, the focus must be shifted from the composer's studio to the performance space. This recognises that the political discourse of the time created less of a dichotomy between composers' engagement and disengagement. For instance, Ben Piekut has documented the intersection between various performative entities that came together in the actual output of the New York avant-garde by providing a composite, and at times disillusioned, 'behind the scenes' picture of the collaborative ventures that shaped events taking place in the 1960s and 1970s (Piekut 2011). The political agenda informing experimentation in theatre writing and performance was the result of multiple agencies, among which the numerous, practitioner-led 'embodied commitments' to experimental forms of representation in music and theatre have often been overlooked. Performers and creative authors from the most diverse backgrounds, from theatre acting to dance and more conventional classical training, engaged in personal quests for embodied practices that drifted away from the pathways of institutional training, self-fashioning their performative personae in unique ways into persuasive vehicles of change and subversion. A newly-found emphasis on the body and the poietic power of its sonic utterance through voice foregrounded the demand for an increasingly varied performative vocabulary, which filtered into the composers' technical and aesthetic spectrum through collaborations with literary authors and philosophers, directors, choreographers, and ultimately individual performers.

Supporting my discussion with performance studies theories that centre the body as a performative space *per se*, in this chapter I explore conceptual intersections spanning experimental and new music theatre, as mediated through the embodied practices of specific theorists and performers. With a commitment to creating alternative forms of staged representation and experimental forms of communication through theorisation and training, these artists sought to promote societal change, presenting as sustainable models the aesthetics and politics developed by their artistic communities. I focus on musical monodramas and music theatre works tailored for a single performer, observing, in particular, the specific experiences of two exceptional vocal performers – Roy Hart and Cathy Berberian – who engaged in training activities that would respond to the increasingly unconventional demands of new music theatre writing, and which mediated between theatre and music practices.

In light of the shared aesthetics of avant-garde composers, theorists and practitioners, my discussion of the making and performance of musical monologues begins with the fundamental notion that text is a 'signifying structure' pertaining to the realms of practice and productivity (Allen 2000: 36). The notion of 'text' thus refers both to the production of a written medium, and the way in which that medium is digested, elaborated and embodied by the performer; the text thus takes shape through multi-agential processes, involving the 'distributed subjectivities' of creative, performative and receptive agents (on 'distributed subjectivity', see Kassabian 2013, and Beard and Gloag 2016: 28). This view, proposed by performance studies and theatre theory, conceives the body as a performative space *per se*, with an agential capacity to determine space and weave the dramaturgical action. Current approaches to 'postopera' similarly emphasise how the body becomes a component – or text – in addition to the music, libretto and staging (Novak 2012: 152). Markus Hallensleben has coined the notion of 'performative body spaces', defining bodies as entities able to mould and redesign the space and tempi of dramatic action:

> Our globalized cultures are based on the European culture of *graphein*, of leaving traces in space. Writing is just one example of making oneself visible in order to be present; walking and dancing are two other instances of

> avoiding the absence of one's own body. But by doing so, we change and in a certain sense not only create, but also destroy spaces. It is an unavoidable, vicious circle. The same can be claimed for the 'body' in that the organic body is always already textual, or is woven and articulated (or disarticulated) like a text, just as any text has a corporeal or cognitive dimension built into it . . . we can only cognitively grasp text in bodily terms and vice versa.
>
> (Hallensleben 2010: 18)

In musical monologues, the solo acting singer stands as a living crucible of musician and actor, and is fully responsible for turning the sonic substance of the literary text into a performative act, single-handedly directing the flow and the dramatic tempi, and thus seeming to embody a drive toward a unitary focus in flesh and blood. Thus, an apparently solipsistic performative form carries a plural trace: the monologue reflects not only the author's construction, but also its representation enacted both through a stage figure and the performer's personage. This enactment results in a polyphonic experience for the audience.

Consistent with these observations, David Graver's concept of 'personage' suggests that, in performance, actors project their representations not only through their impersonation of stage figures, but also through a particular intermediate status deriving from their connection with the performance setting and their visibility to the audience. Personage is thus 'a way of representing oneself within a particular discursive domain' (Graver 2003: 164). This outer projection of the performative self, embedded in live performance, becomes structural in staged solo performances: performers of musical monologues embody at once their musical personae and the various participants' interdependent contributions to the production process, including those of the performance attendee (Auslander 2006). Even though the action is condensed into a single stage figure, the monologue is the result of a combined production process, and thus presents a multi-layered substance. Just like Graver's 'personages', singers perform their musical and theatrical personae within a specific social domain: that of a staged performance, in which the textual and paratextual apparatus fashions the singers' performative identity simultaneously with the dramatic flow. In most cases, twentieth-century musical monodramas were originally tailored to specific vocalists, whose performative power and instrumental qualities, which I will describe here as their 'bodily tessitura', projected a unique dramatic timbre onto the performance, derived from their idiomatic vocal and bodily utterances.[1] In musical monodrama, we see at work the quintessence of the medium of physical performance: the singers' intelligent bodies and voices comprising compelling extra-textual layers that remediate the performer both as musical personage and as stage figure (Duncan 2004: 285). The response of the performer's bodily tessitura to the dramatic interpretation is synesthetic in the resulting alchemy created between voice, body and stage figure.

---

1 I first used the term 'bodily tessitura' in 'Monodramatic immersions: Repositioning the solo performer's voice', a paper delivered at the *Operatic Immersions* International Conference, University of Huddersfield, 22–23 April 2016.

258   *Francesca Placanica*

The explorations of both experimental theatre and new music dramaturgy focused significantly on this new emphasis on the body and its capacity to construct and reconstruct space beyond language. Leading practitioners of the 1960s developed, through their research, a cross-media performative language substantiated by 'corporeal, vocal, gestural and incantational elements' that were able to produce a 'performative generation of materiality' primarily through the 'corporeality, spatiality, and tonality of performance' (Ovadija 2013: 5). In particular, theatre practitioners and theorists strove to infuse spatiality into sound, devising processes devoted to liberating speech, voice and vocal gesture from the written text, and generating physical sound from a voice that was understood as trapped in the corporeal, emotional and psychological subjectivity of the individual. Voice was conceived as an emanation of the materiality of the body, and sound as a self-standing agent in the construction of dramaturgical spatiality. In this newly-expressed materiality, the immanence of the human voice in its bodily wrapping became a principal element of performativity and a crucial agent in the unfolding of dramaturgical devices. The poietic and persuasive power of the performative voice transcended its conventional role as purveyor of language, and developed expressive power by strengthening its intrinsic connections with the body. The voice's capacity to dislocate verbal meaning and make words/sounds resonate both within the body and in space revealed its 'gestural' quality. Sound was no longer conceived only as a medium, or an arbitrary signifier, but as 'an aural object thrown onstage through a performative act – utterance or gesture – that "betrayed" the text of literary drama' (Ovadija 2013: 3). In this newly-launched emphasis on bodily topographies, the unique skills of the interpreter come to the fore, asserting 'the personal and scenic technique of the actor as the core of theatre art' (Barba and Brook 2002: 15). In particular, Jerzy Grotowski's formulation of the Poor Theatre probed the actor's body as a fully performative space which, through discipline, technique and training, could reach a state of self-awareness and self-penetration (Roose-Evans 1989: 145–62; McKaw 2016: 183–214). According to Grotowski, every element that might be defined as representative of theatre in Western culture could be stripped away from the performance, including the stage; the only remaining defining component was the psychological correlation between audience and performer, which could be further deepened through ritualistic stages of participation (Roose-Evans 1989: 147). In Grotowski's theatre, the schism between the actor's self and body was resolved through the capacity of the actor's embodiment to produce semiotic material through movement and sound (McKaw 2016: 203).

For dramaturg and theorist Eugenio Barba (b. 1936) – an Italian author and theatre director based in Denmark, founder of the Odin Theatre and the International School of Theatre Anthropology, both located in Holstebro – dramaturgy was the intercurrence between the literary script, incarnated through the performer's body, and the subsequent reaction of the audience. Dramaturgy was thus conceived as a 'work of action' (from the etymological root of the word), a collective participatory ritual, a reciprocal weaving across audience and stage, which would eventually disclose an unfathomable world through an interactive experience

Embodied commitments   259

(Watson 1993: 43). Theatre sound was a component of this epiphany of materiality, which would allow a total emotional and cognitive immersion and response by the audience: 'Sound, thus, not only reveals dramatic performance: it is perhaps more appropriate to say, sound is performance' (Ovadija 2013: 11). This was the basis of Barba's notion of 'vocal action', a fundamental component of his training method developed predominantly between 1969 and 1972 (see Watson 1993: 66–7). Vocal action posited the voice as an invisible prolongation of the body endowed, as such, with spatial dimensions. Therefore, in training their voices, actors would concentrate not only on expanding or modulating the resonance of their voices, but actually moulding them in ways that would effectively modify the dramaturgical space in relation to the room and other partners.

This avant-garde avowal of the materiality of voice and body as carrier of the theatrical sign was mirrored in explorations led by avant-garde composers. In their vocal and electro-acoustic experimentations, in particular, Bruno Maderna, Luciano Berio, John Cage, Karlheinz Stockhausen, Henri Pousseur and Pierre Boulez, to name but a few, investigated the psychoanalytical roots of language and the deconstruction of sound, often through research informed by semiological and linguistic theories, and postulated new models of communication that supposed the active involvement of the listener (an indicative text is Berio 2013 [1967–70]). These composers brought such instances to the music stage, often borrowing models from other performative languages and applying elements deriving from literature, media and popular culture. Ultimately, they distanced themselves from conventional forms of staged musical representation, and opera in particular, which in their view remained an anachronistic, if not limiting, device.[2]

Looking into ways to render the implicit theatricality implied in the voice, especially in the 1960s and early 1970s, composers such as Berio deployed forms of vocal performance and proposed new types of vocal embodiments especially able to convey a critical portrayal of the intellectual and psychological fragmentation of the subject. Berio's interest in the acoustics and phonetics of a word as a way into a rediscovery of its semantic power echoed the vocal aesthetics of the theatrical avant-garde. His theorisation of the vocal gesture foregrounded the materiality and spatiality of the voice:

> I am not interested in sound by itself – and even less in sound effects, whether of vocal or instrumental origin. I work with words because I find new meaning in them by analyzing them acoustically and musically. I rediscover the word. As far as breathing and sighing are concerned, these are not effect

---

2   In particular, see remarks about opera in Berio 2013 [1967–70]: 425–33 and Bussotti 2014 [2002]: 223–4. Feldman's concept of the musical settings of texts has been widely discussed by the composer himself, and extensively reported by, among others, Claren 2000 and more recently by Laws 2014: 255–8. Mauricio Kagel predicted a dissolution of established music-theatre genres and conventions, explicitly represented in his *Staatstheater* (1971), namely 'an opera to end the opera' (Griffiths 1981: 812), through the caricaturistic portrayal of all agencies involved in a conventional operatic production.

260 *Francesca Placanica*

but vocal gestures which also carry a meaning: they must be considered and perceived in their proper context.

(Berio, cited in Osmond-Smith 1985: 141)

All these elements were to serve the implicit theatricality carried by the voice and its corporeal components, the latter manifesting as vocal gestures. The connection between Barba's concept of vocal action and Berio's idea of vocal gesture based on vocal actions is particularly evident:[3]

> The vocal gesture actually constitutes a collection of all these vocal actions conventionally connected to specific emotions and, for this reason, is to be considered among the most universal aspects of vocal expression. They seldom need to be translated. Because of their tight and organic link with these vocal actions, the conventional singing techniques belong to the cultural inventory of codified attitudes: they are vocal gestures also [. . .] [T]he voice presents such a richness of potential gestures that it becomes possible to use it on its own, like an instrument, to develop a relation with the simultaneity of different actions – that is, a development, simultaneous yet independent, of different performative characteristics that result in a theatre of actions that allows the listener to perceive polyphonically what, by its own specific physical nature, is forced to be monodic.
>
> (Berio 2013 [1967–70]: 431)[4]

One of the key personalities to stand out from the shifting congeries of activity merging music theatre and voice work was Roy Hart, whose impressive vocal range and flexibility were the inspiration for composers including Hans Werner Henze, Peter Maxwell Davies and Karlheinz Stockhausen.[5] Born Ruben Hartstein in 1926, to Polish-Lithuanian parents in South Africa, Hart relocated to England to train as an actor at the Royal Academy of Dramatic Art (RADA), where he soon excelled in principal roles. Hart encountered the German vocal pedagogue Alfred Wolfsohn (1896–1962) almost as soon as he settled in London, and although he felt a discrepancy between Wolfsohn's methods and the training he was receiving at RADA, he furthered his apprenticeship with the German teacher, to the point that he was soon undertaking coaching and teaching duties on Wolfsohn's behalf (Pikes 1999: 67–102; Roose-Evans 1989: 174–86). Wolfsohn had developed experimental forms of vocal training that applied a psychoanalytic perspective to singing; his pupils were looking mainly for vocal resources that would enable them to express their inner selves, and were rarely involved in

---

3 It seems the two figures developed their theories independently yet concurrently.

4 Unless otherwise stated, all English translations are by the author.

5 The Roy Hart Theatre Archives are currently based in Malérargues, France. Numerous resources can be accessed and acquired in digital format online at http://roy-hart-theatre.com/ (accessed 30 May, 2017), and at Paul Silber, *Roy Hart Theatre Archives*, 2009, www.roy-hart. com/ (accessed May 30, 2017).

professional singing. Wolfsohn's training of the 'unchained voice' had a psycho-therapeutic objective; however, it also expanded the trainees' vocal ranges to the extreme, resulting in a crucial landmark in the burgeoning practice of extended vocal techniques.[6] At the beginning of the 1950s, Hart began to experiment with his own teaching method. His pupils of that time described their work in his class as singing lessons incorporating psychoanalytical and self-reflective elements, combining voice technique with music, drama and therapy (Pikes 1999: 73–85). Aiming to develop singing and vocal skills through individualised exercises, this training established a deep connection between body and voice through breath, which, in circular exercises involving all members of the group in succession, was used as a medium to generate a common sense of rhythm and a connection between all participants. According to Hart, it was through breath that the participants were able to overcome their individualistic approaches to societal living, so as to create a strong sense of reciprocity, with the goal of transferring that experience into the everyday lives of those whom he was shaping as his own community of followers:

> [The group's work is] a breaking down of human barriers and the creation of a happier, warmer society [. . .] we believe that people tend to live on a monotonous and unconscious level. When individuals join the group we try to overcome this in a variety of ways. One is by deep and complete breathing.
>
> (Hart, cited in Pikes 1999: 74)

His laboratory work and live performances at the studio he founded in London in the 1960s were attended by key theatre personalities such as Peter Brook and Grotowski himself; Robert Harvey also led dance workshops there (ibid.: 87).

Hart's unique vocal skills and bodily engagement soon attracted the attention of contemporaneous avant-garde composers. In 1968, Hans Werner Henze wrote *Versuch über Schweine* (*Essay on Pigs*) for Hart, to a text by Chilean writer and activist, Gaston Salvatore, expressing the necessity for protest. Hart provided an impressive interpretation (ibid.: 67–102). However, the collaboration that brought Hart to fame was *Eight Songs for a Mad King* (1969) by Peter Maxwell Davies on a text by Randolph Stow, a half-hour monodrama for a vocalist and six instrumentalists explicitly composed using Hart's technical vocabulary. Maxwell Davies had become interested in Roy Hart's techniques, and in 1968 attended a production of Euripides' *Bacchae* at Hart's Abraxas club at the actor's invitation; the performance struck the composer as 'beautiful and disturbing' (Krüger 2014: 24–5). *Eight Songs* was based on the story of King George III, 'Mad King George', depicted at the culmination of his nervous disease, which Hart was to embody using all the potential of his voice.[7] The poems were in fact completed

---

6 The work of both the Roy Hart Theatre and the Alfred Wolfsohn Research Centre was documented in writing, film, photographs and phonograph recordings by author, film maker and archivist Leslie Shepard, who had a key role in the preservation of the legacy of the creators of extended vocal techniques.

7 On the relationship between Maxwell Davies' writing and other aspects of the performer's body, see also Cesare 2006 and Welten 1996.

262 *Francesca Placanica*

at the end of 1968, and Hart then started to build his vocal improvisation upon a few lines of text, providing the composer with an exceptional range of colours and vocal effects from which to select in order to complete the score. Recordings survive from this workshop process, which are currently being investigated by researchers interested in the combined authorship of the pieces (see in particular ibid.: 22–30). The composer worked with Hart's specific vocal physiognomy in mind, including his ability to produce multiphonics and his extreme tessitura. Maxwell Davies described the process of listening to tapes prepared by Hart, in which he experimented on Stow's text:

> I didn't think much. I just listened to them and he was there and I could take down what he was doing on paper and I remembered very well. And I had him, as it were, in my ear, in my head all the time I was composing.
>
> (Maxwell Davies, cited in ibid.: 25).

Hart's creation of the role was premiered by The Pierrot Players, conducted by the composer on 22 April 1969, and was received with great acclaim. In particular, some commentators noted how the work capitalised on Roy Hart's vocal embodiment,[8] a feature of the work that was indeed acknowledged in Maxwell Davies' preface to the monodrama:

> The sounds made by human beings under extreme duress, physical and mental, will be at least in part familiar: with Roy Hart's extended vocal range, and his capacity for producing chords with his voice, the poems presented a unique opportunity to categorize and exploit these techniques to explore certain extreme regions of experience.
>
> (Maxwell Davies, cited in Williams 2000: 81)

However, disputes between Hart and Maxwell Davies arose, apparently as a result of the composer's unwillingness to acknowledge the joint authorship of the work (see Pikes 1989: 87–8; Krüger 2014: 22). The commercial recording of the work made a year later was therefore entrusted to Julius Eastman, who nonetheless produced an outstanding performance.[9] Davies left the score unchanged after his artistic divorce from Hart:

> I just left it. And they can cope with it as best they can. And they do cope in a way. [. . .] Of course, they can't do his multiphonics. But there are plenty of other things that you can do, as we know.
>
> (Maxwell Davies, cited in Krüger 2014: 22)

---

8 For instance, Pikes reports a remark by George Steiner from a letter conserved in the Roy Hart Theatre Archives: 'Last night's performance on the BBC was a stunning experience. I think it may well be a work of genius, but pivoting wholly on your gifts'; George Steiner, letter to Roy Hart, 23 April 1969, cited in Pikes 1999: 87.

9 Peter Maxwell Davies, *Eight Songs for A Mad King*, The Fires of London; Peter Maxwell Davies, Conductor, Julius Eastman, Baritone; Vinyl, LP (London: Unicorn Record/Decca, 1971).

Embodied commitments 263

A collaboration with Karlheinz Stockhausen on *Spiral* (1968), a piece for solo that Stockhausen had devised for an undefined solo instrument, came to a similar end. Roy Hart lent all his *bodily tessitura* to the vocal rendition of the piece, apparently exceeding and even 'betraying' the composer's expectations by launching into unplanned improvisations (Pikes 1999: 88–90). Hart's encounter with contemporary music theatre terminated with these bitter experiences; however, his theories, synthesised at the time with the motto 'Language is dead, long live the voice!', continued to inform his work in Maléargues, where he established a base for his Centre Artistique International (Pikes 1999: 90). He eventually met an untimely death in a car accident in 1975.

Hart's practices were liminal to the work of Peter Brook, another protagonist of the 1960s theatrical avant-garde, who had visited his studio on numerous occasions in the 1960s. In 1964, Brook established a Theatre of Cruelty, after Artaud, at the London Academy of Dramatic Art, and in 1970 he set up The International Centre of Theatre Research in Paris, comprising a number of international performers striving to research alternative methods. Through the embodied research undertaken by his company, he aimed to create a vivid exchange of cultural values springing from the materiality of sound, via an archetypical language of tones and noises without conceptual meaning (Roose-Evans 1989: 184–6). Through embodied practices carried through use of vocalisation and breathing practices, Brook sought to generate a circle of unique intensity and heightened experience shared equally by actor and spectator:

> We call what we are doing 'research'. We are trying to discover something, discover it through what we can make, for other people to take part in. It demands a long, long preparation of the instrument that we are. The question always is: have we good instruments? For that, we have to know: what is the instrument for? The only good purpose is that we should be instruments that transmit truth which otherwise would remain out of sight.
>
> (Brook, cited in Roose-Evans 1989: 185)

The vocalisations and improvisations carried out through embodied practices at the International Centre searched for a universal verbal language stemming from primal instincts that might become accessible and meaningful. Free improvisations based on an ancient Persian ceremonial language became the basis for the monumental production of *Orghast* at the Shiraz Festival in 1971. Experimentation with the voice and its persuasive and demiurgic power to define space and interaction between audience and actor remained central to Brook's methodologies. Acolytes included voice teacher Kristin Linklater, director Joseph Chaikin, theorist and master of body awareness Moshé Feldenkreis, and representatives of the American National Theatre of the Deaf. The daily training routine included the fundamentals of acrobatics, Tai Chi Chuan, Noh movements, Kathakali, and special vocal exercises based on ancient Japanese singing techniques led by actor Yoshi Oida. Most of the voicework was based on the development of ensemble breathing circles through phonetic improvisation, directed toward stripping the

264 *Francesca Placanica*

language of words by concentrating on syllables and vocalisation. All participants, and especially guests, would occasionally share their own knowledge and experience with the rest of the group, and Brook used the feedback received by these artists to devise new sets of exercises based on improvisation and physical action (Croyden 2003: 25).

According to Brook's biographer, Michael Kustow, it was the *Financial Times* music critic Andrew Porter who advocated that Brook be invited to the Shiraz Festival to present *Orghast*, noting similarities between Brook's sound-world and the structures and ethos present in works by Berio and Stockhausen. It was on this occasion that Brook encountered Cathy Berberian, who was then creating a festival commission, *Ausstrahlung* by Bruno Maderna (Kustow 2005: 214). Berberian represents another unicum in the history of twentieth-century performance, soon positioning herself as a vocalist favoured by many composers of the post-World War Two avant-garde. Besides her vocal exploration of neurosis and hysteria, which featured in works such as *Visage* (1961) and *Sequenza III* (1965), she engaged in music theatre monologues tailored to her unchallengeable stage presence and vocal ductility. For instance, Berio's *Recital I (for Cathy)* (1972) is a stream of consciousness based on topoi similar to those of *Eight Songs*; and Roman Haubenstock-Ramati's *Credentials, or Think, Think Lucky* (1960) is a spoken vocal solo with small orchestra based on Lucky's monologue from Act I of Samuel Beckett's stage play *Waiting for Godot*. The latter was not a piece of music theatre, but was implicitly dramatised, as was the case for many solos written for Berberian. In theatre works by Sylvano Bussotti, Berberian's 'personage' imprinted an indelible mark, independently moulding her stage figure. Her playful collaboration with Bussotti on his *La passion selon sade* (1966) allowed her extraordinary physical freedom in her embodied representations.

Following their encounter in Shiraz, Peter Brook invited Berberian to participate in a Paris workshop in March 1972. In an informal, unedited interview, Berberian described the work undertaken in the laboratory, which had been carried out on themed vocal scenic actions based on phonemes. Brook required the participants to experiment with impersonations of birds and birdsong, a lifetime fascination for the director eventually conveyed in *The Conference of the Birds*. Berberian especially highlighted the reciprocity of the experience and the untapped potential it left for her performative self:

> What was important, in retrospect, was the impression that he squeezed our brains [. . .] it should have been a kind of reciprocal experience, and in fact that's what it was, because practically everything I have done in that class served me later on various occasions [. . .] it is a little like those small capsules containing little spinning balls, which work with a delayed input: in 1990 possibly some of these little balls will explode, who knows. I also said another thing: for me the intellectual is one who absorbs the information, and is then capable to deliver them again in turn to others. While I learn

something, I absorb them, and the only way they come out is in my work, because I am not able to explain them in the reasoned way I learnt them.[10]

In the same interview, Berberian described her initial difficulty in trusting and engaging with the technique of singing imparted by actor Yoshi Oida – a Japanese discipline inherited from ancient theatre practices based on modular song scales – because it required a glottal effort and throat rigidity which she initially felt was dangerous for her voice and conflicted with her Western classical vocal training. Apparently, at the end of the course, the group gathered to provide feedback on the experience. Berberian recalled her impressions:

> I remember very well what I said, because it was true and very important. I said that when I entered the course, after a few days I felt lost, distraught, disoriented; I felt like Peter's world was a different planet to which I could never belong. Now the course was over, I felt that Peter's world was the real world, and I feared to go back to life out there, out of it, because I did not know what I'd be there. And then I took Peter aside and I asked him: 'You know, I have been told that I was only a singer, not an actress, and I'd like to have your opinion on that, I'd like for you to be honest with me.' And he said: 'Cathy, the door is open, when you want, you can come and join the group.'[11]

The experiences of Hart and Berberian were eventually transmitted through the later development of their careers as performers and pedagogues, and traces of their work and teaching are left in documents of their research and authored writings. Indeed, their methods of registering their craftsmanship in assertive forms of documentation marked a quite innovative trend in the politics of artistic creation of the era. Both figures self-fashioned their positions in history, seeking to be perceived not only as 'media' in the hands of composers and directors, but as vehicles of embodied knowledge and change. This self-reflective trend foreshadowed the language of ethnographic media used by contemporary theatre collectives to document their research, expressing an authorial drive for embodied performance research.

Hart trained and taught until his untimely death, not only expanding the performative possibilities of the voice, but also imbuing his research with a political and societal scope, devoted to improving the life of his community and creating a model that could be applied to Western societies. His corpus of documentaries, conserved at the Roy Hart Archive in Malérargues, has only recently been subjected to scholarly scrutiny; however, his and Wolfsohn's theories find current

---

10 Cathy Berberian, unedited interview with Silvana Ottieri, tape recording 19 side A, Milan, 1981. Sammlung Cathy Berberian, Paul Sacher Stiftung, Basel, accessed by kind permission. Translation from the original Italian by the author.

11 Berberian, Interview with Silvana Ottieri, tape 19 side A, 1981.

266   *Francesca Placanica*

application in voice therapeutics, while franchised voice training courses for actors continue around the world in his name.[12]

Berberian complemented her role in the avant-garde music-making of the 1960s and 1970s with careful choreographing of her representation in media and press.[13] In 1966, she authored her manifesto on vocal performance, 'La nuova vocalità nell'opera contemporanea', inviting new generations of interpreters to seize their strategic role in the making of experimental vocal compositions by becoming 'composers of their own performances' (Berberian 2007 [1966]: 51–4). Her concept of a 'new vocality' revolved not around a vocabulary of vocal effects invented by the composer and unimaginatively reproduced by the singer, but rather around the singer's independent ability to use the voice in all aspects of the vocal process. In addition, in line with contemporaneous performance practices capitalising on the actor's agency, Berberian highlighted the primacy of the body in vocal performance, postulating 'the artist as a universal fact and the voice as part of the living body, acting and reacting' (Berberian 2007 [1966]: 49):

> I cannot stand the kind of singing that I usually call lace-handkerchief style. I do not think I could sing like that. Yes, perhaps I could. When, however, I enter the stage, I cannot control myself. I need my hands, my arms, my body. I would be desperate if I had to hold the music in my hands.
>
> (Berberian, cited in Varga 2013: 165).

The same conviction made Berberian critical of opera singers who were only concerned with the beauty of their voice, rather than with the meaning of their singing, and so destined to remain empty vessels once the voice had gone with age (see De Swaan 1994). In 'La nuova vocalità', Berberian advocated a holistic physical training that introduced vocal noises, effects and sounds into the singer's performative vocabulary, and would enable the singer to become an independent agent in the creative process. She also blamed the tradition that had fossilised the conventions of operatic and vocal performance – yet another viewpoint she shared with Peter Brook well before their collaboration – while acknowledging the roots of the New Vocality in the overarching authorial attitude that, from Monteverdian singing to the vocality of John Cage, had empowered singers' creativity. The emphasis on the voice as a powerful extension of the body also emerges in Berberian's legacy as a voice teacher. In her instructions, she invited her students to pitch their own interpretations freely through full appropriation of both the text and context of the dramatic action, even if that would cause them to deviate from

---

12 Roy Hart's interviews and recordings are available at the Roy Hart Theatre Archives, and a few are accessible online.

13 The impact of Berberian's persona in contemporaneous culture is still to be comprehensively captured. A corpus of videos of her work on television and radio and in interviews is preserved at the Paul Sacher Stiftung, Basel, while hopefully more footage from the RAI Archives will soon be made available by Nicola Scaldaferri's forthcoming video collection.

tradition and established models.[14] In the terms that she used in her manifesto, by relinquishing convention, and carving in fresh ways their own interpretation, new performers were able to become composers of their own performance (Berberian 2007 [1966]: 49).

The worlds of contemporaneous theatre voicework and experimental music theatre overlapped, met and expressed similar agendas, especially in identifying performance as a communicative act, and in their inquisitive relationship with the audience. These calls, coming from the different angles of composers, directors, theorists and performers, enunciated in various ways a critical need to depart from the old tradition that separated performance from composition. It was evident that the creation of a new performative model would enable greater flexibility and fertility in exchanges between these agencies, as well as triggering new meanings. The training and resources developed by these performers, from the late 1960s well into the 1980s, were indeed auspicious for the creation of an alternative performative politics, in which interpreter, director, writer and composer could share an identical space mediated through the sounding body of the aware performer. Yet this *élan* seems to have lost some of its force along the way. Perhaps this was due to the issues of co-authorship raised by many music compositions, especially when scored for one exceptional interpreter, as well as subsequent clashes between composer and performer, as seen in the case of Hart's collaborations with Stockhausen and Maxwell Davies, not to mention many works written for Berberian (on the question of Berberian and co-authorship, see Vila 2003; Bosma 2006; Placanica 2007 and 2015; Meehan 2011). Not all avant-garde composers were ready to see their authorial voices challenged or moulded, even partially, by their exceptionally accomplished performers.

What is certain, in terms of the scoring of theatrical speech and voice more broadly, is that these influences were interdisciplinary in nature, and often historically interdependent. Konstantin Stanislavski instructed actors to regard a script as a musical score; Brook's instructions were interspersed with musical metaphors. In musical dramaturgy, the performers' vocal experiments informed the composers' writings on psychophysical tropes. However, the legacy of their embodied commitments went far beyond that space and those *topoi*; they factually mediated modes and techniques from one discipline to another, and defined creative territories that future generations of composers/performers would comfortably inhabit with their new performative languages. These performers crafted new intertextual layers, and the authorial attitude with which they pursued their research testifies to their awareness of their historical role in the politics of artistic creation. Theirs were the embodied commitments that underpinned the making of much new music theatre and its multifaceted political agenda, and which informed experimentation in different composition histories and performance practices. The legacy of these performers, who were committed to creative composition in various fields

---

14 An unedited collection of radio documentaries about Berberian's teaching is preserved at the Paul Sacher Stiftung, Basel: *L'atelier de musique de Cathy Berberian*, Radio France, 1983, CD PSS, SLB 67_1; accessed by kind permission.

268 *Francesca Placanica*

of performing arts, deserves to be appreciated more deeply when tracing a broader history of the politics of avant-garde aesthetics. Especially in works that portrayed them as unrivalled soloists, their agency was difficult to separate from the identity of the work as performed on stage. These artists incarnated language and communication, shaping their personages into acting and reacting political bodies. They became flexible instruments in the hands of creative composers and directors, yet were also independent agents able to inflect and lead creative acts, and to leave multiple legacies.

References

Adlington, Robert (2009), 'Introduction', in Robert Adlington (ed.), *Sound Commitments: Avant-Garde Music and the Sixties*, New York: Oxford University Press, pp. 3–15.

Allen, Graham (2000), *Intertextuality*, London: Routledge.

Auslander, Philip (2006), 'Musical personae', *The Drama Review*, 50/1, pp. 100–19.

Barba, Eugenio and Peter Brook (eds) (2002), *Jerzy Grotowski: Towards a Poor Theatre*, New York: Routledge.

Beard, David and Kenneth Gloag (2016), *Key Concepts in Musicology*, Abingdon, UK: Routledge.

Berberian, Cathy (2007 [1966]), 'La nuova vocalità nell'opera contemporanea', transl. Francesca Placanica, in Placanica, 'Cathy Berberian: performance as composition', MM thesis, Dallas: Southern Methodist University, pp. 51–4.

Berio, Luciano (2013 [1967–70]), 'Verso un teatro musicale', in Angela Ida De Benedictis (ed.), *Scritti sulla musica*, Turin: Einaudi, pp. 425–33.

Born, Georgina (1995), *Rationalizing Culture: IRCAM, Boulez, and the Institutionalization of the Musical Avant-Garde*, Berkeley and Los Angeles, CA: University of California Press.

Bosma, Hannah (2006), 'Musical washing machines, composer–performers, and other blurring boundaries: how women make a difference in electroacoustic music', *Intersections: Canadian Journal of Music/Revue canadienne de musique*, 26/2, pp. 97–117.

Bussotti, Sylvano (2014 [2002]), 'Allegory actually. Cathy Berberian . . .', trans. by Francesca Placanica and Pamela Karantonis, in Pamela Karantonis, Francesca Placanica, Anne Sivuoja-Kauppala and Pieter Verstraete (eds), *Cathy Berberian: Pioneer of Contemporary Vocality*, Farnham, UK: Ashgate, pp. 223–4.

Cesare, T. Nikki (2006), '"Like a chained man's bruise": the mediated body in "Eight Songs for a Mad King" and "Anatomy Theater"', *Theatre Journal*, 58/3, pp. 437–57.

Croyden, Margaret (2003), *Conversations with Peter Brook, 1997–2000*, New York: Faber & Faber.

Claren, Sebastian (2000), *Neither: Die Musik Morton Feldmans*, Hofheim: Wolke Verlag.

Duncan, Michelle (2004), 'The operatic scandal of the singing body: voice, performance, performativity', *Cambridge Opera Journal*, 16/3, pp. 283–306.

Graver, David (2003), 'The actor's bodies', in Philip Auslander (ed.), *Performance. Critical Concepts in Literary und Cultural Studies*, volume 2, London: Routledge, pp. 157–74.

Griffith, Paul (1981), 'Unnecessary music: Mauricio Kagel at 50', *The Musical Times* 122/1666, pp. 811–12.

Hallensleben, Markus (ed.) (2010), *Performative Body Spaces*, Amsterdam: Rodopi.

Kassabian, Anahid (2013), *Ubiquitous Listening: Affect, Attention, and Distributed Subjectivity*, Berkeley, CA: University of California Press.

Embodied commitments 269

Krüger, Anne-May (2014), '"If something else works, do it!" Peter Maxwell Davies' und Roy Hart's "Eight Songs for a Mad King"', *Dissonance*, 127, pp. 22–30.

Kustow, Michael (2005), *Peter Brook: A Biography*, London: Bloomsbury.

Laws, Catherine (2014), *Headache among the Overtones: Music in Beckett/Beckett in Music*, Amsterdam: Rodopi.

McKaw, Dick (2016), *Bakhtin and Theatre: Dialogues with Stanislavsky, Meyerhold and Grotowsky*, Abingdon, UK and New York: Routledge.

Meehan, Kate (2011), *Not Just a Pretty Voice: Cathy Berberian as Collaborator, Composer and Creator*, Ann Arbor, MI: UMI Dissertation Publishing.

Novak, Jelena (2012), *Postopera: Reinventing the Voice-Body*, Farnham, UK: Ashgate.

Osmond-Smith, David (ed.) (1985), *Luciano Berio: Two Interviews*, London: Marion Boyars.

Ovadija, Mladen (2013), *Dramaturgy of Sound in the Avant-garde and Postdramatic Theatre*, Montreal: MQUP.

Piekut, Ben (2011), *Experimentalism Otherwise: The New York Avant-Garde and its Limits*, Berkeley, CA: University of California Press.

Pikes, Noah (1999), *Dark Voices: The Genesis of Roy Hart Theatre*, Woodstock: Spring Journal Books.

Placanica, Francesca (2007), 'Cathy Berberian: performance as composition', MM thesis, Dallas: Southern Methodist University.

Placanica, Francesca (2015), '"Unwrapping" the voice: Cathy Berberian's and John Cage's *Aria* (1958)', in Erling E. Guldbrandsen and Julian Johnson (eds), *Transformations of Musical Modernism*, Cambridge, UK: Cambridge University Press, pp. 264–78.

Roose-Evans, James (1989), *Experimental Theatre from Stanislavksy to Peter Brook*, London: Routledge.

Swaan, Carrie de (1994), *Music is the Air I Breathe – Cathy Berberian 1925–1983*, documentary film VHS, Amsterdam: Swaan Productions.

Taruskin, Richard (2005), *The Oxford History of Western Music*, volume 5, *The Late Twentieth Century*, Oxford: Oxford University Press.

Varga, Bàlint Andràs (2013), 'Cathy Berberian', in Bálint András Varga (ed.), *From Boulanger to Stockhausen. Interviews and a Memoir*, New York: University of Rochester Press, pp. 155–66.

Vila, Marie Christine (2003), *Cathy Berberian, cant'actrice*, Paris: Fayard.

Watson, Ian (1993), *Towards a Third Theatre: Eugenio Barba and the Odin Teatret*, New York: Routledge.

Welten, Ruud (1996), '"I'm not ill, I'm nervous": madness in the music of Sir Peter Maxwell Davies', *Tempo*, 196, pp. 21–4.

Williams, Alan E. (2000), 'Madness in the music theatre works of Peter Maxwell Davies', *Perspectives on New Music*, 38/1, pp. 77–100.

Part VI
Analysing new music theatre

12 New music theatre and theories of embodied cognition

Björn Heile

Let us assume that opera is a way of visualising music. This may sound like a rather Wagnerian premise, reminding us of *die ersichtlich gewordenen Taten der Musik* ('deeds of music made visible'), but it responds to a more fundamental principle that appears to have its roots in evolution. Every sound is the result of movement, and as part of our genetic heritage, we constantly analyse all sounds to identify their origins. Without our ancestors' ability to detect the sounds of predator or prey, we wouldn't be here, and we still employ the same skills, if not necessarily for the same purposes. As infants (even as foetuses) we learn to detect sounds, interpret them as movements and imitate them. Music, then, is never 'just' sound; it is movement. Along the same lines, listening, as I will outline in more detail below, does not just involve the perception and cognition of disembodied soundwaves; it is mental or actual bodily re-enactment of sound-producing movements. It is for these reasons, I argue, that we delight in multimodal pairings of music with visual media and movement, whether it is in opera, dance, film, television, music videos or computer games. Indeed, we find it hard not to link the perception of music to visual impulses – and vice versa: witness the urge to employ music in film and television, even where it is not obviously motivated. It may be countered that we're also witnessing a fashion for headphone-listening, the seemingly most abstract and disembodied form of listening. However, it is telling that headphone-listening is so often described as providing a 'soundtrack' to people's lives and consciousness (see, for example, Bull 2007). In other words, music is related at some level to the surrounding environment. As Nicholas Cook put it (pace the philosopher Peter Kivy), 'music is never "alone"' (Cook 1998: 23; see also Cook 2015).

In the following, I want to read new music theatre through the lens of theories of 'embodied cognition', according to which musical perception is governed by the 'mimetic hypothesis', namely that listening involves an actual or imaginary attempt to imitate the sound-producing actions. Although the implications of the theory are pretty much universal, it makes sense to focus on modernist and experimental opera and music theatre. In their emphasis on new, non-hierarchical combinations of text, music and movements (among other elements), these forms can be said to have rediscovered the multimodality that was a hallmark – or at least a promise – of opera from the beginning (Sindoni, Wildfeuer, and O'Halloran

274 *Björn Heile*

2016; Page 2009) but that was seen as stunted by the conventional dramaturgy of traditional opera, with its emphasis on drama and verisimilitude. In this sense, these forms can be seen as the counterpart to or part of the wider development of 'postdramatic theatre' (Lehmann 2006), which replaced the logocentricity of traditional drama with a renewed interest in simultaneity, parataxis and multi-perspectival perception.[1] At the same time, they responded to the disembodiment of music in the classical concert hall. In other words, what Wagner dreamed of – a *Gesamtkunstwerk*, in which all the other arts externalise the inner movement and dynamism of music – could be said to have been brought closer to its realisation by the cross-modal experimentation of the avant-gardes (Shaw-Miller 2004; Rebstock and Roesner 2012). There is a crucial difference, however, in that the latter typically jettisoned the reliance on an illusionist aesthetic and on alignment and congruence between media and art forms that were essential for Wagner.

After providing a short introduction to theories of embodied cognition in music, I will discuss their relevance for an understanding of modernist and experimental opera and music theatre, closing with an analysis of two case studies, Mauricio Kagel's String Quartet II and Luciano Berio's *Sequenza V*. As I will argue, by elucidating our ingrained expectations of the way music is produced through bodily movements, theories of embodied cognition allow us to better understand the *discrepancy* between the actions performed by the musicians in these pieces and the resulting sounds. In this way, these theories allow us to analyse the failures of communication between the members of the string quartet in the Kagel and the alternately amusing and distressing effect of the 'clowning' exhibited by the trombonist in the Berio.

Theories of embodied cognition . . .

In his ground-breaking *Music and Embodied Cognition*, Arnie Cox formulates the 'mimetic hypothesis' in the following terms:

- Part of how we comprehend the behavior of others is by imitating, covertly (MMI) [Mimetic Motor Imagery] or overtly (MMA) [Mimetic Motor Action]
- Part of how we comprehend music is by imitating, covertly or overtly, the observed sound-producing actions of performers.

(Cox 2016: 12)

He further establishes twenty principles governing the mimetic hypothesis, many of which are further subdivided into subcategories (ibid.: 14–15). One of the distinguishing features of theories of embodied cognition is their basis in experimental findings in the neurosciences. We know, for instance, that listening activates the same regions of the brain that are used for motor functions, and that observation

---

1 As is readily apparent, the concerns of theorists of multimodality and postdramatic theatre are closely related, although they tend to come from different traditions or fields.

typically shows the same patterns of neural stimulation as action. For example, Cox has referred to a study by Gazzola, Aziz-Zadeh, and Keysers (2006), which, on the basis of fMRI scans ('Functional Magnetic Resonance Imaging' – a technique for measuring brain activity by detecting changes to blood flow), demonstrated that the same regions of the brain were activated 'both when performing hand actions [such as reaching for and grasping a peanut or a piece of paper, breaking or ripping the object, and replacing the object] and when only hearing such actions.' According to Cox, the implications for music are significant:

> The action of these populations of neurons [in the motor area of the brain] represents an equivalence between goal-oriented (sound-producing) hand actions of musical performers: the sound of the piano, for example, is the sound actions performed on a piano, the sound of hand drums is the sound of drumming actions, and so forth. One of the implications, then, is that whenever we give our attention to such musical sounds, normally we do not simply hear the sounds, but we also feel something of what it would be like to perform the sound-producing actions. (That is, we mimetically represent the sound-producing hand actions, to some degree of fidelity, and such representations have an affective dimension, in what it feels like to perform such actions.)
>
> (Cox 2016: 25–6)

Cox's is one of the most recent formulations of the mimetic hypothesis, and the advantage of his book is that it offers a coherent and very readable synthesis of a wide and often diffuse field, and that it embraces both empirical and music-theoretical approaches. It is worth stressing, however, that there is a growing and diverse body of theory from a number of scholars in different fields and working in different countries. Compare for instance the formulation of the mimetic hypothesis proffered by Rolf Inge Godøy:

> The motor theory (with various variations) claims that perceiving sound is closely linked with mentally simulating the gestures that we believe have been made in the production of that sound. Some recent neurophysiological research suggests that perception and cognition in general is a matter of simulating the actions we assume are related to what we perceive. . . . In our context this means that when listening to music (or even just imagining music with our 'inner ear') we may very well mentally simulate some of the sound-producing gestures that we have previously learned go with the music; for example, energetic movements of the arms with ferocious drum sounds, long protracted gestures with sustained string sounds, and so on. These associations of musical sound with sound-producing gestures could be regarded as integral to music perception, leading to the idea that any sound will be included in some mental image of a gestural trajectory, which is what I previously have termed motor-mimetic cognition.
>
> (Godøy 2013: 70)

276   Björn Heile

To be fair, Godøy's idea of a mental simulation of sound-producing gestures does not appear entirely convincing, and the appendage 'that we have previously learned go with the music' is so general as to muddy the waters (although he has provided more concrete details in some of his other publications). Much of the time, non-musicians can have no concrete idea how sounds are produced. Moreover, most music consists of a multitude of parts and signals, thus, in Cox's words, offering 'multiple mimetic invitations' (2016: 49–50), so it isn't always clear what it is that we may want to respond to. However, the widespread phenomenon of air guitar (and, to a lesser extent, air drum) playing and karaoke demonstrates the impulse to embody the music and the ability of a wide range of listeners, whether trained or untrained, to select between mimetic invitations. While these particular phenomena may be historically, culturally and socially specific (mostly linked to rock music from the 1960s onwards), similar if typically less outward and direct phenomena, are common across cultures and ages. Writing some years after Godøy, Cox provides a useful distinction between 'intramodal' mimesis or 'direct-matching', which refers to a direct imitation of the sound-producing gestures (usually by people playing the same instrument or having the same voice type); 'intermodal' or 'cross-modal' mimesis, which typically involves subvocal imitation (i.e. humming along); and 'amodal' mimesis (abdominal exertions that underlie limb movements and vocalisations) (2016: 45–6).

In other words, whenever we feel the impulse to sing or hum along, play air guitar, dance, tap our feet or nod our head, we engage in mimetic behaviour, whether we actively execute these actions (mimetic motor action – MMA) or suppress them (mimetic motor imagery – MMI). In all these cases, we appear to try to imagine what it feels like to produce the sounds we hear. While not all of us are trained musicians, we all have experience using our voices and producing a range of sounds with our bodies and whatever tools we have at hand, and there is clear evidence that we engage in this behaviour (typically imitating our caregivers) from our infancy and even before (Trevarthen, Delafield-Butt and Schögler 2013). Indeed, according to the long-standing 'motor theory of speech perception', we learn to speak not by learning to analyse sound patterns but through imitation of the vocal tract gestures producing the sounds (Cooper et al. 1967). Although the theory originally argued that speech processing is special, more recent approaches have shown it to be a general phenomenon of perception (Galantucci, Fowler and Turvey 2006).

Cox and most other proponents of the mimetic hypothesis are careful to point out that our motor response offers only a partial explanation of the way we hear and understand music: notice the cautious use of 'part of' in his formulation above (although his book does appear to represent an attempt to create a fairly comprehensive theory of music on that basis). Phenomena such as exact pitch and harmony are probably not sufficiently explained through motor responses alone. Nevertheless, the implications of the theory are far-reaching. That we do respond bodily to music is hardly news, but what the theory suggests – and the empirical evidence for this appears overwhelming – is that this is not an epiphenomenon of music perception that can be ignored in the same way we can suppress the impulse

New music theatre and embodied cognition   277

to sing along or dance to music in the concert hall. Instead, it goes to the very heart of how we experience and make sense of music and why we feel drawn to it. There is related evidence that the way we experience rhythm is based on our corporeal experience of locomotion, notably walking (London 2006), and that our perception of relative pitch is metaphorically related to height and to sensations of bodily strain or relaxation (Cox 2016: 85–108). The clear implication of all this is that, to use the famous thought experiment of brains in a vat used in philosophy, without bodily experience, our minds would not be able to understand music and, in all likelihood, would not have invented or imagined it.

... and their relevance for new music theatre

What implications does a perspective based on embodied cognition of music have for our understanding of modernist and experimental opera and music theatre? Somewhat frustratingly, this is hard to say. The theory is very useful in illuminating why opera has such a hold on audiences and why composers and practitioners kept reinventing it in novel ways when it seemed stifled by convention or ridden with clichés. It is our deeply felt impulse to sing along that makes us empathise with the characters on stage, and it is the bodily movement that we perceive in the music that makes its enactment and visualisation before our eyes so deeply satisfying.

Nevertheless, how the theory can be mobilised to explain the differences between repertoires and pieces and analyse specific examples is somewhat less clear. It seems a general theory of the nature of perception more than a heuristic interpretive or analytical tool. Moreover, it is noteworthy that the theory's proponents have generally stayed away from any multimodal art forms, possibly in an attempt to explicate the nuts and bolts of 'purely' musical perception. Furthermore, we quickly encounter an apparent paradox. If music is the result of sound-performing actions and listening to it means imaginatively re-enacting those movements, then any actual movements accompanying the music can only duplicate our own experience, thus rendering them redundant, or, alternatively, conflict with them, in which case they must be irritating. At heart, the issue is closely related to the dichotomy of conformance vs. conflict between music and visual media as theorised by Nicholas Cook (1998). Although Cox, for example, allows for degrees of congruence between stimulus (the sound heard) and response, this is not developed much further (2016: 45–48).[2] Arguably, an analytical method for the study of opera and other multimodal art forms involving music based on theories of embodied cognition would have to develop ways of describing and theorising levels and forms of congruence.

2 In a private email to me, Cox has drawn attention to the variability of congruence in his model and has recommended this as one of the areas with the greatest potential for multimodal analysis (which, in a sense, I am pursuing in this chapter). I am very grateful for his very helpful and generous response to my enquiries.

278 *Björn Heile*

Apart from analysing congruence between sound-producing actions and music, what such an approach should focus on is the power of identification through the voice, by way of, mostly covert, mimesis (MMI) that opera affords. We can identify with operatic heroes and heroines because we can feel our own vocal folds, our tongues, our diaphragms performing the same (or similar) operations as theirs. This experience obviously depends on our experience with singing and, in some instances, vocal training: despite these significant differences, we all have some experience of using our voices. Most of us know that if we were to actually burst out in song, what we would produce would sound nothing like what opera stars are capable of, but this is just a particular case of theatrical illusion as the willing suspension of disbelief (in Coleridge's celebrated phrase). We can feel in our body what it is like to produce those sounds, and, substituting the real person of the performer for the character they represent, we can imagine what it feels like to perceive the emotions that they express. In other words, although opera is less realistic than most other forms of enacted narrative such as film or drama, it offers potentially more powerful ways of identification with its characters through the peculiar force of mimetic motor action elicited through singing.

Modernist and experimental opera complicates this picture. At issue here is modernism's critique of realism, representation and scenic illusion. From a dramaturgical and wider artistic and cultural perspective these issues matter at least as much as musical style (which tends to be the focus of musicological discussions of opera: copious use of dissonance and 'advanced techniques', whether serial, aleatory, spectralist or electronic, will not make an opera modernist if the music accompanies a conventional drama enacted by singer-protagonists). Although identification is complicated and subverted in such a scenario – Brecht's epic theatre is the most notorious case in point, but the general issue holds true of most if not all modernist theatre – it is not necessarily entirely suppressed. Whereas Violetta in Verdi's *La Traviata* (1853) or Mimì in Puccini's *La Bohème* (1896), to name just two nineteenth-century examples, invite our complete identification – or indeed *require* it for us to derive any enjoyment from the spectacle – we can feel compassion for Mélisande in Debussy's *Pelléas et Mélisande* (1902) or Judith in Bartók's *Bluebeard's Castle* (1918), but we cannot know what they experience. According to Elliot Antokoletz (2004: 30–54), Mélisande may be suffering from trauma, so cannot properly feel, never mind express or communicate emotion. But note how, just as in the case of Verdi's and Puccini's heroines, we get a visceral sense of her bodily if not her mental and emotional experience, through MMI: consider only her famous first phrase: 'Ne me touchez pas, ne me touchez pas!', delivered in two sequential phrases of breathlessly hasty, soft note repetitions, followed by a falling third. We can feel our own throats tightening and our muscles tensing or even trembling in terror.[3] In this way, throughout the

---

3 There is a parallel here to Verdi's Violetta, or, put differently, Verdi to a certain extent foreshadows the modernist emphasis on bodily experience, by capturing Violetta's progressive tuberculosis in her vocal part which becomes increasingly restricted in terms of both range and dynamics. Cf. Cox's comments on Dido's lament in (Cox 2016: 216–17).

New music theatre and embodied cognition   279

work, we can physically experience Mélisande's unease, although, like Golaud, we never learn what ails her. She remains a mystery to us, although we can feel – or think we can – what she feels. In this way, modernist opera does not entirely obliterate identification, but it focuses on corporeal, visceral experience, rather than rational understanding or emotional empathy.

If early modernist opera offers resistance to full identification, later modernist and experimental reinventions of opera have typically further subverted the genre's traditional logocentricity and focused on visual, choreographic and postdramatic elements. While it is still possible, for instance, for a study of Alban Berg's *Wozzeck* (1925) to prioritise 'words and music' in a traditional fashion, such an approach would already be more problematic in the same composer's *Lulu* (1937), with its film interlude, among other theatrical devices. It would be quite absurd for a work such as *Einstein on the Beach* (1976) by Philip Glass, Robert Wilson and Lucinda Childs (the nature of the work requires mention of the director and choreographer alongside the composer). Similar arguments can be made about the operatic works of Luigi Nono, Luciano Berio, Salvatore Sciarrino, Mauricio Kagel, John Cage, Helmut Lachenmann, Kaija Saariaho, Olga Neuwirth or Brian Ferneyhough, to name just some. These works should be seen as postdramatic, multimodal art works, in which music, choreography, text, visual elements, action and movements are combined in different and in principle non-hierarchic ways (which is not to say that one or the other element cannot predominate but that there is no pre-existing expectation that it should). Just as we cannot assume that any element is privileged, we cannot expect synchronicity between them as a norm. Likewise, realism, dramatic representation and scenic illusion may be more exceptions than the rule. But that's not to say that in these operas there is no sense of identification and empathy and that we do not, at one level, connect with the personae on stage, not least through mimetic participation. Indeed, this can be intensified to frightening proportions, as happens in some of Salvatore Sciarrino's works, such as *Lohengrin* (1982) or *L'infinito nero* (1998), in which we appear to hear the articulatory organs or bodily sounds of the protagonists amplified by the instruments. In a way, we don't just get a sense of what it feels like to be the figures we see and hear on stage, we get a sense of what it is to be *inside* them. Put differently, the bodily experience afforded by Sciarrino's work is more akin to Francis Bacon than Botticelli: more real – or rather hyper-real – than idealised.

Modernist opera's challenge to identification is not unlike the resistance to mimetic participation of modernist music as a whole. Cox describes his experience of listening to Brian Ferneyhough's *La chute d'Icare*:

> Upon first listening to this work I was bewildered, but the more I listen to it, the more my experience approaches that of listening to tonal chamber music: I get better at predicting and mimetically participating with ever more details.
> (2016: 50)

This is a good summary of the particular pleasure modernist music affords: a challenge that can be overcome. This music may seem abstract and disembodied – or,

280   *Björn Heile*

as in the case of Sciarrino's work, all too corporeal – but it is never entirely alien to our embodied perception. By contrast, this is what, in my opinion, in an otherwise fascinating contribution, Justin London misses when he argues that Milton Babbitt's Composition for Twelve Instruments

> fail[s] to create this impression of movement; instead the effect is that of stasis, with each cluster of tones merely succeeding each other, without any sense of 'beginning, end, and consummation'. We just do not move like that, nor can we hear ourselves (or others) doing so.
>
> (2006: 136)

Just in case there is any doubt whether this statement implies a value judgement, London clarifies: 'A negative reaction to this music, and other works like it is not simply musical philistinism. Such reactions are borne out of a deep sense of how musical gestures are (and are not) supposed to go' (ibid.: 135). The section in question is admittedly quite abstract and difficult to relate to real-world experiences, such as the movements of our bodies or other naturally occurring rhythms and patterns, but the idea that we *cannot* hear ourselves or others move in this way and that there are certain ways in which musical gestures are supposed and not supposed to go appears dogmatic and narrow-minded. The assumptions here would be that a) musical gestures are directly representative of or congruent with physical movement and that b) all our physical movements take place within fairly narrow confines (regardless of our age, health or possible disability). In my view, both assumptions are unwarranted. While we have a strong tendency to relate musical movements to the movements of our own body, these relations may not be entirely congruent and linear, and we are able to relate quite abstract and irregular movements to our bodily experience. Furthermore, our bodies can move in a great variety of ways and we can imagine the movements of animals, plants and machines. As Cox puts it, '[t]o allow such music [Stockhausen's *Studie II*, on this occasion] to enter and affect us is to take a step, however modest, beyond ordinary human subjectivity and in the direction of the subjectivity of cybernetic organisms' (2016: 211). Even if our body has limitations, our imagination does not.

The pleasure of sections like the Babbitt lies in the attempt to experience different timescales, possibly simultaneously – potentially from the imperceptible movement of glaciers to the heartbeat of a hummingbird, and to try to experience duration without the grid of steady pulse. It is the music's sense of otherness, its resistance to be reduced to our sense of locomotion that makes it interesting.

Musical gestures in Mauricio Kagel's String Quartet II and Luciano Berio's *Sequenza V*

As I pointed out above, the specific contribution that theories of embodied cognition can make to music is by focusing on varying levels of congruence between

New music theatre and embodied cognition 281

what we hear and what we see, between the movements we imagine in response to the sounds we hear and the actual movements, or vice versa, between the imaginary music that would seem congruent with the movements and the actual sounds produced.

One way of doing so is by studying musical gestures. Jensenius *et al.* (2010: 23–24) have distinguished between the following gestures (understood as meaningful movements made by musicians while performing):[4]

- Sound-producing gestures (excitation and modification): e.g. string instrument r.h. excitation, l.h. modification
- Communicative gestures (performer–performer or performer–perceiver): performers signalling to other performers (incl. conducting?) and to audiences
- Sound-facilitating gestures: e.g. swaying motion in upper body
- Sound-accompanying gestures: dancing, foot-tapping, air guitar playing etc. (musicians and audiences).

These are not mutually exclusive; on the contrary, most gestures consist of several components, although one or two may predominate. Consider, for example, a violinist raising their bow in preparation for a stroke. This would be a sound-facilitating gesture, but it may also act as a communicative gesture in giving a cue to other performers or aiding synchronisation. Or, for a contrasting example, imagine a jazz pianist rocking their upper body during performance. This too is primarily a sound-facilitating gesture, and it too performs a communicative function vis-à-vis other musicians, but it also communicates with the audience, inviting entrainment (synchronised movement), which is an important feature of jazz culture and thus aiding a deeper immersion in the music. Finally, the movements can be seen as sound-accompanying, since not all body movements that musicians (particularly jazz and popular musicians) perform necessarily facilitate sound production. It isn't always easy (nor is it necessary) to say where one function ends and the other begins; what matters is that the categories are quite clear and distinct, although they are typically combined in practice. Jensenius *et al.* (2010: 25) have suggested a way of representing the different components of any gesture three-dimensionally (see Figure 12.1).

---

4 Other categorisations of musical gestures have been proposed, but the differences are relatively slight and the one presented here serves present purposes well. One problem with the concept of musical gesture is that a gesture is more than just a movement; instead it is a *meaningful* movement. Traditionally, we use the term more or less synonymously with 'hand signal'. Although some theorists have insisted on the importance of the semantic component, the term is often used for something more akin to movement or motion. In accordance with the source used, I refer to the categories listed by Jensenius *et al.* as 'gestures', although in my discussion I often use the categories as movements. Indeed, my own preferred term is 'action'. The advantage of that term over 'gesture' lies in its not suggesting a semantic function and its advantage over 'movement' lies in its intentional component: it allows us to focus on what musicians are (purposefully) *doing* rather than registering all (incidental) movements that may occur.

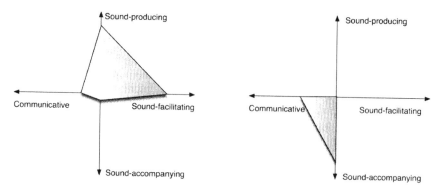

Figure 12.1 Dimension spaces illustrating the gestures of a musician (left) and dancer (right), in Jensenius *et al.* (2010: 25).

One limitation of the categorisation is that it only contains gestures performed in the course of sound-production. But of course musicians carry out a great number of actions that are part of the wider event of performance while not being part of sound-production. This includes setting-up and tuning (and retuning) of instruments and putting on or removing mutes (or other sound-modifying tools). These I call 'preparatory gestures'. Finally, there are gestures, which I call 'formal gestures', such as arranging sheet music and turning pages; entering the stage, adjusting seating (if used), instrument and posture; taking bows or otherwise acknowledging applause and the like. While the previous group of gestures listed by Jensenius *et al.* belong to the performance proper (in the sense of sound production), the latter characterise the frame, separated from the performance proper by a metaphysical divide. Although, as outlined, it is common for performance gestures to combine different functions, it is not normally possible to merge the performance with its framing devices: in other words, it is important to recognise that the filing of performers onto the stage and the tuning of instruments or page-turning are not part of the music concerned. This sounds so obvious that it may not seem necessary to mention it, but it is just the result of a convention. There is an interesting parallel to the role of the Kuroko (or Kōken) in Japanese Kabuki: they act as stagehands (aiding in scene and costume changes and the like) and are typically dressed in black, signifying that they are meant to be invisible and that their actions are not supposed to be part of the play (Salz 2016: 70; see also Kirby 1972: 3–4). But for an uninformed observer, their actions are just as much a part of the totality of the spectacle on stage as those performed by the (fully costumed) actors. Over and above this, the wider point here is that, perhaps not surprisingly, experimental forms have a tendency to overstep the assumed metaphysical divide. The amended table of movement types is presented in Table 12.1.

New music theatre and embodied cognition 283

Table 12.1 Amended table of movement types. The border between performance and frame is the 'metaphysical divide'

Sound-producing	
Excitation	
Modification	
Communicative	**Performance**
Performer–performer	
Performer–perceiver	
Sound-facilitating	
Sound-accompanying	
Preparatory	**Frame**
Formal	

An analysis of musical gesture in accordance with theories of embodied cognition is most usefully executed in experimental music theatre, more than in operatic forms. I have clarified the distinction between opera and experimental music theatre in an earlier publication:

> [E]xperimental music theatre refers to a type of performance in which theatrical actions are created by music making (playing of musical instruments or other sounding objects, singing). This form needs to be distinguished from other types of music theatre, such as opera and related genres, in which music accompanies theatrical action. There are two primary features that distinguish operatic forms, including modernist and avant-gardist ones, from [. . .] experimental music theatre [. . .] : first, a constitutive separation between stage and orchestra pit, which has been described as a metaphysical divide (Abbate 1996, 14–19) and, second, the union of singing and acting, whereby dramatic roles are enunciated through the singing voice. In experimental music theatre as defined here, by contrast, the physical and gestural elements inherent in the music making are the action, and there is no (actual or virtual) separation between stage and instrumental ensemble, nor are there dramatic roles.
>
> (Heile 2016: 335)

This is not to say that the categories of opera and experimental music theatre so defined contain all existing or possible music-theatrical forms: they are more ideal types than descriptive classes. It goes without saying that composers have increasingly explored the boundary between them or combined aspects of them. It is worth noting, however, that the first experiments in experimental music theatre by John Cage, and following him, Mauricio Kagel and others, were distinctly anti-operatic and 'purist' in developing the theatrical elements exclusively from musical gestures and avoiding dramatic roles. Combinations of operatic and

284   *Björn Heile*

experimental music theatre followed later; it is as if they could not have been conceived without the non-operatic mode introduced by experimental music theatre. This is particularly true of most British music theatre. Peter Maxwell Davies's *Eight Songs for a Mad King* (1969) is perhaps symptomatic. The eponymous king (George III) is represented by a baritone; the musicians are on the stage sitting in bird cages (although not all recent productions stick to this). In the composer's own words,

> [t]he flute, clarinet, violin and cello, as well as having their usual accompanimental functions in this work, also represent, on one level, the bullfinches the King was trying to teach to sing. The King has extended 'dialogues' with these players individually [. . .]. The percussion player stands for the King's 'keeper'.
>
> (Davies n.d.)

One of the strengths of the work is the way the musicians embody dramatic personae (if that's the term for bullfinches) and the music – or at least some of the music – is legitimated by the action. The problem (as I see it), however, lies in the phrase 'as well as having their usual accompanimental functions'. Much of the time the musicians might as well be in the pit, and the switching between the roles of dramatic persona and musical accompanist is somewhat awkward. Rather than overcoming Abbate's metaphysical divide, the dramaturgical conception of dialogues with individual instruments accompanied by the rest of the ensemble could be seen to accentuate it. To be fair, what makes the work fascinating is the play with different levels of reality and fantasy, since the performers can be seen to represent figments of George III's hallucinations, but that only partially addresses the dramaturgic problem of 'accompanying music'. Similarly, a lot of music theatre, particularly in the British tradition, has placed the ensemble on the stage but has shied away from drawing radical dramaturgical conclusions as regards the musicians' roles.

It is interesting in this context, too, that many composers gravitated towards more operatic conceptions of music theatre in later parts of their career. This is particularly true of Mauricio Kagel, who largely abandoned experimental music theatre after its apotheosis in *Staatstheater* (1970). In that respect, his *Quatre degrés* (1977), of which 'Dressur' is the most widely performed piece, is a last and somewhat half-hearted attempt, while his 'Theatrical Illusion' *Die Erschöpfung der Welt* (1978) and the 'Lieder-Opera' *Aus Deutschland* (1979) represent new, more operatic (or indeed oratorical) directions – although they were informed by his earlier experiments. Although there may have been institutional reasons for this, the title of the Chair he acceded to in 1974 – Professor for New Music Theatre (seemingly abandoning his earlier insistence on 'Instrumental Theatre') – is significant in this context too. This development is largely mirrored by Luciano Berio, György Ligeti, Harrison Birtwistle and others – even John Cage may be mentioned in this context, if we consider the trajectory from *Theatre Piece* (1960), though *Song Books* (1970) to the *Europera* series (1987–91), for example.

It seems obvious that a focus on gesture is most promising in cases where musicians' movements themselves are at the centre. However, related approaches

New music theatre and embodied cognition   285

can be promising for other genres, in which the stage action is coupled with and responds to music and vice versa, such as dance and opera. The justification for comparing experimental music theatre and opera despite their generic differences lies in the influence that the former arguably exerted on the latter. Although the 'constitutive separation between stage and orchestra pit' largely remains in place (despite its occasional transgression through on-stage music which has been a favourite operatic device from Monteverdi's *Orfeo* onwards) even in works by Sciarrino, Lachenmann and others listed above, the postdramatic emphasis on the non-hierarchic interplay between different media in these works owes a lot to the example set by experimental music theatre and other avant-gardist forms, even if lines of direct influence may sometimes be hard to draw.

The first example is Mauricio Kagel's String Quartet II (1967), specifically a video-recorded performance by the Montréal-based Quatuor Bozzini.[5] In the piece, Kagel plays with a variety of performing gestures, frequently overstepping the metaphysical divide between performance and frame. Indeed, the work begins with formal gestures: the musicians' entries and interactions while sitting down are carefully choreographed. This may not be obvious to an unsuspecting audience member, although the fussiness of the whole procedure is noticeable and would alert most people that something is 'not quite right'. Furthermore, that effect is heightened if the piece is performed after Kagel's String Quartet I, which is an option, since that work choreographs and dramatises the entry and sitting down of musicians even more elaborately: indeed, the whole piece revolves around the casual, individual entries of the musicians like for a rehearsal, and until the end they fail to reach their conventional positions (Zenck 2002; see also Heile 2006: 54–6). Indeed, Walter Levin, the first violinist of the LaSalle Quartet for whom the composition was written, has suggested that the piece is a 'satire' (*Persiflage*) of the Quartet and tailored to its idiosyncrasies, with the cellist, Jack Kirstein, occupying the chair normally reserved for the leader etc. (Spruytenburg 2011: 280–3).[6]

Among the most commonly used devices in String Quartet II are what I would like to call 'virtual preparatory actions': in other words, actions that are performed as if they were meant to have an effect on the sound result, although in actual fact their function is purely theatrical. Some of these also double up as sound-producing gestures. For instance, at one point, the cellist blows into the sound-holes of their instrument (see Example 12.1 for the score passage and Figure 12.2 for a screenshot). This comes across as the kind of thing musicians do to service their instrument; a parallel would be a brass player clearing out water – except that in this case, the action fulfils no discernible function. Instead, it makes an (albeit very faint) sound. So, is the purpose of the action the production of that sound, is it to clean the instrument, or is it essentially an *acte gratuit*? As audience members, we

---

5 I am very grateful to the Bozzini Quartet for sharing this video with me, which is currently not publicly available.

6 I would like to thank Clemens Merkel for alerting me to this book and providing me with a scanned copy of the relevant section.

286 Björn Heile

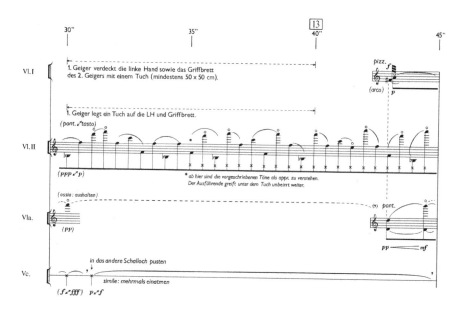

Example 12.1 Mauricio Kagel, String Quartet II, rehearsal number 13, by kind permission of Universal Edition. Translation of instructions: first violin – '1st violin covers the left hand and fingerboard of the 2nd violin with a cloth (at least 50 x 50 cm)'; second violin – '1st violin lays a cloth on LH and fingerboard [...] from here on the prescribed pitches should be regarded as approximate. The performer goes on playing, unperturbed, beneath the cloth'; cello – 'blow into other sound hole [...] simile: breathe in several times'.

cannot be sure, but at the same time, the framing of musical performance requires us to attribute a definitive purpose to every action. After all, it is part of the 'standard protocol' for performance of composed music that any action performed must contribute to the music played, either directly (through sound production) or indirectly (by aiding or preparing for sound production).

The most conspicuous virtual preparatory action consists of the cellist holding their instrument upside down, with the scroll placed on the floor and the spike held aloft. This appears like some kind of in-joke about extended techniques: as the most absurd thing that could be done. And of course, there isn't really any sound-producing action that is enabled or facilitated in this way. Accordingly, the instrument is only played very briefly like this. It would appear as if the performer has antagonised the other players, one of whom moves the cellist's bow from the strings with their own bow – with which the piece ends.

Another very interesting group of actions involves a cloth, which is first placed across the strings of the second violin as a virtual preparatory and sound-modifying action, before it is dropped to the floor in a virtual communicative

New music theatre and embodied cognition   287

Figure 12.2 The Bozzini Quartet during performance of Mauricio Kagel's String Quartet II, around rehearsal number 13.

gesture (see Example 12.1 and Figure 12.2 for the placing of the cloth on the violin and Example 12.2 and Figure 12.3 for its dropping). The moment it falls, a starkly contrasting section in the music starts, so it seems as if the – deliberate – dropping of the cloth is employed as a signal (an obviously absurdly elaborate and impractical one) or, potentially, as if the – accidental – dropping of the cloth somehow changes the nature of the music.[7] Sound-producing gestures are likewise defamiliarised in various ways, with serrated wooden staffs being used as bows and drumming with fingers on strings (excitation) and the use of Sellotape and a coin (modification). In this way, there is another level of non-congruence between what is heard and what is seen; or indeed, the formation of clear expectations is prevented from the start: how can we have any idea what a violin played by serrated wooden staffs sounds like?

Overall, the piece subverts the customary functions of performing gestures and thereby frequently undermines congruence between sound and movement, playing games with our motor imagery. Nothing is quite what it seems: the sound produced is rarely what we expect to hear and the musicians' actions do not have the purpose they suggest (or combine different purposes in bewildering ways)

7 Walter Levin has explained this passage thus: 'In the course of the piece, Henry Meyer [second violinist of the LaSalle Quartet] plays a wonderful melody [*Kantilene*], but I take a towel to cover his fingers and the violin because I don't want to hear it, but he continues playing' (Spruytenburg 2011: 281).

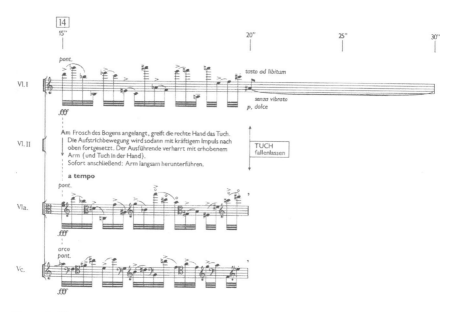

Example 12.2 Mauricio Kagel, String Quartet II, rehearsal number 14, by kind permission of Universal Edition. Translation of instructions: viola – 'Having got to the nut of the bow, the right hand grips the cloth. The upbow movement is then vigorously continued with an upward thrust. The performer 'freezes', with arm raised (and the cloth in his [sic] hand). Immediately afterwards: bring arm down slowly. [. . .] let CLOTH drop.'

Figure 12.3 The Bozzini Quartet during performance of Mauricio Kagel's String Quartet II, around rehearsal number 14.

New music theatre and embodied cognition 289

or the consequences we expect. In this way, the establishment of 'stable performance', in which the musicians play their instruments in more or less customary fashion, producing more or less the results we would expect, is constantly undermined in different ways – whether the gestures performed subvert what I above called the standard protocol or whether they produce sounds that appear non-congruent with the actions performed. Actions such as those involving the handkerchief, holding the cello upside down or the elaborate sitting-down ritual performed go beyond what is necessary for musical performance (although they build on that) and thereby 'theatricalise' the performance. Furthermore, the way many of the gestures such as the actions involving the cloth and, to an extent, holding the cello upside down can be understood both functionally as performing gestures and at the same time as some kind of dream-like and at the same time deeply unsettling surreal theatre can be encapsulated with the term 'metaxis' – 'a state of in-between-ness and a continual process of mediation between two states (Linds 2006, 114)' (Heile 2016: 347). In terms of theories of embodied cognition, it is the non-congruence between performing gesture and sonic result that leads to the 'doubleness' in our perception characteristic of metaxis.

My second example is Luciano Berio's *Sequenza V* for Trombone Solo (1966). It is a fairly well-known, frequently played piece, and a significant number of performances can be found on online sharing sites such as YouTube. In his programme note, Berio has related the composition to the clown Grock. The score specifies a number of actions to be performed by the player, the costume (in the most general terms), and the overall style:

> Walking on the stage and during the performance of section A the performer (white tie, spot from above etc.) strikes the poses of a variety showman about to sing an old favorite. Inspired, he extends his arms, he raises or lowers his instrument [indicated in the notation itself] with movements which should appear spontaneous, he hesitates. Just before section B he utters a bewildered 'why?' and sits down without pausing. He must perform section B as though rehearsing in an empty hall.
>
> (Berio 1968)

Although that is not sanctioned by the score, a performance tradition has arisen whereby the piece is played in clown costume (Webb 2007; cf. also Halfyard 2007).[8] There is an interesting parallel here with Mauricio Kagel's *Match* (1964) for Three Players (two cellists and a percussionist), with which *Sequenza V* shares a number of aspects, and which has similarly been performed by costumed players – the two cellists as tennis players and the percussionist as umpire.

The (admittedly far from clear) performance instructions are interpreted in diverse ways by performers, from nearly straight concert performances to overt clowning. Unfortunately, very few recent performers appear to have taken the

---

8 Abbie Conant has set up a very useful website presenting materials on *Sequenza V*, including videos of Grock in performance: www.osborne-conant.org/Grock.htm (accessed 28 June 2017).

trouble to research Grock's persona, costume and performance style, instead opting for a fairly generic idea of 'clowning' that, furthermore, is probably of rather more recent origin (possibly based on memories of the performers' own childhood) than Grock's heyday during the 1920s and '30s (the 'classic' performances of Dempster, Globokar and Sluchin do not currently seem to be available on video). Although Grock did not shy away from fairly broad comedy, many of his routines and his general persona were quite subtle and understated, and much of his trademark style is reflected in Berio's work. An exception among recent performers who seems to have based their interpretation on a study of Grock's work is Christian Lindberg, whose attire and performance style seem more 'authentic', although the heavy use of makeup around the eyes is not quite accurate (Grock usually wore makeup around the mouth but less around the eyes).[9]

If a costume is worn, the performance comes close to the very definition of 'non-matrixed representation' according to Kirby (1972: 4–5). As he explains, like 'non-matrixed performance' this form of performance does not involve acting in the sense of impersonation, but the performer is placed in a representational framework through external features, such as costume or stage décor. This is exactly what happens in *Sequenza V* if a clown costume is worn, as a consequence of which the whole performance will be viewed differently. This representational framework is heightened by a number of actions the player has to perform. As in Kagel's String Quartet II, some of these actions masquerade as performance gestures, even though they don't fulfil any strictly musical function and in some cases actually create significant additional difficulties. The first of these are formal gestures: the walking onto the stage and striking of poses mentioned in the preface to the score. While some of these actions, such as walking onto the stage, appear to frame the performance, others, such as the raising and lowering of the instrument, uttering of the word 'why?' (followed by a baleful pedal note B♭) and sitting down are part of it; when the poses are to be struck is unclear: there doesn't seem to be any opportunity for this during the performance itself. As for section B, although the character of the music is sharply contrasting – depressive as opposed to the mania of section A – and seated playing is certainly unusual for a solo piece for trombone, it is not clear how a performer can convey the impression of rehearsing in an empty hall, particularly since the musical material is not overly reminiscent of rehearsals and avoids obvious references such as repeated passages, scales or arpeggios.

Another important category is the use of virtual facilitating gestures, in particular exaggerated vertical swaying of the instrument (the raising and lowering of the instrument mentioned in the preface). The most obvious connections to the trickery associated with clowning (and indeed Grock's particular type of humour) go further in externalising the mechanism underlying MMI. At several points, the trombonist visibly prepares for a note only to fall silent; at others, sounds are made seemingly invisibly taking audiences by surprise. These musical jokes are

---

9 Lindberg's performance is available here: www.youtube.com/watch?v=OnfApTtzJmk (accessed 28 June 2017).

obviously aided by the inherent humour of the trombone, which, with its curious shape, seemingly obvious but often misleading mechanism (whereby pitch seems to be controlled by the slide although embouchure is equally important) and propensity for glissandi, is an ideal clown instrument (although it was rarely if ever played by Grock). At other moments, the performer mimics the instrument vocally, changing between sung and played notes so rapidly that it can be hard to distinguish between them. Finally, in a virtuosic passage preceding the apparent breakdown following the utterance of 'why?', what we hear and what we see becomes less and less congruent, as the performer frantically moves the slide up and down, while producing little sound.

In addition, there are virtual communicating gestures. Before imitating the trombone sound vocally, the performer is to move his or her head sideways rapidly. This is of course inaudible and, of all the performances I have seen, only Dave Day carries out the score's instructions.[10] The effect is slightly unsettling: there is no way the gesture can be sound-producing or -facilitating, so, when interpreting it in the framework of musical performance, we can only understand it as communicative – but of what and to whom? On a higher level, the gesture adds to the frantic nature of the performance in the first section (A) of the piece, with the performer visibly and audibly struggling with their instrument and all the different tasks assigned to them – walking, playing, singing, moving the instrument up and down, moving the head.

As has been seen, like Kagel's String Quartet II, *Sequenza V* plays with the customary function of musical gestures, and, like Kagel's *Match*, it also involves simple representation: where *Match* assigns the performers the roles of tennis players and umpire respectively, the reference to Grock establishes a representational framework, even though the primary level of musical performance is never in doubt. In both pieces, this representational framework is subtly confirmed by a number of musical elements and gestures that are difficult to reconcile with 'straight' musical performance, but, again, these are relatively subtle and mostly confined to the beginning. What is perhaps most striking about the Berio is how the element of clowning is mostly represented through non-congruence between sound and movement, with movements that do not result in sound and sounds that do not seem to be the result of movement. It is our strong expectations of congruence between these levels that makes the piece effective, if not as straightforward musical humour, then as an affectionate if unsettling tribute to Grock and other musical clowns.

Conclusion

The categorisation of musical gestures by Jensenius *et al.* or my extension of their taxonomy can aid the analysis of the actions in performances of experimental

10 Day's performance is available here: www.youtube.com/watch?v=ZqlUhN7TbAk&spfreload=10 (accessed 23 June 2017). Although at times very effective, the performance is slightly undermined by overly extrovert clowning and a similarly excessive costume, contrasting with Grock's rather more subtle art.

292 *Björn Heile*

music theatre, facilitating a distinction between actions that serve a conventional musical purpose and those that have a primarily theatrical function. More to the point, it can differentiate the different elements in actions that serve dual purposes and show how theatrical gestures are based on virtual sound-facilitating gestures, such as the swaying of the trombone in Berio's *Sequenza V*; virtual preparatory actions, such as the blowing of the cello's sound holes in Kagel's String Quartet II; or virtual communicative actions, such as the turning of the head in the Berio or the falling cloth in the Kagel. It is the doubleness of these elements – their masquerading as performance elements when they're clearly something else – that, in earlier work, I explained with the term 'metaxis'.

These elements also enable a mobilisation of theories of embodied cognition. What pieces such as those by Berio and Kagel play on is the partial congruence between sound and its response, what is seen and what is heard, what is real and what is imaginary. Seen from this perspective, what Berio and Kagel play with is motor mimetic imagery: the sonic expectations we have if we see certain movements being performed or the movements we want to perform ourselves or see being embodied on hearing certain sounds. The analyses here are offered as preliminary approaches. Future work may have to consider more precise ways of analysing movement than the categorisation of musical gestures, such as Labanotation or motiongrams (Jensenius 2012). Even the methods and tools developed in sports and exercise science may be useful for this purpose.

While these approaches have particular potential for experimental music theatre, specifically based on instrumental performances, another promising approach to the study of more operatic traditions of new music theatre would consist of analysing the opportunities for identification based on MMI proffered by the human voice. Combining these approaches, on the basis of theories of embodied cognition, would offer a rich toolkit for the investigation of a great variety of work within new music theatre.

References

Antokoletz, Elliot (2004), *Musical Symbolism in the Operas of Debussy and Bartok*, Oxford: Oxford University Press.

Berio, Luciano (1968), *Sequenza V, for Trombone Solo*, London: Universal Edition.

Bull, Michael (2007), *Sound Moves: IPod Culture and Urban Experience*, London: Routledge.

Cook, Nicholas (1998), *Analysing Musical Multimedia*, Oxford: Clarendon Press.

Cook, Nicholas (2015), 'Seeing sounds, hearing images: listening outside the modernist box', in Gianmario Borio (ed.), *Musical Listening in the Age of Technological Reproduction*, Farnham, UK: Ashgate, pp. 185–202.

Cooper, F. S., A. M. Liberman, D. P. Shankweiler and M. Studdert-Kennedy (1967), 'Perception of the speech code', *Psychological Review*, 74/6, pp. 431–61.

Cox, Arnie (2016), *Music and Embodied Cognition: Listening, Moving, Feeling, and Thinking*, Bloomington, IN: Indiana University Press.

Davies, Peter Maxwell (n.d.), 'Eight Songs for a Mad King: Work Detail', www.maxopus.com/work_detail.aspx?key=2 (accessed 4 September 2017).

New music theatre and embodied cognition 293

Galantucci, Bruno, Carol A. Fowler and M. T. Turvey (2006), 'The motor theory of speech perception reviewed', *Psychonomic Bulletin & Review*, 13/3, pp. 361–77.

Godøy, Rolf Inge (2013), 'Coarticulated gestural-sonic objects in music', in Elaine King and Anthony Gritten (eds), *New Perspectives on Music and Gesture*, Farnham, UK: Ashgate, pp. 67–82.

Halfyard, Janet K. (2007), *Berio's Sequenzas: Essays on Performance, Composition and Analysis*, Aldershot, UK: Ashgate.

Heile, Björn (2006), *The Music of Mauricio Kagel*, Aldershot, UK: Ashgate.

Heile, Björn (2016), 'Towards a theory of experimental music theatre: "showing doing", "non-matrixed performance" and "metaxis"', in Yael Kaduri (ed.), *The Oxford Handbook of Sound and Image in Western Art*, Oxford: Oxford University Press, pp. 335–55.

Jensenius, Alexander Refsum (2012), 'Some video abstraction techniques for displaying body movement in analysis and performance', *Leonardo*, 46/1, pp. 53–60.

Jensenius, Alexander Refsum, Marcelo M. Wanderley, Rolf Inge Godøy and Marc Leman (2010), 'Musical gestures: concepts and methods in research', in Rolf Inge Godøy and Marc Leman (eds), *Musical Gestures: Sound, Movement, and Meaning*, London: Routledge, pp. 12–35.

Kirby, Michael (1972), 'On acting and not-acting', *The Drama Review: TDR*, 16/1, p. 3.

Lehmann, Hans-Thies (2006), *Postdramatic Theatre*, London: Routledge.

London, Justin (2006), 'Musical rhythm: motion, pace and gesture', in Elaine King and Anthony Gritten (eds), *Music and Gesture*, Aldershot, UK: Ashgate, pp. 126–41.

Page, Ruth (2009), *New Perspectives on Narrative and Multimodality*, London: Routledge.

Rebstock, Matthias and David Roesner (eds) (2012), *Composed Theatre: Aesthetics, Practices, Processes*, London: Intellect Books.

Salz, Jonah (2016), 'Traditional Japanese theatre', in Siyuan Liu (ed.), *Routledge Handbook of Asian Theatre*, London: Routledge, pp. 51–70.

Shaw-Miller, Simon (2004), *Visible Deeds of Music: Art and Music from Wagner to Cage*. New Haven, CT: Yale University Press.

Sindoni, Maria Grazia, Janina Wildfeuer and Kay O'Halloran (2016), *Mapping Multimodal Performance Studies*, London: Routledge.

Spruytenburg, Robert (2011), *Das LaSalle-Quartett: Gespräche mit Walter Levin*, Munich: edition text + kritik.

Trevarthen, Colwyn, Jonathan Delafield-Butt and Benj Schögler (2013), 'Psychobiology of musical gesture: innate rhythm, harmony and melody', in Elaine King and Anthony Gritten (eds), *New Perspectives on Music and Gesture*, Farnham, UK: Ashgate, pp. 11–43.

Webb, Barrie (2007), 'Performing Berio's Sequenza V', *Contemporary Music Review* 26/2, pp. 207–18.

Zenck, Martin (2002), 'Entgrenzungen der Gattungen Kammermusik und Szene in Werken von Michael von Biel, Mauricio Kagel, Bernd Alois Zimmermann Und Luigi Nono', in Christoph-Hellmut Mahling and Christina Pfarr (eds), *Musiktheater Im Spannungsfeld Zwischen Tradition Und Experiment: 1960 Bis 1980*, Tutzing: Hans Schneider, pp. 123–42.

13 Analysing new music theatre

Theme and variations (from a multimedia perspective)

Angela Ida De Benedictis

I would like to begin my contribution with a premise that is terminological in nature (which, however, also ends up relating to more methodological aspects). I am well aware of the difficulty inherent in wanting to define 'new music theatre'. Moreover, it is not a coincidence that almost all the studies on the experimental theatre of the second half of the twentieth century begin by avowing a 'lack of categorization and [a] lack of definition', or by admitting that 'it is not easy to put [it] in a labeled box' (Salzman and Desi 2008: vii). In the present context, I would like to eliminate this problem at its root, setting aside what seem to be the four questions most debated by scholars:

1   'what is and what is not theatre?'
2   'are definitions of genre still possible in the realm of experimental theatre?'
3   'can an instrumental passage be considered theater?', and, finally
4   'what is the difference between musical theatre and musical action?'.[1]

In reflecting on the issues tied to the act of 'analysing new music theatre', I prefer to maintain the distinction between an 'implicit acoustic dramaturgy' (which encompasses also a good part of the instrumental production of the second half of the twentieth century), and an 'explicit theatrical dimension' that necessarily requires the mediation of a physical location designated for the enactment. Thus, in speaking about 'music theatre' I will refer unambiguously to 'stage works' that:

a)   presuppose a scenic, spatial, and visible dimension that interacts with the music, and
b)   in which the audience has a fixed (albeit not precise) constitutive role in the chain developing the 'theatre meaning'.[2]

I will speak, that is, in reference to *forms of representation* in which more than one acoustic (musical, verbal, etc.) and visible (movable scenes, given locations,

---

1   See among others Adlington 2005: 227ff.
2   See Rozik 2008, especially p. 8: 'theatre occurs when a person A *represents* X while S looks on', an assumption based on Erika Fischer-Lichte's theory.

Analysing new music theatre   295

costumes, gestures, movements, postures, projections, etc.) component or sign act simultaneously. In other words, I will speak of a heterogeneous collection of signs ('plurisignation'; see Rozik 2008: 8) in the very artefact in which (to cite Berio) a 'musical drama – that is, the form of the musical processes – can begin again to identify itself with scenic dramaturgy – that is, with the form of "representational" processes and behaviors' (Berio 1980, in Maurizi 2004: 27).

From this perspective, it matters little that we can recognize in these artefacts direct descendants or clear juxtapositions with regards to an 'operatic form', whether they be narrative or anti-narrative, linear or non-linear, and so on. Nor is it decisive whether the 'dramatic roles are enunciated through the singing voice' (Heile 2016: 335), or are acted in the scene by mimes or actors, or else are completely absent. What interests me most here is to reflect on the analytical issues arising from forms of experimental musical theatre in which, in the *final staged work*, there should be no precise hierarchies between the acoustic and visible dimensions, and in which the 'perceptive strategies'[3] may not necessarily give priority to the music.

This premise is necessary because, from an analytical standpoint, the difficulties encountered when one speaks of 'new music theatre' concern, after all, the existence of a stage and of a visible dimension that is, as a whole, a 'meaningful structural element' (Berio 1967: 11). Indeed, it is by reflecting on the artistic forms where sounds, actions and scenic-spatial dimensions converge that a sort of inherent contradiction comes to the fore in almost all the analyses I have consulted – and, I add, also in many of those I myself have conducted thus far. Whether it be by choice or by necessity, all these analyses are limited, in fact, nearly indiscriminately to single components or to the music alone.[4] These analyses can be dedicated to the compositional structure, to the creation, to the compositional process, to the music/text relationship, to the reception history. They can be analyses based on historical-documentary facts that precede the composition or that follow the premiere. They can take into consideration possible changes introduced by the author in the compositional process or between one performance and the next. They can be dedicated to the peculiarities of the stage-technical solutions of a specific performance or to the relationships between the composer and various collaborators. Further, they can investigate the impact of the first performance, or of subsequent restagings through the lens of contemporary criticism.[5] Or, they can combine a few of these typologies. Rarely, however, does one end up analysing the work as a 'unified whole', which is to say beginning with the 'final staged product' in order to analyse the dimension of the performance understood as a complex whole (as an acoustic and visible *text* in itself), rather than as a plurality of single structural components (which may be analysable on their own regardless

---

3 See in this connection Hans-Thies Lehmann, quoted in Heile 2016: 337.
4 Numerous examples will be found in the list of references accompanying other chapters in this volume.
5 In such cases it may happen that the chronological distance is levelled or ignored, thus causing the analytical approach to be uncritical.

296   *Angela Ida De Benedictis*

of an actual onstage destination). Despite the complexity, involving ever more multimedia, that musical theatre reached in the second half of the twentieth century, the 'theatrical fact' (the staged work) still struggles to be understood as a starting point (a *cause*) of an analytical process and not as a sum (*effect*) of disparate analyses at various levels, bundled together.[6]

It is clear that, with such premises, terminological differences take on little importance. In defining (and analysing) new music theatre, to me the only element that assumes undisputed priority is the one regarding the 'creative intentionality' of the author (or authors). I believe, in other words, that in approaching a musical work hermeneutically, and in interpreting its greater or lesser efficacy in terms of dramatic or *theatrical* performance, the dividing line in the choice of analytical instruments and methods should depend above all on the evaluation of the *destination* intended by the author(s).[7] The interrogation of the documents used for analysis, that is, should necessarily be distinguished according to whether one speaks of works destined to be performed in concerts, or mediated by a *stage* (irrespective of the greater or lesser conventionality of the representational space). Beyond the catchphrases used by the composers themselves (one thinks of Donatoni when he stated that he would not write for theatre, since 'everything is theatre'), or of interpretative assumptions – sometimes banal, sometimes more articulated – that the music of Cage is 'always theatre', just as are likewise the *Sequenze* of Berio or a quartet of Kagel, the only fact that can help in making some distinctions is precisely the intentionality of the author with regards to an artefact that is destined for a specific *medium*: the theatrical one. This is a medium that can assume a thousand forms, real or imaginary, but that is always 'acted' and reconstructed mentally, by association, by the audience. One might object that, in some analyses devoted to music in which the performers' 'action' contributes as much as the sound of their instruments to build a specific 'dramaturgy', it was nevertheless the author's intention to confer those works with some further metaphors of meaning in a theatrical sense.[8] This objection confirms the peculiarity and difficulty of analyses aimed at forms of stage representation in which the intentionality of the composer already contains, in a nutshell, the awareness of an intention (often conflicting) with other levels of authorship.

Eric Salzman and Thomas Desi correctly revealed the complexity of the various steps that a message devised by an author must take on its way *towards* the stage (Salzman and Desi 2008). Figure 13.1a shows the scheme they propose in

---

6 Moreover, when an interpretation of the 'whole' is reached, it remains mostly in the field of music criticism. About the concept of 'performance' as a whole see also Schechner 2001, especially p. 4: 'The literary, dramatic [musical] text is but one part of a complex whole that includes mise-en-scène, acting styles, stage design and technology, and directing theory.'

7 I shall not discuss in this context aspects related to the well-known debate on the 'intentional fallacy', which would raise questions that are not directly relevant to the present essay.

8 This objection confirms my premise (discussed further below) that the analysis of 'staged music' often implies a confusion between 'gesture' and 'theatricality' – very different concepts that sometimes are erroneously employed as synonyms.

order to synthesize this path from the intentionality of the composer to the arrival of the 'message meaning' with the audience.[9] The system is irreproachable, and yet in my view it fails to grasp one key aspect of the 'new music theatre', one that directly influences (and limits) all analytical approaches. This is because the intentionality of the author, as already mentioned, must be reinterpreted and projected into a final product in which more than one intentionality combine. Indeed, as shown in Figure 13.1b, in the final work one can recognize a *cluster* of different intentionalities, at times already expected in the preparatory phases of the theatrical project (this, for example, is the case of works such as *Esposizione* by Berio-Sanguineti-Halprin, discussed later). Or, as in Figure 13.1c (which outlines the most common case), one can see a stratification of different authorial contributions that end up combining in the various phases of the staging, in most cases the cause of conflict or of changes to the work made while underway or between one staging and another.[10]

By speaking of definitions of genre and of specificity of 'message' regarding works of new music theatre, we are already accomplishing an analytical discourse, or rather, one that is meta-analytical. This is a discourse that permits us to recognize, in the many studies of the theatre of the second half of the twentieth century, the custom of giving priority to the individuation of genres, categories,

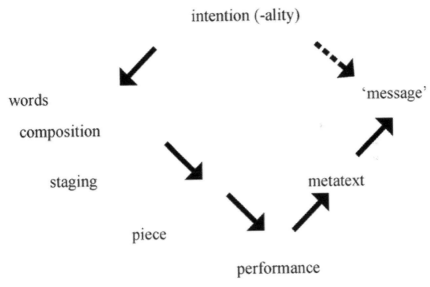

The message an author wants to pass on is many steps away.

Figure 13.1a Diagram from Salzman and Desi 2008: 322.

---

9 Salzman and Desi 2008: 322. In Figures 13.1b and 13.1c I freely modify this model.
10 'Composer/author', in their turn, can be two distinct persons, if the composer is not the author of the text (put another way: when he or she is his or her own librettist).

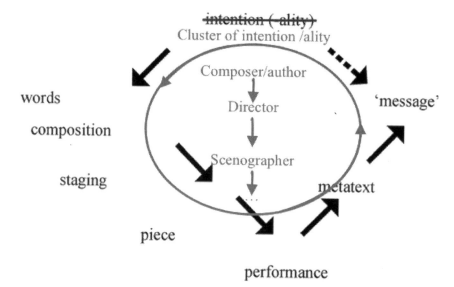

The message ~~an author~~ many authors want to pass on is many steps away.

Figure 13.1b 1st variation.

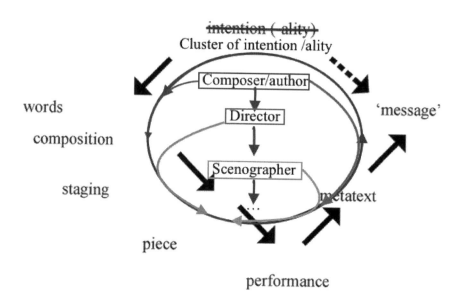

The message an author wants to pass on is many steps away.
and other people involved in the staging

Figure 13.1c 2nd variation.

Analysing new music theatre 299

classes or sub-classes in the most variegated repertoire, each one recognizing in a given work or in a given composer a more or less marked level of 'theatricality'. Or else, it permits us to analyse single steps of the compositional process, or single parts of the established work(s), often borrowing analytical approaches from the most diverse disciplines (sometimes of very little pertinence to music). Not infrequently, one witnesses a unique equation: if one speaks of musical structure, one does not speak of the scenic element; and conversely, if one speaks of the scenic element, one does not speak of the musical structure. The possible approaches are so manifold that Eric Salzman and Thomas Desi (2008: 310) have come to pose the question: 'What is analysis good for?' It is unfortunate that, besides hinting at the necessity of arriving at a method that calls for a 'dense net of cross-references', in fact they do not end up giving convincing answers.

Maybe, instead of asking oneself 'which analyses should be used', the question to pose should start from a more basic 'what are we talking about when we talk about analysis of new music theatre?'[11] This question, on closer inspection, was already posed in 1983 by Carl Dahlhaus in reference to the contemporary theatre clearly derived from opera. In order to disentangle himself from the heterogeneity of contemporary productions, he proposed to group the works of the twentieth century in four 'trends', with the full awareness that the 'operation [. . .] comprises in itself some violence', but nevertheless glimpsing in this criterion a 'most useful [. . .] analytical starting point' (Dahlhaus 1983: 149). The proposed groupings followed the evaluation of four points of view:

1   the relationship that the new theatrical productions had with traditional operatic genres;
2   whether they did or did not follow aesthetic and technical-compositional postulates of the musical avant-garde;
3   the way in which the authors approached the problem of the libretto;
4   whether the new productions supported or rejected the tendencies of director's theatre (Regietheater).

This proposal, already barely adaptable to the theatre of the early twentieth century, reveals itself to be completely unsuitable for the works realized between the 1950s and 1970s, even if we were willing to expand or modify the grouping criteria. This is because each of these points, even the fourth one, inevitably leads one to analyses directed 'to the form and musical processes', and consequently far from an objective interpretation of what Berio called the 'representational behaviors' (Berio 1980, in Maurizi 2004: 27).

Encountering the name of Dahlhaus, one might think that, from 1983 to now, nearly forty years of detailed study and researches have passed, sprinkled with new publications and numerous analytical proposals. Nonetheless, this simple consideration leads us to observe a subtle inconsistency. Despite the evident

11   This question has nothing to do with the problematic issue of the 'scientific validity of the analysis' (Cook 1987; cited in Salzman and Desi 2008: 314).

300   *Angela Ida De Benedictis*

inadequacy of these four categories, in the end almost all of the analyses dedicated to the musical theatre of the 1950s–1970s can be framed within these categories (sometimes even turning the assumptions of Dahlhaus into a negative formulation). The examples are numerous and range from analyses that investigated the intersections with European and non-European avant-garde theatre (from Grotowski to the Living Theatre, to the Open Theater, and so on), to those that analysed the collaboration with painters and new artistic tendencies (Nono-Vedova, Clementi-Perilli, Maderna-*pop art*, and so on). Other examples range from investigations aimed at the recognition of forms of interaction and/or of fusion with new or different musical expressions such as jazz, popular music, folk or ethnic music (as in some studies dedicated to Berio's *Allez-hop*, or to the theatre of Kagel, Nono, Maderna, to name but a few), to reflections on the influence and/or the consequences of a political *engagement* more or less reflected in the use of certain linguistic choices (a topic that immediately brings to mind notably some analyses of Nono's experimental theatre, but also certain studies on Manzoni, on Maderna's *Hyperion*, or Guaccero's *Scene del potere*, and so on). There are even cases of analyses directed at the observation of formulae of mannerism or 'aestheticising attitudes' (as in the theatre of Bussotti), or of aleatory formulae, that is to say the study of the 'virtualities' and of the dramatic potentials that arise when parts or sections of works are intentionally left open by the author (and, again, Maderna's name returns). This medley on the various analytical levels can continue even to include studies on the interferences with the comic genre or with the theatre of the absurd (Ligeti); or it could include analyses that focus on the enlargement of the scenic space thanks to the use of electro-acoustic technology and of projections, or, alternatively, on the definitive dissolution of scenic spaces, obtained in the name of a reversal between the internal and external spaces of the theatre (the premiere of Berio's *Esposizione* could be mentioned here). By extension, it is even possible to fit into one of the categories proposed by Dahlhaus those analyses in which it is observed that the action-performance sometimes overruns into the happening, or those in which the same concept of 'gesture' often becomes a synonym of 'theatricality'.[12]

Wishing to reflect on some short-circuits implicit in these categories, or on facts that are often missing in the analyses dedicated to forms of experimental music theatre, one may begin by considering the importance, for some composers, of experiences realized in contexts different from that of a traditional 'stage'. For many, for example, the experience of the radio and later the television served as a 'trigger' for the imagination and for experimentation with new expressive-dramatic formulae, transported (or applied) only subsequently in a more traditional scenic space. Among the various examples that might be cited, I would like to recall those of Berio and Maderna: for both, analyses carried out on the theatrical

---

12 See note 8. Some other analyses, based on the 'szenischen Verstehens' theorized by the psychoanalyst Alfred Lorenzer (see Heilgendorff 2002) deserve to be debated in another context. They are in fact aimed at the perceptive level and at 'decoding' thought processes, rather than explaining the 'musical object' itself.

Analysing new music theatre 301

works composed between the 1960s and 1970s (*Passaggio, Esposizione, Opera* for Berio; *Hyperion* and *Satyricon* for Maderna) are misleading or partial if one does not expand the interpretative and analytical view to a perspective of *cross-mediality*, one that also makes reference to the composers' other multimedia or audiovisual experiences of the same years, which often prepared the ground or constituted the basis for the experimentation of the most successful expedients of their musical theatre.[13] This aspect will be further discussed later in the text. First, I would like to take on that which, for me, is the most evident short circuit in analyses dedicated to avant-garde theatre, one concerning the predominance of investigations relating to the 'technical-compositional' level and to the observation of the adherence (or non-adherence) to what Dahlhaus calls the 'aesthetic postulates of the musical avant-garde' (Dahlhaus 1983: 149). The viewpoint of compositional technique often ends up acquiring a central importance in analyses dedicated to musical theatre, sometimes far exceeding reflection on the scenic destination of those composed musical structures, composed in view of a stage performance in a specific space, involving live singers, actors, mimes, instruments and so on. Even in the description of the conference session at which I offered a first version of the present thoughts, the mention of 'serial or parametrical thought' stood central, alongside the question of whether 'For those [composers] accustomed to serial or parametrical thought, the representational domain could in itself be problematic for its introduction of levels of extra-musical association'.

As regards analyses of new music theatre, the question of compositional technique needs, in my opinion, to be downsized or to be seen as *one* component within an analytical process which, as a consequence of the interaction of more than one level of intentionality beyond that of the composer, should be 'multi-layered,' if not interdisciplinary.[14] By this I do not wish to negate the importance of the musical style, or of the degree of 'novelty in the compositional language' that grounds the work, especially if the linguistic register then has a direct consequence at the level of the representation of characters or scenic situations.[15] What I would like to observe, however, is that the compositional techniques and their degree of experimental originality do not suffice, on their own, to establish the success or to ratify the innovative capability of the *stage work* as a whole. The case of *Intolleranza 1960* by Nono is, from this perspective, highly instructive: at the beginning of the 1960s, few works could boast a more innovative musical

---

13 Among the compositions for radio or television that influenced subsequent stage works in different ways, we could recall, among other examples, Berio's radio play *Il malato immaginario* (1973, then abridged and revised in the radio-opera *Diario immaginario*, 1975); his radiophonic documentary *A-Ronne* (1974), and the diaporama work *La voix des voies* (1977); and Maderna's radio dramas *Il mio cuore è nel sud* (1950) and *Don Perlimplin* (1961), or his television-opera *From A to Z* (1969).

14 A similar approach may be found in Beard 2012; see especially p. 1: 'the stage works [...] demand interpretation from multiple, inter-disciplinary perspectives'.

15 A different case is when the analysis of the musical structure of a stage work is meant as a more general or comparative investigation of the compositional techniques used by a composer in different works at a given time.

302 *Angela Ida De Benedictis*

language; however, few works could boast a more evident dramaturgical and scenic failure.[16] A failure not avoided, I might add, by the equally innovative staging and scenographic set-up devised by Kašlik, Svoboda and Vedova. Just as the scenic/dramaturgic result cannot be evaluated only by the measure of musical technique, so too the very concepts of new vocality, of diversification or poly-stratification of the sound texture – often at the heart of many analyses – do not suffice to give justice to an overall evaluation of the works. When one speaks of new music theatre, in short, one cannot refer only to the 'new music', but also, necessarily to a 'new theatre'. As obvious as this simple observation may sound, we must not forget that in new music theatre the music gradually stops being the structural element *par excellence*. The interaction with other 'forming agents' (direction, scenography, and so on) acquires ever more importance and often the role of the director or of the choreographer, far from being secondary, becomes equal to that of the composer (on this point see also Salzman and Desi 2008: 96–102).

In this context, the numerous analyses dedicated to the compositional process and to the genesis of the works deserve a separate discussion. Whoever has analysed a work by evaluating its premises and results through the study of its sketches can subscribe to David Beard's observation in the opening section of his volume on the theatre of Birtwistle:

> as ideas evolve, from the composer's musical sketches to the final production, multiple meanings accrue that are particular to each drama. Original intentions and priorities change, become compromised [. . .], leading to tensions and contradictions that are instructive and distinctive to each work.
>
> (Beard 2012: 1)

In many of the theatrical works I have analysed, and in particular those of composers such as Nono and Sciarrino (but also in part those of Maderna or Manzoni), I have often noticed that the compositional process developed in an almost 'abstract' way with regards to the scenic destination (almost as if they were instrumental or vocal compositions).[17] Or, yet still, that the changes and second thoughts that occurred in the course of the staging sometimes were a direct consequence of the difficulty in making those musical structures 'interact' with an added 'visual' dimension.[18] With due caution, though, and after many years'

---

16 This failure might almost be considered a first step towards Nono's gradual withdrawal of the visual-scenic dimension, culminating in the 1980s with *Prometeo*, a 'tragedy of listening' that intentionally dispensed with any staging plan.

17 See, among others, De Benedictis 2002 and 2012. My observations here are also based also on unpublished research that I have conducted on the entire theatre production of Nono and Berio from the 1950s to the 1970s, on Maderna's *Satyricon*, Sciarrino's *Macbeth, Da gelo a gelo* and *Superflumina*, Penderecki's *Die Teufel von Loudon*, and other theatrical experiences by Nino Rota, Luigi Dallapiccola, and others.

18 Nono's documented struggle with the visual dimension is perhaps the best illustration of this phenomenon. See, for example, the entire body of textual and photographic material published in De Benedictis and Mastinu (eds) 2011, and the chapters dedicated to *Prometeo* in Nielinger-Vakil 2016, especially pp. 191–316.

experience in analysing new music theatre on the basis of sketch studies, I would like to ask a crucial question: is the study of the creative process and of compositional techniques really necessary for comprehending the dramatic dynamics that develop on stage? Does recognizing on paper, for example, certain tone rows or series that identify a character (later abandoned, as in some case by Nono or Birtwistle; see Beard 2012: 51 and De Benedictis 2007), or does following step-by-step the creation of a text and its setting in music have a real effect on the evaluation of the whole scenic result? While recognizing the importance of this interpretative approach, in the present context my answer must be that the rigorous analysis of the musical structures does not in itself suffice to explain the resulting associative dynamics (dramatic, gestural, etc.) that the music will have on stage. And if only the analysis of the musical structures sufficed, it would mean that that music is 'theatre' in itself; that those structures work at the dramatic level even without the scene. And then we would be back at the starting point: in music everything is theatre, and nothing is theatre.

Rather, remaining within the framework of the creative process, studies of unfinished theatre works, or of theatrical projects that were transformed into instrumental or vocal works along the way, turn out to be of primary importance: like 'torsos' that, in their unfinished state, permit us to comprehend some at times surprising or innovative details. (From this perspective, I will limit myself to citing the importance that, for the analysis of Nono's *Al gran sole carico d'amore*, the knowledge and the analysis of all the theatrical projects following *Intolleranza 1960*, from the so-called 'project of Campo Sant'Angelo' to *Un diario italiano*, etc., can have.[19] I could also cite the importance that the experience of *Esposizione* had for Berio with regard to what followed next, from *Laborintus II* to *Opera*, or the role of the 'group improvisation' *Trimalchio* for Maderna's *Satyricon*.[20]) Of equal importance is the research on pre-compositional material that answers the question: 'in composing a theatrical work, does the composer *think* in "visual terms"?' Speaking of music scores destined for the stage, it is indeed legitimate to presume the existence of documentary evidence that might allow us to evaluate the effective peculiarity of compositional procedures conceived to mediate a 'musical understanding of dramaturgy', or a 'dramatic understanding of music' (Berio 1967: 8). Or even to observe the interaction or the effective integration within a score of musical structures and scenic ideas.

From this perspective, the sketches often give unequivocal answers. Let us take, for example, the case of Nono, for whom, as I have already stressed, the visual dimension was always a sort of 'Achilles' heel'.[21] In the very early

---

19 Moreover, one should consider that almost all of Nono's vocal and instrumental works from the 1960s either stemmed or derived from theatrical projects that never materialized. I discuss these projects in a forthcoming essay entitled 'The first dramaturgical ideas and engagement in Luigi Nono's theatrical projects of the 1950s'.

20 The experiment of *Trimalchio* took place in the summer of 1971 at the Berkshire Center of Tanglewood and is documented by materials preserved among the manuscripts of *Satyricon* in the Maderna Collection at the Paul Sacher Stiftung. The project was reviewed in Hammerich 1971.

21 See note 18.

304 *Angela Ida De Benedictis*

planning phases of *Intolleranza 1960* one can recognize many annotations dedicated to an ideal representation of the auditory, visible and gestural events on stage. Figure 13.2, for example, shows a page sketched in the very early stages of the composition, well before defining any musical material whatsoever. Nono subdivides here the (imaginary) scenic space so as to make more than one level of action (physical and visual) interact with more than one kind of media (projection of photographs, films, graphics, actors, mimes, and so on).[22] The concept is as much futuristic as it is abstract, just as successive attempts to pre-programme, in an almost serial manner, the use of the scenic space are abstract. In Figure 13.3 we see, in a notebook of 1962, the conception of a series of seven scenic sequences in a dimension of 'total space' that abolishes the separation between the audience and the stage. This is one of several pages in which Nono organizes a 'spatial density' of the audience/stage relationship ('pubblico/scena'), following a permutational logic that is almost serial (see numbers 1–7 and the diagram added at the bottom of the Figure 13.3).[23] This logic is confirmed by the following sketch shown in Figure 13.4, where the retrograde-mirror type structure of the elements is clarified with the definition of the central 'stage situation' (numbered as '4' in Figure 13.3) as the axis of the mirror and 'highest' climax of the entire sequence.[24] It is interesting to note how the planning of a serial density of spatial (and scenic-sonorous) situations, as well as the decisions concerning the visual dimension or the multimedia context on stage (also of a permutational character) such as those that can be observed in Figure 13.4, are always made by Nono independently of a finished or already defined dramaturgical plan. In these cases, they are made even before the definition of the verbal text. These are *a priori* annotations that, rather than true decisions, bespeak a desire: to control the global event (or the space) along with the music. Or, to control the different levels of the performance as different 'parameters'.[25] This is perhaps a legitimate desire, but one that, simply because it is abstract, is very far from being transportable to the multi-decisional dynamics pertaining to scenic performances. If it might surprise us, then, to ascertain that, in *Intolleranza 1960*, the same control over musical structures underwent modifications on the way, becoming eventually a true exercise in 'compositional liberty', it does not surprise us at all, on the other hand, to note that not one of the scenic ideas taken by Nono in the early abstract stage of the compositional process was then put into practice in the actual score and

---

22 The sketch is dedicated to the 'suddivisione della scena' (stage subdivision) 'a) between simultaneous actions and empty parts, b) between actions and graphs or pictures or films' for projection.

23 In the same notebook 'B.017' Nono sketched some ideas related to a project with Giuliano Scabia, as well as notes on his theoretical text 'Some Clarifications on "Intolleranza 1960"' (English translation in Nono 2018: 193–208).

24 'MASSIMO / con scena tutta in teatro / pubblico sulla scena' (maximum, with complete stage in the hall [and] audience on the stage).

25 Heinemann 1970: 410 talks about different levels of performance in the new music theatre as if they were different parameters, thus implicitly suggesting the application of a 'parametrical' analysis to the interpretation of sub-structures. Although this suggestion is extremely interesting, it does not appear to take sufficiently into account the visual dimension of the performance.

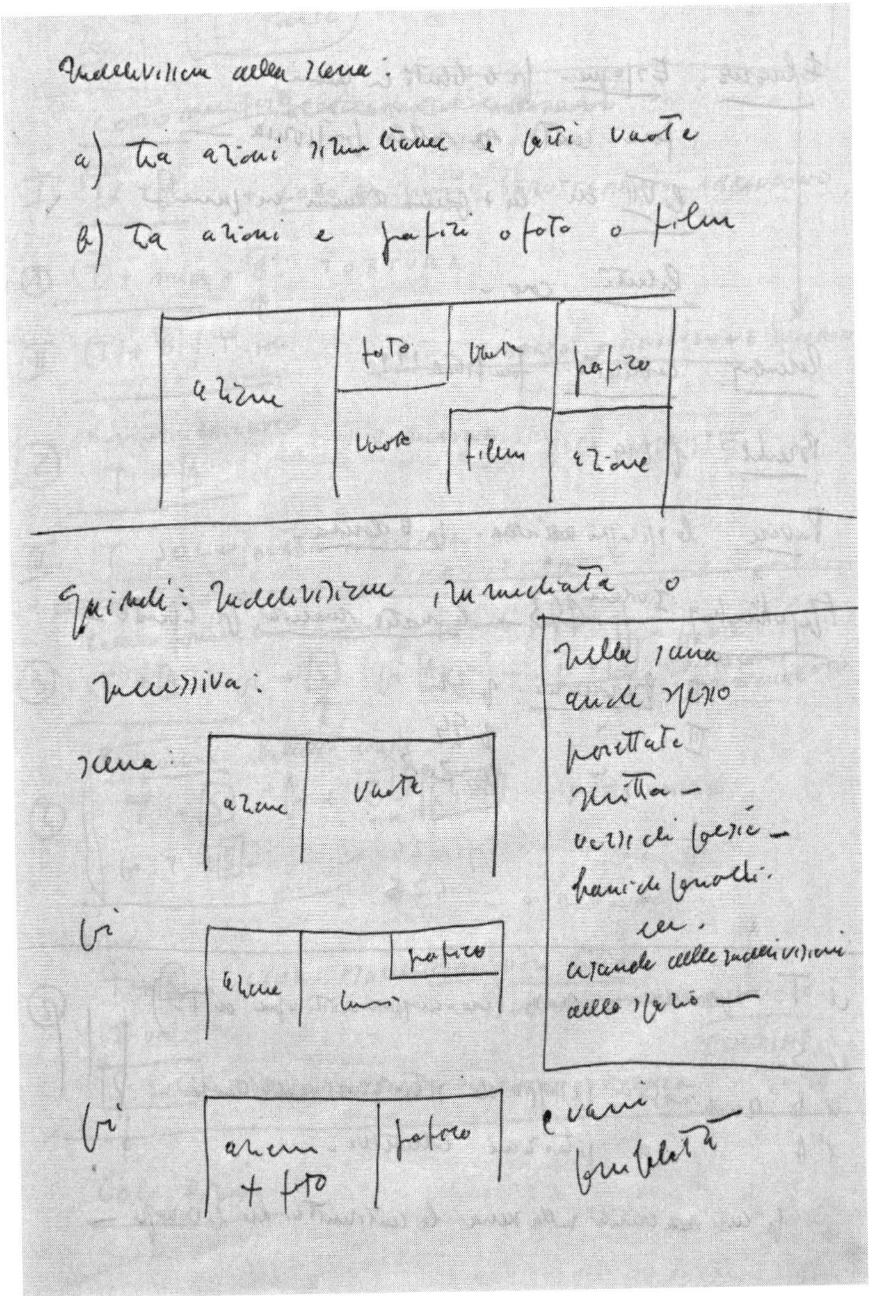

Figure 13.2 Luigi Nono, preparatory sketch for a 'theatrical work 1961'; notebook 'Q.007', f. 5 *recto*, ref. cat. 23.06.01/05r (*Intolleranza 1960*); courtesy of the Archivio Luigi Nono.

306 *Angela Ida De Benedictis*

during the performance of the work. It is even more striking that in his theoretical texts from the same period, Nono was fully aware that a 'new music theatre' should imply 'an encounter . . . in which music, painting, poetry, and stage dynamism . . . contribute not to a synthesis of the arts . . . but to a new freedom for the creative imagination', against the 'univocal despotism of one constituent element over the others: music over text and staging' (Nono 2018 [1962a]: 209; see also Nono 2018 [1962b]).

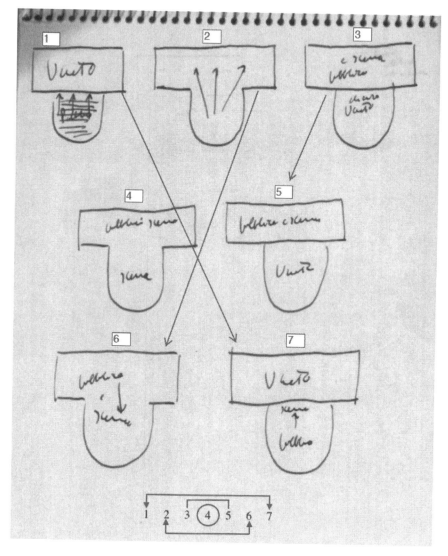

Figure 13.3 Luigi Nono, sketch in notebook 'B.017', f. 2 *recto*, ref. cat. 26.05.01/18 (*Da un diario italiano*), with numbers added; courtesy of the Archivio Luigi Nono.

Analysing new music theatre 307

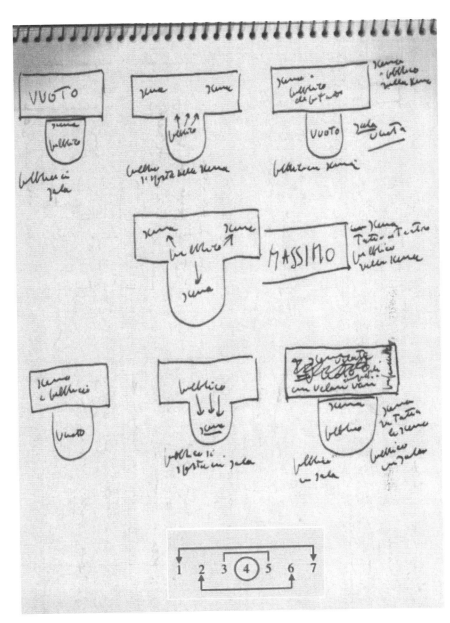

Figure 13.4 Luigi Nono, sketch in notebook 'B.017', f. 3 *recto*, ref. cat. 26.05.01/19 (*Da un diario italiano*), with numbers added; courtesy of the Archivio Luigi Nono.

Altogether different is the case of Luciano Berio, whose knowledge of the conventions and dynamics pertaining to theatrical spaces is undeniable, and can be summarized in his certainty that to achieve new scenic expressions that go beyond those handed down by tradition, 'nothing is more useful and

308 *Angela Ida De Benedictis*

effective than [. . .] using dialectically some of the instruments of your "enemy"' (Berio 1967: 11).[26] In many theatrical works by Berio the scenic space, even the more traditional one, gets bent to the precise necessities of the sonorous performance, and, often, it gets used specifically as an additional 'meaningful structural element' (ibid.).[27] This is not a mere thought jotted down in a theoretical text: hints at the use of space as a structural element of the work are present in many of Berio's pre-compositional materials. Figure 13.5 reproduces a sketch of the first version of *Opera*, dating from 1969, where the composer describes the action of a group of kids running, scared, on stage until they freeze 'squashed and terrified against "a wall" for at least a minute – Always yelling!' ['stanno schiacciati e atterriti contro "un muro" per almeno 1 minuto – Sempre urlando!']. And, already imagining the potential afforded by traditional stage spaces, Berio adds: 'use the acoustics of the theatre' ['usare l'acustica del teatro'], visualizing with some drawings the effects of the spatial movement of the yells.

The importance that the 'theatrical design and architecture play in the creation of theatrical meaning' (Low 2016: 1) is evident in all the phases of realization of the stage works by Berio, from the sketches to the premieres, to the various restagings in different places than the premiere. I just mentioned *Opera*, which is from this perspective an exemplary experience. The impact that the venue (and the space) chosen for the first performance had on the structure and on the articulation of the musical text is apparent in the pages of the first version of *Opera*, which was performed in Santa Fe with the Open Theater group of New York in 1970 (see Ottomano 2016; Maurin 2016). For subsequent performances (Florence 1977, Nanterre/Lyon 1979, Turin 1980, and Rome 1981), where the American experimental theatre group was not present, Berio drew up a new version: all passages or parts that in Santa Fe were characterized by the onstage presence of the Open Theater were revised or eliminated, and were replaced by new materials, partially elaborated in collaboration with the stage directors according to the new theatrical spaces. These decisions often consciously placed the music in a relationship of 'action and contradiction' with respect to the visual dimension, to quote Gae Aulenti who, together with Luca Ronconi, directed Berio's *Opera* in the productions of 1979–1981.[28] This illustrates how the space can become a

26 Right since his first theatrical experiences (*Mimusique No. 2, Allez-hop, Passaggio* etc.) Berio showed a thorough awareness that 'theatre' means a complex whole of history, dynamics, relationships, places, and signs.

27 The whole sentence states: 'If the destination of a music theater work is the operatic stage it is because *that* space is still the most convenient and efficient theatrical space available or because the reference to operatic convention is a meaningful structural element. It can also happen that a work is clearly set in opposition to the opera theater . . . In a case like that we must realize that nothing is more useful and effective than giving voice to your criticism in the right place, dialectically, using some of the instrument of you "enemy". Finally, musical theater negates opera, but it can continually absorb and use it among the infinite, staged and unstaged, aspects of reality'. Next to this sentence, Berio added by hand: 'PASSAGGIO!'.

28 The quotation is from a video interview held with Gae Aulenti in 1980, where she shows a number of schemes that illustrate in an extremely significant way the stage concept for *Opera* (clip from the thirteenth episode of the programme *Teatromusica*, edited by R. Leydi, RAI Archive). These schemes have not yet been found in any archives to date.

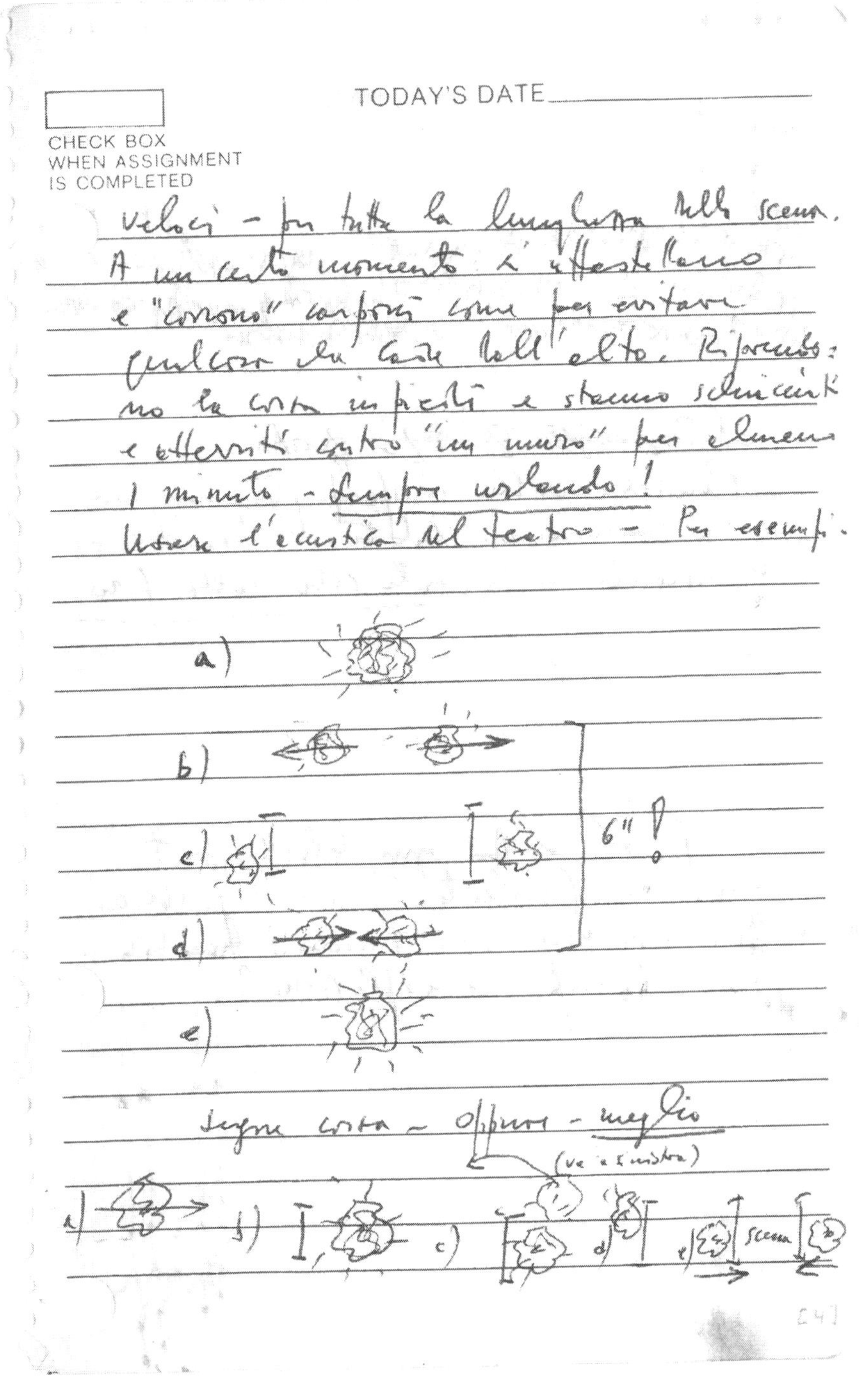

Figure 13.5 Luciano Berio, sketch for *Opera*, 1st version (*c.* 1969); Luciano Berio Collection, Paul Sacher Foundation (with kind permission).

310   *Angela Ida De Benedictis*

'meaningful structural element' and how decisions related to the setting and stage (approached by Aulenti and Ronconi in Turin as 'metatheatrical' levels of signification) can end up interacting with the musical structures and can add to them meanings not decipherable from the score alone.[29]

That the knowledge of the scenic locations or their integration in the compositional process plays a very important role, despite the indifference of many analyses conducted at this level, is confirmed by those works of new music theatre that overflow into the field of multiauthoriality, such as the aforementioned *Esposizione* by Berio, Sanguineti and Halprin (1962–63).[30] The work was withdrawn by Berio after its premiere, but this should not lead to hasty value judgments: its preparation and its staging were a very important milestone in Berio's search for new solutions to experimental music theatre. After the first and only performance at Venice's La Fenice (on April 18, 1963), he rethought and amplified the same musical structures within another multimedia container, *Laborintus II* (1964–65), initially conceived 'to be performed on stage, on television, outdoors, on the radio etc.,' and open to 'different musical solutions' in the case of 'presence (or absence, as in the case of a radio performance) of a visual and spatial development'.[31] These constant adaptations reveal an incessant attention to and reflection upon the importance of the spaces chosen for the representation of a given message. This awareness led him to understand right at the start that the experience of *Esposizione*, born *with* a given group of actor and dancers (Ann Halprin's Dancers' Workshop Company of San Francisco) and *for* a specific location, that of La Fenice in Venice, would nevertheless become something different if performed again by different companies and in different places.

Before we go any further with *Esposizione*, this latter point allows me to open a brief parenthesis on the implicitly 'ephemeral' nature of every production of musical theatre, which has serious consequences also on the analytical level. Almost all of the relevant experiences (or 'turning points') of new music theatre in the second half of the last century have often remained tied to the event of the first performance, and have been analysed with reference to *those* scenes and *that* directorial-spatial dimension, most of the time no longer reproducible, or lost.

---

29 Salzman and Desi argued that 'Music theater can be considered the confluence or adding up of language-like expressions: verbal or spoken language (the story; the libretto), physical movement or body language (gesture, dance), images or visual language (*décor* or design), and sound or musical language (pitch and rhythm; vocal and instrumental)' (2008: 13). In my opinion, music theatre can be considered a lot more: the existing scenic space (whether traditional or not) is in any case part of the performance and it often affects (or contributes to) the dramaturgy, regardless of the indications specified in the score (or in the text). In works like *Opera* and *Esposizione* (where the open space outside La Fenice in Venice was as much a 'component' of the performance as the hall and the stage inside) the visual dimension goes far beyond the *décor* and the scenery. Another issue is the attribution of these different levels to a single author (the composer) or to the multiplicity of creative minds involved in the production of a music theatre work.

30 For more detailed information on this work see De Benedictis 2016, esp. pp. 181–200 and 228–35.

31 Luciano Berio, introductory notes to *Laborintus II* (first version, 'Partitura A'), 1965; preserved in the Luciano Berio Collection, Paul Sacher Foundation, Basel; reproduced in De Benedictis 2016: 246 (facsimile) and 215 (English translation).

After all, it is not a coincidence that, as in traditional operas, at each performance, the work can change sometimes quite substantially, giving life every time to new versions, each newly projected in the 'ephemeral' dimension of the performative event.[32] On closer inspection, the history of new music theatre can be seen as a chain of *unique* events, whose interpretation cannot be based exclusively on the analysis of the musical (and textual) materials, but must equally concern itself with an analysis of the performance and of audiovisual documents. Let us not forget, however, that sometimes the analysis of theatrical works that had a single performance only – and of which there is no extant video documentation – corresponds *tout court* to a genetic and/or structural investigation, or to a study of the coeval reception of a music artefact that only retrospectively could be recognized as 'music theatre'. Since we are unable to 'ascertain' the work's dramaturgical scope within the scenic space, it follows that we are free to investigate those notes or that score with whatever analytical method is suitable for any kind of instrumental, vocal, or orchestral music. A good case is the 'azione musicale' *Collage* (1961), by Aldo Clementi and Achille Perilli, whose premiere in Rome was its first and only performance, and was not documented on video.[33] The discovery in the early 2000s of Perilli's draft and sketches for the scenery (see Lux and Tortora (eds) 2005) should have led to its revival, but this also came to nothing. In my opinion, the fact that the only existing document is the score (and any related musical material) places such works 'off limits' for any kind of real analysis within a scenic-theatrical frame.

This digression brings us directly to the analysis of a work such as *Esposizione*, an activity that necessarily implies philological research into a single performance, a *unicum* which, however, offers various starting points for a broader reflection on the analytical methodologies of new expressions of musical theatre. I mentioned the limitations that analysis of the score alone yields in the realm of new music theatre. In the case of *Esposizione*, these limitations are evident even from a first glance at the pages deposited by Berio at Universal Edition at the time. Example 13.1 reproduces page 4 of the score, which in total comprises only nine pages, whereas the entire work lasted over an hour. A few of

---

32 Berio's *Opera*, Manzoni's *Atomtod*, Nono's *Al grande sole carico d'amore*, or the same *Intolleranza 1960*, are examples of works that were changed and updated with each new performance. Let us also think about Stockhausen's *Originale*: for this work (that makes use of previously composed instrumental works), Stockhausen prepared a score for the staging, with precise indications for every aspect of the performance; then – as he himself testified – already for the first performance in Cologne (1961), 'he changed entries and durations in an improvisational manner during the performances, that Name June Paik never repeated a single one of his actions and that other performers refused to perform some of the required actions' (Salzman and Desi 2008: 146). It is interesting that a subsequent performance of *Originale* that took place in 1964 in New York was contested by artists from the Fluxus group who accused Stockhausen of 'poaching on their turf' (ibid.; see also the documentary video on www.youtube.com/watch?v=p6-rVxLwlEc, accessed 22 February 2019).

33 An autonomous orchestral score, *Sette scene da 'Collage'* (published in 1964, also performed only once), was subsequently extracted from the original stage work.

the instructions present on this page allow us to understand, however, that the score was nothing but a partial element to be taken as a mere performative base for the instrumentalists (which had to repeat some modules several times in the course of the performance, in an 'always slightly varied' way, as we read on the bottom).[34] This partial layer, in addition, interacted with another sounding level, pre-recorded on magnetic tape (the word 'tape' is clearly legible at the top right of the Example 13.1). Similar to a television or radio score, this too presents itself as a prescriptive base, not complete in all its parts, and to be completed at the moment of performance, making it interact with other elements not prescribed in the score (or indicated only as generic annotations). Certainly, analysing *Esposizione* beginning with these nine pages, or on the basis of partial magnetic tapes kept in the Luciano Berio Collection, would lead to a distorted interpretation of a stage work of great complexity. Berio himself described it as such in a letter written in 1962 to the superintendent of La Fenice, Mario Labroca:

> It is difficult [. . .] for me to explain to you in a few words the nature of the work. There will be three actor-dancers, one singer [. . .] and a few children. There isn't an actual story, but a polyphony of 'stories,' of apparently independent facts and actions. The exclusively musical part is [also] recorded [. . .] the actor-dancers and the children must be Americans, from here in San Francisco. They are the best theatre group that I know:[35] the only ones that know how to think of theatre outside any predetermined category: that which they do can be 'opera,' 'drama,' 'comedy,' 'dance,' 'farce' etc.: a true 'total theater' [. . .] with the simplest and most rigorous tools.[36]

In the preparation of the Venetian performance, the role of Ann Halprin was as fundamental as that of Berio. The two artists collaborated, for the most part long-distance, via few but essential exchanges that allowed each to develop in freedom their own performative part. In order to study their 'singing' parts and to practice the choreography, the dancers started out with the architecture of the Venice Opera House and used 'time scores' sent to them by Berio himself (see Benedictis 2016: 187 and 189). It has only recently become possible to understand the nature of these 'temporal scores', mentioned by Halprin in several interviews, following the recent rediscovery of the scheme (shown as Figure 13.6) among a number of manuscripts by Berio preserved in Cathy Berberian's personal archive.[37] Space precludes a full description of this interesting scheme here: it will suffice to point out that it comprises a sort of framework in which Berio signals, moment by

---

34 'Ogni sezione ripetuta deve essere lievemente variata, nella dinamica e nel tempo'.

35 Namely, Ann Halprin's Dancers' Workshop Company.

36 Luciano Berio to Mario Labroca, 21 March 1962, original in Italian, Archivio Storico delle Arti Contemporanee (Historical Collection, Music section; hereafter ASAC), Venice, reproduced by kind permission. See also Berio's letter to Labroca from 30.7.1962 reproduced in De Benedictis 2016: 234.

37 Berberian's archives, previous stored by Cristina Berio in Los Angeles and Radicondoli, were acquired in 2016 by the Paul Sacher Foundation, Basel.

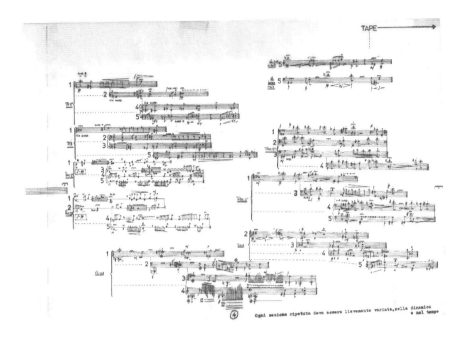

Example 13.1 Luciano Berio, *Esposizione*, score previously deposited in the archive of Universal Edition, Wien (now preserved in the Paul Sacher Foundation, Luciano Berio Collection), p. 4. By kind permission.

moment, the evolution of single temporal blocks, indicating within each of them the names of the actors-dancers and their expected actions, the sung or instrumental parts, the scenic situations, and so on. Each block is distinguished by a precise duration (indicated in minutes) and, at times, even internally subdivided temporally. From this, little by little, emerges the possibility to analyse *Esposizione* – as a work conceived for a stage – not limiting oneself any longer to a partial aspect (the score), but juxtaposing also the directions supplied by this page, and making the whole interact with the documentary traces and the testimonies left by Halprin and Berio himself.

However, the document that makes possible a more rounded interpretation and comprehension of *Esposizione* (i.e. an analysis of its 'new theatrical' dimension) is the existence of a video recording that, although incomplete and limited to a few minutes, permits us to develop discussions of 'performative action' and to allow all the constitutive levels of the work to interact in a wider hermeneutic process, one that is projected towards a context of multidimensional signification:[38] the music, ambient sounds, voices, gestures, spaces inside

---

38 The term 'multidimensional' is intended here to imply layers of signification that go beyond the audiovisual contents, relating to the three-dimensional presence of spatial aspects destined not only for vision and hearing but also for the other senses (there is participation, spatialized vision, real space, bodies and the elements 'onstage', and so on).

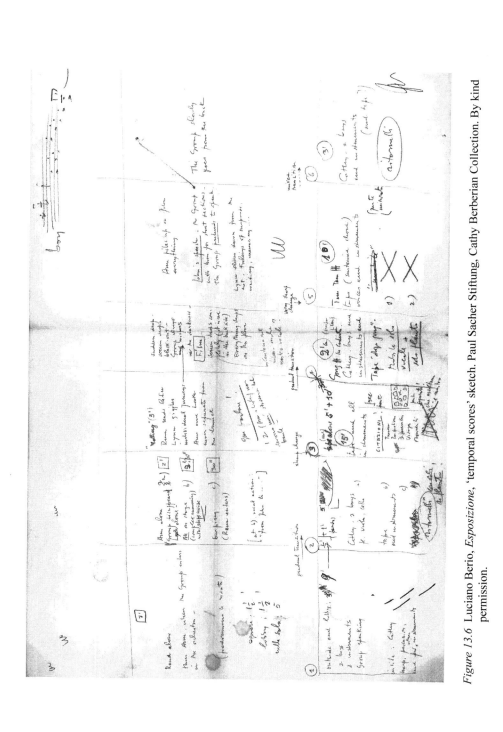

Figure 13.6 Luciano Berio, *Esposizione*, 'temporal scores' sketch. Paul Sacher Stiftung, Cathy Berberian Collection. By kind permission.

Analysing new music theatre   315

and outside the theatre, scenery, props, and so on.[39] It is thanks to a document of this type that, for *Esposizione*, we can undertake an analytic approach that moves from the video (though fragmentary and partial) to pre-compositional materials, aiming at an analysis of the dramatic structures that follows not the process of its becoming (inductive, from the sketches to the final work), but in its 'asserting itself on stage' (deductive, from the work back to the sketches).[40]

It is clear that the discussion, by now, has completely shifted to the dimension of performance analysis, and, as a result, to the necessity of giving priority to analytical instruments that do not take off only from the score, but above all from the performance documentation. Which is to say: from a documentation that may be, in the most fortunate of cases, audiovisual, but which, even if it is limited to only audio and/or photographic documents, allows us – as Philip Auslander affirms – to 'arrive at an understanding of the performance and the product of this understanding' (Auslander 2009: 95).[41] Taking advantage of what Auslander argues in his theoretical approach, though, I would see in the performance documentation more than a body of 'texts from which we can imaginatively reactivate historical performances *in the present*' (ibid.; my emphasis).[42] Rather, I would see in it a 'complex whole' of different sources (audiovisual and non-audiovisual), which should interact in an analytical process that takes into account globally all the performative and theatrically significant levels involved in the moment of a given staging *in the past*. Just as in recent studies on theatre, where there is an attempt to separate theatre from the field of literature, reclaiming for it the status of an independent 'art form', so too in the realm of music we should finally separate the forms of representative expression from conventional analytical theories in order to develop 'analytical forms' pertinent to the complexity of the staged events. These analytical approaches, in my opinion, should proceed not from the

39 The video of the premiere of *Esposizione* comprises a fragment of about 5 minutes from the broadcast *Valori espressivi della musica contemporanea*, RAI, 1969, unpublished.

40 As well as for the sketches and musical structures, it goes without saying that the video recording alone cannot suffice for an exhaustive analysis: it serves for reconstructing, but not for intercepting the analytical object with sufficient cogency. The 'object' to be analysed is not the audiovisual trace as such, but the theatrical-scenic situation that the recording documents.

41 In this context it is worth mentioning the intense and interesting debate on performance, liveness, and mediatized culture developed since the 1990s by Philip Auslander, Peggy Phelan, and Erika Fischer-Lichte.

42 In the field of prose theatre, Eli Rozik makes a distinction between the study of theatre as a medium (the text that generates its performance) and the analysis of performance as a text. The former is confronted with all the semiotic levels that underlie the generation of a performance, while the latter is compared to the generation of 'theatre meaning', not only 'by its medium, but also by the nature of its described fictional worlds, and the vital complementation of the spectator' (Rozik 2008: 3). On the basis of the analytical theories developed by Mukarovsky, Fischer-Lichte, De Marinis and others, Rozik comes to theorize the 'textual nature of the theatre performance': if an artistic product is a structure made up of signs, and therefore an autonomous artifact, the performance (understood as a text: the *performance-text*), or rather the theatrical artifact, is also an object of analysis (ibid.: 7). Although this is certainly an interesting analytical hypothesis, in my view it is not really viable for music theatre, since the study (limited to structure) would then become a 'structural study of performance'.

316 *Angela Ida De Benedictis*

compositional process to the stage, but should make the journey in the opposite direction, attempting not to find in the final work the mirrors of the musician's ideas alone, but to analyse the final work as *theatrical object*,[43] as an interactive sum of different decisional levels that 'necessitates new modes of reading' according to models that are not only structural but that, above all, go beyond the (semantically charged) concept of 'text'.[44]

To conclude, I would like to return briefly to radio theatre; this is a genre which, in the same years (the 1950s to the 1970s), was understood by a few composers (including Berio, Kagel and Maderna) as an actual *new music (acoustical) theatre* without stage. During my research dedicated to radio theatre (e.g. De Benedictis 2004; De Benedictis and Novati (eds) 2012), I noticed that often the imaginary theatre functions in an even more immediate manner than the real one, and not only on the level of perception or reconstruction of a meaning. Analysing works of radio theatre was, for me, always a more immediate experience than analysing staged works, where the dimension of listening intersects and often collides with a hyper-interpretative threshold conditioned by eyesight (and by a lived experience). For radio works I was 'forced' to begin with the sound document (the 'final work' on tape), a fact that led me to question whether, as for radio theatre, it would be preferable also for the analysis of the new musical theatre to begin from the aural and visual (audiovisual) documentation – that is, from the performance. The difference in analytical approach mirrors a more general difference regarding the theoretical foundations of the work ('das Werk'). In radio theatre, in fact, the work is to be seen in the recorded audio document, in the 'performed work'; in the musical theatre it is tantamount to the prescriptive text, to the score. Certainly, in radio theatre often the recording (the audio document) assumes an importance that is not just primary but absolute, since often the score of the works does not exist, or it comprises only a partial or incomplete prescriptive base that, during the process of recording/finalization of the work, is completed with layers not fixed on paper and not analysable with 'traditional' methods.[45] But this does not suffice to explain such a substantial difference in analytical approach or to give reasons for the type of vacuum in musicological studies dedicated to new musical theatre, where video or auditory documents continue to be considered at times as almost secondary sources. And where, with often brilliant results and with great philological or interpretative competence, scholars continue to conduct analytical investigations that are valid and

---

43 This could be taken as alternative proposal to Rebstock and Roesner, who with the same concept mean an event in which 'the musicality of theatrical performance and the theatricality of musical performance' get confused (2012: 9). In my opinion, when speaking of a 'theatrical object' one should avoid thinking in terms of a reification of the theatrical performance; it should instead be understood in terms of a 'process' taking place in (real) time and space, more than a 'product'.

44 See also, in relation to quite other repertoires, Levin 2007, especially p. 3: 'Reconceived as a text, ([. . .] as a text *in performance*), opera has emerged as an agitated or unsettled site of signification, one that encompasses multiple modes of expression and necessitates new modes of reading.'

45 For example, the staging of Maderna's *Don Perlimplin* on the basis of the published score (a new edition was published by Suvini Zerboni in 2002) may lead to something quite different from the work the author originally created and established on tape (now published on CD in De Benedictis and Novati (eds) 2012). In a case like this, the analysis of the score and of a stage performance based on it could end in contradictions and diverge from the 'real work'.

Analysing new music theatre   317

useful for the understanding of single elements of a stage production. Interesting as they may be, such analyses remain partial and particularized.

Acknowledgements

I wish to thank Giacomo Albert, Alessandro Cecchi, Maurizio Corbella, Emilio Sala and all the participants at the Italian study group on 'Multi- and Cross-Mediality' launched in September 2017 in Gargnano (http://leavlab.com/berio-and-beyond/) for the many interesting contributions and ideas arising from the discussion of a first draft of this text; and Talia Pecker Berio and Veniero Rizzardi for their unwavering friendship and support.

References

Adlington, Robert (2005), 'Music theatre since the 1960s', in Mervyn Cooke (ed.), *The Cambridge Companion to Twentieth-Century Opera*, Cambridge, UK: Cambridge University Press, pp. 225–43.

Auslander, Philip (2009), 'Toward a hermeneutics of performance art documentation', in Jonas Ekeborg (ed.), *Kunsten A Falle: Lessons in the Art of Falling*, Horten: Preus Museum, pp. 93–5.

Beard, David (2012), *Harrison Birtwistle's Operas and Music Theatre*, Cambridge, UK: Cambridge University Press.

Berio, Luciano (1967), 'Problems of musical theater', lecture held in Harvard University (Cambridge) on 11 January 1967; typescript of 15 pp., original in English, unpublished; Luciano Berio Collection, Paul Sacher Foundation, Basel. Published in Italian translation as 'Problemi di teatro musicale', in Luciano Berio (2013), *Scritti sulla musica*, ed. Angela Ida De Benedictis, Torino: Einaudi, pp. 42–57.

Berio, Luciano (1980), interview, in Maurizi, Paola (2004), *Quattordici interviste sul 'nuovo teatro musicale' in Italia. Con un elenco cronologico delle opere (1950–1980)*, Perugia: Morlacchi, pp. 27–8.

Berio, Luciano (2013), *Scritti sulla musica*, ed. Angela Ida De Benedictis, Torino: Einaudi.

Cook, Nicholas (1987), *A Guide to Musical Analysis*, London: Dent.

Dahlhaus, Carl (1983), 'Oper und Neue Musik. Versuch einer Problemskizze', in *Von Musikdrama zur Literaturoper. Aufsätze zur neueren Operngeschichte*, München-Salzburg: Katzbichler, pp. 145–52.

De Benedictis, Angela Ida (2002), 'La sentenza impossibile: un primo 'banco di prova' tra compromesso e attualità', in Carmelo Di Gregorio and Luigi Pestalozza (eds), *Per Giacomo Manzoni*, Milan: Lim, pp. 81–95.

De Benedictis, Angela Ida (2004), *Radiodramma e arte radiofonica. Storia e funzioni della musica per radio in Italia*, Turin: EDT-De Sono.

De Benedictis, Angela Ida (2007), 'Intervals at the service of dramaturgy: the conception of "character-rows" in "Intolleranza 1960" by Luigi Nono', in Giordano Ferrari (ed.), *L'écriture musicale et son expression scénique au XXe siècle*, Paris: L'Harmattan, pp. 49–68.

De Benedictis, Angela Ida (2012), 'The dramaturgical and compositional genesis of Luigi Nono's *Intolleranza 1960*', *Twentieth-Century Music*, 9/1–2, pp. 101–41.

De Benedictis, Angela Ida (2016), 'From "Esposizione" to "Laborintus II": transitions and mutations of a "desire for theatre"', in Giordano Ferrari (ed.), *Le théâtre musical de Luciano Berio: De 'Passaggio à La Vera Storia'*, Paris: L'Harmattan, pp. 177–246.

318 *Angela Ida De Benedictis*

De Benedictis, Angela Ida and Giorgio Mastinu (eds) (2011), *Intolleranza 1960 a cinquant'anni dalla prima assoluta*, Venice: Marsilio.

De Benedictis, Angela Ida and Maria Maddalena Novati (eds) (2012), *Imagination at Play. The Prix Italia and Radiophonic Experimentation*, Milan: Rai-Trade – Die Schachtel.

Hammerich, R. C. (1971), 'Defying arts. Maderna proves committee can create musical work of art', *The Republican*, 8 August.

Heile, Björn (2016), 'Toward a theory of experimental music theatre: "showing-doing", "non-matrixed performance" and "metaxis"', in Yael Kaduri (ed.), *The Oxford Handbook of Sound and Image in Western Art*, Oxford: Oxford University Press, pp. 335–55.

Heilgendorff, Simone (2002), *Experimentelle Inszenierung von Sprache und Musik: vergleichende Analyses zu Dieter Schnebel und John Cage*, Freiburg im Breisgau: Rombach.

Heinemann, Rudolf (1970), 'Das neue Musiktheatre zwischen Absürdität und Engagement', *Melos*, 10, pp. 406–10.

Levin, David J. (2007), *Unsettling Opera. Staging Mozart, Verdi, Wagner, and Zemlinsky*, Chicago, IL: University of Chicago Press.

Low, Jennifer A. (2016), *Dramatic Spaces: Scenography and Spectatorial Perception*, London: Routledge.

Lux, Simonetta and Daniela Tortora (eds) (2005), *Collage 1961: un'azione dell'arte di Achille Perilli e Aldo Clementi*, Rome: Gangemi.

Maurin, Frederic (2016), 'L'embarquement pour Santa Fe: la contribution de l'Open Theater à la création d'"Opera"', in Giordano Ferrari (ed.), *Le théâtre musical de Luciano Berio: De "Passaggio à La Vera Storia"*, Paris: L'Harmattan, pp. 285–320.

Maurizi, Paola (2004), *Quattordici interviste sul "nuovo teatro musicale" in Italia. Con un elenco cronologico delle opere (1950–1980)*, Perugia, Morlacchi.

Nielinger-Vakil, Carola (2016), *Luigi Nono: A Composer in Context*, Cambridge, UK: Cambridge University Press.

Nono, Luigi (2018 [1962a]), 'Possibility and necessity of a new music theater', in *Nostalgia for the Future: Luigi Nono's Selected Writings and Interviews*, ed. Angela Ida De Benedictis and Veniero Rizzardi, Berkeley, CA: University of California Press, pp. 209–23.

Nono, Luigi (2018 [1962b]), 'Play and truth in the new music theater', in *Nostalgia for the Future: Luigi Nono's Selected Writings and Interviews*, ed. Angela Ida De Benedictis and Veniero Rizzardi, Berkeley: University of California Press, pp. 224–8.

Nono, Luigi (2018), *Nostalgia for the Future: Luigi Nono's Selected Writings and Interviews*, ed. Angela Ida De Benedictis and Veniero Rizzardi, Berkeley, CA: University of California Press.

Ottomano, Vincenzina C. (2016), 'Luciano Berio's "Opera" or a kind of "miroir de moi-même"', in Giordano Ferrari (ed.) (2016), *Le théâtre musical de Luciano Berio: De "Passaggio à La Vera Storia"*, Paris: L'Harmattan, pp. 247–84.

Rebstock, Matthias and David Roesner (eds) (2012), *Composed Theatre: Aesthetics, Practices, Processes*, Bristol, UK: Intellect.

Rozik, Eli (2008), *Generating Theatre Meaning: A Theory and Methodology of Performance Analysis*, Brighton, UK: Sussex Academic Press.

Salzman, Eric and Thomas Desi (2008), *The New Music Theater: Seeing the Voice, Hearing the Body*, Oxford: Oxford University Press.

Schechner, Richard (2001), 'What is "performance studies" anyway?', in Günter Berghaus (ed.), *New Approaches to Theatre Studies and Performance Analysis*, Tübingen: Niemeyer, pp. 1–11.

Index

Abbado, Claudio 115
Abbate, Carolyn 98, 284
Abel, Lionel 7, 66, 66n8, 72
acousmatic 91–2, 102, 107, 114–16;
  see also electronic music; listening;
  magnetic tape; vocality
actor 25, 35–6, 62, 67–8, 148, 208, 223,
  227, 237, 245, 252, 267; *see also* mime
Adamov, Arthur 18, 203
Adlington, Robert 46n30, 73, 79–80, 84,
  93, 95, 151, 255
Aeschylus 42; *L'Orestie* 42
Albert, Giacomo 317
Albert, Walter 110n14
alienation 60, 68, 83, 94, 109, 112, 130,
  136; *see also Verfremdungseffekt*
Alovisi, Ezio 199n37
Alvarado, Velasco 159–61
Ambrosino, Nuccio 24n6
American Hurrah 209
Amodio, Amedeo 180, 198
Andriessen, Louis 81, 129, 140, 141n51,
  144; *La Commedia* 81; *Contra tempus*
  141n51; *see also Reconstructie*
Ann Halprin's Dancers' Workshop
  Company 46, 310, 312n35, 67
Antheil, George 101, 118; *Transatlantik*
  101, 118
Antokoletz, Elliot 278
Aperghis, Georges 155, 204, 223–4;
  Histoire de Loup 224
Appia, Adolphe 245
Aristotele 65
Arrigo, Girolamo 204, 219, 223; *Orden*
  219, 223; *Wacjwa* 219
Artaud, Antonin 7, 16–7, 22–4, 29, 34,
  34n4, 36, 42, 42n20, 46, 54, 60, 135,
  193–5, 210, 219, 223, 237, 245, 263;
  Les Cenci 42
Assayag, Gérard

Aszodi, Jessica 4
Atelier de Composition du Groupe de
  Recherches Musicales 219, *222*
Auber, Daniel 147, 169; *La muette de
  Portici* 142, 147–8, 169, 172
Auden, W. H. 136–7, 150
audience 2–3, 15–19, 39, 45, 112, 129,
  137, 185– 88, 193, 209, 234, 277, 294,
  304; audience participation 6–7, 16,
  21–2, 24, 26–7, 29, 34, 41–3, 45, 63–5,
  87, 93–4, 210, 246–48, 258
Augias, Corrado 24n6
Aulenti, Gae 308, 308n28, 310
Auslander, Philip 315, 315n41
authorship 9, 198, 262, 267, 296
avant-garde 6, 21, 25, 98, 154–6, 180,
  189–90; avant-garde music 2, 255,
  266; avant-garde theatre 15–16, 18–20,
  25–6, 44, 54, 139, 203, 228, 301;
  definitions of 15, 17–18, 24
Aziz-Zadeh, Lisa 275

Babbitt, Milton 280; Composition for
  Twelve Instruments 280
Bach, Johann Sebastian 23, 124, 241
Bachmann, Ingeborg 188n18
Bacon, Francis 279
Balestrini, Nanni 189
Ball, Hugo 55
Barba, Eugenio 25, 29, 258–60
Baroni, Mario 149
Barrat, Pierre 219, 224
Barrault, Jean-Louis 34, 35n13, 36, 42–3,
  46, 245
Barthes, Roland 15, 18, 26, 223
Bartók, Béla 241–2, 278, 207; *Bluebeard's
  Castle* 278
Bartolucci, Giuseppe 16, 24, 24n6, 27; *see
  also* scenic writing
Baruchello, Gianfranco 198

320 *Index*

Bastard Assignments 6
Bataille, Georges 153
Baudelaire, Charles 154, 209
Bayle, François 219
Bazin, André 83
Beard, David 4–5, 9, 302
Beauvoir, Simone de 153, 160
Beck, Julian 17, 22, 47, 209–10, 212–13
Beckett, Samuel 7, 18–20, 53, 55, 59–60, 64, 203, 237, 249; *Acte sans paroles I* 55, 237; *Acte sans paroles II* 237; *En attendant Godot* 18–19, 264
Bedford, David 249; *The Wheel* 246, *246*
Beethoven, Ludwig van 81, 153, 165; *Fidelio* 81, 163
Béjart, Maurice 107, 119, 121–4, 196n32, 204, 206–7, 209–10, 212–13, 215–16, 219; *A la Recherche de Dom Juan* 206–9, 213; *Baudelaire* 122; *L'Art de la barre* 207; *Bacchanale* 207; *Bhakti* 122; *Boléro* 207; *Chant du compagnon errant* 122; *The Green Queen* 206; *Messe pour le temps présent* 121, 206, 208, 212–13; *Nijinsky, Clown de Dieu* 123; *Notre Faust* 124; *Pas de deux* 207; *Peter and the Wolf* 207; *Sonate à trois* 207; *Stimmung* 123; *Symphonie pour un homme seul* 107, 119; *Variations pour une porte et un soupir* 207
Bellini, Vincenzo 123
Bellocchio, Marco 24n6
Bene, Carmelo 19–20, 24n6, 27; *Amleto o le conseguenze della pietà filiale da Laforgue secondo Carmelo Bene* 20; *Basta con un 'Vi amo' mi ero quasi promesso. Amleto o le conseguenze della pietà filiale* 20; *Hamlet* 20
Bentoiu, Pascal 123; *Hamlet* 123
Berberian, Cathy 9, 24n6, 46, 109, 195, 256, 264–6, 266n13, 266n14, 267, 312, 312n37
Berg, Alban 41, 65, 101, 118, 165, 196, 279; *Lulu* 41, 65, 101, 118, 165, 279; *Wozzeck* 65, 279
Bergen, Beverly 150
Berio, Cristina 312n37
Berio, Luciano 7, 46, 46n30, 53–5, 61–2, 64–7, 67n9, 67n11, 68, *70–1*, 72, 122, 195–7, 209, 214, 234, 241, 259–60, 264, 274, 279–80, 284, 289–92, 295, 299–301, 301n13, 302n17, 303, 307–8, 308n26, 308n27, *309*, 311, 311n32, 312–13, *313–14*, 316; *Allez-hop* 65, 196–7, 197n35, 197n36, 241, 300, 308n26; *A-Ronne* 301n13; *Circles*

65; *Cronaca del Luogo* 66; *Diario immaginario* 301n13; *Esposizione* 46, 46n30, 297, 299–301, 310–11, 310n29, 311n32, 312–13, *313–14,* 315–16, 315n39; *Laborintus II* 122, 310; *Il malato immaginario* 301n13; *Mimusique No. 2* 65, 241, 308n26; *Omaggio a Joyce* 55; *Opera* 66–7, 67n11, 68, *70–1*, 72, 209, 301, 308, 308n28, *309*, 310n29; *Outis* 66; *Passaggio* 65, 195–6, 214, 301, 308n26; *Un re in ascolto* 66; *Recital I (for Cathy)* 264; *Sequenza III* 264; *Sequenza V* 274, 280, 289, 289n8, 290–2; *Sequenze* 296; *La vera storia* 66; *Visage* 55, 195, 264; *La voix des voies* 301n13
Bernard, Roger 137
Bernstein, Leonard 101, 119; *Fancy Free* 101, 119
Bertolani, Valentina 73
Bertoncini, Mario 178, 184, 189, 193–4; *Epitaffio alla memoria di un concerto* 189; *Spazio-Tempo* 184, 194
Beuys, Joseph 22
Bialas, Günter 121; *Hero und Leander* 121
Bibalo, Antonio 111; *Das Lächeln am Fuße der Leiter* 111
Birtwistle, Harrison 3, 9, 227, 232, *232*, 232n7, 239–40, *239*, 240n15, 241, 242, 242n21, 245n30, 249–51, *251*, 251n39, 284, 302–3; *Bow Down* 250, 251, *251*, 251n39; *Down by the Greenwood Side* 242; *For O, For O, the Hobby-Horse is Forgot* 232, *232*; *The Mask of Orpheus* 227, 232n7; *Oresteia* 250, 251n39
Blacher, Boris 101, 111, 114, 121; *Zwischenfälle bei einer Notlandung* 111, 114, 121
Blanco, Hugo 159
Blin, Roger 18
Bloch, Ernst 7, 63, 63n6m, 64, 64n7, 72; *Das Prinzip Hoffnung* 63n6
Blomdahl, Karl-Birger 101, 111–12, *113*, 120; *Aniara* 111, 112n16, *113*, 120;
body 4, 6, 22, 25, 106, 208, 227, 230, 250, 256–9, 266, 268; bodily tessitura 257, 263; *see also* embodiment
Boehmer, Konrad 141–2
Boerman, Jan 121; *Alchemie* 121; *Monument voor een gestorven Jongen* 121
Boito, Arrigo 59
Bonalumi, Agostino 197
Bond, Edward 148; *We Come to the River* 148

Borio, Gianmario 1, 36
Börlin, Jean 118; *Relâche/Cinéma* 118
Born, Georgina 227
Bornhoff, Jack 214
Borzykh, Jennie 245n31
Borzykh, Jennie 250n37
Botticelli, Sandro 279
Boulez, Pierre 42–3, 46, 52–3, 156, 164, 207, 209–10, 219, 242, 259; *Le marteau sans maître* 43; *L'Orestie* 42; *Pli selon pli* 43; *Second Piano Sonata* 46
Bourgeade, Pierre 219, 223
Bourseiller, Antoine 209–10
Branchi, Walter 185, 193; *Synergy* 193
Brecht, Bertolt 7, 16–8, 22, 24, 44, 44n24, 63–5, 72, 83–5, 88, 92, 94–5, 97, 195, 204, 210, 215, 223, 234, 249, 278; *Der brave Soldat Schwejk* 44n24; *Die Dreigroschenoper* 18; *Mutter Courage und ihre Kinder* 17–18, 204; *Rasputin* 38, 39, 84; *Rise and Fall of the City of Mahagonny* 65; *The Seven Deadly Sins* 195; *see also Verfremdungseffekt*
Brecht, George 22
Brod, Max 114
Brook, Peter 22, 22n4, 25, 29, 29n8, 219, 239, 245, 249, 261, 263–4, 266–7; *The Conference of the Birds* 264; *Marat/Sade* 22; *The Tempest* 245
Bruno, Stefania 2, 6–7, 185n12
Brunsvick, Yves 214
Brüstle, Christa 36
Bucchi, Valentino 177n1, 195, 198; *Il coccodrillo* 198
Buch, Esteban 5, 8
Burian, Jarka M. 85–6
Burton, Humphrey 242n21
Bussotti, Sylvano 5, 22–3, 24n6, 27, 29, 121, 155, 181, 183, 187, 189, 192n26, 193–6, 198, 264, 300; *Bergkistall* 198; *Lorenzaccio* 194, 194n30; *Passion selon Sade* 5, 23, 121, 155, 187, 264; *La più rararara* 189; *Raramente* 182; *Sette fogli* 195; *Solo* 189
Butor, Michel 61–3, 205, 215, 219; *Votre Faust* 43, 61–4, 108n12, 122, 205–6, 215, 219

Cage, John 16–7, 22, 46, 53, 79, 88, 103, 103n5, 119, 179, 184, 188, 190, 192n26, 195, 215, 228–9, 241, 259, 266, 279, 283–4, 296; *0'00"* 229; *Aria* 195; *Europera* 284; *Fontana Mix* 195; *Song*

Books 284; *Theatre Piece* 188, 192n26, 284; *Water Music* 119
Calder, Alexander 196
Calder, John 249
Caldwell, Sarah 89–90, 98
Calenda, Antonio 24n6
Calvino, Italo 197, 241
Camerlo, Humbert 153–4, 153n1, 158, 160, 172
Capriolo, Ettore 24, 24n6
Carael, Georges 205–6
Cardew, Cornelius 234, 240–1, 252; *The Great Learning* 234; *Schooltime Compositions* 234
Carlos, Wendy 112n16
Casarès, Maria 206, 209
Castellani, Enrico 189
Castiglioni, Niccolò 195–6; *Tre misteri* 195
Castro, Fidel 8, 130–1, 131n8, 147n73, 157, 161
Cavani, Liliana 24n6
Cecchi, Alessandro 317
censorship 88–9, 96–7, 134, 148, 213
Centre Internationale de Recherche Théâtrale (CIRT) 29, 29n8; *Orghast* 29, 263–5
Cesari, Renato 110n14
Chaikin, Joseph 67, 263
Chailly, Luciano 122; *L'Idiota* 122
Chanoine, Jeanne 136n27
Charbonnier, Jeannine 219; *Conditionnement* 219
Chase, Gilbert 34, 38n16
Cheskoo the Clown *see* Mark Furneaux
Chiari, Giuseppe 22, 189; *Whisky* 189
Childs, Lucinda 279; *Einstein on the Beach* 279
Cicognini, Alessandro 83
Clair, René 118; *Relâche/Cinéma* 118
Clarke, Arthur C. 112n16
Clarke, Elizabeth 235
Claudel, Paul 35n13, 224; *Le Soulier de Satin* 224
Claus, Hugo 129–30, 130n5, 131–7, 134n19, 137n30, 140, 140n49, 146n70, 148; *Masscheroen* 130n5; *Morituri* 132–3, 133n17, 136; *see also Reconstructie*
Clementi, Aldo 21, 177–9, 181n9, 192, 196–7, 300, 311; *Collage* 21, 177, 179, 180, 181n9, 195, 197, 311; *Ideogrammi* 179
Cluzel, Raphaël 219

322   Index

cognitive process 3; 227, 230, 280; *see also* embodiment
Cohen, Milton 195n31
Cole, Bruce 240, 240n19, 244
Coleridge, Samuel Taylor 278
Colombo, Furio 68
compositional process 3, 80, 85, 88, 158, 165, 180, 242,295, 299, 302, 310, 315–17
compositional technique 5, 37, 144, 156, 164–5, 301, 303, 312–13
Conant, Abbie 289n8
Constantinedes, Photes 240n17
Cook, Nicholas 2–3, 228n4, 273, 277
Corbella, Maurizio 317
Corneille, Pierre; *Le Cid* 204
Corvin, Michel 203
Cosman, Milein *239*, 240
Cox, Arnie 274–7, 277n2, 278n3, 279–80
Cox, John 234
Cranko, John 122; *Présence* 122
Crénom 209
Cresci, Marco *191*
Cunningham, Merce 184
Curran, Alvin 184, 188, 188n19, 199n39; *La lista del giorno* 184; *Songs and Views from the Magnetic Garden* 188

D'Ornjhelm, Christel 204, 216
Da Ponte, Lorenzo 59
Dahlhaus, Carl 299–301
dance 30–7, 46, 53, 67, 79–81, 183, 189, 194, 196–8, 205–10, 228–31, 235
Dantzig, Rudi van 121; *Monument voor een gestorven Jongen* 121
Davies, Peter Maxwell 5, 9, *239*, 240, 240n15, 240n18, 241, 243, 243n24, 243n25, 249, 260, 261n7, 262, 262n9, 267, 284; *Antechrist* 241; *Blind Man's Buff* 242; *Eight Songs for a Mad King* 240n18, 261, 262n9, 264, 284; *Le Jongleur de Notre Dame* 243; *Missa Super L'Homme Armé* 241; *Renaissance Scottish Dances* 241; *Psalm 124* 241; *Vesalii icons* 5, 240n18
Davis, Charles *239*
Davis, Miles 242
Day, Dave 291, 291n10
De Baecque, Antoine 214
De Benedictis, Angela Ida 10, 44n27, 46n30, 61, 64, 88
De Bernardinis, Leo 24n6
De Gaulle, Charle 210
De Jong, Piet 146

De Kooning, Willem 17
De Leeuw, Reinbert 129, 145; *see also Reconstructie*
De Marinis 315n42
De Seta, Vittorio 178n3; *Un uomo a metà* 178n3
De Sica, Vittorio 83; *Bicycle Thieves* 83
De Vita, Massimo 24n6
Debussy, Claude 278, 122; *Pelléas et Mèlisande* 278
Decourdemanche, Jacques 208
Decroupet, Pascal 64
Degli Espinosa Francesco 190n22
Dempster, Thomas J. 290
Den Daas, Jaap 145
Desi, Thomas 79, 296, *297*, 299, 310n29
Désormière, Roger 42
Dessau, Paul 122–3, 160; *Einstein* 123; *Lanzelot* 122
Devreese, Frédéric 133n17
Dewey, Ken 193n28
DeZutter, Stacy 228n2, 244, 244n26
Diacono, Mario 23, 193
Diamand, Peter 132
Dilthey, Wilhelm 106
Donald Duck 136
Donatoni, Franco 296
Donizetti, Gaetano 165
Donovan, William J. 136n26
Dorazio, Piero 184; *Klangfarbenspiel* 184
Dort, Bernard 18
Dostal, Nico 119; *Manina* 119
Downes Bob 123; *Troy Game* 123
drama: theories of 52–3, 64, 72
Drott, Eric 155
Dubin, Al 124
Duchamp, Marcel 17, 198

Eastman, Julius 262, 262n9
Ebbeke, Klaus 38n15, 39, 39n17
Eco, Umberto 26, 63, 68
Egk, Werner 101, 118; *Peer Gynt* 101, 118
electronic music 7, 37, 92, 101–3, 106, 112, 116, 131, 195, 208, 223
Elzenheimer, Regine 41n19
embodiment 5, 9–10, 93, 228, 256–7, 273–4, 276, 280; embodied cognition 273–4, 277, 283, 292; embodied technique 230, 235, 238, 250; *see also* body
Endrich, Archer (Tom) *236*, 237n11
engagement 8–9, 81, 83, 86–7, 91–2, 95, 133, 148, 154, 172, 255, 300; political engagement 134, 145–6, 300

Ensemble Aisthesis 154n2
Ensemble Instrumental de Musique Contemporaine de Paris 219
Ensemble Musique Vivante 208, 215n20
Enzensberger, Hans Magnus 130, 130n4, 143
Erasmus 146, 146n70
Erismann, Guy 9, 204, 204n2, 215, 215n21, 215n22, 216, 219, 223
Ernst, Max 17
Euripides 261; *Bacchae* 261
Evangelisti, Franco 178, 181, 181n9, 185, 192; *Die Schachtel* 181n9, 185
Evers, A. *143*
experimentation 16, 20, 22–3, 25, 29–30, 36–8, 46, 52–3, 92, 141, 192, 199, 214–15; *see also* film

Fabian, Imre 59
Fadini, Edoardo 24, 24n6
Fearn, Raymond 85
Feldenkreis, Moshé 263
Feldman, Morton 259n2
Fellegara, Vittorio 195; *Una gita in campagna* 195
Fenn, Karen 208
Ferneyhough, Brian 279; *La chute d'Icare* 279
Ferrari, Giordano 1
Fialka, Ladislav 241
film 34, 39, 81–2, 110, 178, 192, 194, 198, 228, 245; experimental film 80, 83–4, 88, 98; film projection 35, 38–9, 41, 81, 84, 86, 101, 188–9, 193
Finney, Jack 242
Finnissy, Michael 236–7, *238*, 241; *Bouffe* 236, *238*, 237
Fischer-Lichte, Erika 294n2, 315n41, 315n42
Flanagan, Hallie 44n25
Flindt, Flemming 123; *Dødens triumf* 123
Flusser, Vilém 105n8
Fluxus 21, 189, 311n32
Focus Opera Group 244n29
Forti, Simone 190
Fortner, Wolfgang 120; *In seinem Garten liebt Don Perlimplín Belisa* 120
Fox, Erika 233, *233*; *Round for Fourteen Strings* 233, *233*
Freccia, Massimo 110n14
Frenzel, Karl 137
Friend, Lionel 250n37
Fülöp-Miller, René 44, 44n23
Fure, Ashley 5; *The Force of Things* 5
Furneaux, Mark 9, 240–4, 244n28

Gayer, Catherine 136
Gazzelloni, Severino 109, 136
Gazzola, Valeria 275
Gazzolo, Virginio 24n6
Gélas, Gérard 212; *La paillasse aux seins nus* 212
Gelber, Jack 22; *The Connection* 22
Gelmetti, Vittorio 178, 184, 189, 193; *La descrittione del gran paese* 184
Genet, Jean 64, 203
Gentele, Göran 59
Georgi, Claudia 85
gesture *see* musical gesture; vocality
Ghelgerode, Michel 59–60; *La Balade du Grand Macabre* 59–60
Giaccari, Luciano 190n22
Giesekam, Greg 89
Ginastera, Alberto 123, 155; *Beatrix Cenci* 123
Glass, Philip 279; *Einstein on the Beach* 279
Glăveanu, Vlad Petre 227
Globokar, Vinko 290
Gluck, Christoph Willibald 109; *Orfeo ed Euridice* 109
Godøy, Rolf Inge 275–6
Goebbels, Joseph 36
Goehr, Alexander 9, 111, 121, 234, 242; *Arden muß sterben* 111, 121; *Naboth's Vineyard* 234; *Sonata About Jerusalem* 234; *Triptych* 234, 242
Goehr, Laelia 234n10
Goethe, Johann Wolfgang 61, 208; *Triumph der Empfindsamkeit* 208
Gogol, Nikolaj 35n11; *The Revisor* 35n11
Gorky, Maxim 86; *The Last Ones* 86
Goya, Francisco de 161, *162*, 163; *Caprichos* 161; *Todos caerán 162*
Grammatica Teatro No-Stop ore 12 189
Gramsci, Antonio 134
Grassi, Paolo 17
Graver, David 257
Gregor, Joseph 44n23
Grifi, Alberto 189n21; *Anni '60 No Stop* 189n21
Grock 289, 289n8, 290–1, 291n10
Gropius, Walter 34, 34n3, 36–7, 41, 42n20, 249
Grosz, George 44
Grotowski, Jerzy 24–5, 28–9, 52–3, 72, 148, 188, 245, 249, 258, 261, 300
Groupe instrumental à Percussion de Strasbourg 207
Gruppo 63 19, 23, 26, 188n18, 189, 193, 193n28

324 *Index*

Gruppo Altro 193; *Altro-Experimenta* 193
Guaccero, Domenico 29–30, 178, 180–1,
  181–3, 185, *186*, 187–8, 192, 192n26,
  193, 197, 199, 199n37, 300; *Fatti
  d'amore e di guerra* 199; *Kombinat
  Joey* 181n7, 185; *Novità assoluta* 185,
  186; *Rappresentazione et Esercizio*
  188; *Rot* 180, 197, *Scene del potere* 30,
  181–3, 187, 192, 300
Guevara, Ernesto Che 129–31, 130n3, 132,
  132n12, 140, 141n51, 142–3, *143*, 149,
  157, 163
Guicciardini, Roberto 24n6
Gunn, Ronald 249

Hacker, Alan 240, 240n19
Haefliger, Ernst 114
Haitink, Bernard 132, 132n14
Hall, Michael 228, 233n9, 244n29
Hallensleben, Markus 256
Halprin, Anna 46, 67, 195, 215, 310,
  312–13; *Esposizione* 46, 46n30, 297,
  299–301, 310–11, 310n29, 311n32,
  312–13, 315–16, 315n39; *Parade and
  Changes* 215
Hamsun, Knut 36; *Hunger* 36
Hansen, Al 22
happening 16–17, 21, 26, 46–7, 68, 84, 94,
  97, 154, 179, 184, 194, 241, 300
Harrap, Peter *236*
Harrison, Jonty 251n39
Harrison, Tony 250
Hart, Roy 9, 240n18, 256, 260–3, 265,
  266n12, 267
Hartley, Hal 81; *La Commedia* 81
Hartstein, Ruben 260
Harvey, Robert 261
Haubenstock-Ramati, Roman 114, 121,
  264; *Amerika* 114, 121; *Credentials, or
  Think, Think Lucky* 264
Hay, Debora 190
Haynes, John *251*
Hegel, Wilhelm Friedrich 18
Heidegger, Martin 106, 106n11
Heile, Björn 3, 5, 10, 103n5, 229, 231
Heineman, John 178, 193
Heisenberg, Werner 105–6
Heister, Werner 102–3, 103n3
Helms, Hans G. 109
Henry, Pierre 102, 107, 109, 119, 123–4,
  206, 208; *Messe pour le temps présent*
  121, 206, 208; *Nijinsky, Clown de Dieu*
  123; *Orphée 53* 108, 119; *Symphonie
  pour un homme seul* 102, 107, 119

Henze, Hans Werner 108, 119, 123, 130,
  130n4, 143, 148, 177n1, 196, 241,
  260–1; *Boulevard Solitude* 196n32;
  El Cimarrón 143; *La Cubana* 143;
  Das Ende einer Welt 108, 119; *Der
  langwierige Weg in die Wohnung der
  Natascha Ungeheuer* 123; *Tristan* 123;
  Versuch über Schweine (Essay on Pigs)
  261; *We Come to the River* 148; *Der
  junge Lord* 196n32
Hergé (Georges Prosper Remi) 161;
  Tintin 161
Hiekel, Jörn Peter 102, 103n3
Higgins, Dick 22
Hölderlin, Friedrich 135–7, 150; *Hyperion-
  Fragment* 150; *Thalia-Fragment* 137
Holliger, Heinz 122; *Der magische
  Tänzer* 122
Hood, Morag *251*
Horner, Keith 249
Huisman, Jacques 205
Huisman, Maurice 131, 132, 132n12, 133,
  135, 137, 139–40, 142
Hulsker, Jan 142

immersion 4, 7, 41, 81–5, 90–1, 96, 98,
  111, 245, 259, 281
improvisation 45, 144, 154, 195, 207, 210,
  243–4, 248, 252, 262–4, 303
instrumental theatre 35–7, 156, 177, 179,
  231, 284
Ionesco, Eugène 7, 18, 53–6, *58*, 59, 59n4,
  60, 72, 209; *La cantatrice chauve* 18,
  55–6, *58*; *La Leçon* 55; *Macbett* 59

Janáček, Leoš 122
Jarry, Alfred 35n13, 42, 54–60; *Père Ubu*
  42; *Ubu Roi* 59
Jaskulski, Pawel 245n31
jazz 37, 116, 120–1, 144, 209, 281
Jensenius, Alexander Refsum 281, 281n4,
  282, 282, 291
Joffrey, Robert 121; *Astarte* 121
Jona, Emilio 115
Jonic, Bettina 249
Joyce, James 26, 54, 55; *Finnegan's Wake*
  54; *Ulysses* 54
Judson Dance Theater 199
Juliana, Queen of The Netherlands 141

Käb, Wilhelm 36
Kabeláč, Miroslav 207
Kafka, Franz 114; *Amerika* 115; *Der
  Verschollene* 114

Kagel, Mauricio 3–4, 7, 34–7, 45, 55, 79, 101, 103n5, 106–7, *107*, 111, 120, 122, 184, 187, 193n27, 215, 219, 224, 229, 231, 234, 237, 259n2, 274, 279–80, 283–5, *286–8*, 289–92, 296, 300, 316; *Anagramma* 55; *Antithese* 107, 120; *Aus Deutschland* 284; *Dressur* 224, 284; *Die Erschöpfung der Welt* 284; *Himmelsmechanik* 35; *Montage à titre de spectacle* 193n27; *Mare Nostrum* 224; *Match* 289, 291; *Pas de Cinq* 219; *Phonophonie* 193n27; *Quatre Degrés* 284; *Sonant 1960/...* 231; *Staatstheater* 111, 122, 231, 237, 259n2, 284; String Quartet I 285; String Quartet II 274, 280, 285, *286–8*, 290–2; *Sur scène* 35, 106–7, *107*, 120, 215, 231; *La Trahison orale* 224; *Variaktionen über Tremens* 193n27
Kahan, Roger 219
Kapp, Volker 35n13
Kašlík, Václav 85, 87, 98, 120, 302; *Krakatit* 120
Kelemen, Milko 34, 34n11, 111, 122; *Der Belagerungszustand* 111, 122
Kelietio, Joan 123; *Troy Game* 123
Keller, Hans *239*, 240
Keysers, Christian 275
Kiesler, Friedrich 37
Kirby, E. T. 34, 47
Kirby, Michael 229, 290
Kirchner, Volker David 124; *Die Trauung* 124
Kirstein, Jack 285
Kitchen, The 199
Kivy, Peter 273
Klompé, Marga 145, 147, 147n73, 147n74, 148–9
Kohl, Lia 6; *sorry, thanks* 6
Koppel, Thomas 123; *Dødens triumf* 123
Kounellis, Jannis 23, 195
Kovács, Inge 37, 64
Křenek, Ernst 101, 111, 118, 121; *Der goldene Bock* 111, 121; *Johnny spielt auf* 118
Kronenburg, Hubert 145
Kubrick, Stanley 112n16; *2001 – A Space Odyssey* 112n16
Kustow, Michael 264
Kylián, Jiří 123; *The Odd One* 123

Labroca, Mario 312
Lachenmann, Helmut 279, 285
Laforgue, Jules 20; *Hamlet, ou les suites de la piété filiale* 20

Langenkamp, Harm 5, 8
LaSalle Quartet 285, 287n7
Latino-Metronio 19
Lavelli, Jorge 208–10, 219, 223–4
Laws, Catherine 227n1
Le Cercle 224
Lebel, Jean-Jacques 211–12
Lecoq, Jacques 241–2
LeFanu, Nicola 244; *Anti-world* 244
Lehmann, Hans-Thies 295n3
Leibowitz, Cora 153n1
Leibowitz, René 8, 153, 153n1, 154–8, 158n7, 157n8, 159–61, 163–4, *164*, 165, *166–71*, 172–3, 216n23; *La circulaire de minuit* 154; *Les Espagnols à Venise* 154, 156, 158; *Four songs Che Guevara in memoriam op. 80* 157 *Labyrinthe* 154; *La nuit close* 154; *Todos caerán* 8, 154, 157–8, 160–1, 163–4, *164*, 165, *166–71*, 169, 172–3
Leibowitz, Tamara 153n1
Leiris, Michel 157, 160, 172
Lenz, Jacob 38
Leonardi, Alfredo 189, 199n39; *Organum multiplum* 199n39
Lerici, Roberto 24n6
Les Guetteurs de son 224
Lévi-Strauss, Claude 153n1, 157–8, 158n8, 159–61, 172
Lévi-Strauss, Monique 153n1, 158–9, 172
Levin, Walter 285, 287n7
Liberovici, Sergio 24n6
Liebermann, Rolf 111
Ligeti, György 3, 7, 54–6, *57*, 59, 59n4, 60, 72, 215, 284, 300; *Artikulation* 54; *Aventures* 54–6, *57*, 59–60, 215; *Le Grand Macabre* 54, 59–60, 59n3; *Nouvelles Aventures* 54, 56, 59
Lim, Liza 5
Limbour, Georges 154, 158
Lindberg, Christian 290, 290n9
Lindegren, Erik 111–12
Linklater, Kristin 263
listening 41–2, 93, 273–4, 316–17
Living Theatre 9, 17, 22, 24, 27, 47, 52–3, 67, 148, 188, 204, 208–10, 212–13, 300; *Antigone* 22, 212; *Frankenstein* 22, 24; *Mysteries and Smaller Pieces* 22, 210; *Paradise Now* 17, 22, 210, 212–13
Loan, Nguyen Ngoc 96
London, Justin 280
Lorca, Federico García 136–7
Lorenzer, Alfred 300n12

326 *Index*

Louafi, Alain 235
Louther, William 240n18
Loyer, Emmanuelle 214
Lutyens, Elisabeth 250n37; *The Linnet From the Leaf* 250n37
Luzzati, Emanuele 24n6
Lyon, Raymond 214

Mac Low, Jackson 22
Macchi, Egisto 23, 23n5, 29, 81, 178, 181, 181n7, 181n8, 187–8, 192–3, 195; *A(lter)A(ction)* 23, 23n5, 193, 195; *Anno Domini* 181n7; *Parabola* 181n7; *Processo a Giovanna* 181n7
Maciunas, George 22
Maderna, Bruno 5, 89, 101, 109, 116n19, 121, 123, 132–3, 133n17, 134, 134n19, 135, 135n23, 135n24, 136, 136n27, 137, 139–40, 146n70, 148–50, 196, 215, 259, 264, 300–1, 301n13, 302, 302n17, 303, 303n20, 316, 316n45; *Ausstrahlung* 264; *Contrasti* 150; *Dimensioni II* 109, 150; *Dimensioni III* 149–50; *Don Perlimplin* 301n13, 316n45; *From A to Z* 301n13; *Hyperion* 109, 116n19, 121, 135n23, 136, 149–50, 215, 300–1; *Hyperion en het geweld* 5, 132–3, 136, 138, 139–40, 147–9; *Il mio cuore è nel sud* 301n13; *Psalm* 150; *Le rire* 116n19, 149; *Satyricon* 123, 302n17, 301, 303, 303n20; *Stele per Diotima* 150
magnetic tape 7, 37, 62, 101–3, 108–11, 114–17, 185, 197, 205, 223, 312; *see also* acousmatic; electronic music
Maguire, Jan 164–5
Mahler, Gustav 122
Malina, Judith 17, 22, 47, 210
Malipiero, Gian Francesco 196n33; *Torneo notturno* 196n32
Malraux, André 207, 209
Mann, Thomas 61
Mantegna, Gianfranco 189
Manzoni, Giacomo 43, 81, 85, 87, 94, 101, 115–16, 116, 121, 123, 214, 300, 302, 311; *Atomtod* 43, 87, 115–17, 116, 121, 214, 311; *Per Massimiliano Robespierre* 123
Marcuse, Herbert 137, 141, 149
Marlowe, Christopher 249
Marsh, Roger 236, 237n11
Martin, Frank 119; *Le vin herbé* 119
Martinson, Harry 111–12
Marx brothers 169
Mason, Benedict 251n39

Massias, Gérard 204, 219; *Tjurunga* 219
Masson, Diego 208, 215n20, 216
Mastropietro, Alessandro 5–7, 9
Matossian, Nouritza 43n21
McBean, Angus 248
McLuhan, Marshall 8, 101, 103, 104, 105–7, 112, 112n16, 117
media 38, 53, 91, 93–4, 97, 101, 106–7, 109, 117, 177, 179–3, 265, 274, 285; cross-media 194, 198, 285, 301; mixed-media 179, 181, 184, 189, 192, 195, 304; moving image media 80–6, 89, 94, 96–8, 312–13; new media 102–3, 105 107–8, 115, 117; theatrical media 36–7, 45, 102, 107; theory of 104–5, 117; visual media 102, 273, 277; *see also* film; multimediality; radio; television
Mendel, Deryk 133n17, 137
Mengelberg, Misha 129, 140, 141n51; *Hello Windyboys* 141n51; *see also Reconstructie*
Menotti, Gian Carlo 101, 119; *The Consul* 101; *The Telephone, or L'amour à trois* 119
Merkel, Clemens 285
Meschke, Michel 59
Meyer-Eppler, Werner 103
Meyer, Henry 287
Meyerhold, Vsevolod 7, 21, 23, 35, 35n11, 35n13, 38, 41n18, 44, 245, 249; *The Revisor* 35n11
Mihalovici, Marcel 53; *The Last Tape* 53
Milhaud, Darius 101, 103n3, 118; *Christophe Colomb* 103n3, 117
Milloss, Aurel 183
mime 9, 53, 227, 230, 238, 241–3, 252; and music 231–2, 234–5, 243–4
Mime Action Group 239
mimetic motor theory 274–6, 278–9, 287, 291–2
Miroglio, Francis 204
Missiroli, Mario 197
Mitchell, W. J. T. 92
Mnouchkine, Ariane 217
Mobutu, Sese Seko 134
Mocrep 6
modernism 3, 153–4, 179, 274, 277–9
Moholy-Nagy, László 34–5, 38, 39n17, 41, 45
Molinié, Antoinette 153, 153n1 159, 159n13, 160, 161, 172
Mondelli, Peter 172
Monteverdi, Claudio 68, 109, 154, 199n37, 266, 285; *Orfeo* 68, 109, 285

Index 327

Moorman, Charlotte 184, 199n38
Moravia, Alberto 188n18
Morricone, Ennio 178; *Requiem per un destino* 178
movement 10, 227, 235–7, 273, 277, 283, 287–9; *see also* mimetic motor theory
Mozart, Wolfgang Amadeus 143, 204; *Le nozze di Figaro* 204
Mrozek, Slawomir 209
Mukarovsky, Jan 315n42
Mulisch, Harry 129–32, 131n8, 140, 146n70; *see also Reconstructie*
multimediality 2–4, 7, 30, 37, 80, 85, 88, 102, 179–81, 189, 205, 299–301
multimodality 2, 273–4, 277, 279
Mundry, Isabel 5
Münzmay, Andreas 7–8
Murray Schafer, R. 121; *Loving* 121
Musgrave, Thea 123; *The Voice of Ariadne* 123
Music Theatre Ensemble 242
Musica Elettronica Viva (MEV) 184, 188n19, 190, 190n23, *191*, 195, 195n31, 199n39; *Zuppa 191*
musical gesture 280–3, 285, 289–91
Musiques Éclatées 219–20, *222*
MW2 193

Nauman, Bruce 83
Neuwirth, Olga 279
new theatre 15–16, 21, 24–5, 28–30, 203, 208, 214, 223, 302
Nikolais, Alwin 120; *Imago – The City Curious* 120
Nitsch, Hermann 22, 27
Nixon, Richard 129
Noller, Joachim 102
Nonnis, Franco 24n6, 180, 181n9; *Die Schachtel* 181n9, 185
Nono, Luigi 3, 5, 7, 21, 23, 34, 34n6, 43–4, 44n23, 44n26, 44n27, 45, 45n28, 47, 53, 81, 85, 86–98, 101–2, 114, 120, 123, 130–1, 134–5, 214, 249, 279, 300–2, 302n16, 302n17, 302n18, 303, 303n19, 304, 304n23, *305–7*, 306, 311n32; *Al gran sole carico d'amore* 102, 123, 303, 311n32; *A floresta é jovem e cheja de vida* 47, 135; *Da un diario italiano* 24, 303, *306–7*; *Intolleranza 1960* 5, 7, 21, 23, 44, 81, 87–8, 91–2, 94–5, 98, 102, 114, 120, 134, 214, 301, 303–4, *305*, 311n32; *Non consumiamo Marx* 135; *Prometeo* 302n16, 302n18; *Y entonces comprendió* 135

Nordheim, Arne 123; *Solitaire* 123
Nordwall, Ove 59
North, Robert 123; *Troy Game* 123
Nussbaum, Walter 154n2
Nyman, Michael 234

Odin Teatret 25, 29, 258
Offenbach, Jacques 85, 153, 163, 172; *La Duchesse de Gérolstein* 163; *La Périchole* 172; *Syllabaire pour Phèdre* 219 *The Tales of Hoffmann* 85
Ohana, Maurice 219
Oida, Yoshi 263, 265
Olivero, Magda 110n14
ONCE group 195, 195n31
Open Theater 53, 66–7, 67n9, 67n10, 67n11, 68, 300, 308
opera 65–6, 72, 91, 102–3, 110, 153–7, 172, 188, 196–7, 204, 216, 259, 266, 274, 284; opera house 8, 33, 36–7, 41–2, 59–60, 111, 164, 172, 192, 194, 312; opera singer 249, 266; operatic genre 61, 68, 144, 285, 295
Orff, Carl 87, 93, 101, 119–20, 122; *Ludus de nato Infante mirificus* 120; *Der Mond* 101, 119; *Prometheus* 87, 93, 122
Orton Richard 236, *236*, 237; *Mug Grunt* 236, *236*, 237
Otera, Lisandro 147n73
Ottomano, Vincenzina C. 7

Paik, Nam June 83, 311n32
Panizza, Oscar 208; *The Council of Love* 208
Panni, Marcello 178, 184, 192, 192n24; *Klangfarbenspiel* 184; *La Partenza dell'Argonauta* 192n24
Panni, Nicoletta 110n14
Paxton, Steve 190
Pearcey, Eilean 240n18
Pecker Berio, Talia 67n9, 317
Penderecki, Krzysztof 111, 122, 302n17; *Die Teufel von Loudon* 111, 122, 302n17
Pennisi, Francesco 178, 183, 183n10, 192; *Sylvia Simplex* 183, 192n24
performance 17, 19, 23, 27–30, 55, 64, 185–7, 214, 230, 252, 304–7; performance analysis 228–9, 285–92; performance art 2, 46, 79–81, 190; performance space 2, 16, 18, 20–1, 24, 27–8, 33, 36–7, 87, 89, 97, 115, 185, 187, 208, 219, 233, 256, 300
Perilli, Achille 21, 177, 179, 179n5, 185, 189, 197, 300, 311; *Collage* 21, 177, 179, 180, 181n9, 195, 197, 311

328 Index

Perlini, Memé 192n24, 214
personage 257, 264, 268
Pes, Aurelio 185n11
Peskó, Zoltán 52
Peter Shaffer 245, *248*; *The Royal Hunt of the Sun* 245, *248*
Petitpierre, Claude 208
Petrassi, Goffredo 178, 178n4, 179, 195; *Morte dell'aria* 178
Phelan, Peggy 315n41
Philippot, Michel 215, 215n21, 215n22
Picabia, Francis 118; *Relâche/Cinéma* 118
Picasso, Pablo 17
Piekut, Ben 255
Pierrot Players 240n18, 240n19, 262
Pikes, Noah 262n8
Pinter, Harold 59
Pirandello, Luigi 22, 64
Pirie, Peter J. 234
Piscator, Erwin 7, 17–18, 21, 34, 34n2, 35, 38–9, *39*, 39n17, 41–2, 42n20, 43–4, 44n24, 44n27, 84
Pistoletto, Michelangelo 190, 190n23
Placanica, Francesca 5, 9
Planchon, Roger 209
Plissezkaja, Maja Michailowna 123; *Anna Karenina* 123
Polak, Wim 142
Poli, Liliana 136n27, 150
Pollock, Jackson 17, 23
Ponente, Nello 20n2
Popoli, Tiziano 149
Porter, Andrew 264
Pörtner, Paul 39, 39n17, 45
Poulenc, Francis 120; *La voix humaine* 120
Pousseur, Henri 7, 43, 54, 61–4, 72, 108n12, 122, 205, 215, 259; *Répons* 63; *Scambi* 63; *Votre Faust* 43, 61–4, 108n12, 122, 205–6, 215, 219
Prampolini, Enrico 23
Prandelli, Giacinto 110n14
Pratella, Francesco 118; *L'aviatore Dro* 118
Preetorius, Emil 106
Prey, Claude 155, 204, 219, 223; *On veut la lumière, allons-y* 219
Prieberg, Fred 108
Příhodová, Barbora 91–3
Pritchett, Wayne 242
Prokofiev, Serge 207
protest 15, 25, 28, 87, 133, 135, 139, 141, 147, 210–12, 255
Puaux, Paul 203–4, 209–10, 212–13, 216
Puccini, Giacomo 153–4, 163–5, 278; *La Bohème* 278; *Tosca* 154, 164; *Turandot* 163, 165

Puecher, Virginio 136
Puig, Michel 155, 204, 207, 216, 216n23, 223; *Provisoires Agglomérats* 207; *Stigmates* 156

Quadri, Franco 24, 24n6
Quartucci, Carlo 19, 23–4, 24n6, 28, 30; *Camion* 28; *Zip-Lap-Lip-Vap-Mam-Crep-Scap-Plip-Trip-Scrap e la Grand Mam alle prese con la società contemporanea* 23–4
Quatuor Bozzini 285, 285n5, *287–8*

radio 7, 53, 102, 105, 108, 110, 177, 300, 310, 312, 316–17; radio opera 102, 108, 301; radio theatre 185, 316
Radok, Alfréd 85, 88
Rain, Douglas 112n16
Rands, Bernard 236–7
Raree Show 241
Ravel, Maurice 158, 207; *Boléro* 207; *L'heure espagnole* 158
Rebstock, Matthias 35, 35n12, 316n43
Reconstructie 5, 129, 130, 132, 132n12, 133, 140, 142, 142n56, *143*, 143n57, 144–7, 147n79, 148–9
Reehorst, Jan 142
Reeser, Eduard 142
Reeves, Geoffrey 249
Reinink, Hendrik Jan 142n55
Remondi, Claudio 19
Remshardt, Ralf 82, 95
Renaud, Madelein 42
Renosto, Paolo 178
Resnik, Salomon 159
revolution 130–1, 144, 157–8, 161, 163, 172–3, 255
Ricci, Mario 20n2, 184; *Klangfarbenspiel* 184; *Movimento n.1 per marionette sola* 20n2
Richards, M. C. 46
Riethmüller, Albrecht 33n1
Rilling, Lydia 37n14
Ripellino, Angelo Maria 21, 44, 44n26, 45, 114
Rizzardi, Veniero 317
Robbins, Jerome 101; *Fancy Free* 101
Roesner, David 79–80, 316n43
Rogers, Holly 7
Rolling Stones 122
Ronconi, Luca 24n6, 308, 310
Ross, Alex 4
Rossellini, Renzo 101, 110, 110n4, 111, 114, 120; *La guerra* 110, 110n4, 114, 120
Roßmann, Karl 115

Roustan, Joëlle 137
Rowley, Caitlin 6; *Aides memoire* 6
Royal Shakespeare Company 22, 245
Rozik, Eli 315n42
Rucker, August 105
Russolo, Luigi 118
Rzewski, Fredric 184, 189, 195;
   Impersonation 184; *Portrait* 184, 195;
   Selfportrait 184, 189, 195; *Variations* 184

Saariaho, Kaija 279
Sala, Emilio 317
Salazar, António de Oliveira 213
Salvatore, Gaston 261
Salzman, Eric 79–80, 296, *297*, 299,
   310n29
Samuel, Claude 54
Sanguineti, Eduardo 19, 68, 267, 310;
   Esposizione 46, 46n30, 297, 299–301,
   310–11, 310n29, 311n32, 312–13,
   315–16, 315n39; *Laborintus* 19
Santini, Andrea 91
Sargentini, Fabio *191*
Sartre, Jean-Paul 86, 135, 153–4, 157, 160,
   163, 172
Satie, Erik 101, 118, 122, 241; *Parade*
   196n32; *Relâche* 101, 118
Sawyer, R. Keith 228n2, 228n3, 244,
   244n26
Scabia, Giuliano 23–4, 24n6, 28, 30,
   304n22; *Zip-Lap-Lip-Vap-Mam-Crep-*
   Scap-Plip-Trip-Scrap e la Grand Mam
   alle prese con la società contemporanea
   23; *Teatro Vagante* 28
Scaldaferri, Nicola 266n13
scenic writing (Bartolucci) 7, 16, 27–8,
   30, 185
Schaeffer, Bogusław 193
Schaeffer, Pierre 101–2, 107–9, 119, 124;
   Orphée 53 108, 119; *Orphée 51 ou*
   Toute la lyre 102, 108, 109; *Symphonie*
   pour un homme seul 102, 107, 119
Schat, Peter 43, 81, 85, 129–30, 130n5,
   131–2, 132n12, 140–1, 141n51, 142,
   142n56, 144–5, 145n63, 146n70,
   215; *Labyrint* 43, 132, 142, 144,
   215; *On Escalation* 141n51; *see also*
   Reconstructie
Schechner, Richard 26, 29, 229
Schellen, Fernand 144, 147n73
Scherchen, Hermann 44, 134
Schlemmer, Oskar 44–5
Schmidt, Dörte 1, 38n15, 41, 41n19
Schnebel, Dieter 4, 36, 192n24, 192n26,
   231; *Glossolalie 61* 192n24; *Maulwerke*

36; *Réactions (Abfälle I.1)* 192n26;
   Visible Music 1–2 231
Schneemann, Carolee 88; *Night Crawlers* 88
Schoenberg, Arnold 65, 118, 154, 156,
   165; *Erwartung* 154; *Die glückliche*
   Hand 118, 154; *Moses und Aron* 65,
   165, 196n32
Schola Heidelberg 154n2
Schönbach, Dieter 122; *Wenn die Kälte in*
   die Hütten tritt 122
Schröder, Julia 6, 7
Schtschedrin, Rodion 123; *Anna*
   Karenina 123
Schuler, Manfred 41
Schuller, Gunther 111, 121; *Die*
   Heimsuchung 111, 121
Schwitters, Kurt 54, 179n5; *Ursonate* 54
Sciarrino, Salvatore 184, 185n11, 279–80,
   285, 302, 302n17; *Amore e Psiche*
   184; *L'infinito nero* 279; *Lohengrin*
   279; *Macbeth, Da gelo a gelo* 302n17;
   Superflumina 302n17
screen 3, 21, 35, 81–8, 90–8, 115, 135,
   149, 179, 195; *see also* film; media;
   television; visuality
Searle, Humphrey 53; *The Photo of the*
   Colonel 53
Seawright, James L. 120; *Imago – The City*
   Curious 120
Shakespeare, William 20, 158, 249
Shankar, Ravi 122
Shelley, Mary 24; *Frankenstein* 24
Shepard, Leslie 261n6
Sills, Beverly 90
Simonovitch, Konstantin 209, 219
Sitsky, Larry 121; *The Fall of the House of*
   Usher 121
Skalický, Jan 89
sketches *see* compositional process
Sklar, Roberta 67n11
Sluchin, Benny 290
Smith, Bessie 121, 179
Šmok, Pavel 122; *Listy duverné* 122
Sollers, Philippe 156
Somoza, Anastasio García 161
Sophocles 210; *Antigone* 210
Soro, Loreto 189
space 44, 53, 55, 68, 117, 190–2, 194–5,
   204, 258, 294, 304; *see also* audience;
   performance
Spatz, Benjamin 230, 230n6, 235
Spinoza, Baruch 230
spoken theatre 4, 37, 52–4, 60–3, 72, 204,
   206, 216
stage *see* performance; space

330 *Index*

Stanislasvki, Konstantin 239, 267
Steiner, Clyde 195
Steiner, George 262n8
Stibilij, Milan 207
Stockhausen, Karlheinz 3, 33, 33n1, 55,
63, 123, 199n39, 215, 227, 231, 235,
235, 236, 259–60, 263–4, 267, 280,
311n32; *Gesang der Jünglinge* 55;
Harlekin 231; *Inori* 235, *235*, 236–7;
Licht 33, 227; *Originale* 199n39, 215,
311n32; *Spiral* 263; *Stimmung* 123;
Stimmung für 6 Vokalisten 123; *Studie
II* 280
Storming of the Winter Palace, The 43
Stow, Randolph 261–2
Strauss, Richard 65; *Der Rosenkavalier* 65
Stravinsky, Igor 219, 241; *L'histoire du
soldat* 215, 219
Strehler, Giorgio 17–19
Striggio, Alessandro 68
Stroessner, Alfredo 161
Stuckenschmidt, Hans Heinz 34, 37, 46
subjectivity 27, 258, 280
Subotnick, Morton 122; *Silver Apples of
the Moon* 122
Svoboda, Josef 7, 85–91, 93–4, 96–8,
115, 302
Sylvestre, Brigitte 224
Syrcus, Chrome 121; *Astarte* 121
Szondi, Peter 18

Taddei, Ottavio 110n14
Tairov, Aleksandr 44
Tal, Josef 111, 116, 123; *Ashmedai* 111,
116, 123
Tasso, Torquato 199n37
Tau, Sergio 23
Taylor, Elizabeth 136
Tchaikovsky, Pyotr Ilyich 123
Teatr Laboratorium 24, 148
Teatro Immagine 30, 192n24
Teatrogruppo 24n6
television 7, 37, 81, 83–4, 87, 89, 91–7,
102, 116, 139, 215, 273, 300, 310, 312
Tetley, Glen 122; *Embrace Tiger and
Return to Mountain* 122; *Tristan* 123
text: approaches to 53–4, 59–61, 68,
256, 258
theatre *see* avant-garde; instrumental
theatre; opera; total theatre
Thomalla, Hans 5
Titone, Antonino 181n8
Toch, Ernst 101, 118; *Der Fächer* 101,
118; *Die Prinzession auf der Erbse* 118

Toller, Ernst 44, 44n24; *Hoppla, wir
leben!* 44n24
Tortora, Daniela 1
total theatre 30, 31, 33–8, 41–3, 45, 47,
115, 216
Townsend, Brenda 233n9
Tradimenti 241
Trionfo, Aldo 24n6
Trubert, Jean-François 6, 9
Trujillo, Rafael 161
Tudor, David 46, 184, 190
Turner, Victor 29

Vachtangov, Evgenij 44
Valobra, Franco 23
Van der Aa, Michel 81; *Sunken Garden*
81–2, 84
Van Itallie, Jean-Claude 67, 209; *The
Serpent* 67, 67n9
Van Manen, Hans 122; *Situation* 122;
Squares 122
Van Vlijmen, Jan 129, 140, 146n70; *see
also Reconstructie*
Vanden Brugge, Oscar *138*
Varèse, Edgard 210, 245; *Poéme
électronique* 120
Vasulka, Steina 83
Vedova, Emilio 21, 88, 300, 302
Verdi, Giuseppe 66, 155–6, 164–5, 204, 278,
278n3; *Don Carlos* 164, 204; *Jérusalem*
204; *Macbeth* 204; *La Traviata* 278
Verfremdungseffekt 7, 83, 91, 95
Vergine, Bibiana 73
Viard, Martine 224
video art 80, 98
Vilar, Jean 9, 17, 203–4, 204n2, 205–10,
212–13, 213n16, 214–15, 215n22, 219,
220, 223, 224
visuality 4, 7, 16, 21, 35, 37, 55, 95, 101,
179, 185, 194, 273, 278–9, 302–3, 308
Vitez, Antoine 224
Vlad, Roman 195
vocality 20, 36, 52, 68, 114, 203, 246, 257,
263–4, 266, 283; vocal gesture 259–60,
292; vocal techniques 262–3, 265; vocal
training 260–1, 263, 265–7; *see also*
acousmatic
Von Hagen, Victoria 158
Vostell, Wolf 83

Wagemans, B. P. 144
Wagner, Richard 23, 33, 37, 47, 82, 93,
122, 158, 207, 273–4; *Parsifal* 37; *Der
Ring des Nibelungen* 33

Index 331

Wake-Walker, Frederic 251
Walshe, Jennifer 3–5
Warder, Fred *251*
Warren, Harry 124
Webern, Anton 207
Weill, Kurt **88**, 101, 118, 195, 215;
  Aufstieg und Fall der Stadt Mahagonny
  118; *Die Dreigroschenoper* 18;
  Royal Palace 118; *The Seven
  Deadly Sins* 195; *Der Zar läßt sich
  photographieren* 101, 118
Weininger, Andor 37
Weiss, Peter 22, 43, 59, 141; *Die
  Ermittlung* 43; *Die Verfolgung
  und Ermordung Jean Paul Marats
  dargestellt durch die Schauspielgruppe
  des Hospizes zu Charenton unter
  Anleitung des Herrn de Sade* 22; *Viet
  Nam Diskurs* 141
Werle, L. J. 86; *The Journey* 86
Westerberg, Stig 112n15
Whitman, Robert 88; *Prune Flat* 88
Wilcox, Dean 88, 90–2, 94–6
Wilkinson, Marc 245, 245n30, *248*, 249;
  The Royal Hunt of the Sun 245, *248*
Williams, William Carlos 22; *Many
  Loves* 22

Wilson, Bob (Robert) 30, 279; *Deafman
  Glance* 30; *Einstein on the Beach* 279
Wilson, Georges 209–10
Wilson, Jeremy 240n16
Wolfsohn, Alfred 260–1, 265
Work in progress 196, 197n35
Wrigley, Amanda 250n38
Wyle, Nancy 235, *235*

Xenakis, Iannis 34, 43, 43n21, 120;
  Oresteia 43; *Poéme électronique* 120

Yankowitz, Susan 66, 67n10; *Terminal*
  66, 68
Young, La Monte 22, 188n19

Zazeela, Marian 188n19
Zenck, Martin 42–3
Zhdanov, Andrei 131
Zimmermann, Bernd Alois 7, 34, 37,
  37n14, 38, 38n15, 39, 39n17, *40*, 41,
  41n18, 41n19, 42, 45, 86–7, 102, 103n3,
  108, 115, 121–2, 214; *Présence* 122;
  Die Soldaten 37–8, *40*, 41–2, 45, 86,
  102, 103n3, 108, 115, 121, 215
Zimmermann, Heidy 153n1
Zosi, Giuliano 178

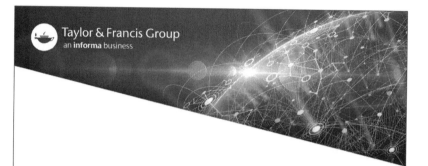

Taylor & Francis eBooks

www.taylorfrancis.com

A single destination for eBooks from Taylor & Francis with increased functionality and an improved user experience to meet the needs of our customers.

90,000+ eBooks of award-winning academic content in Humanities, Social Science, Science, Technology, Engineering, and Medical written by a global network of editors and authors.

TAYLOR & FRANCIS EBOOKS OFFERS:

- A streamlined experience for our library customers
- A single point of discovery for all of our eBook content
- Improved search and discovery of content at both book and chapter level

REQUEST A FREE TRIAL
support@taylorfrancis.com

9780367730949